THE FIENDS WHO PREY
ON HUMANITY

- **JOHN WAYNE GACY** entertained children as ''Pogo the Clown'' . . . and buried 28 bodies in his basement.

- **DAVID ''SON OF SAM'' BERKOWITZ** was ordered to kill by his neighbor's Labrador retriever.

- **RAYMOND MARTINEZ FERNANDEZ and MARTHA BECK** swindled lonely women out of their life savings . . . then robbed them of their lives.

- **DEAN ARNOLD CORLL** bought his victims for $200 a head . . . and homemade candy.

- **CHRISTINE LAVERNE SLAUGHTER FALLING** graduated from killing kittens to child murder.

''A veritable *Who's Who* of who-dunits in serial slayings . . . Should be hunted down by anyone and everyone who is aware of the menace of murder in our midst.''

Robert Bloch, author of *Psycho*

HUNTING HUMANS

The Encyclopedia of Serial Killers

Volume 1

MICHAEL NEWTON

AVON BOOKS ◆ NEW YORK

AVON BOOKS
A division of
The Hearst Corporation
1350 Avenue of the Americas
New York, New York 10019

Copyright © 1990 by Michael Newton
Published by arrangement with Loompanics Unlimited
Library of Congress Catalog Card Number: 91-93026
ISBN: 0-380-76396-6

First Avon Books Printing: April 1992

AVON TRADEMARK REG. U.S. PAT. OFF. AND IN OTHER COUNTRIES, MARCA
REGISTRADA, HECHO EN U.S.A.

Printed in the U.S.A.

RA   10 9 8 7 6 5 4 3 2 1

To Barbara Howell.
More grist for the mill . . .

ACKNOWLEDGMENTS

I am indebted to the following individuals and institutions for their kind assistance in the preparation of this work. Geographically, they include:

ALABAMA: John Fay, Associate Executive Editor, Mobile *Press-Register;* Sgt. Wilbur Williams, Mobile Police Dept.

ALASKA: Brenda Files, Anchorage *Daily News;* Investigator Mark Stewart, Alaska State Troopers, Criminal Investigation Bureau

ARIZONA: Tucson *Citizen*

ARKANSAS: Lt. R.L. Jenkins, Little Rock Police Dept.; Lt. Doug Stephens, Arkansas State Police; Chief James Vandiver, Little Rock Police Dept.

CALIFORNIA: Robert Andrew, Librarian, Long Beach *Press-Telegram;* Lt. Ray Biondi, Sacramento County Sheriff's Dept.; David Cappoli, Librarian, Los Angeles *Herald Examiner;* Sgt. Garry Davis, Kern County Sheriff's Dept.; D.A. Dicaro, Librarian, Beale Memorial Library (Bakersfield); Joan Douglas, Librarian, Riverside *Press-Enterprise;* Capt. Robert Grimm, Los Angeles County Sheriff's Dept.; John Irby, the Bakersfield *Californian;* Rhonda Kruse, Senior Librarian, San Diego Public Library; Sgt. A. Thurston, Kern County Sheriff's Dept.; Union-Tribune Publishing Co., San Diego

CANADA: Alberta—Patricia Garneau, Librarian, Edmonton *Journal;* British Columbia—Pacific Press

Limited; the Vancouver *Sun;* Ontario—Deborah Jessop, Librarian, the Windsor *Star;* Quebec—the Montreal *Gazette;* Saskatchewan—Eric Jenkins, head librarian, Regina *Leader Post*

COLORADO: Eleanor Geheres, Manager, Denver Public Library; James Jordan, Senior Agent, Colorado Dept. of Public Safety

CONNECTICUT: Hartford *Courant;* Barbara White, Editor, Meriden *Record-Journal*

DELAWARE: Col. Daniel Simpson, Director, Delaware State Police

ENGLAND: Kevin Wilson

FLORIDA: Vernon Bradford, Florida Dept. of Corrections; Hernando County Library; J.E. McMillen, Jacksonville Sheriff's Dept.; Heath Meriwether, Editor, Miami *Herald;* Lt. Mark Schlein, Broward County Sheriff's Dept.; Arnold Summers, General Manager, Park Newspapers of Florida

GEORGIA: K. Wayne Ford, Staff Writer, Athens *Banner-Herald;* Starr Holland, Librarian, Albany *Herald;* Diane Hunter, Librarian, *Atlanta Journal;* E.P. Peters, Director, Georgia Bureau of Investigation

HAWAII: Charles Memminger, Staff Writer, Honolulu *Star-Bulletin*

IDAHO: Jon Jensen, Staff Writer, Idaho Falls *Post-Register*

ILLINOIS: Bill Behrens, Investigator, Cook County Sheriff's Dept.; David L. Morse, Illinois State Library

INDIANA: Cecil Smith, Editor, Salem *Leader*

IOWA: Thomas R. Ruxlow, Director, Iowa Division of Criminal Investigation; Eugene Thomas, Editor, Nevada *Journal*

KANSAS: Jack H. Ford, Assistant Director, Kansas Bureau of Investigation; Ethel J. Hunt; Davis Merritt, Jr., Executive Director, Wichita *Eagle-Beacon;* Capt.

Ken Pierce, Shawnee County Sheriff's Dept.; Lt. Tom Sargent, Shawnee County Sheriff's Dept.

KENTUCKY: Morgan T. Elkins, Commissioner, Kentucky State Police

LOUISIANA: Helen C. Hudson and Susan Parmer, Shreve Memorial Library; New Orleans Public Library; Gwen Pearce, Reference Librarian, Bossier Parish Library

MARYLAND: Susan E. Stetina, Deputy Clerk, Circuit Court of Cecil County; Sgt. Paul D. Waclawski, Baltimore County Police Dept.

MASSACHUSETTS: Worcester *Telegram & Gazette*

MICHIGAN: *The Detroit News;* P.W. Dukes, Librarian, Detroit *Free Press;* Vonda Jamrog, Dept. of Corrections; Kalamazoo *Gazette;* Jim Shanahan, Managing Editor, St. Joseph *Herald Palladium;* Maj. Lewis G. Smith, Michigan State Police; Lt. Paul H. Wood, Michigan State Police

MINNESOTA: Meredith R. Cook, Blue Earth Community Library

MISSISSIPPI: Cleveland *Bolivar Commercial;* Beverly Canerdy, Jackson *Clarion-Ledger;* Maj. Walter Tucker, Dept. of Public Safety

NEBRASKA: Capt. J.E. Burnett, Nebraska State Patrol; Sheriff David R. Schleve, Scotts Bluff County

NEVADA: Carroll Edward Cole; Las Vegas *Review-Journal;* Jenny Scarantino, Librarian, Las Vegas *Sun*

NEW JERSEY: Eloise Lehnert, Blairstown *Press;* Mary Ann McDade, Morristown Library; Howard A. McGinn, Prosecutor, Warren County

NEW YORK: Detective Al Sheppard, NYPD Intelligence Division

NORTH CAROLINA: Fayetteville *Observer;* Ken Reading, Public Library of Johnston County

NORTH DAKOTA: Dick Hickman, Special Agent, Bureau of Criminal Investigation

OHIO: J. Richard Abell, Cincinnati Public Library; James Bates, Assistant Prosecuting Attorney, Lucas County; Det. Donald Bradley, Cleveland Police Dept.; Lee McLaird, Reference Archivist, Bowling Green State University; Margaret Marten, Cleveland *Plain Dealer;* Medina County *Gazette;* J. Bradford Tillson, Editor, Dayton *Daily News*

OKLAHOMA: Ted Limke, Director, Oklahoma State Bureau of Investigation

OREGON: Capt. Robert J. Brickeen, Oregon State Police

PENNSYLVANIA: Marcia Morelli, New Castle Public Library; Scranton *Times;* Carol Thomas, Librarian, Wilkes-Barre *Times-Leader*

SOUTH CAROLINA: M.S. Crockett, Librarian, Charlotte *Evening Post*

TENNESSEE: Ellen Henry, Librarian, Jackson *Sun;* Nashville *Banner;* Steve O. Watson, Director, Tennessee Bureau of Investigation

TEXAS: Sheriff Larry R. Busby, Live Oak County; Opal Miller, Librarian, County of Live Oak; Robert Sadler, Associate Editor, Waco *Tribune-Herald;* Dennis Spies, Managing Editor, Amarillo *Globe-News;* Patricia Starr, Austin *American-Statesman;* Larry Todd, Public Information Officer, Dept. of Public Safety; Richard Veit, Librarian, Texas Collection, Baylor University

UTAH: Chief Swen C. Nielsen, Provo Police Dept.

VIRGINIA: Lucy Proctor, Senior Staff Writer, Christianburg *News Messenger;* Julian Pugh, Dept. of Corrections

WASHINGTON: Jeanne Engerman, Librarian, Washington State Library; Tacoma Public Library; Harold D. Wilson, Librarian, Seattle Public Library

WISCONSIN: La Crosse *Tribune;* Kate Lorenz, Jefferson Public Library; Milwaukee *Journal;* Newspapers, Inc., Milwaukee; the *Wisconsin State Journal*

WYOMING: Christopher A. Crofts, Director, Wyoming Division of Criminal Investigation; Bess Sheller, Director, Carbon County Library

With special thanks to my wife, Judy, for her assistance in the final preparation of the manuscript.

"Society's had their chance.
I'm going hunting. Hunting humans."

—JAMES OLIVER HUBERTY, 1984

PREFACE

The face of modern homicide is changing. We are caught up in the midst of what one expert calls an "epidemic of homicidal mania," victimized by a new breed of "recreational killers" who slaughter their victims at random, for the sheer sport of killing. In the years since World War II, our annual solution rate for homicides has dropped from 90% to 76%, indicating that one in every four domestic murders goes unsolved. In human terms, that means 5,000 victims—13 each and every day—will be dispatched by murderers who walk away, scot free. According to the FBI's best estimate, at least 3,500 of those will be slain by "serial killers," a special breed of predator who kill repeatedly, without remorse, sometimes for years on end.

Initially, we run afoul of definitions. Self-proclaimed "authorities" butt heads in endless arguments about the mandatory body count and length of intervals between specific crimes that are presumed to qualify a "genuine" serial killer. Most such guidelines have been arbitrary and entirely artificial, stacking the odds in favor of this or that pet theory. In an effort to restore common sense to the subject, I have adopted the definition published in a 1988 report from the National Institute of Justice. The NIJ report defines serial murder as "a series of two or more murders, committed as separate events, usually, but not always, by one offender acting alone. The crimes may occur over a period of time ranging from hours to years. Quite often the motive is psychological, and the offender's behavior and the physical evidence observed at the crime scenes will reflect sadistic, sexual overtones."

Serial murder is the crime of the 1990s, but is it really new? The term is certainly of recent vintage, coined around 1980 to differentiate between "mass murderers"—who slaughter several victims in a single, frantic outburst—and the more insidious, methodical killers who spin out their crimes over time. New terminology, however, does not signify a new phenomenon. Criminologist Melvin Rheinhardt discussed the subject of "chain killers" as early as 1962, and the problem was already ancient. Gilles de Rais, the richest man in France and confidante to Joan of Arc, was executed in the 15th century for slaying upwards of 100 children. Several interesting cases were prosecuted under the Inquisition, cloaked in the theological trappings of witchcraft, vampirism, and lycanthropy. Elizabeth Bathory was convicted, in 1611, of personally killing some 650 young women, for the purpose of bathing herself in their blood. Joseph Phillipe slaughtered Parisian prostitutes in the 1860s, and Jack the Ripper carried the game to London twenty years later, inspiring a host of imitators over the next decade. In short, the problem seems to be as old as human history. The work in hand confines itself, for practical reasons, to a survey of 20th-century serial killers.

Geographically, serial killers are found on every continent except Antarctica, with North America claiming 76% of the total and Europe running a distant second with 19%. Easily leading the field, the United States boasts 74% of the world total—and 97% of the North American gross—in serial murders. Europe's leaders are England (with 36%), Germany (with 29%), and France (trailing with 11%). Communist nations contribute a mere 1.8% of the total, with ten cases recorded since 1917, a fact explained in equal parts by cultural differences and the tendency of state-owned media to "lose" bad news.

Who are the murderers among us? In America, 85% are male and 8% female; sex remains undetermined in another 7% of cases, where the killers are still at large. Ethnically, 82% of American serial killers are white, 15% are black, and 2.5% are Hispanic. (Native Americans and Orientals figure in one case each, with the Oriental killer serving as accomplice to a white man.) Few of them are legally insane, and all are cunning, indicated by the fact that some 18% of cases in this century remain unsolved.

In operational terms, 87% of American serial killers are loners, while only 10% hunt in pairs or packs. Of the "social" killers, 59% represent all-male groupings (ranging from two-man teams to gangs of a dozen of more), while 23 percent are male-female couples, and 18% include mixed groups of varying sizes.

Generalizations are dangerous, but serial killers may be loosely classified in terms of their hunting techniques. *Territorial* killers stake out a defined area—a city or county, sometimes a particular street or municipal park—and rarely deviate from their selected game preserve. An estimated 58% of American serial killers fall into this category, including 65% of all blacks and 44% of all female killers. *Nomadic* slayers travel widely in their search for prey, confounding authorities as they drift aimlessly from one jurisdiction to another. The nomad ranks include 34% of America's "recreational" killers, with 30% of black killers and 28% of lethal ladies falling into this category. *Stationary* killers crouch like spiders in a web, committing murders mainly in their homes or places of employment—clinics, nursing homes, and hospitals included. Only 8% of America's serial killers belong in this category, including a bare 3% of black killers and a substantial 28% of female practitioners.

As defined above, the motives for serial murder are "quite often" psychological, with strong sado-sexual overtones and evidence of compulsive behavior. Coolly professional killers-for-hire are excluded from the definition, but that does not preclude a profit motive in serial crimes. Approximately 6% of cases here described are exercises in greed run amok, incorporating what psychologist Stanton Samenow has called a "double voltage"—that is, the amplified thrill of killing for profit *and* pleasure. (Significantly, 31% of female serial killers have murdered for gain, compared to 3% of their male counterparts.) Since 1969, a disturbing 8% of American serial cases have involved practitioners of Satanism or black magic, while another 5% involve members of the medical profession—doctors, dentists, nurses, nursing aides.

Ancient or otherwise, serial murder is clearly escalating in modern society. In the first half of this century, American police recorded an average of 1.2 serial cases per year. Since 1960, the figure has leaped to 12 cases per year, and by the 1980s new cases were capturing headlines at an average rate of two per month. While new police investigative methods and wider journalistic coverage clearly account for some of the phenomenal increase, it remains obvious that serial crimes *are* multiplying dramatically.

The work in hand suggests no ultimate solutions to our "murder epidemic." The FBI's Violent Criminal Apprehension Program (VICAP) is a long step in the right direction, coupled with early diagnosis of potential killers and referral of their cases for competent treatment. We have known for years that many future murderers display a tell-tale "triad" of symptoms—bedwetting, arson, and cruelty to animals—in their childhood years, but parents, teachers, and physicians must be trained to spot the warning signs. More recent evidence establishes that child abuse and early trauma to the brain may help to launch a killer on his way. At least four of the male killers considered here were subjected to identical childhood abuse, forced to dress in girl's clothing by sadistic relatives who sought to "teach them a lesson." (At this writing, a California woman, Mary Bergamasco, faces trial on child abuse charges, after dressing her seven-year-old son as a pig and staking him out in the front yard, to teach him that "lying and stealing makes you ugly like Pinocchio.")

Prevention is essential, then . . . but is it practical? Psychologists inform us that the human character is rather firmly set between years two and five—that is, before a child leaves home for public school. Carroll Edward Cole murdered his first victim at age nine, and a significant number of serial slayers are hard at work in their teens. Once having killed, they are apparently immune to psychiatric therapy. Confined, they are a constant danger to their keepers, fellow prisoners, and to society at large, inevitably claiming further victims if they manage to escape or win parole. Such cases, sadly, are not rare, and the deliberate release of psychopathic killers to the street

CASE HISTORIES

Allam, Ibrahim

Trim and fit at fifty-five, Herbert Kavale was a bachelor who enjoyed the ladies, and Vienna had no shortage of attractive, willing women. It was not uncommon for his cleaning lady to discover him in bed, exhausted from the night before, when she arrived at eight a.m., and he was seldom found alone. The morning of September 19, 1983, was therefore doubly strange; there was no trace of any female visitor about Kavale's flat, and he did not respond when she came tapping at his bedroom door. Concerned, she risked a peek inside and found Kavale stretched out, nude, across the bed, a bathrobe cord wound tight around his neck.

Police initially suspected that a burglar had surprised Kavale, killing him when he resisted, but a coroner's report revealed the victim had engaged in sex ten minutes prior to death. Kavale's car was missing from the parking lot downstairs, and homicide detectives tried another theory on for size, suggesting that Kavale might have hired a prostitute who brought her pimp along for purposes of robbery and murder.

Through investigation, Viennese detectives learned Kavale had secured a number of his female playmates through the ads in certain "swinger's" magazines. The magazines kept records that enabled them to forward on replies to different ads. Kavale's latest contacts were Egyptian aliens, Ibrahim and Dahlia Allam, who advertised their availability for "unconventional games"—a euphemism for spec-

7

tator sex. Immigration records listed Ibrahim Allam as twenty-five, his wife a mere sixteen; they had been married in July of 1983, in Munich. When detectives called upon their address in Vienna, they discovered that the couple had departed swiftly, on the day Kavale's body was discovered.

Background checks with the authorities in Munich showed that Ibrahim Allam was born in Cairo, emigrating to West Germany at age fifteen. He ran afoul of the police in 1977, as the direct result of his betrothal to a 15-year-old girl. Omar Khalifa, father of Allam's intended, was violently opposed to the engagement. Furious at the rejection, Ibrahim had drawn a gun and shot Khalifa through the head, in front of twenty witnesses. A murder charge was bargained down to manslaughter, and he had been released in less than four years' time, on the condition that he leave West Germany forever.

Viennese investigators knew that they were dealing with a killer, now, and matters went from bad to worse with the discovery of Kavale's car along the Marseilles waterfront. Detectives in the seaport city learned that Ibrahim and Dahlia had struck a deal with two young yachtsmen—Jean Lefebvre and Maurice Delvaux—to sail as passengers en route to the United States. Their 42-foot ketch was found in New York harbor six weeks later, but no trace could be discovered of the owners or their lethal passengers.

American police received their break in mid-July of 1985, when Egyptian Ali Bengaza was violently assaulted on a Chicago street corner. Bystanders intervened, and his attacker fled at the approach of a policeman, but Bengaza knew him well enough. The victim had been friends with Ibrahim and Dahlia Allam in Egypt and West Germany. His friendship had developed into love for Dahlia, and Ibrahim had flown into a homicidal rage when Ali had suggested Dahlia should divorce her husband to become Mrs. Bengaza. Prior to the explosion, Ibrahim informed Bengaza he had killed three men since his release from prison in West Germany.

The fugitives were run to earth in New York City, shortly after the Chicago incident, and were delivered to the Austrian authorities. Both Ibrahim and Dahlia signed confessions prior to the commencement of their trial in early 1986. According to their statements, Ibrahim had changed his mind about participating in the ''games'' Kavale had commissioned. After Dahlia chose to follow through, Allam had gone berserk with jealousy and choked Kavale with his bathrobe sash.

For Dahlia, charges of abetting murder were reduced to those of failure to assist a person facing mortal danger; she was sentenced to a year in prison. Ibrahim, convicted on May 9 of second-degree murder, received a term of twenty years. Upon release, he faces extradition to Marseilles, with murder charges waiting in the deaths of Jean Lefebvre and Maurice Delvaux.

Angelo, Richard

An Eagle Scout and 1980 high school graduate, Richard Angelo signed up for service as a volunteer fireman at the earliest permissible age. Neighbors admired his courage, but none suspected his underlying motivation—an obsessive need for recognition as a ''hero''—that would drive him to commit a string of vicious crimes in later years.

Angelo graduated from New York state university as a registered nurse in May 1985, working briefly at two Long Island hospitals before he landed a job at Good Samaritan Hospital, in West Islip, during April 1987. As the new recruit and low man on the totem pole, he worked the hours from 11 P.M. to 7 A.M., in the small ward reserved for cardiac patients and other cases requiring intensive care. Angelo never complained about the hours; if anything, he seemed to like the graveyard shift.

The loss of patients in intensive care is not surprising, given the severity of illness and the traumatic nature of their injuries, but doctors on the staff at Good Samaritan recorded some unusual cases in the latter months of 1987. Patients who appeared to be recovering from surgical procedures at a normal pace were dying off without apparent cause, and hospital administrators were alarmed, to say the least. Six suspicious deaths between September 16 and

October 11 left doctors bewildered—until the killer made a critical mistake.

On October 11, following the deaths of two post-operative subjects in a single day, patient Girolamo Cucich was approached by a bearded, heavy-set man who informed him, "I'm going to make you feel better." The visitor injected something into Cucich's intravenous tube, producing immediate numbness and labored breathing. The patient had strength enough to buzz for a nurse, and his life was saved, providing authorities with their first witness in a mystifying case.

On October 12, police routinely questioned Richard Angelo. As the only male nurse on the graveyard shift—and a bearded one, at that—he was a natural suspect in the Cucich attack. By November 3, laboratory test results confirmed that Cucich had received a shot of Pavulon, inducing muscular paralysis that could have led to death by suffocation. A search of Angelo's hospital locker, on November 13, turned up hypodermic needles and a vial of potassium chloride, a drug that produces massive heart problems if used incorrectly. The next day, searchers visited Angelo's apartment, seizing vials of Pavulon and a similar drug, Anectine.

Arrested on November 15, while attending an out-of-town conference for emergency medical technicians, Angelo was held without bail pending further investigation. In custody, he swiftly confessed to a series of murders, estimating that he used Pavulon or Anectine to poison an average of two patients per week during September and early October 1987. His motive? Richard sought to make himself a "hero" by arriving on the scene in time to "save" his victims.

As the records clearly indicate, his plan had lethal flaws. In Angelo's last six weeks on the job, his ward had experienced thirty-seven "Code Blue" emergencies, with a loss of twenty-five patients. Prosecutors were more conservative in their estimate, numbering Angelo's victims "in excess of ten," while other published reports placed the body-count as high as thirty-eight.

A legal technicality barred Angelo's confession from the courtroom, and the only charge immediately filed was one of first-degree assault, involving Girolamo Cucich. Angelo was granted bail, but chose to stay in custody, citing various threats against his life. By mid-December, laboratory tests were under way on nineteen corpses, and the end results brought further charges. On January 4, it was announced that victims Milton Poulney and Frederick LaGois had each been injected with Pavulon prior to death. Charges of second-degree murder were filed against Angelo, in the LaGois case, on January 13, with more indictments pending.

Archerd, William Dale

Born in 1912, William Archerd cherished a lifelong fascination with medicine. Lacking the cash and self-discipline required for medical school, he sought work as a hospital attendant, learning what he could of drugs and their effects through practical experience. During 1940 and '41, Archerd worked at Camarillo State Hospital, in California, serving in departments where insulin shock therapy was used to treat mental illness. In 1950, he pled guilty to illegal possession of morphine in San Francisco, receiving five years probation. A second offense revoked his probation, and Archerd was confined to the minimum-security prison at Chino; escaping in 1951, he was swiftly recaptured and transferred to San Quentin. By October 1953, he was free on parole.

Archerd's "bad luck" extended into other aspects of his life. Married seven times in fifteen years, he lost three wives to mysterious bouts of illness between 1956 and 1966. If that were not enough, his friends and other relatives were also dying.

On July 27, 1967, Archerd was arrested in Los Angeles, charged with three counts of first-degree murder. The victims included: his fourth wife, Zella, who collapsed two months after their marriage, on July 25, 1956; a teenaged nephew, Burney Archerd, dead at Long Beach on September 2, 1961; and wife number seven, authoress May Brinker Arden, who died on November 3, 1966. As charged in the indictment, Archerd was suspected of injecting each victim with an overdose of insulin, thereby producing lethal attacks of hypoglycemia.

At least three other victims were suspected in the murder series. Archerd's first known victim, according to police, was a friend named William Jones, who died in Fontana, California, on October 12, 1947. Archerd's fifth wife, Juanita, had also displayed classic symptoms of hypoglycemia at her death, in a Las Vegas hospital, on March 13, 1958. Another of Archerd's friends, Frank Stewart, died in the same hospital two years later, on March 17, 1960.

On March 6, 1968, William Archerd was convicted on three counts of murder, the first American defendant convicted of using insulin as a murder weapon. His death sentence was affirmed by California's Supreme Court in December 1970.

Atlanta "Child Murders"

The curious and controversial string of deaths that sparked a two-year reign of terror in Atlanta, Georgia, have been labeled "children's" murders even though a suspect, ultimately blamed for 23 of 30 homicides, was finally convicted only in the deaths of two adult ex-convicts. Today, nearly a decade after that suspect's arrest, the case remains, in many minds, an unsolved mystery.

Investigation of the case began, officially, on July 28, 1979. That afternoon, a woman hunting empty cans and bottles in Atlanta stumbled on a pair of corpses, carelessly concealed in roadside undergrowth. One victim, shot with a .22-caliber weapon, was identified as Edward Smith, 14, reported missing on July 21. The other was 13-year-old Alfred Evans, last seen alive on July 25. The coroner ascribed his death to "probable" asphyxiation. Both dead boys, like all of those to come, were black.

On September 4, Milton Harvey, age 14, vanished during a neighborhood bike ride. His body was recovered three weeks later, but the cause of death remains officially "unknown." Yusef Bell, a 9-year-old, was last seen alive when his mother sent him to the store on October 21.

Found dead in an abandoned school November 8, he had been strangled manually by a powerful assailant.

Angel Lenair, age 12, was the first recognized victim of 1980. Reported missing on March 4, she was found six days later, tied to a tree with her hand bound behind her. The first female victim, she had been sexually abused and strangled with an electric cord; someone else's panties were extracted from her throat.

On March 11, Jeffrey Mathis vanished on an errand to the store. Eleven months would pass before recovery of his skeletal remains, advanced decomposition ruling out a declaration on the cause of death. On May 18, 14-year-old Eric Middlebrooks left home after receiving a telephone call from persons unknown. Found the next day, his death was ascribed to head injuries, inflicted with a blunt instrument.

The terror escalated into summer. On June 9, Christopher Richardson, 12, vanished en route to a neighborhood swimming pool. Latonya Wilson was abducted from her home on June 22, the night before her seventh birthday, bringing federal agents into the case. The following day, 10-year-old Aaron Wyche was reported missing by his family. Searchers found his body on June 24, lying beneath a railroad trestle, his neck broken. Originally dubbed an accident, Aaron's death was subsequently added to the growing list of dead and missing blacks.

Anthony Carter, age 9, disappeared while playing near his home on July 6, 1980; recovered the following day, he was dead from multiple stab wounds. Earl Terrell joined the list on July 30, when he vanished from a public swimming pool. Skeletal remains discovered on January 9, 1981, would yield no clues about the cause of death.

Next up on the list was 12-year-old Clifford Jones, snatched off the street and strangled on August 20. With the recovery of his body in October, homicide detectives interviewed five witnesses who named his killer as a white man, jailed in 1981 on charges of attempted rape and aggravated sodomy. These witnesses provided details of the crime consistent with the placement and condition of the victim's body, but detectives chose to file their affidavits, listing Jones with other victims of an "unknown" murderer.

Darron Glass, an 11-year-old, vanished near his home on September 14, 1980. Never found, he joins the list because authorities don't know what else to do about his case. October's victim was Charles Stephens, reported missing on the ninth and recovered next day, his life extinguished by asphyxiation. Capping off the month, authorities discovered skeletal remains of Latonya Wilson on October 18, but they could not determine how she died.

On November 1, 9-year-old Aaron Jackson's disappearance was reported to police by frantic parents. The boy was found on November 2, another victim of asphyxiation. Patrick Rogers, 15, followed on November 10. His pitiful remains, skull crushed by heavy blows, were not unearthed until February 1981.

Two days after New Year's, the elusive slayer picked off Lubie Geter, strangling the 14-year-old and dumping his body where it would not be found until February 5. Terry Pue, 15, was missing on January 22 and was found the next day, strangled with a cord or piece of rope. This time, detectives said that special chemicals enabled them to lift a suspect's fingerprints from Terry's corpse. Unfortunately, they were not on file with any law enforcement agency.

Patrick Baltazar, age 12, disappeared on February 6. His body was found a week later, marked by ligature strangulation, and the skeletal remains of Jeffrey Mathis, were found nearby. A 13-year-old, Curtis Walker, was strangled on February 19 and found the same day. Joseph Bell, 16, was asphyxiated on March 2; Timothy Hill, on March 11, was recorded as a drowning victim.

On March 30, police added their first adult victim to the list of murdered children. He was Larry Rogers, 20, linked with younger victims by the fact that he had been asphyxiated. No cause of death was determined for a second adult victim, 21-year-old Eddie Duncan, when his body was found on March 31. On April 1, ex-convict Michael McIntosh, age 23, was added to the roster on the grounds that he had also been asphyxiated.

By April 1981, it seemed apparent that the "children's

murder'' case was getting out of hand. Community critics denounced the official victims list as incomplete and arbitrary, citing cases like the January 1981 murder of Faye Yearby to prove their point. Like ''official'' victim Angel Lenair, Yearby was bound to a tree by her killer, hands tied behind her back; she had been stabbed to death, like four acknowledged victims on the list. Despite these similarities, police rejected Yearby's case on grounds that (a) she was a female—as were Wilson and Lenair—and (b) at 22, she was ''too old''—although the last acknowledged victim had been 23. (Dave Dettlinger, examining police malfeasance in *The List,* suggests that 63 ''pattern'' victims were capriciously omitted from the ''official'' roster, twenty-five of them after a suspect's arrest supposedly ''ended'' the murders.)

During April, spokesmen for the FBI declared that several of the crimes were ''substantially solved,'' outraging blacks with suggestions that some of the dead had been slain by their own parents. While that storm was raging, Roy Innis, leader of the Congress of Racial Equality, went public with the story of a female witness who described the murders as the actions of a cult involved with drugs, pornography and Satanism. Innis led searchers to an apparent ritual site, complete with large inverted crosses, and his witness passed two polygraph examinations, but by that time the police had focused their attention on another suspect, narrowing their scrutiny to the exclusion of all other possibilities.

On April 22, Jimmy Payne, a 21-year-old ex-convict, was reported missing in Atlanta. Six days later, when his body was recovered, death was publicly ascribed to suffocation and his name was added to the list of murdered ''children.'' William Barrett, 17, went missing May 11; he was found the next day, another victim of asphyxiation.

Several bodies had, by now, been pulled from local rivers, and police were staking out the waterways by night. In the predawn hours of May 22, a rookie officer stationed under a bridge on the Chattahoochee River reported hearing ''a splash'' in the water nearby. Above him, a car rumbled past and officers manning the bridge were alerted. Police and FBI agents halted a vehicle driven by Wayne

Bertram Williams, a black man, and spent two hours grilling him, poking through the car, before they let him go. On May 24, the corpse of Nathaniel Cater, a 27-year-old convicted felon, was fished out of the river downstream, the authorities putting two and two together as they focused their probe on Wayne Williams.

From the start, he made a most unlikely suspect. The only child of two Atlanta schoolteachers, Williams still lived with his parents at age twenty-three. A college dropout, he cherished ambitions of earning fame and fortune as a music promoter. In younger days, he had constructed a working radio station in the basement of the family home.

On June 21, Williams was arrested and charged with the murder of Nathaniel Cater, despite testimony from four witnesses who reported seeing the victim alive on May 22 and 23, *after* the infamous "splash." On July 17, Williams was indicted for killing two adults—Cater and Payne—while newspapers trumpeted the capture of Atlanta's "child killer."

At his trial, beginning in December 1981, the prosecution painted Williams as a violent homosexual and bigot, so disgusted with his race that he hoped to wipe out future generations by killing black children before they could breed. One witness testified that he saw Williams holding hands with Nathaniel Cater on the night of May 21, a few hours before "the splash." Another, 15 years old, told the court that Williams had paid him two dollars for the privilege of fondling his genitals. Along the way, authorities announced the late addition of a final victim, 28-year-old John Porter, to The List.

Defense attorneys tried to balance out the scales with testimony from a woman who admitted having "normal" sex with Williams, but the prosecution won a crucial point when the presiding judge admitted testimony on ten other deaths from The List, designed to prove a pattern in the murders. One of those admitted was the case of Terry Pue, but neither side had anything to say about the fingerprints allegedly recovered from his corpse in January 1981.

The most impressive evidence of guilt was offered by a team of scientific experts, dealing with assorted hairs and fibers found on certain victims. Testimony indicated that some fibers from a brand of carpet found inside the Williams home had been identified on several bodies. Further, victims Middlebrooks, Wyche, Cater, Terrell, Jones and Stephens all bore fibers from the trunk liner of a 1979 Ford automobile owned by the Williams family. The clothes of victim Stephens *also* yielded fibers from a second car—a 1970 Chevrolet—owned by the family. Jurors were *not* informed of eyewitness testimony naming a different suspect in the Jones case, nor were they advised of a critical gap in the prosecution's fiber evidence.

Specifically, Wayne Williams had no access to the vehicles in question at the times when three of the six "fiber" victims were killed. Wayne's father took the Ford in for repairs at 9 a.m. on July 30, 1980, nearly five hours *before* Earl Terrell vanished that afternoon. Terrell was long dead before Williams got the car back on August 7, and it was returned to the shop next morning, still refusing to start. A new estimate on repair costs was so expensive that William's father refused to pay, and the family never again had access to the car. Meanwhile, Clifford Jones was abducted on August 20 and Charles Stephens on October 9, 1980. The defendant's family did not purchase the 1970 Chevrolet until October 21, twelve days after Stephen's death.

On February 27, 1982, Wayne Williams was convicted on two counts of murder and sentenced to a double term of life imprisonment. On March 1, 1982, the Atlanta "child murders" task force officially disbanded, announcing that 23 of 30 "List" cases were considered solved with his conviction. The other seven cases, still open, reverted to the normal homicide detail.

In November 1985, a new team of lawyers uncovered formerly-classified FBI documents from 1980 and '81, describing surveillance of a militant Ku Klux Klansman suspected of murdering several victims on The List. Despite that evidence and glaring flaws throughout the prosecution's case, all appeals filed on behalf of Wayne Williams have been rejected by the courts.

"Ax Man of New Orleans, The"

In the predawn hours of May 23, 1918, New Orleans grocer Joseph Maggio and his wife were murdered in bed by a prowler who chiseled through their back door, used Joseph's ax to strike each victim once across the skull, then slit their throats with a razor to finish the job. Maggio's brothers discovered the bodies and were briefly held as suspects, but police could find no evidence of their involvement in the crime and both were soon released.

A few blocks from the murder scene, detectives found a cryptic message chalked on the sidewalk. It read: "Mrs. Maggio is going to sit up tonight just like Mrs. Toney." Police could offer no interpretation, so the press stepped in. The *New Orleans States* reported a "veritable epidemic" of unsolved ax murders in 1911, listing the victims as Italian grocers named Cruti, Rosetti (killed with his wife), and Tony Schiambra (whose spouse was also murdered). Over seven decades, half a dozen authors have accepted the report as factual, relying on the "early" crimes to bolster this or that proposed solution in the case. Unfortunately, none of them saw fit to look beyond the headlines, or they might have learned the truth and spared themselves embarrassment.

Examination of contemporary documents reveals that no such crimes were noted in newspaper obituaries, coroner's records, or police homicide reports for the year 1911. In fact, no Crutis or Schiambras died that year from any cause, while the death of May Rosetti—a black woman—was blamed on disease. Ironically, there *were* unsolved ax murders in Louisiana during 1911, claiming a total of sixteen lives, but the victims were all black and none were killed in New Orleans.

On June 28, a baker delivering bread to the grocery of Louis Besumer found a panel cut from the back door. He knocked, and Besumer emerged, blood streaming from a head wound. Inside the apartment, Besumer's "wife"— Anna Lowe, a divorcee—lay critically wounded. She lingered on for seven weeks, delirious, once calling Besumer a German spy and later recanting. On August 5 she died, after naming Besumer as her attacker, prompting his arrest on murder charges. (Nine months later, on May 1, 1919, a jury deliberated all of ten minutes before finding him innocent.)

Returning late from work that evening, August 5, Ed Schneider found his pregnant wife unconscious in their bed, her scalp laid open. She survived to bear a healthy daughter, but her memory of the attack was vague, at best. A hulking shadow by her bed, the ax descending—and oblivion.

On August 10, sisters Pauline and May Bruno woke to sounds of struggle in the adjacent room occupied by their uncle, Joseph Romano. They rushed next door to find him dying of a head wound, but they caught a glimpse of his assailant, described in official reports as "dark, tall, heavy-set, wearing a dark suit and a black slouch hat."

The rest of August was a nightmare for police, with numerous reports of chiseled doors, discarded axes, lurking strangers. Several of the latter were pursued by vengeful mobs but always managed to escape. At last, with time and the distraction of an armistice in war-torn Europe, the hysteria began to fade.

On March 10, 1919, the scene shifted to Gretna, across the river from New Orleans. A prowler invaded the home of Charles Cortimiglia, helping himself to the grocer's own ax before wounding Charles and his wife, killing their infant daughter. From her hospital bed, Rose Cortimiglia accused two neighbors, Iorlando Jordano and his son Frank, of committing the crime. Despite firm denials from Charles, both suspects were jailed pending trial.

Meanwhile, on March 14, the *Times-Picayune* published a letter signed by "The Axeman." Describing himself as "a fell demon from the hottest hell," the author announced his intention of touring New Orleans on March 19—St. Joseph's night—and vowed to bypass any home where jazz was playing at the time. "One thing is certain," he declared, "and that is that some of those people who do not jazz it (if there be any) will get the axe!" On the appointed night, already known for raucous celebration, New Orleans was even noisier than usual. The din included numerous performances of "The Mysterious

Axman's Jazz," a song composed for the occasion, and the evening passed without a new attack.

On May 21, the Jordano trial opened in Gretna. Charles Cortimiglia did his best for the defense, but a jury believed his wife, convicting both defendants of murder on May 26. Father Jordano was sentenced to hang; his elderly father drew a term of life imprisonment.

And still the raids continued. Grocer Steve Boca was wounded at home on August 10, 1919, his door chiseled through, the bloody ax discarded in his kitchen. On September 3, the Ax Man entered Sarah Laumann's bedroom through an open window, wounding her in bed, dropping his weapon on the lawn outside. Eight weeks later, on October 27, grocer Mike Pepitone was murdered at home; his wife glimpsed the killer, but offered detectives no helpful description.

On December 7, 1920, Rose Cortimiglia publicly confessed to perjury in the Jordano trial, explaining that she blamed her neighbors for the slaying out of spite and jealousy. Both prisoners were pardoned and released, unconscious of events that had unfolded five days earlier, in California.

On December 2, Joseph Mumfre, late of New Orleans, was ambushed and shot to death on a Los Angeles street corner. His female assailant, veiled and dressed in black, was identified as the widow of Mike Pepitone. At her murder trial, resulting in a ten-year sentence, she would finger Mumfre as the slayer of her husband—and, by implication, as the Ax Man.

Homicide investigators scoured Mumfre's record and discovered he was serving time in jail, for burglary, during the Ax Man's hiatus from August 1918 to March 1919. Various authors have noted that Mumfre was also locked up between 1911 and early 1918—thus implying a connection with the nonexistent "early" murders—but the suspect's motive still remains a mystery.

In 1973, author Jay Robert Nash "solved" the case by calling Mumfre a Mafia hit man, allegedly pursuing a long vendetta against "members of the Pepitone family." The explanation fails when we recall that only one of eleven victims—the last—was a Pepitone. Likewise, speculation

on a Mafia extortion plot against Italian grocers overlooks
the fact that four victims were non-Italians, while several
were unconnected with the grocery business. At this writing, the Ax Man's case remains a mystery.

"Babysitter, The"

The terror came to Oakland County, Michigan, in 1976.
Authorities would later disagree on body-counts and motives, even the description of their suspect, but there was
no argument about the impact that a string of grisly murders had upon the wealthy bedroom communities northwest of Detroit. Someone was killing children, claiming
one victim after another with seeming impunity, while police watched helplessly from the sidelines.

The first to die was Cynthia Cadieux, 16, abducted from
Roseville on January 15, found naked and dead the next
morning, lying on a rural road in Bloomfield Township.
Raped and bludgeoned with a blunt instrument, she had
been dragged some distance over snow-covered pavement,
her clothing piled fifteen feet from the body.

Four days later, in Birmingham, 14-year-old Sheila
Shrock was raped and shot to death inside her home. Police made the discovery while checking out a prowler call.
Two blocks away, John McAuliffe had been terrorized,
bound, and robbed of five dollars by a gunman who invaded his house. Police were left with a description of the
killer, but they had no other leads.

On February 13, 12-year-old Mark Stebbins left the
American Legion hall in Ferndale, heading homeward
shortly after noon. He never got there, and his lifeless
body would be found in Southfield six days later, lying in
the snowy parking lot behind an office building. Dead at
least 36 hours when found, Stebbins had been sexually
assaulted, then smothered, his body cleaned with metic-
ulous care before he was laid out for discovery.

The pattern seemed to break with 13-year-old Jane Allan, abducted while hitchhiking in Royal Oak, on August 8,
1976. Her body was found three days later at Miamis-
burg, Ohio, with the cause of death listed as carbon mon-

oxide poisoning. Thus far, police saw no link between the four murders, nor could they find a connection with the September 1972 strangulation of teenager Donna Serra, in Ray Township. Unique methods of murder, along with the rape of both sexes, suggested different killers—at least two, and perhaps as many as four.

The pattern was established in December, with 12-year-old Jill Robinson's disappearance from Royal Oak, three days before Christmas. Her body was discovered on December 26, near Troy in southern Oakland County, laid out neatly in a roadside snow bank. The cause of death had been a single short-range shotgun blast—another deviation—but the victim's body had been scrubbed before she died. The coroner could find no evidence of sexual assault.

On January 2, 1977, 10-year-old Kristine Mihelich left her Berkley home to buy a magazine and vanished on the three-block walk. Her body was discovered January 21, in Franklin Village, near the spot where Cynthia Cadieux had been discarded one year earlier. Unlike her predecessor, Kristine had not been raped; instead, she had been suffocated, body washed and laid out in a funeral position, as with victims Robinson and Stebbins.

Homicide detectives were convinced of a connection in at least three cases now, and they did not have long to wait for number four. On March 16, 11-year-old Timothy King disappeared in Birmingham, his case igniting a general panic throughout Oakland County. Witnesses recalled seeing Tim with a shaggy-haired man who drove a blue Gremlin compact, but no one had noted the license number. Appearing on local television, Timothy's mother begged for the safe return of her child, promising that his favorite chicken dinner would be waiting.

The search ended on March 23, with discovery of the boy's corpse in a roadside ditch, near Livonia. Another victim of suffocation, Timothy had been scrubbed and manicured after death, with his clothing cleaned and pressed. Medical examiners reported evidence of sexual assault, but they ''detected no proof that the killer was a male.'' Examination of the stomach contents showed that Timothy had been allowed one final chicken dinner prior to death. The media began to call their man the "Baby-sitter," after the apparent care he lavished on his victims while he held them captive. Authorities could not agree upon the killer's motives, some suggesting that he scrubbed the bodies to remove incriminating evidence, while others read the act as a ritual exorcism of guilt. The molestation of male victims pointed to a homosexual killer, but why, then, were female victims chosen? The shotgun death of Jill Robinson was another riddle. One source hypothesized that Jill had survived attempted suffocation, suddenly reviving on the roadside; another theory noted that she had begun to menstruate, suggesting the killer had altered his pattern to cope with the only "adult" victim.

On March 27, Dr. Bruce Danto, a Detroit psychiatrist, published an open letter to the "Babysitter," theorizing on his motives, pleading with the man to call for help or turn himself in to police. Among the predictable rash of crank calls, one stood out. The male caller told Danto simply, "The article was wrong. You better hope it doesn't snow any more."

In short order, Danto began receiving letters and calls from a man who gave his name as "Allen," describing himself as the murderer's roommate. According to the caller, he and his friend had soldiered together in Vietnam, the Babysitter returning home with a deep bitterness toward affluent America. Suburban children were selected as the victims, he explained, in a twisted effort to "bring the war home" and educate wealthy slackers to the suffering of combat veterans. On one occasion, "Allen" made a date to meet with Danto, but he never showed.

In Oakland County, spring and summer passed without another "pattern" homicide, parents growing apprehensive as autumn turned to winter and the snow began to fall. Aside from cleanliness, fresh snow appeared to be the killer's chief obsession. Safety programs instituted the previous winter were revived, police patrols beefed up in grim anticipation of another crime that never came. To date, there have been no more calls from "Allen," no more homicides attributed to the Babysitter. Whether he is dead, locked up on other charges or at large today, the case remains unsolved.

Baker, Stanley Dean

On July 13, 1970, California Highway Patrol officers received reports of a hit-and-run accident at Big Sur. Three persons had been injured in one car, while two long-haired males sped away in another, fleeing the scene of the crash. Patrolmen found two long-hairs walking down a nearby road and noted similarities in the descriptions. Under questioning, one suspect readily confessed involvement in the accident, startling police as he added, "I have a problem. I'm a cannibal."

To prove the point, Stan Baker turned his pockets out and palmed a human finger bone—removed, he said, from his most recent victim in Montana. Baker's sidekick, Harry Allen Stroup, was also carrying a bony digit, and the pair were taken into custody on suspicion of homicide. Investigators in Montana found the mutilated remains of victim James Schlosser in the Yellowstone River, his heart and several fingers missing from the scene.

The case was grim enough, but Baker was not finished talking, yet. According to his statement, he had been recruited by Satanic cultists from a college campus in his home state of Wyoming. An alleged member of the homicidal "Four Pi movement," Baker had sworn allegiance to the cult's master—known to intimates as the "Grand Chingon"—and he had committed other slaying on the cult's behalf. There had been human sacrifices, he reported, in the Santa Ana Mountains, south of Los Angeles. Displaying supposed cult tattoos, Baker also confessed participation in the April 20, 1970 murder of Robert Salem, a 40-year-old lighting designer in San Francisco. Salem had been stabbed 27 times and nearly decapitated, his left ear severed and carried away in a crime that Baker attributed to orders from the Grand Chingon. Slogans painted on the walls in Salem's blood—including "Zodiac" and "Satan Saves"—were meant to stir up panic in an atmosphere already tense from revelations in the Manson murder trial.

Baker, 22, and his 20-year-old companion were returned to Montana on July 20. Convicted of murder, both were sentenced to prison, where Baker continued his efforts on behalf of the cult. Authorities report that he actively solicited other inmates to join a Satanic coven, and full moons seemed to bring out the worst in Stanley, causing him to howl like an animal. He sometimes threatened prison guards, and was relieved of homemade weapons on eleven separate occasions, but administrators still saw fit to let him travel through the prison system, teaching transactional analysis to other inmates. Harry Stroup discharged his sentence and was released in 1979; Stanley Baker was paroled to his native Wyoming six years later, requesting that his present whereabouts remain confidential. (See also: "Four Pi Movement;" Manson, Charles; "Son of Sam")

Ball, Joe

Born in 1892, Joe Ball was a one-time bootlegger and tavern owner at Elmendorf, Texas, near San Antonio. In the 1930s, Ball ran the Sociable Inn, distinguished by its lovely waitresses and alligator pit out back, where Joe would daily entertain his patrons with the ritual of feeding time. He seemed to have a problem keeping waitresses—and wives—but the variety was part of what made Ball's establishment so popular.

There was a darker side to Joe, however, and according to reports from other residents of Elmendorf, Ball sounded anything but sociable. One neighbor, a policeman by the name of Elton Crude, was threatened with a pistol after he complained about the stench emitted by Joe's alligator pool. (The smell, Ball normally explained, was due to rotting meat he used for 'gator food.) Another local was so terrified of Ball that he packed up his family one night and fled the state, without a word of explanation.

In September 1937, worried relatives reported Minnie Gotthardt's disappearance to authorities in Elmendorf. The missing 22-year-old had been employed with Ball before she dropped from sight, but under questioning the tavern keeper said that she had left to take another job. Police were satisfied, until another waitress—Julia Turner—was reported missing by her family. Ball's answer was the

same, but this time there were problems, since the girl
had failed to take her clothes along. Joe saved the day by
suddenly remembering an argument with Julia's roommate; Turner had been anxious to get out, and Ball had
given her $500 for the road.

Within a few short months, two other women joined the
missing list; one of them, Hazel Brown, had opened up a
bank account two days before she disappeared, then ''left''
without retrieving any of the cash. Texas Rangers entered
the case, compiling a roster of Ball's known employees
over the past few years. Many were found alive, but at
least a dozen were permanently missing, along with Joe's
second and third wives. Ball stood up well under questioning, but his elderly handyman cracked, reporting that
he had helped Ball dispose of several female corpses, acting under threat of death when he fed their dismembered
remains to the alligators. From the safety of his new location, Joe's ex-neighbor joined the litany, describing an
evening in 1936 when he had seen Ball chopping up a
woman's body, tossing the fragments to his hungry pets.

The Rangers had enough to win indictments, but they
needed solid evidence for a conviction. On September 24,
1938, they dropped by the Sociable Inn to examine Joe's
meat barrel, and Ball realized the game was up. Stepping
behind the bar, he rang up a ''No Sale'' on the cash register, drew a pistol from the drawer, and killed himself
with one shot to the head. His handyman was later jailed
for two years, as an accessory after the fact, while Joe's
alligators were donated to the San Antonio zoo.

Barfield, Margie Velma

Born October 23, 1932, in Cumberland County, North
Carolina, Margie Bullard would look back on her childhood as a cruel period of ''permissible slavery,'' made
worse by the attentions of a father who began molesting
her at age thirteen. The stories are refuted categorically
by seven siblings, who deny all charges of abuse in any
form, by either parent, and it must be granted that Margie's early development seemed normal for the given time

and place. Dropping out of high school in her junior year, she eloped with Thomas Burke at seventeen, settling in Paxton, where she bore two children without incident.

The trouble started after fifteen years of marriage, when Burke's luck turned sour almost overnight. Discharged from his job and subsequently injured in a car crash, he began drinking heavily to drown his sorrows, the ever-present liquor an affront to Margie's fundamentalist religion. Marriage became a sort of guerrilla warfare, with Margie hiding her husband's whiskey, sometimes pouring it down the sink, finally committing him to Dorothea Dix Hospital, in Raleigh, as an alcoholic. Working at a local mill to support the family, she relied on prescription tranquilizers for peace of mind.

Thomas came home from the hospital sober and sullen, bitter at his wife's "betrayal." In 1969, when he burned to death in bed, authorities dismissed the death as accidental, caused by careless smoking, but later, with the advantage of hindsight, there would be dark suspicions of foul play.

In 1971, Margie married Jennings Barfield. He lasted six months, his sudden death ascribed to "natural causes," but exhumation and autopsy in 1978 would reveal lethal doses of arsenic in his system.

By the time she murdered Barfield, Margie was already dependent on prescription drugs, carelessly mixing her pills, with the result that she was four times hospitalized for overdose symptoms. In contrast to her addiction, she maintained an active interest in religion, teaching Sunday school at the local Pentecostal church on a regular basis.

Short on cash, Margie was writing rubber checks to cover her "medical" expenses, and her several trips to court produced judicial wrist-slaps. in 1974, she forged her aged mother's name to a $1,000 loan application, panicking when she realized the bank might try to contact the real Lillie Bullard for verification. Margie eliminated the problem by feeding her mother a lethal dose of insecticide, and again the death was attributed to natural causes.

Two years later, Margie Barfield was employed by local matron Dollie Edwards as a live-in maid. A fringe benefit of the job was Dollie's nephew, Stuart Taylor, who began

dating Margie on the side, but their romance did not stop
Barfield from poisoning her employer in February 1977.
Her motive remains unclear—there were no thefts involved—and physicians ascribed the sudden death to
"acute gastroenteritis."

Margie next moved in with 80-year-old John Lee and
his wife Record, age 76. After forging a $50 check on
Lee's account, she sought to "make him sick" and thereby
gain some time to cover the shortage, but her plans obviously went awry. First poisoned in April 1977, John Lee
lost 65 pounds before his eventual death, on June 4. After
the funeral, Margie began feeding poison to Lee's widow,
but she gave up her job in October 1977, leaving a frail
survivor behind.

Moving on to a Lumberton rest home, Barfield was
twice caught forging checks on Stuart Taylor's account.
He forgave her each time, but they argued fiercely after
her third offense, on January 31, 1978. That night, Margie
spiked his beer with poison, keeping up the dosage until
Taylor died on February 4. Relatives rejected the diagnosis
of "acute gastroenteritis" and demanded a full autopsy,
resulting in the discovery of arsenic.

Under interrogation, Margie confessed the murders of
Taylor, her mother and second husband, Dollie Edwards
and John Lee. Aside from the motiveless Edwards slaying,
they were all "accidents," bungled attempts to cover up
for forgery and theft. A jury deliberated for less than an
hour before convicting Barfield of first-degree murder, and
she was executed by lethal injection on November 2, 1984.

Bartsch, Juergen

Born out of wedlock in post-war Germany, Juergen
Bartsch lost his mother at the tender age of five months.
He was adopted after spending eleven months in a found-
ling home, but the selection of a new family was unfortunate. Enrolled in a parochial school, Bartsch was
seduced by a homosexual priest who also delighted in filling his mind with sadistic stories from medieval times.
Back in his adopted home, the boy was alternately treated

with contempt and extravagant attention. His "mother" insisted on bathing Juergen through adolescence and beyond, a practice she continued to the date of his arrest on murder charges.

By 1967, Bartsch—now 17—was working as a butcher's apprentice, still living with his adoptive parents in Bonn, West Germany. He was also a sadistic pedophile, responsible for the torture-slayings of four young boys he had lured to an abandoned mine shaft, killing each in turn after they were brutalized and sexually abused. On arrest and conviction, he was sentenced to a term of life imprisonment, the German death penalty having been outlawed after World War II.

On April 10, 1971, the Supreme Court of Germany overturned Juergen's conviction, on grounds that the lower court improperly ignored psychiatric evidence and Bartsch was a minor when the crimes took place. Psychiatrists informed the high court that Bartsch's actions were a product of sexual compulsion, beyond his conscious control. His sentence was reduced from life to ten years, with credit for time already served.

In April 1976, seeking to curry favor for early parole, Bartsch submitted to voluntary castration as part of his overall rehabilitation program. He died on April 28, following surgery, with doctors attributing his death to heart failure.

Bateson, Paul

In 1977 and '78, New York homosexuals were terrorized by a series of "bag murders," in which six male victims were mutilated and dismembered, their remains wrapped in black plastic bags and dumped in the Hudson River. Some of the grisly fragments washed up on the New Jersey shore, others coming to ground near the World Trade Center. Police traced items of recovered clothing to a shop in Greenwich Village, catering to gays, and distinctive tattoos identified one of the victims as a known homosexual. Lacking identities and confirmed cause of death in several cases, the crimes were not officially classified as homicides, but were listed as CUPPI's—circumstances undetermined pending police investigation.

A solution in the case derived from evidence collected in an "unrelated" case. On September 14, 1977, film critic Addison Verrill was beaten and stabbed to death in his New York apartment. Charged with the slaying, Paul Bateson, a 38-year-old X-ray technician, confessed to meeting Verrill in a Greenwich Village gay bar. After having sex at Verrill's flat, Bateson crushed his victim's skull with a metal skillet, afterward stabbing Verrill in the heart. Convicted of the homicide on March 5, 1979, Bateson drew a term of 20 years to life in prison.

While in custody, awaiting trial, Paul Bateson bragged of killing other men "for fun," dismembering their bodies, and dropping the bagged remains in the Hudson River. Detectives satisfied themselves of Bateson's guilt, but he was never charged, and the "bag murders"—that later inspired the movie *Cruising*—remain technically unsolved.

Bell, Mary Flora

Mary Bell was born in May of 1957, when her unwed, mentally unstable mother was, herself, a child of seventeen. Though Betty Bell would subsequently wed the baby's father, marriage did not guarantee a stable home. Mary's father was frequently out of work, occasionally in trouble with the law. Betty, for her part, frequently left her daughter with relatives or acquaintances, once "giving" the child to a woman she met on the street, outside an abortion clinic. The Bell home in Newcastle, England, was filthy and sparsely furnished. At school, Mary became known as a chronic liar and disruptive pupil. On occasion, she voiced her desire "to hurt people."

The cruel urge surfaced on May 11, 1968, when Mary and Norma Bell (no relation) were playing with a three-year-old boy on top of a Newcastle air raid shelter. The boy fell and was severely injured, but the incident was written off as accidental. On May 12, the mothers of three young girls informed police that Mary had attacked and choked their children. She was interviewed and lectured by authorities, but no juvenile charges were filed.

On May 25, two boys playing in an old, abandoned house found the corpse of four-year-old Martin Brown, lying in an upstairs room. Mary and Norma Bell had followed the boys inside, and had to be ordered out when police arrived. With no obvious cause of death, it was assumed that Martin Brown had swallowed pills from a discarded bottle, found nearby.

On May 26, Norma Bell's father caught Mary choking his 11-year-old daughter; he slapped her face and sent her home. Later that day, a local nursery school was vandalized. Police discovered notes that read "Fuch of, we murder, watch out, Fanny and Faggot," and "We did murder Martain brown, fuckof you Bastard."

Four days later, Mary Bell appeared at the Brown residence, asking to see Martin. Reminded of the tragedy, she told his grieving mother, "Oh, I know he's dead. I wanted to see him in his coffin."

On May 31, a newly-installed burglar alarm at the vandalized nursery school brought patrolmen rushing back to the scene, where they found Mary and Norma Bell loitering beside the building. Both girls fervently denied involvement in the previous break-in, and they were released to the custody of their parents.

Two months elapsed before the disappearance of three-year-old Brian Howe, in Newcastle. An immediate search was mounted, and Mary Bell told Brian's sister that he might be playing on a heap of concrete blocks that had been dumped out on a nearby vacant lot. In fact, he was discovered there, among the tumbled slabs, but he was dead, a victim of manual strangulation, legs and stomach mutilated with a razor and a pair of scissors that police recovered at the scene. A medical examiner suggested that the killer might have been a child, since relatively little force was used.

Detectives started circulating questionnaires among the local children, asking suspects to account for their movements at the time of Brian's death. Answers from Mary and Norma Bell were inconsistent, and both girls were brought in for questioning. While Mary claimed that she

had seen an older boy abusing Brian, Norma soon broke
down and told of watching Mary kill the boy. At trial, in
December 1968, Norma was acquitted of all charges, while
Mary Bell was convicted on two counts of manslaughter.

Described by court psychiatrists as "intelligent, manip-
ulative, and dangerous," Mary proved herself a problem
inmate. In 1970, she fabricated charges of indecent assault
against one of her warders, but the man was acquitted in
court. In September 1977, she escaped from Moor Court
open prison with another inmate, but the runaways were
captured three days later. In the meantime, they had met
two boys with whom they spent the night, a circumstance
that placed the egocentric Mary back in tabloid headlines,
offering a blow-by-blow account of how she gave up her
virginity.

Berdella, Robert A.

By his own admission, 39-year-old Robert Berdella was
a strange character. The owner of Bob's Bizarre Bazaar in
Kansas City, Missouri, Berdella carried business cards that
advertised that he had "poison" in his head. Around the
house, he showed a milder side, helping his Hyde Park
neighbors establish a local community crime watch program. His strange behavior on the job was written off as
so much advertising hype—until the afternoon of April 2,
1988.

That day, a neighbor of Berdella's stepped outside to
find a naked stranger crouching on his porch. The 22-year-
old wore nothing but a dog collar, buckled around his
neck, and he blurted out a tale of sexual abuse that sent
Berdella's neighbor racing for the telephone, to call police.

According to the victim, he had been held captive in
Berdella's home the past five days, subjected to repeated
sexual assaults before he finally clambered through a
second-story window and escaped. Detectives picked Berdella up and searched his home for evidence. In doing so,
they opened up a grim Pandora's box of horror.

In the house, police discovered some 200 photographs

of naked men, the subjects bound and clearly suffering from cruel abuse. Torture devices were also seized in the raid, along with a pair of human skulls, occult literature, and a Satanic ritual robe. That weekend, deputies unearthed bone fragments and another human head in Berdella's yard.

On April 4, 1988, Robert Berdella was arraigned on seven counts of sodomy, one count of felonious restraint, and one count of first-degree assault. Bail was initially set at $500,000, revoked the next day, when officers testified that one of the men in Berdella's photographs—trussed up and hanging by his heels—appeared to be dead. While excavation continued on Berdella's property and prosecutor's contemplated murder charges, homicide investigators started checking out their list of missing persons dating back to 1984. A bargained guilty plea on one account of murder consigned Berdella to prison for life, but authorities suspected him in at least seven other deaths.

On December 19, 1988, Berdella pled guilty to first-degree murder in the death of victim Robert Sheldon, and to four counts of second-degree murder involving additional male victims. He was sentenced to a term of life imprisonment.

Besnard, Marie

Around Loudon, in France, she is remembered as the "Queen of Poisoners," with thirteen victims charged against her name. She is a legend in the district—for her crimes, and for the way in which she managed, finally, to cheat the executioner.

The only child of frugal parents, born in 1896, Marie Davaillaud was educated at a convent school where classmates would remember her as "vicious and immoral." She was "wild with boys," detractors said, adept at "snitching other people's things and lying to cover up." In 1920, already a spinster at the age of 23, Marie was married to her cousin, one Auguste Antigny, who was known to suffer from tuberculosis. When he died in 1927, it was blamed on "pleurisy." The undertaker buried him

with shoes on, an aesthetic oversight that would rebound
against his grieving widow 22 years later.

During August 1929, Marie was married to Leon Besnard. The newlyweds were quick to realize that fortune
lay beyond their grasp while certain of their relatives were
still alive, but clearing out the family tree takes time. There
were rewards in store when two of Leon's great-aunts died,
in 1938 and 1940, but the bulk of the inheritance was
claimed by Leon's parents, leading the Besnards to change
their plans. In May, her wealthy father stricken down by
a "cerebral hemorrhage," Marie insisted that her mother
come to live with Leon and herself.

The stage was set for action. In November 1940, Leon's
father died from eating "poison mushrooms." Three
months later, he was orphaned when his mother fell prey
to "pneumonia." Locals had begun to joke about the
"Besnard jinx," but Leon and Marie were more concerned with their inheritance, a sum that was unfortunately, split between themselves and Leon's sister Lucie.
Counting on the jinx, they merely had to bide their time
and wait. A "suicide" removed the final obstacle a few
months later, bringing Lucie's share of the inheritance to
Leon and Marie.

The family curse was turning out to be a gold mine.
Next in line, a childless couple, the Rivets, were taken in
by the Besnards, expressing their sincerest gratitude by
altering their wills to make Marie their only heir. The ink
was barely dry before Messr. Rivet was stricken by
"pneumonia," dying in his bed. His widow's death, a
short time later, marked by nausea and convulsions, was
attributed by her physician to "the chest sickness."

Two elderly cousins, Pauline and Virginie Lalleron,
were the next to go. Pauline, according to Marie, mistook
a bowl of lye for her dessert one evening. Her excruciating
death apparently made no impression on Virginie, who
repeated the identical "mistake" a short week later. Careless as they may have been, the cousins had been clear
about remembering Marie and Leon in their wills.

For all of its adventure, married life was paling for Marie. By 1947, she had fallen for a handsome German
P.O.W. living in Loudon. In late October, Leon died at

home, but not before confiding in a friend, Madame Pintou, that he was being poisoned by his wife. "She murdered me," he gasped as he lay dying, and the story swiftly made its way around Loudon.

Marie's decrepit mother died in January 1949, her last surviving relative to fall before the "jinx." By now, the local rumor mill was working overtime, but the authorities remained aloof. Marie attempted to intimidate her various accusers, sending garbled death threats through the mails. A burglar invaded Madame Pintou's home by night, selectively destroying every gift she had received from the Besnards. The Massip brothers, having passed the Pintou rumors on, were forced to leave Loudon when arsonists destroyed their home.

Enough was finally enough. Police were summoned, and on May 11, Leon was exhumed by order of the court. According to the coroner's report, his body had absorbed approximately twice the arsenic required to kill a man. A dozen other victims were exhumed, including the Rivets, Auguste Antigny, and assorted members of the Davaillaud and Besnard families. Each, it seemed, had managed to ingest a fatal dose of arsenic before succumbing to the family "jinx." (In Auguste's case, the test was run on toenails, accidentally preserved for more than twenty years inside his shoes.)

From jail, Marie made last-ditch efforts to arrange her alibi. A friend was asked to spike the family's stock of wine with arsenic, creating reasonable doubt of accidental death, but he refused. In desperation the defendant tried to put a contract out on Madame Pintou and the Massip brothers, but her contacts ran to the police, in search of leniency in other cases. Shaken by her failures, the defendant told a visitor, "I am lost. I am guilty."

Brought to trial in February 1952, on thirteen counts of homicide, Marie Besnard displayed a different face in court. She had retained a battery of high-priced Paris lawyers, who demanded new examinations to confirm that all the victims had been slain with arsenic. A mistrial was declared, and bodies were unearthed a second time. As luck would have it, testable remains of seven victims had been totally consumed in previous examinations, and the counts of murder were reduced to six for Besnard's second trial, in March of 1954. This time, the jury failed to reach a verdict, and Marie was freed on bond until a third trial could be scheduled. In the meantime, further exhumations, further tests, reduced the dwindling supply of evidence.

The case was finally disposed of in December 1961. Determined to proceed, the state reinstituted thirteen counts of homicide against Marie Besnard, but prosecutors failed to sell their case. Despite the evidence of arsenic in thirteen corpses, her confessions and attempts to murder witnesses, Marie Besnard was finally acquitted by a jury on December 12. The "Queen of Poisoners" had managed to commit the perfect crime.

Bianchi, Kenneth A. and Buono, Angelo

Born to a prostitute mother in Rochester, New York, during May 1951, Ken Bianchi was given up for adoption as an infant. By age eleven, he was falling behind in his school work, given to furious tantrums in class and at home. Married briefly at 18, two years later he would write to a girlfriend, claiming he had killed a local man. She laughed it off, dismissing it as part of Ken's incessant macho posturing, but homicide was preying on Bianchi's mind. By 1973, he was certain police suspected him of involvement in Rochester's brutal "alphabet murders."

The case got its popular name from the initials of three young victims, raped and murdered over a two-year period. Carmen Colon, age 11, had been the first to die, in 1971. Wanda Walkowicz was next, in 1972, and the killer's victim for 1973 had been 10-year-old Michelle Maenza. In fact, police were not suspicious of Bianchi while he lived in Rochester; it would be six more years before they realized his car resembled one reported near the scene of one "alphabet" slaying.

In January 1976, Bianchi pulled up stakes and moved to Los Angeles, teaming up with his adopted cousin, Angelo Buono, in an amateur, white-slave racket. Born at Rochester in October 1934, Buono was a child of divorce, transported across country by his mother at age 5. By fourteen, he was stealing cars and displaying a precocious obsession with sodomy. Sentenced for auto theft in 1950, he escaped from the California Youth Authority and was recaptured in December 1951. As a young man, Buono idolized convicted sex offender Caryl Chessman, and in later years he would emulate the so-called "red-light" rapist's method of procuring victims. In the meantime, though, he fathered several children, viciously abusing several wives and girlfriends in the process. Somehow, in defiance of his violent temper and an almost simian appearance, he attracted scores of women, dazzling cousin Kenneth with his "harem" and his method of recruiting prostitutes through rape and torture.

Two of Buono's favorite hookers managed to escape his clutches during 1977, and Bianchi would later mark their departure as a starting point for L.A.'s reign of terror. In precisely two months time, the so-called "Hillside Stranglers" would abduct and slay ten women, frequently abandoning their naked bodies in a kind of grim display, as if to taunt authorities.

Rejected by the Glendale and Los Angeles police departments, longing for a chance to throw his weight around and show some "real authority," Bianchi fell in line with Angelo's suggestion that they should impersonate policemen, stopping female motorists or nabbing prostitutes, according to their whim. Along the way, they would subject their captives to an ordeal of torture, sexual assault and brutality, inevitably ending with a twist of the garrote.

Yolanda Washington, a 19-year-old hooker, was the first to die, murdered on October 17, her nude body discovered the next day near Universal City. Two weeks later, on October 31, police retrieved the corpse of 15-year-old Judith Miller from a flowerbed in La Crescenta. Elissa Kastin, a 21-year-old Hollywood waitress, was abducted and slain November 5, her body discovered next morning on a highway embankment in Glendale. On November 8, Jane King, aspiring actress and model, was kidnapped, raped, and suffocated, her body dumped on an off-ramp of the Golden State Freeway, undiscovered until November 22.

By that time, female residents of Los Angeles were living a nightmare. No less than three victims had been discovered on November 20, including 20-year-old honor student Kristina Wechler, dumped in Highland Park, and two classmates from junior high school, Sonja Johnson and Dolores Cepeda, discovered in Elysian Park a week after their disappearance from a local bus stop. Retrieval of Jane King's body increased local anxiety, and Thanksgiving week climaxed with the death of Lauren Wagner, an 18-year-old student, found in the Glendale hills on November 29.

By that time, police knew they were looking for dual suspects, based on the testimony of eyewitnesses including one prospective victim—the daughter of screen star Peter Lorre—who had managed to avoid the stranglers' clutches. On December 9, prostitute Kimberly Martin answered her last out-call in Glendale, turning up nude and dead on an Echo Park hillside next morning. The last to die, at least in California, was Cindy Hudspeth, found in the trunk of her car after it was pushed over a cliff in the Angeles National Forest.

Bianchi sensed that it was time to try a change of scene. Moving to Bellingham, Washington, he found work as a security guard, flirting once more with the police work he craved. On January 11, 1979, Diane Wilder and Karen Mandic were raped and murdered in Bellingham, last seen alive when they went to check out a potential house-sitting job. Bianchi had been their contact, and inconsistent answers led police to hold him for further investigation. A search of his home turned up items stolen from sites he was paid to guard, and further evidence finally linked him with the Bellingham murders. Collaboration with L.A. authorities led to Bianchi's indictment in five of the Hillside murders, during June 1979.

In custody, Bianchi first denied everything, then feigned submission to hypnosis, manufacturing multiple personalities in his bid to support an insanity defense. Psychiatrists saw through the ruse, and after his indictment in Los Angeles, Ken agreed to testify against his cousin. His guilty plea to five new counts of homicide was followed by Buono's arrest, in October 1979, and Angelo was indicted on ten counts of first-degree murder. A ten-month preliminary hearing climaxed in March 1981, with Angelo ordered to stand trial on all counts.

Bianchi, meanwhile, was desperately seeking some way to save himself. In June 1980, he received a letter from Veronica Lynn Compton, a 23-year-old poet, playwright, and aspiring actress, who sought Ken's opinion on her new play (dealing with a female serial killer). Correspondence and conversations revealed her bizarre obsession with murder, mutilation, and necrophilia, encouraging Bianchi to suggest a bizarre defense strategy. Without a second thought, Veronica agreed to visit Bellingham, strangle a woman there, and deposit specimens of Bianchi's sperm at the scene, leading police to believe the "real killer" was still at large.

On September 16, 1980, Compton visited Bianchi in prison, receiving a book with part of a rubber glove inside, containing his semen. Flying north to Bellingham, she picked out a female victim but bungled the murder attempt. Arrested in California on October 3, Compton was convicted in Washington during 1981 and sentenced to prison, with no hope of parole before 1994.

(In confinement, she soon tired of writing to Bianchi and turned her attentions to serial slayer Douglas Clark, awaiting execution at San Quentin. Their torrid correspondence struck a consistently ghoulish note, as when Compton wrote to Clark, "Our humor is unusual. I wonder why others don't see the necrophilic aspects of existence as we do." On July 27, 1988, Veronica Compton escaped from the woman's prison at Gig Harbor, Washington. She remains at large.)

As Buono's trial date approached, Bianchi began a series of contradictory statements, leading prosecutors to seek dismissal of all charges in July 1981. A courageous judge, Ronald George, refused to postpone the trial, which eventually lasted from November 1981 to November 1983. Convicted on nine counts of murder—excluding Yolanda Washington's—Buono was sentenced to nine terms of life without parole. His cousin was returned to Washington, for completion of two corresponding terms in the Bellingham case.

Biegenwald, Richard

Born on Staten Island in 1940, Biegenwald was the target of countless beatings from his alcoholic father. At age five, he torched the family home and was packed off for observation at the Psychiatric Center in Rockland county, New York. Drinking and gambling by age eight, a year later Biegenwald received a series of electro-shock-therapy treatments at New York's Bellevue Hospital. Richard's next institutional stop was the State Training School for Boys at Warwick, New York, where he was accused of theft and inciting other inmates to escape. On visits home to Staten Island, he stole money from his mother and, at age 11, set himself on fire. He was released from custody in time to graduate from the eighth grade, at age sixteen.

Biegenwald lasted only a few weeks in high school. Soon after dropping out, he drifted to Nashville, Tennessee, stole a car there, and was arrested by federal agents for transporting the vehicle across state lines. Released from custody a few months later, during 1958, he stole another car on Staten Island, drove to Bayonne, New Jersey, with a male accomplice, and there tried to hold up a grocery store. In the process, he killed proprietor Stephen Sladowski, a father of four who was also Bayonne's assistant prosecuting attorney. Biegenwald and his partner were picked up in Maryland two days later, after firing a shotgun at state troopers who stopped them for speeding. Convicted of murder and sentenced to life in New Jersey, Richard served seventeen years before his parole in 1975.

Back on the streets, he worked odd jobs and developed a curious relationship with a pretty 16-year-old neighbor of his mother's. The girl was an outstanding student, seemingly normal in all respects, and her parents were stunned when she announced her engagement to Biegenwald, a scarfaced ex-convict more than twice her age. By that time, Richard had more trouble on his hands. He had not reported to his parole officer since mid-1977, and he was suspected of rape on the side. Arrested in Brooklyn during June 1980, Biegenwald married his girlfriend in the Brooklyn House of Detention.

Rape charges were dropped when the victim failed to pick Biegenwald out of a lineup, but he served six more months on a charge of parole violation. Upon release, he found work as a maintenance man, moving his wife to an aging apartment house in Asbury Park, New Jersey. One of their neighbors was Dherran Fitzgerald, a prison acquaintance and career criminal now on parole, sought by police on charges that included shoplifting and interstate gun-running.

On January 4, 1983, the body of 18-year-old Anna Olesiewicz was found behind a restaurant in Ocean Township, north of Asbury Park. Shot four times in the head, the girl was fully clothed, and police found no evidence of rape. She had last been seen alive on Labor Day weekend, 1982, along the crowded boardwalk at Asbury Park.

Upon hearing the news, a girlfriend of Biegenwald's wife placed an urgent call to police, fingering Richard as a suspect in the murder. According to the caller, she had accompanied Biegenwald on several trips to the boardwalk, trolling for victims, and he had once shown her a young woman's body hidden in his garage, giving her one of the victim's rings as a present.

Police surrounded the apartment house on January 22, surprising Biegenwald, his wife, and Dherran Fitzgerald. A search of the premises turned up pipe bombs, pistols, a machine gun, knockout drops and marijuana, a live puff adder snake, and the floor plans of various local business establishments. In custody, Fitzgerald began to sing, remarking that Biegenwald had once shown him a woman's corpse in the garage, explaining that she had been killed "for business reasons." Fitzgerald had helped bury the victim at the home of Biegenwald's mother, on Staten Island, accidentally uncovering a second dead woman as he was digging the grave. Following his directions, police unearthed the remains of 17-year-old Maria Ciallella, last seen in October 1981, and Deborah Osborne, also 17, missing since April 1982. Ciallella had been shot twice in the head, while Osborne had been stabbed in the chest and

abdomen. Another field trip with Fitzgerald brought officers to the grave of a 17-year-old Betsy Bacon, shot twice
in the head, at a point north of Asbury Park.

As the investigation proceeded, new charges were filed
against Biegenwald in the murder of prison escapee William Ward, shot five times in the head and buried outside
Neptune City, New Jersey. Biegenwald was also suspected, but never charged, in two other killings. One involved the shooting death of John Petrone, an ex-convict
and sometime police informer, unearthed—minus his jaw-
bone—on a remote New Jersey wildlife preserve. The other
case involved Virginia Clayton, 17, abducted and killed on
September 8, 1982, her body found three days later, four
miles from the site where Petrone was buried.

Richard Biegenwald was indicted by New Jersey authorities on five counts of first-degree murder. Dherran
Fitzgerald turned state's evidence, pleading guilty on
counts of weapons possession and hindering Biegenwald's
arrest (by concealing bodies), receiving a sentence of five
years on each count. Upon conviction of murdering Anna
Olesiewicz, Biegenwald was sentenced to death by lethal
injection. A second conviction, in the case of William
Ward, earned him a sentence of life imprisonment.

Bishop, Arthur Gary

Raised by devout Mormon parents in Salt Lake City,
Utah, Bishop was an Eagle Scout and honor student in
high school, afterward serving his church as a missionary
in the Philippines. On his return to Utah, he graduated
with honors from Steven Henager College, with a major
in accounting. Friends and family members were stunned
by his February 1978 conviction for embezzling $8,714
from a used car dealership, but Bishop seemed repentant,
pleading guilty and winning a five-year suspended sentence on his promise of restitution. Instead of paying the
money back, however, he dropped from sight, and a warrant was issued for his arrest. When Bishop refused to
surrender, he was formally excommunicated from the
Mormon church.

By that time, in October 1978, he was living as "Roger Downs" in Salt Lake City, signing up with the Big Brother program to spend time with disadvantaged youth. Wherever Bishop settled, his charisma lured children into spending time around his home or joining him on camping expeditions. Over time, it led five victims to their deaths.

The first to vanish, four-year-old Alonzo Daniels, was reported missing from his Salt Lake City apartment complex on October 14, 1979. "Roger Downs" lived just across the hall, and he was questioned by police, but it was all routine. Detectives had no leads, no body, and no suspect in the case.

On November 9, 1980, 11-year-old Kim Peterson disappeared in Salt Lake City, last seen when he left home to sell a pair of skates. The buyer was alleged to be a male adult, but neither of Kim's parents had seen the man, and they had no clue to his identity.

Eleven months later, on October 20, 1981, four-year-old Danny Davis disappeared from his grandfather's side while shopping at a busy supermarket in southern Salt Lake County. "Roger Downs," residing half a block from the store, was routinely questioned by authorities, but they made no connection with previous cases and did not consider him a suspect.

Another eighteen months elapsed before the killer struck again, abducting Troy Ward on June 22, 1983—his sixth birthday. On July 14, 13-year-old Graeme Cunningham vanished from home, two days before he was scheduled to go on a camping trip with a classmate and their adult chaperone, 32-year-old "Roger Downs."

After questioning "Downs," police began quietly checking his background, discovering his almost unnatural fondness for neighborhood children. They also learned that he was wanted—under the alias of "Lynn Jones"—for embezzling $10,000 from a recent employer, stealing his own personnel file from the office before he disappeared.

In custody, Bishop quickly admitted his true identity, confessing to five counts of murder. Next morning, he led authorities to the Cedar Fort section of Utah County, pointing out graves where the remains of victims Daniels, Peterson, and Davis were recovered. A drive to Big Cottonwood Creek, 65 miles further south, turned up the bodies of Troy Ward and Graeme Cunningham.

The continuing investigation revealed that Bishop had molested scores of other children through the years, sparing their lives for reasons known only to himself. Several parents had knowledge of his activities, but none had come forward while the four-year search for a child killer was in progress. A search of Bishop's home uncovered a revolver and a bloody hammer, snapshots of one victim taken after his abduction, and various other photographs of nude boys, focused on their torsos to prevent identification.

In court, jurors listened to Bishop's taped confession, including his admission of fondling victims after death. At some points he giggled, at other times mimicking a boy's final words in a high, falsetto voice. The clincher was his statement that, "I'm glad they caught me, because I'd do it again." Convicted and sentenced to die, Bishop waived all appeals and was executed, by lethal injection, on June 9, 1988.

Bittaker, Lawrence Sigmund and Norris, Roy Lewis

Lawrence Bittaker was serving time for assault with a deadly weapon in 1978, when he met Roy Norris at the California Men's Colony at San Luis Obispo. A convicted rapist, Norris recognized a soul-mate in Bittaker, and they soon became inseparable. While still confined, they hatched a grisly plot to kidnap, rape and murder teenage girls "for fun," as soon as they were freed. If all went well, they planned to kill at least one girl of each "teen" age—from 13 through 19—recording the events on tape and film.

Paroled on November 15, 1978, Bittaker began making preparations for the crime spree, obtaining a van that he dubbed "Murder Mack." Norris was released on June 15, 1979, after a period of observation at Atascadero State Hospital, and he hurried to Bittaker's side, anxious to implement their plans.

On June 24, 1979, 16-year-old Linda Schaeffer vanished following a church function, never to be seen again. Joy Hall, 18, disappeared without a trace in Redondo Beach on July 8. Two months later, on September 2, Jacqueline Lamp, 13, and Jackie Gilliam, 15, were lost while thumbing rides in Redondo Beach. Shirley Ledford, 16, of Sunland, was the only victim recovered by authorities; abducted on October 31, she was found the next morning in a Tijunga residential district. Strangled with a coat hanger, she had first been subjected to "sadistic and barbaric abuse," her breasts and face mutilated, arms slashed, her body covered with bruises.

Detectives got their break on November 20, when Bittaker and Norris were arrested on charges stemming from a September 30 assault in Hermosa Beach. According to reports, their female victim had been sprayed with Mace, abducted in a silver van, and raped before she managed to escape. The woman ultimately failed to make a positive I.D. on Bittaker and Norris, but arresting officers discovered drugs in their possession, holding both in jail for violation of parole.

Roy Norris started showing signs of strain in custody. At a preliminary hearing, in Hermosa Beach, he offered an apology "for my insanity," and he was soon regaling officers with tales of murder. According to his statements, girls had been approached at random, photographed by Bittaker, and offered rides, free marijuana, jobs in modeling. Most turned the offers down, but others were abducted forcibly, the van's radio drowning their screams as they were driven to a remote mountain fire road for sessions of rape and torture. Tape recordings of Jacqueline Lamp's final moments were recovered from the "Murder Mack," and detectives counted 500 photographs of smiling young women among the suspects' effects.

On February 9, 1980, Norris led deputies to shallow graves in San Dimas Canyon and the San Gabriel Mountains, where skeletal remains of Lamp and Jackie Gilliam were recovered. An ice pick still protruded from Gilliam's skull, and the remains bore other marks of cruel mistreatment. Charging the prisoners with five counts of murder, Los Angeles County Sheriff Peter Pitchess announced that

Bittaker and Norris might be linked to the disappearance of 30 or 40 other victims. By February 20, the stack of candid photographs had yielded nineteen missing girls, but none were ever traced, and Norris had apparently exhausted his desire to talk.

On March 18, Norris pled guilty on five counts of murder, turning state's evidence against his confederate. In return for his cooperation, he received a sentence of 45 years to life, with parole possible after thirty years.

Bittaker, meanwhile, denied everything. At his trial, on February 5, 1981, he testified that Norris first informed him of the murders after their arrest in 1979. A jury chose to disbelieve him, returning a guilty verdict on February 17. On March 24, in accordance with the jury's recommendation, Bittaker was sentenced to die. The judge imposed an alternate sentence of 199 years and four months, to take effect in the event that Bittaker's death sentence is ever commuted to life imprisonment.

Boden, Wayne Clifford

A sexual sadist, obsessed with the desire to bite female breasts, Canadian Wayne Boden became infamous as the "Vampire Rapist," after his distinctive *modus operandi*. Stalking his victims in the neighborhood of Montreal, he sparked a two-year reign of terror with attacks that drew particular attention for their brute ferocity.

On July 23, 1968, Norma Villancourt, a 21-year-old teacher, was found dead in her Montreal apartment. She had been raped and strangled, her breasts savaged with bite marks, but police reported no evident signs of a struggle. In fact, a pathologist noted the victim had died with a passive, faint smile on her face.

The best part of a year elapsed before the killer struck again, in 1969, strangling Shirley Audette and dumping her corpse at the rear of an apartment complex in West Montreal. Though fully clothed when found, she had been raped, and there were bite marks on her breasts. A conversation with the victim's former boyfriend brought to light her fears that she was "getting into something dangerous" with someone she had started dating, but the suspect's name had not been mentioned.

On November 23, Marielle Archambault left her job at a Montreal jewelry store, departing with a young man she addressed as "Bill." When she did not appear for work the next morning, Marielle's employer went to see if she was ill. He found her on the floor of her apartment living room, the victim of a strangler who had raped her, ripping off her bra to gnaw her breasts. A crumpled photograph discovered in the wreckage of her flat was readily identified as that of her companion, "Bill," but homicide detectives still could not connect the smiling face with any real-life suspect.

On January 16, 1970, the killer struck again, picking off Jean Wray, 24, in her Montreal apartment. On arrival for a scheduled date, Wray's boyfriend found her door unlocked, her naked body on the sofa, bloody bite marks on her breasts. Despite the clear-cut evidence of violence, officers could find no sign of a protracted struggle; once again, the victim looked serene in death.

The fear in Montreal was little more than an unpleasant memory by 1971, when the Vampire Rapist made his next appearance some 2,500 miles away, in Calgary. His victim was Elizabeth Pourteous, a teacher, reported missing from work on May 18. Her apartment manager was called, and found her body on the bedroom floor, surrounded by wreckage of a struggle. Raped and strangled, she had also suffered the familiar bite marks on her breasts. A broken cufflink was discovered near the body.

Two colleagues at her school recalled that Pourteous had been seen with a young man, in a blue Mercedes, on the night she died. The car had featured a bull-shaped decal, advertising beef, in one window. A friend of the victim also informed police that Pourteous had recently started dating a new acquaintance—named "Bill"—who fit descriptions of the Vampire Rapist.

On May 19, patrolmen found the suspect car parked near the murder scene. Wayne Boden was arrested half an hour later, moving toward the car on foot. He told police that he had moved from Montreal a year earlier, admitted seeing Elizabeth Pourteous on the night she died, and

identified the cufflink as his own. The final confirmation
was delivered by an orthodontist, who compared a cast of
Boden's teeth with bite marks on the victim, earning
Wayne a term of life imprisonment.

Returned to Montreal for trial, he openly confessed to
three of the related murders, oddly balking in the case of
Norma Villancourt. It was enough, regardless, and his four
life sentences appeared to guarantee that Boden would be
permanently out of circulation.

Bombeek, Cecile

Early in 1977, nurses employed at the public hospital in
picturesque Wetteren, Belgium, began comparing notes on
curious events in the 38-bed geriatric ward. For openers,
the death rate had increased dramatically in recent months,
with twenty-one patients lost in the span of a year. Other
cases revealed signs of sadistic mistreatment, including
catheters ripped from the bladders of elderly patients by
"persons unknown." In time, suspicion focused on 44-
year-old Sister Godfrida, a Josephite nun assigned to the
geriatric ward.

Born Cecile Bombeek, the product of a staunchly Catholic home, Sister Godfrida adopted her religious name after joining the Apostolic Order of St. Joseph. Her behavior
appears to have been exemplary before 1976, when the
aftermath of brain surgery left her addicted to morphine.
Narcotics are available in Wetteren, despite stiff criminal
penalties, but they are not inexpensive. Neither were Sister
Godfrida's bisexual love affairs with a retired missionary
and a local teacher; her lovers enjoyed expensive food,
vintage wine, and Cecile was anxious to oblige.

In time, police contended, she began to loot the savings
and personal property of her aged patients, embezzling
more than $30,000 in a year's time. On the side, she began
to display sadistic tendencies, abusing her charges, killing
at least three with insulin overdoses when they became
"too difficult at night." In retrospect, it was impossible
to estimate the lethal sister's body-count. Dr. Jean-Paul

De Corte, spokesman for the hospital's governing board, declared, "It could just as well be thirty people as three."

In custody, Cecile's confession to three homicides was sufficient to bring an indictment. In March 1978, she was committed for psychiatric observation, to determine her fitness for trial.

Brady, Ian Duncan and Hindley, Myra

Born on January 2, 1938, Ian Stewart was the illegitimate son of a Scottish waitress. He never met his father, and despite sporadic visits from his mother he was raised by foster parents in Gorbals, Glasgow's toughest slum. In early years, he earned a reputation as a budding sadist, torturing other children and maiming animals "for fun." He also tried his hand at petty crime, earning several terms of probation on charges that included housebreaking and theft. In 1954, the courts sent him to Manchester, to live with his mother and her new husband, Patrick Brady. Ian would use his stepfather's surname in the future, continuing his criminal activities as he blossomed into a full-fledged teenage alcoholic. A week after his eighteenth birthday, Ian was sentenced to two years on conviction for theft. His last arrest, before indictment on murder charges, was settled by payment of a fine for drunk and disorderly conduct, in 1958. Along the way, he had acquired new interests, building up a library of books on Nazi Germany, sadism, and sexual perversion.

Born in July 1942, Myra Hindley was sent to live with her grandmother after the birth of her younger sister. Homely and shy, she was still a virgin in January 1961, when she found work as a typist for a chemical supply company in Gorbals. Ian Brady was the invoice clerk, and Myra fell for him on sight, penning endless professions of love in her diary, afraid to approach him directly. Brady impressed her as an intellectual, reading *Mein Kampf* at lunch in the original German, and she was thrilled when he finally asked her out. They took in a movie—about the

Nuremburg war crimes tribunal—and then returned to her grandmother's house, where Brady introduced her to sex.

Soon, they were inseparable, Myra bleaching her hair to please Ian, dressing in Nazi-style boots and leather, with Brady dubbing her "Myra Hess." They used Ian's automatic camera to pose for obscene photos—complete with hoods, whips, and a dog—but Brady was unsuccessful in his efforts to crack the local pornography market. Next, they toyed with the idea of armed robbery, but Brady's nerve failed in the crunch, leaving Myra to take shooting lessons, purchase two pistols, and pass a driver's test in expectation of wheeling the getaway car. Finally, unable to go through with the plan, they turned their attention to kidnapping, child molestation, and murder.

Police did not connect the crimes, at first. Pauline Reade, 16, was the first to vanish, missing from her Gorton home—two doors from the residence of Myra Hindley's brother-in-law—on July 12, 1963. Four months later, on November 23, 12-year-old John Kilbride disappeared from Ashton-under-Lyne. Keith Bennett, also 12, was reported missing from Manchester on June 16, 1964, last seen near the home occupied by Brady's mother. Another Manchester victim, 10-year-old Leslie Ann Downey, disappeared without a trace on December 26, 1964.

Authorities were baffled by the "unrelated" cases, left without a single piece of solid evidence. The twisted lovers, meanwhile, were intent on a campaign to corrupt Myra's brother-in-law, David Smith, and recruit him into their circle. A petty criminal with several arrests of his own, Smith was amused when the conversation turned to murder, and he questioned Brady's ability to follow through. On October 6, 1965, Brady offered a practical demonstration with Edward Evans, a 17-year-old homosexual, striking him fourteen times with a hatchet before finishing the job by means of strangulation.

Horrified, Smith phoned police next morning, directing them to Brady's address. The raiders caught Ian and Myra at home, retrieving a fresh corpse from the bedroom, along with the bloody hatchet and Brady's library of volumes on perversion and sadism. A 12-year-old neighbor girl recalled several trips she had made with the couple to Saddleworth Moor, northeast of Manchester, near the Penine Way, and authorities launched a search which uncovered the body of Leslie Ann Downey on October 16.

Four days later, another search of Brady's flat turned up two left-luggage tickets for Manchester Central Station, leading police to a pair of hidden suitcases. Inside, they found nude photographs of Leslie Ann, along with tape recordings of her final tortured moments, pleading for her life as she was brutally abused. A series of seemingly innocent snapshots depicted portions of Saddleworth Moor, and detectives paid another visit to the desolate region on October 21, unearthing the body of John Kilbride.

In custody, Brady seemed proud of his crimes, boasting of "three or four" victims planted on the moors. Police announced that they were opening their files on eight missing persons, lost over the past four years, but no new charges had been added by the time Ian and Myra went to trial. Jurors were stunned by the Downey tape, and by Brady's bland description of the recording as "unusual." On May 6, 1966, both defendants were convicted of killing Edward Evans and Leslie Ann Downey; Brady was also convicted of murdering John Kilbride, while Myra was convicted as an accessory after the fact. Brady was sentenced to concurrent life terms on each count, while Hindley received two life terms plus seven years in the Kilbride case.

Nineteen years later, in November 1985, Brady was transferred from prison to a maximum-security hospital, there confessing the Reade-Bennett murders in an interview with tabloid reporters. Another year passed before searchers returned to the moors, with Myra Hindley joining them for an abortive outing on December 15, 1986. The remains of Pauline Reade were uncovered on June 30, 1987, nearly a quarter-century after her disappearance. It took pathologists a month to decide that the girl had been sexually assaulted, her throat slashed from behind.

In August 1987, Brady mailed a letter to the BBC, containing sketchy information on five "new" murders. In the letter, Brady claimed another victim buried on the moor, a man murdered in Manchester, a woman dumped in a canal, and two victims gunned down in Scotland, at

Glasgow and Loch Long. None of the victims were identified, but police announced that they were reopening the
files on two ancient murders, including the 1963 beating
death of 55-year-old Veronica Bondi in Manchester, and
the 1965 strangulation of Edith Gleave, a 38-year-old prostitute, in Stockport. No further information is forthcoming
in those cases, but it was announced—on January 14,
1988—that no prosecution is anticipated in the cases of
Pauline Reade and Keith Bennett.

Briggen, Joseph

Born around 1850, Joseph Briggen was a product of
farming stock and he followed in the family tradition,
working hard to scratch a living from his remote Sierra
Morena Ranch, in northern California. All things considered, he had little to show for his labor. Briggen's crop
was invariably poor, and the effort might have been a complete waste of time, except for his prize Berkshire hogs.

So perfect were his swine, that Briggen soon became
the odds-on favorite for winning honors at the annual state
fair in Sacramento. His pork brought top dollar, and every
year Briggen was pestered by questions from envious
breeders. In answer, he would only say that his stock
received the finest possible care—and the best feed
—available.

The feed, in fact, was Briggen's specialty, although he
dared not share the recipe. For years, the rancher made
repeated, periodic trips to San Francisco, touring the
Embarcadero district in search for homeless men and
transients. These he hired, throwing in a pledge of room
and board. Sometimes the new employees lasted weeks,
before they grew suspicious and demanded something
more than food and lodging for their pay. When cash was
called for, Briggen simply killed his latest victim,
chopped the body up, and fed it to his hogs. In Briggen's
mind, the ''special'' diet was responsible for his success
in raising swine, and he was not prepared to change a
winning system.

In early 1902, Briggen hired a young man named Steven

Korad, the latest in a series of expendable employees, but the rancher's carelessness was showing. Checking out his room that night, before retiring, Korad found two severed fingers on the floor behind his bed. The young man slipped away to notify authorities, and excavations at the ranch unearthed an estimated dozen victims in the next few days. A human skull and other bones were found inside the sty itself.

Authorities did not suggest that Briggen's body-count was limited to twelve or thirteen victims, but they had enough to win conviction. Tried in August, Briggen drew a term of life imprisonment and died a short time later, in San Quentin. The identify and final number of his victims stands as an enduring mystery.

Brudos, Jerome Henry

Born in South Dakota during January 1939, Brudos moved to California with his family, as a child. He grew up with a deep, abiding hatred for his domineering mother and a strange, precocious lust for women's shoes. Discovering a pair of high-heels at the local dump, he brought them home, where they were confiscated and burned by his mother. By the time he entered first grade, Brudos was stealing shoes from his sister; at age sixteen, now living in Oregon, he branched out into burglary, making off with shoes from neighboring homes, sometimes snatching women's undergarments from clothes lines.

In 1956, at seventeen, Brudos beat up a girl who resisted his crude advances on a date, winding up in juvenile court. Ordered to visit the state hospital in Salem, as an out-patient, while continuing his high school education, Brudos apparently gained nothing from therapy. Joining the army in March 1959, he was troubled by dreams of a woman creeping into his bed at night. A chat with an army psychiatrist led to Jerome's discharge on October 15, 1959, and he went home to live with his parents, in Salem, moving into their tool shed.

Unknown to members of his family, Brudos had begun to prey on local women, stalking them until he found a chance to knock them down or choke them unconscious, fleeing with their shoes. Still virginal in 1962, he met his future wife and quickly made her pregnant, trooping to the altar from a sense of obligation. By 1967, settled in the Portland suburb of Aloha, Brudos began complaining of migraine headaches and "blackouts," relieving his symptoms with night-prowling raids to steal shoes and lacy undergarments. On one occasion, a woman awoke to find him ransacking her closet and Brudos choked her unconscious, raping her before he fled.

On January 26, 1968, 19-year-old Linda Slawson was selling encyclopedias door-to-door when she called on Jerry Brudos. Bludgeoned and strangled to death in his basement, she became the first of five known victims killed in Oregon. The second, 16-year-old Stephanie Vikko, disappeared from Portland in July. A third, student Jan Whitney, 23, vanished on November 26, during a two-hour drive from Eugene to McMinnville, her car turning up north of Albany, Oregon.

So far, authorities were working on a string of disappearances, with no hard proof of homicide. That changed on March 18, 1969, with the discovery of Stephanie Vikko's remains, in a wooden area northwest of Forest Grove. Nine days later, 19-year-old Karen Sprinker vanished from a Salem parking garage, leaving her car behind. Two witnesses reported same-day sightings of a large man, dressed in women's clothing, loitering in the garage.

While the police were searching for their suspect, Brudos faced a minor crisis in his own back yard. While cleaning house, his wife had turned up photographs of Jerry dressed in drag, and she had also found a "plastic" breast, described by Brudos as a "paperweight." (In fact, it was a hunting trophy, treated with preservative.) She missed the *other* photographs, depicting Brudos with his victims, posing with their bodies, dressing them in frilly underwear like life-sized dolls, but dark suspicion had begun to fester, all the same.

On April 23, 1969, Brudos claimed his final victim, picking off 22-year-old Linda Salee at a Portland shopping mall. Her body, weighted down with an auto transmission, was pulled from the Long Tom River on May 10. Two days later, fifty feet downstream, a team of divers turned up victim Karen Sprinker, weighted with an engine block. The second body wore a brassiere several sizes too large, padded with paper towels to conceal the fact that her breasts had been amputated.

Interviews with local co-eds yielded several stories of an aging, self-described "Vietnam veteran" who frequently approached girls on campus, asking for dates. Police staked out the scene of one such rendezvous, in Corvallis, on May 25, questioning Jerry Brudos closely before they let him go. Picked up on a concealed weapons charge five days later, Brudos broke down and confessed to the murders in detail, directing authorities to evidence that would clinch their case. On June 27, 1969, Brudos pled guilty on three counts of first-degree murder and was sentenced to a term of life imprisonment. His popularity with fellow inmates is recorded in a string of prison "accidents," including one that left him with a fractured neck in 1971.

"BTK Strangler, The"

The residents of Wichita were ill-prepared to cope with monsters in the early days of 1974. Their lives were by and large conservative, well-ordered, purposeful. They had no previous experience to help prepare them for the coming terror, and it took them absolutely by surprise.

On January 15, four members of the Otero family were found dead in their comfortable suburban home, trussed up like Thanksgiving turkeys and strangled with lengths of cord cut from old venetian blinds. Joseph Otero, 38, lay face-down on the floor at the foot of his bed, wrists and ankles bound with samples of the same cord that was wrapped around his neck. Close by, Julie Otero lay on the bed she had once shared with her husband, bound in similar fashion and already cooling in death. Joseph II, age nine, was found in his bedroom, duplicating his father's position at the foot of his bed, a plastic bag encasing his skull. Downstairs, 11-year-old Josephine hung by her neck from a pipe in the basement, dressed only in sweatshirt and socks.

Aside from the killer's ritualistic M.O., police knew the attack had been planned in advance. Someone had severed phone lines outside, bringing an ample supply of cord for binding and strangling his victims when he entered the house. The neighbors filed reports of a "suspicious looking" stranger in the area, but published sketches of the suspect led police precisely nowhere.

Ten months later, in October, a local newspaper editor received his first anonymous call from the killer, directing him to a particular book in the Wichita public library. Inside the book, he found a letter filled with numerous misspellings, claiming credit for the massacre, promising more victims to come. Signing himself the "BTK Strangler," the killer provided his own translation in a post script. He wrote: "The code words for me will be . . . Bind them, Torture them, Kill them."

Police requested that the letter be withheld, against the possibility of false confessions in the case, but no one came forward. No evidence materialized. Twenty-nine months would pass before the killer showed his hand again.

On March 17, 1977, 26-year-old Shirley Vian was murdered in her home, stripped, bound and strangled on her bed, left with a plastic bag over her head, the traditional cord wrapped tight around her neck. Vian's three children, locked in a closet by the armed intruder who invaded their home, managed to free themselves and call police. Again, the crime was clearly premeditated: the killer had stopped one of Vian's sons on the street that morning, displaying photographs of a woman and child, allegedly seeking directions to their home.

On December 9, 1977, Nancy Jo Fox, 25, was found dead in the bedroom of her Wichita apartment, a nylon stocking twisted around her neck. Unlike previous victims, she was fully clothed. An anonymous caller directed officers to the scene, and police traced the call to a downtown phone booth, where witnesses vaguely recalled "someone"—perhaps a blond six-footer—using the booth moments later.

The killer mailed a poem to the local press on January 31,

but it was routed to the advertising section by mistake and overlooked for days. Disgruntled at the absence of publicity, he shifted targets, firing off a letter to a local television station on February 10. "How many do I have to kill," he asked, "before I get my name in the paper or some national attention?"

In his latest note, the strangler claimed a total of seven victims, naming Vian and Fox as the latest. Number seven remained anonymous, with a taunting punch line: "You guess the motive and the victims." Unable to document the killer's claim, authorities still took him at his word, announcing theoretical acceptance of the body-count.

Alternately blaming his crimes on "a demon" and a mysterious "factor X," the strangler compared his work with that of Jack the Ripper, Son of Sam, and the Hillside Strangler. Psychiatrists who analyzed the letters felt the killer saw himself as part of some nebulous "grand scheme," but they were unable to pinpoint his motive or predict his next move.

In fact, there was none. With a decade and more having passed since his last, whining plea for attention, the strangler has claimed no more victims in Wichita, penned no more poems or notes to the press. He has vanished, as if from the face of the earth, leaving questions and riddles behind.

Bullock, David

Born in New York City on November 13, 1960, Bullock had a history of trouble with the law that dated from his adolescent years. In February 1977, he was arrested in Monroe, New York, on charges of criminal mischief and petty larceny. Five months later, in Manhattan, he pled guilty to attempted grand larceny and was committed to a home for delinquent youths, receiving a conditional discharge in November. A burglary arrest in January 1978 led to his adjudication as a youthful offender in Goshen, New York. Over the next three years, Bullock logged adult arrests for robbery and grand larceny, drifting into the seamy underworld of male prostitution. Between December 1981 and January 1982, he killed at least six times, without apparent provocation from his victims.

Number one was 42-year-old James Weber, an actor shot to death in Central Park the evening of December 4. Nine days later, Bullock told prostitute Edwina Atkins about the murder and she "laughed in (his) face," refusing to believe the story. After sex, Bullock covered her face with a pillow, shot Atkins in the head and set her apartment on fire. On December 15, Bullock used a similar method with Stephen Hassell, a 29-year-old businessman who took him home for sex. As Bullock told detectives, there was "no particular reason" for Hassell's murder, it was "something to amuse myself."

Bullock's fourth victim was roommate Michael Winley, shot in the head on December 23 and dumped in the Harlem River. (Police accepted Bullock's version of the crime, despite the fact that Winley's corpse had never been recovered.) Heriberto Morales, age 50, took Bullock home after a Christmas party and paid for the mistake with his life. According to Bullock, Morales "started messing with the Christmas tree, telling me how nice the Christmas tree was, so I shot him." As an afterthought, he also set the place on fire.

Thus far, all of Bullock's victims had been murdered with a .38 revolver, shot without apparent motive. On the fourth of January, Bullock needed cash and he was carrying a sawed-off shotgun when he met 28-year-old Eric Fuller in Mount Morris Park. Charged with six counts of murder on January 15, Bullock told detectives that there might be other victims: he had tried to shoot at least four more, but might have missed. Without specific details, bodies, or complaints from living targets, no more charges were appended to the list.

On October 26, 1982, Bullock pled guilty to six counts of second-degree murder. Asked for a motive, he told the court, "It's fun." To David Bullock, murder was a kind of sport that "makes me happy." Facing terms of 25 years to life on each murder count, he was advised of the judge's intention to mete out a sentence that "guarantees you never get out of jail as long as you shall live."

Bundy, Theodore Robert

Ted Bundy is a striking contrast to the general image of a "homicidal maniac": attractive, self-assured, politically ambitious, and successful with a wide variety of women. But his private demons drove him to extremes of violence that make the gory worst of modern "slasher" films seem almost petty by comparison. With his chameleon-like ability to blend, his talent for belonging, Bundy posed an ever-present danger to the pretty, dark-haired women he selected as his victims.

Linda Healy was the first fatality. On January 31, 1974, she vanished from her basement lodgings in Seattle, leaving bloody sheets behind, a blood-stained nightgown hanging in her closet. Several blocks away, young Susan Clarke had been assaulted, bludgeoned in her bed a few weeks earlier, but she survived her crushing injuries and would eventually recover. As for Linda Healy, she was gone without a trace.

Police had no persuasive evidence of any pattern yet, but it would not be long in coming. On March 12, Donna Gail Manson disappeared en route to a concert in Olympia, Washington. On April 17, Susan Rancourt vanished on her way to see a German language film in Ellensburg. On May 6, Roberta Parks failed to return from a late-night stroll in her Corvallis neighborhood. On June 1, Brenda Ball left Seattle's Flame Tavern with an unknown man and vanished, as if into thin air. Ten days later, Georgann Hawkins joined the list of missing women, lost somewhere between her boyfriend's apartment and her own sorority house in Seattle.

Now detectives had their pattern. All the missing women had been young, attractive, with their dark hair worn at shoulder length or longer, parted in the middle. In their photos, laid out side-by-side, they might have passed for sisters, some for twins. Homicide investigators had no corpses yet, but they refused to cherish false illusions of a happy ending to the case. There were so many victims, and the worst was yet to come.

July 14. A crowd assembled on the shores of Lake Sammamish to enjoy the sun and water sports of summer.

When the day was over, two more names would be appended to the growing list of missing women: Janice Ott and Denise Naslund had each disappeared within sight of their separate friends, but this time police had a tenuous lead. Passers-by remembered seeing Janice Ott in conversation with a man who carried one arm in a sling; he had been overheard to introduce himself as "Ted." With that report in hand, detectives turned up other female witnesses who were themselves approached by "Ted" at Lake Sammamish. In each case, he had asked for help securing a sailboat to his car. The lucky women had declined, but one had followed "Ted" to where his small Volkswagen "bug" was parked; there was no sign of any sailboat, and his explanation—that the boat would have to be retrieved from a house "up the hill"—had aroused her suspicions, prompting her to put the stranger off.

Police now had a fair description of their suspect and his car. The published references to "Ted" inspired a rash of calls reporting "suspects," one of them in reference to college student Theodore Bundy. The authorities checked out each lead as time allowed, but Bundy was considered "squeaky clean;" a law student and Young Republican active in law-and-order politics, he once had chased a mugger several blocks to make a citizen's arrest. So many calls reporting suspects had been made from spite or simple overzealousness, and Bundy's name was filed away with countless others, momentarily forgotten.

On September 7, hunters found a makeshift graveyard on a wooded hillside several miles from Lake Sammamish. Dental records were required to finally identify remains of Janice Ott and Denise Naslund; the skeleton of a third woman, found with the others, could not be identified. Five weeks later, on October 12, another hunter found the bones of two more women in Clark County. One victim was identified as Carol Valenzuela, missing for two months from Vancouver, Washington, on the Oregon border; again, the second victim would remain unknown, recorded in the files as a "Jane Doe." Police were optimistic, hopeful that discovery of victims would eventually lead them to the killer, but they had no way of knowing that their man had given them the slip already, moving on in search of safer hunting grounds and other prey.

The terror came to Utah on October 2, 1974, when Nancy Wilcox disappeared in Salt Lake City. On October 18, Melissa Smith vanished in Midvale; her body, raped and beaten, would be unearthed in the Wasatch Mountains nine days later. Laura Aime joined the missing list in Orem, on October 31, while walking home in costume from a Halloween party; a month would pass before her battered, violated body was discovered in a wooded area outside of town. A man attempted to abduct attractive Carol Da Ronch from a Salt Lake City shopping mall November 8, but she was able to escape before he could attach a pair of handcuffs to her wrists. That evening, Debbie Kent was kidnapped from the auditorium at Salt Lake City's Viewmont High School.

Authorities in Utah kept communications open with police in other states, including Washington. They might have noticed that a suspect from Seattle, one Ted Bundy, was attending school in Utah when the local disappearances occurred, but they were looking for a madman, rather than a sober, well-groomed student of the law who seemed to have political connections in Seattle. Bundy stayed on file, and was again forgotten.

With the new year, Colorado joined the list of hunting grounds for an elusive killer who apparently selected victims by their hairstyles. Caryn Campbell was the first to vanish, from a ski lodge at Snowmass on January 12; her raped and battered body would be found on February 17. On March 15, Julie Cunningham disappeared en route to a tavern in Vail. One month later to the day, Melanie Cooley went missing while riding her bicycle in Nederland; she was discovered eight days later, dead, her skull crushed, with her jeans pulled down around her ankles. On July 1, Shelly Robertson was added to the missing list in Golden; her remains were found on August 23, discarded in a mine shaft near the Berthoud Pass.

A week before the final, grim discovery, Ted Bundy was arrested in Salt Lake City for suspicion of burglary. Erratic driving had attracted the attention of police, and an examination of the car—a small VW—revealed peculiar items such as handcuffs and a pair of panty hose with eyeholes cut to form a stocking mask. The glove compartment yielded gasoline receipts and maps that linked the suspect with a list of Colorado ski resorts, including Vail and Snowmass. Carol Da Ronch identified Ted Bundy as the man who had attacked her in November, and her testimony was sufficient to convict him on a charge of attempted kidnapping. Other states were waiting for a shot at Bundy now, and in January 1977 he was extradited to Colorado for trial in the murder of Caryn Campbell, at Snowmass.

Faced with prison time already, Bundy had no time to spare for further trials. He fled from custody in June, and was recaptured after eight days on the road. On December 30 he tried again, with more success, escaping all the way to Tallahassee, Florida, where he found lodgings on the outskirts of Florida State University. Suspected in a score of deaths already, Bundy had secured himself another happy hunting ground.

In the small hours of January 15, 1978, he invaded the Chi Omega sorority house, dressed all in black and armed with a heavy wooden club. Before he left, two women had been raped and killed, a third severely injured by the beating he inflicted with his bludgeon. Within the hour, he had slipped inside another house, just blocks away, to club another victim in her bed. She, too, survived. Detectives at the Chi Omega house discovered bite marks on the corpses there, appalling evidence of Bundy's fervor at the moment of the kill.

On February 6, Ted stole a van and drove to Jacksonville, where he was spotted in the act of trying to abduct a schoolgirl. Three days later, twelve-year-old Kimberly Leach disappeared from a schoolyard nearby; she was found in the first week of April, her body discarded near Suwanee State Park.

Police in Pensacola spotted Bundy's stolen license plates on February 15, and were forced to run him down as he attempted to escape on foot. Once Bundy was identified, impressions of his teeth were taken to compare with bite marks on the Chi Omega victims, and his fate was sealed. Convicted on two counts of murder in July 1979, he was sentenced to die in Florida's electric chair. A third conviction and death sentence were subsequently obtained in the case of Kimberly Leach.

After ten years of appeals, Bundy was finally executed in February 1989. In his last interview, he confessed to a total of 28 murders.

Cannibal Murders—Illinois

It was a case with all the grisly drama of a Hollywood production. A serial slayer, predictably dubbed "Jack the Ripper" by newsmen, was stalking young women in Chicago and environs, discarding their mutilated corpses like so much cast-off rubbish. Homicide detectives had no inkling of the killer's motive or identity; they couldn't even manage to agree upon a body-count. The speculation published daily in Chicago's press was bad enough; the truth, when finally exposed, was infinitely worse.

On May 23, 1981, 28-year-old Linda Sutton was abducted by persons unknown from Elmhurst, a Chicago suburb. Ten days later, her mutilated body—the left breast missing—was recovered from a field in Villa Park, adjacent to the Rip Van Winkle Motel. The evidence suggested Sutton had been kidnapped by a sadist, but police had nothing in the way of solid clues.

A year would pass before the next acknowledged victim in the series disappeared. On May 15, 1982, 21-year-old Lorraine Borowski was scheduled to open the Elmhurst realtor's office where she worked. Employees turning up for work that morning found the office locked, Borowski's shoes and scattered contents from her handbag strewn outside the door. Police were called at once, but five more months elapsed before her corpse was found, on October 10, in a cemetery south of Villa Park. Advanced decomposition left the cause of death a mystery.

Two weeks later, on May 29, Shui Mak was reported missing from Hanover Park, in Cook County, her mutilated body recovered at Barrington on September 30. On June 13, prostitute Angel York was picked up by a "john" in a van, handcuffed, her breast slashed open before she was dumped on the roadside, alive. Descriptions of her attacker had taken police nowhere by August 28, when teenage hooker Sandra Delaware was found stabbed and strangled to death on the bank of the Chicago River, her left breast neatly amputated. Rose Davis, age 30, was in identical condition when police found her corpse in a Chicago alley, on September 8. Three days later, 42-year-old Carole Pappas, wife of the Chicago Cubs' pitcher, vanished without a trace from a department store in nearby Wheaton, Illinois.

Detectives got the break they had been waiting for October 6. That morning, prostitute Beverly Washington, age 20, was found nude and savaged beside a Chicago railroad track. Her left breast had been severed, the right deeply slashed, but she was breathing, and emergency treatment would save her life. Hours later, in a seemingly unrelated incident, drug dealer Rafael Torado was killed, a male companion wounded, when the occupants of a cruising van peppered their phone booth with rifle fire.

Two weeks later, on October 20, police arrested unemployed carpenter Robin Gecht, age 28, and charged him with the cruel assault on Beverly Washington. Also suspected of slashing prostitute Cynthia Smith before she escaped from his van, Gecht was an odd character, once accused of molesting his own younger sister. Authorities immediately linked him with the "Ripper" slayings, but they had no proof, and he made bail October 26.

Meanwhile, detectives had learned that Gecht was one of four men who rented adjoining rooms at Villa Park's Rip Van Winkle Motel, several months before Linda Sutton was murdered nearby. The manager remembered them as party animals, frequently bringing women to their rooms, and he surprised investigators with one further bit of information. The men had been "some kind of cultists," perhaps devil-worshippers.

Two of the Rip Van Winkle tenants—brothers Thomas and Andrew Kokoraleis—had been kind enough to leave a forwarding address, for any mail they might receive. Police found 23-year-old Thomas at home when they called, and his inconsistent answers earned him a trip downtown. The suspect promptly failed a polygraph examination, cracking under stiff interrogation to describe the "Satanic chapel" in Gecht's upstairs bedroom, where captive women were tortured with knives and ice picks, gang-raped, and finally sacrificed to Satan by members of a tiny cult including Gecht, the Kokoraleis brothers, and 23-year-old Edward Spreitzer. As described by the prisoner, cultic rituals included severing one or both breasts with a thin wire garrote, each celebrant "taking communion" by eating a piece before the relic was consigned to Gecht's trophy box. At one point, Kokoraleis told detectives, he had counted fifteen breasts inside the box. Some other victims had been murdered at the Rip Van Winkle, out in Villa Park. He picked a snapshot of Lorraine Borowski as a woman he had picked up, with his brother, for a one-way ride to the motel.

Police had heard enough. Armed with search and arrest warrants, they swept up Robin Gecht, Ed Spreitzer, and 20-year-old Andrew Kokoraleis on November 5, lodging them in jail under $1 million bond. A search of Gecht's apartment revealed the Satanic chapel described by Tom Kokoraleis, and lawmen came away with a rifle matched to the recent Torado shooting. Satanic literature was also retrieved from the apartment occupied by Andrew Kokoraleis. With their suspects in custody, authorities speculated that the gang might have murdered 18 women in as many months.

Tom Kokoraleis was charged with the slaying of Lorraine Borowski on November 12, formally indicted by a grand jury four days later. Brother Andrew and Edward Spreitzer were charged on November 14 with the rape and murder of victim Rose Davis. When the mangled body of 22-year-old Susan Baker was found on November 16, at a site where previous victims had been discarded, police were worried that other cult members might still be at large. No charges were filed in that case, however, and authorities now connect Baker's death with her background of drug and prostitution arrests in several states.

Facing multiple charges of attempted murder, rape, and aggravated battery, Robin Gecht was found mentally competent for trial on March 2, 1983. His trial opened on September 20, and Gecht took the witness stand next day, confessing the attack on Beverly Washington. Convicted on all counts, he received a sentence of 120 years in prison.

Tom Kokoraleis had suffered a change of heart since confessing to murder, attorneys seeking to block the reading of his statements in forthcoming trials, but on December 4, 1983, the confessions were admitted in evidence. Meanwhile, on April 2, 1984, Ed Spreitzer pled guilty on four counts of murder—including victims Davis, Delaware, Mak and Torado. Sentenced to life on each count, he received additional time on conviction for charges of rape, deviant sexual assault, and attempted murder.

Tom Kokoraleis was convicted of Lorraine Borowski's murder on May 18, 1984. While awaiting sentencing, he led police to a field where Carole Pappas was allegedly buried, but searchers could find no remains. On September 7, the killer's helpful attitude was rewarded with a sentence of life imprisonment. Eighteen days later, Kokoraleis, his brother, and Ed Spreitzer were indicted for the murder of Linda Sutton. Andrew Kokoraleis and Spreitzer were also named in a second indictment, covering the murder of Lorraine Borowski.

On February 6, 1985, a statement from Andrew Kokoraleis was read to the jury in his trial for the Davis murder. In his confession, the defendant admitted he was "cruising" with fellow cultists Gecht and Spreitzer when they kidnapped Davis, with Andrew stabbing her several times in the process. Convicted on February 11, he received his life sentence on March 18.

A year later, on March 4, 1986, Edward Spreitzer was convicted of murdering Linda Sutton, formally sentenced to death on March 20. Authorities declared that Spreitzer had agreed to testify against Gecht in that case, but at this writing no further charges have been filed in Chicago's grim series of cannibal murders.

Carpenter, David J.

It took some time for brooding rage to surface in the case of David Carpenter, but when it reached the surface there were no holds barred. In 1961, when he was thirty-three years old, the future "Trailside Killer" brutally attacked a woman with a hammer, earning fourteen years in prison for his trouble. Back in circulation by the latter part of 1970, he drew another seven years on two counts of kidnapping and robbery. Before his transfer to the penitentiary, he joined four other inmates in escaping from the Calaveras County jail. Recaptured by the FBI, he did his time and was paroled in 1977. He found a job in San Francisco, working for a photo print shop, and gave evidence of "going straight." In fact, his brief hiatus was the calm before a lethal storm.

The terror began with Edda Kane, age 44, whose naked, violated body was discovered on a hiking trail in Mt. Tamalpais State Park, near San Francisco, on August 20, 1979. According to forensics experts, she was murdered execution-style, shot through the head while kneeling, possibly while pleading for her life.

March 7, 1980, Barbara Swartz, age 23, went hiking in the park. Her body was recovered one day later on a narrow, unpaved trail. She had been stabbed repeatedly about the chest, while kneeling in the dirt.

Anne Alderson went jogging on the fringes of the park, October 15, 1980, and did not return. The 26-year-old was found next afternoon; three bullets in the head had snuffed her life while she was kneeling at her killer's feet.

November 27, Shauna May, age 25, did not show up to keep a lover's rendezvous in the parking lot at Point Reyes Park, a few miles north of San Francisco. Two days later, searchers found her body in a shallow grave. Beside her lay the decomposing corpse of a New Yorker, 22-year-old Diana O'Connell, who had disappeared while hiking in the park a full month earlier. Both women had been killed by gunshots to the head.

Mere hours before the corpses at Point Reyes were unearthed, November 29, two other victims were discovered in the park. Identified as Richard Stowers, 19, and Cynthia Moreland, 18, they had been missing since September, when they told friends of their plans for hiking in the area. Again, both victims had been murdered execution-style.

As panic gripped the Northern California camping areas, the media indulged in speculation linking the sadistic

"Trailside Killer" with the "Zodiac," another serial assassin—still at large—responsible for seven murders in the latter 1960s. Homicide detectives had not linked the Zodiac with any documented crimes since 1969, and now the press began to speculate on his return, perhaps from serving time in prison or a sanitarium. Unlike the Zodiac, however, the elusive "Trailside Killer" felt no need to taunt police with mocking letters. He was satisfied to let his actions speak out, loud and clear.

On March 29, 1981, the killer struck again, this time in Henry Cowle State Park, near Santa Cruz. He ambushed hikers Stephen Haertle and Ellen Hansen, brandishing a .38, announcing to the woman that he meant to rape her. When she warned him off, the gunman opened fire, killing her outright and leaving young Haertle for dead. Surviving wounds that ripped his neck, a hand, and one eye, the lone survivor crawled for help. He had been close enough to offer homicide detectives a description of the killer's crooked, yellow teeth. Upon release of the description, other hikers told police that they had seen a man resembling the gunman in a red, late model foreign car.

Despite the new, important leads, police had reason for concern. From all appearances, publicity had caused their man to change his hunting ground and weapon. All the other gunshot victims had been murdered with a .45, and if the pistol was destroyed or lost, a major portion of their case might well go up in smoke.

On May 1, 1981, a resident of San Jose informed detectives that his girlfriend, Heather Scaggs, was missing. She had last been seen en route to buy a car from fellow print shop worker David Carpenter, who lived in San Francisco. Carpenter, she said, had made a special point of asking her to come alone when she dropped by to get the car. Police dropped in to question Carpenter, immediately noticing his strong resemblance to composite sketches of the Trailside Killer. In his driveway sat a small, red, foreign car. A background check revealed his felony arrests, and Stephen Haertle picked the suspect's mug shot as a likeness of the Santa Cruz assailant.

Carpenter was taken into custody on May 14, and ten days later, the remains of Heather Scaggs were found by hikers in Big Basin Redwood State Park, north of San Francisco. She had been executed with the pistol used on Stephen Haertle and his girlfriend, Ellen Hansen, back in March.

Despite a search of Carpenter's belongings, homicide investigators still had not recovered any weapons.

Finally, they got a break, discovering a witness who remembered selling Carpenter a .45—illegal, in itself for a convicted felon—and although they never found the gun, at least a link, of sorts, had been established to the early homicides. A short time later, testimony from a suspect facing trial for robbery revealed that Carpenter had sold the thief a .38 revolver back in June. The weapon was recovered, and its barrel markings matched the bullets fired at Ellen Hansen, Heather Scaggs, and Stephen Haertle.

As detectives worked to build their case, they linked their suspect with another unsolved homicide. On June 4, 1980, Anna Menjivas had been discovered, dead, in Mt. Tamalpais State Park. Her murder had not been connected with the "Trailside" slayings at the time, but now investigators learned she was a long-time friend of David Carpenter, who often let him drive her home from work. The link appeared too strong for mere coincidence, and Anna's name was added to the murder chain, for ten in all.

Publicity led Carpenter's defense attorneys to request a change of venue. When his trial convened in April 1984, he faced a jury in Los Angeles, but relocation did not change the damning evidence of guilt. Convicted of the Scaggs and Hansen murders on July 6, Carpenter was sentenced to die in the gas chamber at San Quentin. Judge Dion Morrow, in pronouncing sentence, told the court, "The defendant's entire life has been a continuous expression of violence and force almost beyond exception. I must conclude with the prosecution that if ever there was a case appropriate for the death penalty, this is it."

On May 10, 1988, a San Diego jury convicted Carpenter of first-degree murder in the slayings of Richard Stowers, Cynthia Moreland, Shauna May, Diana O'Connell, and Anne Alderson. Carpenter was also pronounced guilty of raping two of the women and attempting to rape a third.

Catlin, Steven David

Adopted as an infant, during 1944, by Glenn and Martha Catlin, of Kern County, California, Steven moved to Bakersfield with his new parents in the early 1950s. Dropping out of high school, he showed no interest in honest work and was arrested on forgery charges at age nineteen, serving nine months in a California Youth Authority camp.

Catlin's first marriage was stormy and violent, domestic problems exacerbated by his abuse of drugs. In 1966, he acquired a second wife without divorcing the first, employing a pseudonym on the marriage license. A few months after the second, bogus wedding, he was picked up for stealing a credit card at the gas station where he worked. The judge called Catlin an addict and packed him off to the state prison at Chino, where he spent the next three years.

Upon release, Catlin divorced his first wife and legally remarried his second, using his real name, but the relationship was already doomed. The couple separated after ten months, and Catlin was married a third time, divorcing that wife eight months later. A fourth wife—Joyce—was acquired in short order, but she would prove less fortunate than her predecessor in escaping from a dead-end marriage.

Catlin's fascination with cars led to a job with the pit crew of racer Glendon Emery, based in Fresno, California. Infatuated with Emery's step-daughter, Catlin began to court her while still married to Joyce. In April 1976, Joyce Catlin was admitted to Bakersfield's Mercy Hospital with a severe case of "flu"; she seemed to improve, then took a sudden turn for the worse and died, of "pneumonia," on May 6. Husband Steve ordered her body cremated without delay.

A year later, in May 1977, Catlin married his fifth wife—Kaye—and moved to Fresno, finding employment at a local garage. Quick promotions placed him in charge of forty employees, but Catlin had expensive tastes and cash was always short. On October 28, 1980, his adoptive father died suddenly, the fluid in his lungs attributed to pre-existing cancer. Once again, the body was swiftly cremated on orders from Catlin.

In 1981, Catlin's employers at the Fresno garage noticed a sudden rash of missing auto parts. A routine background check on various employees turned up Steven's unreported record, and he was forced to resign, though no charges were filed. Financially, the strain began to mount.

On February 17, 1984, Kaye Catlin suddenly fell ill while visiting Las Vegas with her mother. Returning to Fresno, she was hospitalized with fluid in her lungs. Physicians were still trying to diagnose her illness when she died on March 14. Catlin, meanwhile, had acquired another fiancee, encountered on a visit to the hospital. His grief was tempered by her love—and by the $57,000 he received from life insurance payments.

Back in Bakersfield, his third ex-wife had followed Catlin's eerie run of luck, and she approached the local sheriff with her dire suspicions. Joyce Catlin had been cremated after death, but Mercy Hospital still retained certain tissue samples, and these were submitted for analysis in November 1984. A few days later, on December 8, Catlin's mother collapsed and died—from "a stroke"—shortly after a visit by Steve and his latest girlfriend. Catlin ordered the body cremated, but disposal was postponed until an autopsy could be performed.

The noose was closing rapidly on Catlin, now. Analysis of tissue samples from his mother and his two late wives revealed that all had suffered poisoning from Paraquat, an herbicide so lethal that its use was banned in the United States. A bottle of the stuff, complete with Catlin's fingerprints, was found in his garage. Indicted shortly after marrying his sixth—and final—wife, the killer went to trial at Monterey, in May of 1986. Convicted on a single murder count—for killing Kaye—he drew a term of life imprisonment. In Bakersfield, where other charges waited, prosecutors hoped to see him executed.

Chadd, Billy Lee

A self-styled "death merchant" who enjoyed killing for pleasure, Chadd had confessed to three murders and various rapes in at least two states. In 1974, according to his own statement, the 20-year-old drifter invaded the home of a San Diego woman, choked and raped his victim, then slashed her throat and continued the sexual assault as she lay dying. She may have been his first victim, but she would not be the last.

A year later, in August 1975, Chadd was working at a Las Vegas restaurant when he met Delmar Bright, 29, employed as a porter at a nearby hotel. As Chadd tells the story, Bright offered him twenty dollars and a six-pack of beer in return for a nude photo-modeling session. Chadd agreed, but claimed that Bright attempted homosexual assault, compelling Chadd to kill in self-defense. In fact, when found, the victim lay face-down and naked on his bed, hands and feet bound with electrical cord, stabbed in the back with his throat slashed. ("I'd heard that stabbing someone in the kidney would kill him," Chadd explained, "but I didn't know, so I went ahead and cut his throat, too.")

By 1978, serving with the Marine Corps, Billy Chadd was back in San Diego. There, he kidnapped and raped another woman, along with her teenage daughter, after tying up the victim's elderly parents and her younger children. Arrested on that charge and sentenced to thirteen years in prison, he also confessed the 1974 slaying and a second local murder, in 1978. His sentence of life in the first homicide was later overturned by the California Supreme Court.

Talkative in custody, Chadd leaked his involvement in the murder of Delmar Bright, and officers sent his fingerprints off to Las Vegas, where they matched latent prints from the 1975 murder scene. Chadd was a persistent problem for his keepers, twice setting his cell on fire in December 1981, sitting in the middle of the floor with a towel over his face while smoke curled around him. By April 1982, he claimed to be "born again," a new man, but the old Billy Chadd was convicted of murder and sentenced to life, the term to run consecutive with his 13 years in California.

Chase, Richard Trenton

No one should have been surprised at the identity of Sacramento, California's "vampire killer" when he was arrested in the final days of January 1978. As a young man, Richard Chase was known to eat live birds, and while residing in Nevada he had several times been found in farmers' fields, stark naked, covered with the blood of cattle he had slaughtered. Chase finally shifted to human victims during four days of madness, shooting and slashing six persons to death between January 23 and 27. In custody, he openly confessed to drinking one victim's blood, carrying pieces of others home with him, to be fondled and gnawed on at leisure. Despite his apparent mental aberration, Chase was convicted of murder and sentenced to prison for life.

Christenson, William Dean

A native of Bethesda, Maryland, born in 1945, Christenson logged his first felony conviction in 1969, charged with assault and battery in the stabbing of a teenage girl in Washington, D.C. Two years later, he pled guilty to raping a Maryland go-go dancer, serving nine years before his parole in 1980. On April 16, 1981, traveling as "Richard Owen," he was picked up for rape in Montreal, bargaining down to a guilty plea on charges of indecent assault. A year later, he was "inadvertently" released by Canadian authorities, despite a request that he be delivered to Maryland as a parole violator and suspect in other violent rapes.

On April 27, 1982, the decapitated, dismembered body of 27-year-old Sylvie Trudel was found in the Montreal apartment occupied by "Richard Owen." That same afternoon, the sectioned corpse of Murielle Guay, 26, was found wrapped in trash bags at Mille-Isles, 50 miles northwest of Montreal. Police were initially reluctant to connect the crimes, noting that Trudel's killer displayed "a certain amount of expertise," while victim Guay was "really butchered," but their doubts were resolved by April 29, with murder warrants issued in the name of William Christenson.

Back in the United States, Christenson met his parents at Lancaster, Pennsylvania, tapping their bank account for a $5,000 grub stake. (Both were charged with harboring a fugitive.) With cash in hand, the killer started drifting over the eastern half of the country, spending time in Florida, Georgia, Kentucky, Maryland, New Jersey, New York, and Pennsylvania.

He was living in Scranton, as "Stanley Holl," when go-go dancer Michelle Angiers was stabbed 30 times in a tavern parking lot at nearby Dickson, her body recovered on September 13, 1982. Nine months later, in Trenton, New Jersey, Christenson shot and wounded two black men whom he had befriended in a local saloon. On December 4 of that year, in Philadelphia, he used the same gun to kill another black, 51-year-old Jeffrey Schrader, in a barroom altercation. Arrested in that case, Christenson sat in jail while police searched his apartment, retrieving a bloody mattress and a hacksaw, matted with blood and hair. (No trace has been found to this day of the dancer with whom he had once shared the flat.) Convicted of the Schrader homicide, he drew a prison term of life without parole.

By the summer of 1984, felony charges were piling up against Christenson. Trenton authorities wanted him for trial on the double shooting, while Montgomery County, Maryland, sought to try him on another rape charge. That August, Canadian authorities closed their file on the Montreal murders, citing Christenson's present life sentence, but he was already suspect in two other slayings, the victims dismembered with a hacksaw. Nationwide, police named him as a suspect in at least thirteen deaths with suggestions that the final count might reach thirty. Pennsylvania officers dubbed him "a real American Jack the Ripper."

Christenson responded to the attention by striving to

make himself mysterious, signing court documents with a check mark and challenging prosecutors to prove his identity. In November 1984, he spoke to Philadelphia newsmen about his "extreme mental and alcohol problems," voicing the fear that he would be charged by police in numerous unsolved murders.

On February 16, 1985, Christenson left state prison in a heavily-armed convoy, complete with helicopter escort, bound for Philadelphia and his arraignment in the murder of Michelle Angiers. Convicted of third-degree murder in that case, on August 5, 1987, the killer faced a new term of twenty years on completion of his existing life sentence. The investigation in Christenson's case continues, with further prosecutions anticipated by authorities in several states.

Christie, John Reginald Halliday

Yorkshire born in April 1898, Christie endured a stern childhood, with little or no visible affection from his parents. Developing chronic hypochondria in a bid for attention, he also ran afoul of police as a juvenile, resulting in beatings at home. Christie left school at fifteen to become a police clerk, but was fired for petty theft. Next, he went to work in his father's carpet factory, but was caught stealing again and banished from home.

Wounded and gassed in World War I, Christie was blind for five months and suffered hysterical loss of his voice spanning three and a half years. Marriage, in 1920, seemed to hold his bad luck at bay for a time, but in 1934 Christie was struck by an automobile, suffering serious head injuries along with other, lesser wounds. Briefly employed at the post office, he spent seven months in jail for stealing money orders. In 1938, Christie and his wife moved into a flat at 10 Rillington Place, in London. A year later, he joined the War Reserve Police, earning a bully's reputation for throwing his weight around and punishing neighbors for minor blackout offenses.

Christie's several homicides were all committed in the flat on Rillington Place, with the early crimes occurring in the midst of wartime. His initial victim was Ruth Fuerst, an Austrian immigrant who called on Christie while his wife was visiting with relatives; he strangled her while having sex and buried her that evening, in his garden. Number two was Muriel Eddy, one of Christie's co-workers at a London radio factory. Stopping by the flat with Christie's wife away, Muriel complained of feeling ill. Her host prescribed a "cure" which consisted of inhaling lethal gas, and Eddy joined Ruth Fuerst in Christie's busy garden.

In late November 1949, a neighbor, illiterate truck driver Timothy Evans, approached police and said, "I would like to give myself up. I have disposed of the body of my wife." Following his directions, police searched the drains below Rillington Place, but in vain. A second visit found the body of Beryl Evans in a shed behind the house, together with her strangled infant daughter, Geraldine. (During the search, Christie stood talking with two detectives in his garden, while a dog rooted around their feet and turned up a skull. Christie shooed the animal away and trod the skull back under, with his visitors none the wiser!)

Upon recovery of the bodies, Evans first confessed to killing both his wife and daughter, later altering his statement to blame Christie. In his new affidavit, the trucker claimed that his wife died during an abortion, performed by Christie, after which Christie offered to arrange for the "unofficial adoption" of baby Geraldine. Detectives and a jury chose to believe Christie, described by prosecutors in court as "this perfectly innocent man." Convicted of strangling his daughter only, Evans was sentenced to death and eventually hanged.

By this time, married life was wearing thin on Christie. On the night of December 14, 1952, he strangled his wife with a stocking and wedged her body under the floorboards, afterward claiming that she had suffered spontaneous convulsions and he "could not bear to see her suffer."

With the nuisance of a live-in spouse removed, Christie's murder schedule escalated. On January 2, 1953, he brought home Rita Nelson, a London prostitute, plying her with liquor before he induced her to sit in a deck chair, covered with a canopy, which he had planted above an open gas pipe. When Nelson fell unconscious, Christie strangled her and raped her corpse before concealing it in a cupboard. The method worked so well that he repeated it with prostitute Kathleen Maloney, on January 12, and Hectorina McLennan, on March 3.

Christie left Rillington Place on March 20, 1953, and the new tenants began renovations four days later. They found his cupboard, hidden by a layer of wallpaper, with three female corpses inside. Police responding to the call soon found his wife, beneath the floor, and unearthed Christie's first two victims in the garden. Searchers found a human femur propping up the fence, out back, and in the flat a tin was found containing pubic hair removed from four different women. (Curiously, the hair matched none of Christie's known victims.)

Arrested on March 31, Christie soon confessed to the series of murders, contending that Beryl Evans traded sex in return for his help in committing suicide. At his trial, in June, the jury rejected Christie's insanity defense, and he was sentenced to die. He mounted the gallows on July 15, 1953.

Christopher, Joseph G.

A pathological racist, Christopher launched a one-man war against blacks in September 1980, claiming victims from upstate New York to southwestern Georgia. In his wake, he left an atmosphere of bigotry and violence that provoked a string of hostile confrontations in communities not known for racial animosity. His legacy of death and hatred lingers to the present day, as several of the crimes connected to his rampage—or inspired by his example—are officially unsolved.

The war began September 22, when 14-year-old Glenn Dunn was shot and killed outside a Buffalo supermarket. The victim was sitting in a stolen car when he died, and witnesses described his assailant as an unidentified "white youth." The following day, 32-year-old Harold Green was shot while dining at a fast-food restaurant in suburban

Cheektowaga. That night, Emmanuel Thomas, age 30, was killed by a sniper while crossing the street to his home, seven blocks from the scene of Dunn's murder. On September 24, the action shifted to nearby Niagara Falls, with the murder of a fourth black, Joseph McCoy.

Investigators found that all four victims were killed with the same gun, and headlines followed their fruitless search for the elusive ".22-caliber killer." Buffalo blacks complained of nonexistent police protection, and there were sporadic incidents of blacks pelting white motorists on the streets. A cross was burned in Buffalo, and fears were voiced that the murders might be a preview of things to come, paving the way for some paramilitary racist group's campaign of local genocide.

Things got worse on October 8, when 71-year-old Parler Edwards, a black taxi driver, was found in the trunk of his car, parked in suburban Amherst, his heart cut out and carried from the scene. Next day, another black cabbie, 40-year-old Ernest Jones, was found beside the Niagara River in Tonawanda, the heart ripped from his chest. His blood-spattered taxi was retrieved by police in Buffalo, three miles away.

The local black community was verging on a state of panic now, made worse by an incident in Buffalo hospital on October 10. A black patient, 37-year-old Collin Cole, was recuperating from illness when a white stranger appeared at his bedside and snarled, "I hate niggers." A nurse's arrival saved Cole from death by strangulation, but his condition was listed as serious, with severe damage done to his throat. Descriptions of the would-be strangler roughly matched eyewitness reports on the ".22-caliber killer."

The action shifted to Manhattan on December 22, with five blacks and one Hispanic victim stabbed—four of them killed—in less than thirteen hours. John Adams, 25 years old, was the first to fall, narrowly escaping death when he was knifed by a white assailant around 11:30 a.m. Two hours later, 32-year-old Ivan Frazier was accosted on the street, deflecting a blade with his hand, sustaining minor injuries before he fled on foot. The next four victims were less fortunate. Messenger Luis Rodriguez, 19, was stabbed to death around 3:30 p.m. in what police described as "an apparent holdup." No motive was suggested in the deaths of 30-year-old Antone Davis, knifed around 6:50 p.m., or 20-year-old Richard Renner, killed less than four hours later. The last victim, discovered just before midnight, was a black "John Doe" stabbed to death on the street near Madison Square Garden.

Police were still searching desperately for the elusive "Midtown Slasher" when 31-year-old Roger Adams, a black man, was stabbed to death in Buffalo on December 29. Wendell Barnes, 26, was fatally wounded in Rochester, on December 30, but Buffalo native Albert Menefee was luckier the next day, surviving a thrust that nicked his heart. On January 1, Larry Little and Calvin Crippen survived separate attacks, fighting off their white assailant with only minor injuries.

On January 6, police announced that the recent stabbings were "probably linked" with Buffalo's unsolved .22-caliber shootings, but still they seemed no closer to a suspect. The case broke twelve days later, in Georgia, when Pvt. Joseph Christopher, age 25, was arrested at Fort Benning, charged with slashing a black GI. A search of his former residence, near Buffalo, turned up quantities of .22-caliber ammunition, a gun barrel, and two sawed-off rifle stocks. More to the point, authorities learned that Christopher had joined the army on November 13, arriving at Fort Benning six days later. He was absent on leave from December 19 to January 4, with a bus ticket recording his arrival in Manhattan on December 20.

Hospitalized with self-inflicted wounds on May 6, 1981, Christopher bragged to a nurse of his involvement in the September slayings around Buffalo. Four days later, he was charged with three of the local shooting deaths, a fourth murder count added to the list on June 29, plus charges related to nonfatal Buffalo stabbings in December 1980 and January 1981. In New York City, indictments were returned in the murder of Luis Rodriguez and the nonfatal stabbing of Ivan Frazier.

In October 1981, Christopher waived his right to a jury trial in Buffalo, placing his fate in the hands of a judge. Two months later, he was found mentally incompetent for trial, but the ruling had been reversed by April 1982. On April 27, after twelve days of testimony, he was convicted on three counts of first-degree murder, drawing a prison term of 60 years to life.

In September 1983, Christopher sat for an interview with Buffalo journalists, estimating that his murder spree had claimed a minimum of thirteen lives. Reporters noted that he "did not deny" the grisly murders of Parler Edwards and Ernest Jones, but no charges have yet been filed in those cases. In July 1985, Christopher's Buffalo conviction was overturned on grounds that the judge had improperly barred testimony pointing toward mental incompetence. Three months later, in Manhattan, a jury rejected the killer's insanity plea, convicting him in the murder of Luis Rodriguez and the wounding of Ivan Frazier.

Clark, Douglas Daniel
and Bundy, Carol

Born in 1948, the son of a retired navy admiral turned international engineer, Douglas Clark had lived in 37 countries by the time he settled in Southern California. He liked to call himself "the king of the one-night stands," supplementing his machinist's income through affairs with frowsy matrons, reserving his leisure time for kinky liaisons with underaged girls and young women. In private moments, he cherished dark fantasies of rape and murder, mutilation and necrophilia, yearning for the moment when his dreams could graduate to stark reality.

At age 37, Carol Bundy was typical of Clark's conquests. A vocational nurse, the overweight mother of two had left her abusive husband in January 1979, quickly falling in love with the manager of her new apartment building. A native of Australia, 45-year-old John Murray sang part-time in a local country-western bar, but he was never too busy to help out a tenant in need. Noting that Bundy suffered from severe cataracts, Murray drove her to a Social Security office and had her declared legally blind, bringing in $620 each month for Carol and her sons. Next, he took her to an optometrist, where she was fitted for glasses, enabling her to discard her white cane. Enraptured, Carol began deliberately clogging the toilets and drains in her apartment, anything at all to bring the manager around. Soon they were lovers, but Murray was married, refusing to give up his family. In October, Carol approached his wife, offering $1,500 if the woman would disappear, but the effort backfired, with Murray berating her, coldly suggesting she find other lodgings.

Three months later, during January 1980, Carol was pining in the country-western bar when she met Douglas Clark, and he immediately swept her off her feet. Clark moved into her home the same night, working by day in the boiler room of a Burbank soap factory, devoting his nights to a crash course in ecstasy that made Carol his virtual slave. She swallowed her pride when he brought younger women home for sex, dutifully snapping photographs on command. One of his conquests was an eleven-year-old, picked up while roller skating in a nearby park, but Carol made no complaint as kinky sex gave way to pedophilia, increasingly spiced with discussions of death and mutilation.

On June 11, 1980, half-sisters Gina Narano, 15, and Cynthia Chandler, 16, vanished from Huntington Beach, en route to a meeting with friends. They were found next morning, beside the Ventura Freeway near Griffith Park, in Los Angeles; each had been shot in the side of the head with a small-caliber pistol. At home, Clark gleefully confessed the murders to Bundy, regaling her with details of how he had forced the girls to fellate him, shooting each in the head as she brought him to climax.

In the predawn hours of June 24, Karen Jones, a 24-year-old hooker, was found behind a Burbank steakhouse, murdered by a single gunshot to the head. Later that morning, police were summoned to Studio City, where another female victim—this one headless—had been found by horrified pedestrians. Despite the missing head, she was identified as Exxie Wilson, 20, another veteran streetwalker.

That afternoon, while Carol Bundy's sons were visiting relatives, Clark surprised her by plucking a woman's head from the refrigerator, placing it on the kitchen counter. He ordered Carol to make up the twisted face with cosmetics, and she later recalled, "We had a lot of fun with her. I was making her up like a Barbie with makeup." Tiring of the game, Clark took his trophy to the bathroom, for a shower and a bout of necrophilic oral sex.

Newspaper headlines were already touting the crimes of a new "Sunset Slayer" by June 27, when Exxie Wilson's head was found in a Hollywood alley, stuffed inside an ornate wooden box. Authorities noted that it had been thoroughly scrubbed before it was discarded by the killer. Three days later, a group of snake hunters near Sylmar, in the San Fernando Valley, turned up a woman's mummified corpse, identified as Sacramento runaway Marnette Comer. Last seen alive on June 1, the 17-year-old prostitute had been dead at least three weeks when she was found. Like other victims in the series, she was known to work the Sunset Strip.

And the murders continued. On July 25, a young "Jane Doe" was found on Sunset Boulevard, killed by a shot to the head. Two weeks later, hikers in the Fernwood area, near Malibu, turned up another unidentified corpse, dismembered by predators, a small-caliber bullet hole visible in the skull.

Despite her hot romance with Clark, Carol Bundy had continued visiting John Murray at the country-western bar where he performed by night. She did not hold her liquor well, and after dropping several hints about her newest lover's criminal activities, she was appalled by Murray's comment that he might report Doug Clark to the police. On August 5, she kept a midnight rendezvous with Murray in his van, parked two blocks from the bar, and she killed him there. Found four days later, the singer had been stabbed nine times and slashed across the buttocks, his head severed and missing from the murder scene.

It had become too much for Carol Bundy. Two days after Murray's body was discovered, she broke down on the job, sobbing out to a fellow nurse, "I can't take it anymore. I'm supposed to save lives, not take them." Her friend tipped police and they called on Bundy at home, retrieving three pairs of panties removed from victims as trophies, along with snapshots of Clark and his eleven-year-old playmate. Arrested on the job in Burbank, Clark was still in jail four days later, when police retrieved a pistol from the boiler room. Ballistics tests would link the gun with bullets recovered from five of the known "Sunset" victims.

At his trial, serving briefly as his own attorney, Clark blamed Carol Bundy and John Murray for the slayings, contending that they had patterned their crimes after the case of Theodore Bundy. Jurors saw through the flimsy ruse, and on January 28, 1983, they convicted Clark across the board, including six counts of first-degree murder with "special circumstances," plus one count each of attempted murder, mayhem, and mutilating human remains. Strutting before the jury during the penalty phase of his case, Clark declared, "We have to vote for the death penalty in this case. The evidence cries out for it." The panel agreed with his logic, and he was sentenced to death on February 15.

At her own trial, for murdering Murray and one of the unidentified females, Carol Bundy first pled insanity, then reversed herself and admitted the slayings. According to her statement, John Murray was shot in the head, then decapitated to remove ballistic evidence. She had also handed Clark the gun with which he shot an unnamed prostitute, found dead along the Sunset Strip in July 1980. Convicted on the basis of her own confession, Bundy received consecutive terms of 27 years to life on one count, plus 25 years to life on the other.

Cole, Carroll Edward

A death wish, once in custody, is not unusual among compulsive killers. Carroll Edward Cole, admitted murderer of thirteen persons, was securely serving out a term of life in Texas, with parole a possibility in seven years, when he elected voluntarily to face a pair of murder charges in Nevada, fully conscious of the fact that he would be condemned to die upon conviction. Once the sentence had been passed, facilitated by his guilty plea, Cole staunchly fended off appeals and efforts of assorted liberal groups to interpose themselves on his behalf. His execution, in December 1985, immediately paved the way for others in the Western states, but Cole's significance lies elsewhere—in the man himself, and in "the system's" failure to prevent his crimes.

When Cole was five years old his mother forced him to accompany her on extramarital excursions in his father's absence, using torture to extract a pledge of silence, making him a bruised accomplice to her own adultery. As he grew older, Cole was forced to dress in frilly skirts and petticoats for the amusement of his mother's friends, dispensing tea and coffee at sadistic "parties" where the women gathered to make sport of "mama's little girl." Enrolled in elementary school two years behind his peers, Cole grew up fearing for his masculinity, intensely sensitive to jokes about his "sissy" given name. At nine, he drowned a playmate who made fun of him, avoiding punishment when careless officers dismissed the murder as an accident. He had begun to fight habitually at school, and once contrived to maim the winner of a yo-yo contest in which Cole had come out second-best: while playing on a piece of road equipment, he engaged the gears and crushed his rival's hand inside the dozer's massive treads.

In adolescence, Cole accumulated numerous arrests for drunkenness and petty theft. He joined the Navy after dropping out of high school, but was discharged for the theft of pistols, which he used to fire at cars along the San Diego highways. Back at home in Richmond, California, during 1960, he attacked two couples with a hammer as they parked along a darkened lover's lane. Increasingly, he cherished fantasies of strangling girls and women who reminded him of his adulterous mother.

Finally, alarmed by violent fantasies which would not let him rest, Cole flagged a squad car down in Richmond and confessed his urges to police. On the advice of a police lieutenant, Cole surrendered voluntarily to mental health authorities, and spent the next three years in institutions where he was regarded as an "anti-social personality" who posed no threat to others. Finally discharged in 1963, he moved to Dallas, Texas, and exacerbated matters by immediately marrying an alcoholic prostitute.

The grim relationship was doomed to failure, filled with screaming battles, beatings, the occasional resort to weapons. Finally, in 1965, persuaded that his wife was servicing the tenants of a motel where they lived, Cole torched the place and was imprisoned on an arson charge. Upon release, he drifted northward, through Missouri, and was jailed again for the attempted murder of Virginia Rowden, age eleven. Cole had chosen her at random, crept inside her room while she was sleeping, and had tried to strangle her in bed; her screams had driven him away, and he was readily identified by witnesses as her assailant when police arrived.

Missouri offered Cole more psychiatric treatment through assorted inmate programs, but it didn't take. In 1970, he once again surrendered to authorities—this time in Reno, Nevada—confessing his desire to rape and strangle women. Learned doctors wrote him off as a malingerer and set him free, on the condition that he leave the state. Cole's file contains the telling evidence of psychiatric failure: "Prognosis: Poor. Condition on release: Same as on admittance. Treatment: Express bus ticket to San Diego, California."

The problem was exported, but it would not go away. Within six months of his return to San Diego, Cole would kill at least three women. (On the day before his execution in Nevada, he suggested that there might have been two others in this period, the details of their murders blurred by massive quantities of alcohol.) His victims, then and later, shared the common trait of infidelity to husbands, fiancees, or boyfriends; each approached Cole in a bar, accompanied him to lonely roads for sex, and laughed about the skill with which they "put one over" on their regular companions.

Moving eastward, Cole picked off another victim in Casper, Wyoming, during August 1975. Assorted jail terms often interfered with hunting, but he surfaced in Las Vegas during 1977, staying long enough to kill a prostitute and get himself arrested on a charge of auto theft, which was dismissed. A few weeks later, after days of drinking, Cole awoke in Oklahoma City to discover the remains of yet another woman in his bathtub; bloody slices of her buttocks rested in a skillet on the stove.

Returning once again to San Diego, Cole remarried—to another "drunken tramp"—and sought the help of local counselors to curb his drinking. Given the conditions of his home life, it was hopeless, and the urge to murder was consuming him, inevitably fueled by alcohol, a ravenous obsession. During August 1979, he strangled Bonnie Stewart on the premises of his employer, dumping her nude body in an alleyway adjacent to the store. For weeks, he had been threatening to kill his wife—the threats reported to an officer in charge of supervising his parole—but when he finally succeeded in September, the authorities refused to rule her death a homicide. Despite discovery of her body, swaddled in a blanket and reposing in a closet of Cole's home, despite Cole's own arrest while drunkenly attempting to prepare a grave beneath a neighbor's house, detectives viewed the death of Diane Cole as "natural," related to her own abuse of drink.

Taking no chances, Cole hit the road. He claimed another victim in Las Vegas, gravitating back to Dallas where, within eleven days in 1980, he would strangle three more victims. Though discovered at the final murder scene, the victim stretched out at his feet, he was again regarded merely as a "casual suspect" by detectives. Weary of the game at last, Cole startled them with his confession to a string of unsolved homicides; at trial, in 1981, his guilty plea insured a term of life with possible parole, and he was counting down the days to freedom when reports of a potential extradition to Nevada changed his mind.

The case of Carroll Edward Cole deserves a place among the classics as a showcase of "the system's" abject failure. As a child, young Eddie Cole was failed by educators who ignored his late enrollment, failed to recognize the signs of chronic child abuse, and dealt with adolescent violence as a problem to be swept away, referred to other agencies. As a potential murderer who sought the help of mental institutions, he was failed by the psychologists and psychoanalysts of half a dozen states, repeatedly discharged as a malingerer, a harmless fake, "no danger to society.'' On two occasions, officers in San Diego literally caught Cole in the act of an attempted murder—and, on each occasion, they accepted his ridiculous assertion of a lover's quarrel, offering the would-be killer transportation to his home. When violent fantasies became reality, investigators with the same department stubbornly ignored persuasive evidence, rejecting even Cole's confession, passing off two homicides as drunken accidents, dismissing others as the handiwork of angry pimps. In Texas, Cole might very well have slipped the net again, if he had not elected to confess in cases where detectives were inclined to view his homicides as ''accidental deaths.'' In such a case, the system fails not only Carroll Edward Cole. It fails us all.

Coleman, Alton

Born Elton Coleman in November 1955, the middle of five children from a prostitute in the Waukegan ghetto, the future terror of the Midwest was raised by his maternal grandmother. Dubbed ''Pissy'' by his playmates, for a childhood tendency to wet his pants, Coleman grew up running with street gangs, cultivating an unsavory reputation. A black who preferred blacks as victims, his numerous arrests were concentrated in the area of sex crimes, a propensity which led him on a lethal crime spree and, eventually, to the death house.

In January 1974, Coleman was arrested for the abduction, rape, and robbery of an elderly woman in Waukegan. A bargained guilty plea to simple robbery earned him a sentence of two to six years in Joliet prison, where he was later accused of molesting male inmates. A prison psychiatric profile dubbed Coleman a ''pansexual, willing to have intercourse with any object, women, men, children, whatever.'' Free on parole, he was charged with rape again in 1976 and 1980, winning acquittal each time when a jury believed that his victims consented to sex. His record reveals a total of four rape charges, two counts of deviate sexual assault, five of unlawful restraint, and one count for indecent liberties with a child. The latter victim was a niece of Coleman's; an angry mother filed the charge, but later changed her mind in court. The judge, dismayed, branded her new story "completely implausible." "I think," he declared, "the woman as she stands here today is terrified by this man."

Briefly married, Coleman was abandoned by his teen-aged wife, who sought police protection when she went to claim her various belongings from their home. She "just couldn't take it no more," and years later, in court, she would offer descriptions of Coleman's obsession with bondage, young girls, and perverse, violent sex.

In February 1980, Coleman was accused of raping a Waukegan girl at knifepoint, and while never indicted, he was also suspect in the rape and strangling of Gina Frazier, age 15, in 1982. Reduction of his bail in the Waukegan case put Coleman on the street in time to launch a rampage which would place him on the FBI's "Most Wanted" list.

Coleman's young accomplice in the weeks to come was Debra Denise Brown, age 21. The fifth of eleven children from a respectable home, she had been engaged to marry another man when she met Coleman and fell into a semblance of love. Breaking off her engagement, she became Coleman's live-in lover—and, later, his confederate in crime.

On May 29, 1984, Vernita Wheat, age nine, convinced her mother to let her accompany "Robert Knight" and his girlfriend to Waukegan, fifteen miles from their home in Kenosha, Wisconsin. The purpose of the trip was to retrieve a stereo, described by Vernita and "Knight" as a belated Mother's Day present. When the three had not returned the next morning, officers were notified. A photo lineup readily identified "Robert Knight" as Alton Coleman; his companion had been Debra Brown.

With Coleman's sinister record in mind, a federal grand jury indicted both suspects on kidnapping charges, and the FBI went to work. On June 18, Tamika Turks, age seven, and her nine-year-old aunt were walking near their home in Gary, Indiana, when Coleman and Brown pulled in to the curb, asking directions. Money was offered in exchange for help, and both girls climbed into the car. Confronted with a knife, they were driven to a wooded area twelve miles away, where Coleman raped and choked Tamika Turks, while Debra held her down. Tamika's aunt was also raped and beaten, but she managed to escape. Selection of familiar photographs by the survivor added further charges to the growing list, and still the fugitives remained elusive.

The strangled body of Vernita Wheat was found on June 19, in an abandoned building in downtown Waukegan. That same afternoon, police in Gary received a missing-person report on Donna Williams, 25, a local beauty operator. She had last been seen en route to pick up a "nice young couple from Boston," who had agreed to visit her church. None of them showed for the service, but witnesses identified photos of Coleman and Brown as recent visitors to the salon where Williams worked. On June 27, the missing woman's car was located in Detroit, but Coleman and Brown had already surfaced in Motor City, with a vengeance.

On June 24, the couple accosted a Detroit woman outsider her home, brandishing knives and demanding that she drive them to Ohio. The intended victim saved herself by deliberately crashing into a parked truck, fleeing on foot while the killers took off in her damaged vehicle.

On June 28, Coleman and Brown invaded the home of Palmer and Maggie Jones, in Dearborn Heights, surprising the middle-aged couple at breakfast. The latest victims were beaten with a club, robbed of $86, and left bleeding on the floor while the fugitives fled in their car. Two days later, a pair of Detroit men offered the couple a ride. When Coleman drew a gun, the driver grappled with him briefly and escaped. His passenger, an invalid, was tossed out on the street, amazingly unharmed.

Verified sightings of Coleman and Brown were recorded every day between July 2 and 7. On July 2, a middle-aged Detroit couple were attacked in their home, beaten with a pipe and subjected to Coleman's incoherent harangue on how blacks were forcing him to murder other members of his race. The victims' stolen car was dropped off in Toledo, where another couple was assaulted, handcuffed in their home, relieved of transportation. A Toledo bartender reportedly exchanged shots with Coleman, after the fugitives tried to abduct one of the bartender's patrons.

On July 7, Coleman and Brown spent the night with Virginia Temple, 30, and her ten-year-old daughter, Rochelle, in Toledo. Before they left next morning, both were strangled, the girl raped, their bodies stuffed into a crawlspace beneath the looted home.

Four days later, on July 11, the remains of Donna Williams were discovered in Detroit. She had been strangled with a pair of pantyhose. That afternoon, the FBI announced that Coleman had been elevated to a most unusual eleventh place on its "Most Wanted" list, an option used when vicious crimes in progress mark a suspect as particularly dangerous.

And the body-count kept rising. In Cincinnati, Tonnie Storey, age 15, had last been seen with individuals resembling Brown and Coleman; four days later, when her corpse was found, she had been stabbed repeatedly, with two shots in the head. On July 13, Marlene Walters, 44, became the first white victim of the crime spree, bludgeoned in her home at Norwood, Ohio, a Cincinnati suburb. Harry Walters, gravely injured, managed to describe the killers of his wife as two young blacks who had arrived on ten-speed bikes and talked their way inside the house, expressing interest in the purchase of a camper. When they fled, they had been driving Harry's car.

On July 16, Coleman and his sidekick abducted Oline Carmichal, a Lexington college professor, driving him back to Dayton, Ohio, where they left him unharmed, locked in the trunk of his car. Rescued on July 17, Carmichal described his kidnappers as *two* black men and a woman. The mystery was cleared up shortly, with the arrest of Lexington native Thomas Harris, who explained that he was "kind of forced" to help the fugitives. Harris claimed he had talked Coleman and Brown out of killing their latest prisoner.

A half hour after Carmichal was freed, an elderly minister and his wife were found, battered but breathing, in their Dayton home. Investigation showed that Coleman and Brown, using pseudonyms, had met the couple a week earlier, spending two nights in their home and parting on amiable terms when the minister drove them to Cincinnati "for a prayer meeting." On July 17, the couple had returned, beating their former hosts severely and making off with the minister's station wagon.

The latest stolen vehicle was dumped the next day in Indianapolis, beside a car wash, where owner Eugene Scott, 77, and *his* car were reported missing. Scott was found by searchers hours later, in a ditch near Zionsville; he had been stabbed repeatedly, shot four times in the head.

The long trail reached its end in Evanston, Illinois, on July 20, 1984. An anonymous tip from a "friend" of the fugitives alerted police to their presence in the neighborhood, and they were soon spotted at a local park. Five officers surrounded the couple, relieving Coleman of two bloody knives and lifting an unloaded .38 from Brown's purse. That afternoon, Eugene Scott's missing car was found in Evanston, five blocks from where the suspects were arrested. Debra Brown had left her fingerprints inside.

In Chicago, a federal magistrate set bond in the Wheat case at $25 million cash. "This nation has been under a siege," he declared. "This nation has been under a reign of terror not knowing when the next victim was going to be taken. I am going to make sure no other victim will be subject to this man." Another bond of $20 million cash was set for Debra Brown.

The magistrate need not have worried. Tried separately for the murders of Marlene Walters and Tonnie Storey, in Cincinnati, both were convicted and sentenced to death in each case. In Indiana, Coleman picked up another death sentence for the murder of Tamika Turks; 100 years was added for the rape and the attempted murder of her aunt. Debra Brown was also convicted in that case, hoping for a lighter sentence when she slipped the judge a note that read: "I am a more kind and understanding and lovable person than people think I am." Unmoved, the judge pronounced matching sentences of death, on the murder charge, and consecutive 40-year terms on charges of kidnapping and child-molesting. Illinois supplied the *coup de grace*, sentencing Coleman to die for the kidnap and murder of Vernita Wheat.

"I'm dead already," Coleman told the court before pronouncement of his sentence in Waukegan. "You are talking to a dead man." Satisfied that he was right, authorities declined to prosecute the couple in their four outstanding homicides.

Collins, John Norman

Seven years before Ted Bundy launched his one-man war against brunettes in Washington, attractive co-eds in the state of Michigan were targeted as victims by another human monster. In a two-year period, the hunter struck repeatedly, at random, savaging his prey with the abandon of a rabid animal. The killer's downfall, when it came, was more dependent on coincidence and carelessness than any slick deductions on the part of homicide investigators.

First to die was Mary Fleszar, in July of 1967. Vanished from the campus of Eastern Michigan University at Ypsilanti, she was found by teenaged boys on August 7, stabbed to death and decomposing, with her hands and feet hacked off. Two days after her remains had been identified, a young man turned up at the mortuary, asking for permission to take snapshots of the body (which was angrily refused). Employees at the mortuary could not offer any clear description of the man.

A year elapsed before the second victim was abducted, on July 1, 1968. Discovered five days later in Ann Arbor, student Joan Schell had been raped and stabbed no less than 47 times. Detectives learned that she was seen with fellow student John Norman Collins on the night she disappeared, but Collins was a personable youth, and the police accepted his alibi at face value. Another eight months slipped away before the body of a third co-ed, Jane Mixer, was discovered in a cemetery south of Ypsilanti. Mixer had been strangled with a nylon stocking, and a bullet had been fired into her brain at point-blank range before her corpse was found on March 21, 1969. It was the end of quiet times and the beginning of a ruthless siege in Ypsilanti, as the co-ed killer stepped up his attacks in both ferocity and frequency.

On March 25, construction workers near the scene of Joan Schell's murder stumbled on another corpse. The victim, sixteen-year-old Maralynn Skelton, had been killed by crushing blows about the head; a stick had been rammed into her vagina, and police reported evidence of flogging with a heavy strap or belt before she died. Three weeks later, young Dawn Basom, just thirteen, was found half-naked in Superior Township, strangled with a black electric cord. Her sweater was discovered in an old, abandoned farmhouse roughly one mile from the point where Mary Fleszar's body had been found in 1967.

Driven by some unknown urge, the killer now began to taunt police. Officers returned to search the empty farmhouse for a second time in early April, and discovered articles of female clothing which had not been there before. A short time later, someone torched an old barn on the property where lengths of black electric cord had been retrieved; lined up across the driveway, officers discovered five clipped lilac blossoms—one for each of the outstanding murders on their books.

On June 9, 1969, some teenaged boys found Alice Kalom, graduate of EMU, discarded like some broken plaything in a vacant field near Ypsilanti. She had been raped and stabbed repeatedly, her throat slashed, with a bullet fired into her brain before the killer's rage was finally spent.

The final victim, Karen Beineman, went missing from her dorm at EMU on July 23. Her body was discovered three days later, in a wooded gully, strangled, beaten savagely, her breasts and stomach scalded with some caustic liquid. Karen's panties had been wadded up and stuffed in her vagina, as a sort of grisly afterthought; detectives found the garment to be thick with short, clipped hairs from someone other than the victim.

Three days after the discovery of Karen Beineman's body, State Police Corporal David Leik returned to his home in Ypsilanti from a family vacation. He discovered black paint splashed across the basement floor, surmising that it had been spilled by his wife's nephew, John Collins, who had cared for the family dog in their absence. Checking in for duty after his vacation, Leik was told that Collins had been questioned as a suspect in the co-ed murders, whereupon he spent an evening scraping up the paint, uncovering peculiar brownish stains beneath it. Lab analysis reported that the stains were only varnish, but in scraping up the paint, Leik had been forced to relocate a washer in the basement. Underneath it, he discovered tufts of hair belonging to his sons, the relics of a family haircut session prior to their vacation. Curious, he turned the samples over to detectives, and a new report confirmed the clippings were identical to hair recovered from the panties left with Karen Beineman. In his apparent haste to cover what he thought were bloodstains, Collins led detectives to the evidence for which they had been waiting all along.

Pretrial investigation showed that Collins was a chronic thief who sometimes suffered violent rages, usually directed toward some female who had managed to offend him. Intimate acquaintances described the suspect as an over-sexed and sometimes brutal lover who was "into" bondage and repulsed by any contact with a woman in her menstrual cycle. (Several of the victims had been murdered in their menstrual periods.) In June of 1969, he used a worthless check to rent a trailer which was later found in California, near the scene of yet another unsolved rape and homicide. At trial, he was convicted of the Beineman murder and consigned to prison for a term of twenty years.

Corll, Dean Arnold

Indiana born, on Christmas Eve of 1939, Dean Corll grew up in a combative home, his parents quarreling constantly. They were divorced while Corll was still an infant, then remarried after World War II, but Dean's father provided no stabilizing influence, regarding his children with thinly-veiled distaste, resorting to harsh punishment for the smallest infractions. When the couple separated a second time, Corll and his younger brother were left with a series of sitters, their mother working to support the family on her own. Rheumatic fever left Dean with a heart condition, resulting in frequent absence from school, and he seemed to welcome the change when his mother remarried, moving the family to Texas. A part-time business making candy soon expanded to become their livelihood, and Corll was generous with samples as he sought to win new friends.

In 1964, despite his heart condition, Corll was drafted into military service, where he displayed the first signs of flagrant homosexuality. On turning thirty, in December 1969, he seemed to undergo a sudden shift in personality, becoming hypersensitive and glum. He had begun to spend his time with teenage boys, like David Owen Brooks and Elmer Wayne Henley, passing out free candy all around, hosting glue- and paint-sniffing parties at his apartment in Pasadena, a suburb of Houston. At the same time, he displayed a sadistic streak, leaning toward bondage in his sexual relationships with young men and boys. On one occasion, during 1970, Brooks entered the apartment to find Corll nude, with two naked boys strapped to a homemade torture rack. Embarrassed, Corll released his playmates and offered Brooks a car in return for his promise of silence. Later, as his passion turned to bloodlust, Corll would use Brooks and Henley as procurers, offering $200 per head for fresh victims.

The date of Corll's first murder is uncertain. Brooks would place it sometime in mid-1970, the victim identified as college student Jeffrey Konen, picked up while hitchhiking. Most of Corll's victims were drawn from a seedy Houston neighborhood known as the Heights, their disappearances blithely ignored by police accustomed to dealing with runaways. Two were friends and neighbors of Henley, delivered on order to Corll, and sometimes the candy man killed two victims at once. In December 1970, he murdered 14-year-old James Glass and 15-year-old David Yates in one sitting. The following month, brothers Donald and Jerry Waldrop joined the missing list, with Wally Simineaux and Richard Embry slaughtered in October 1972. Another pair of brothers—Billy and Mike Baulch—were killed at separate times, in May 1972 and July 1973, respectively. Corll's youngest known victim was a nine-year-old neighbor, residing across the street from Dean's apartment.

On August 8, 1973, a tearful phone call from Elmer Henley summoned Pasadena police officers to Corll's apartment. They found the candy man dead, six bullet holes in his shoulder and back, with Henley claiming he had killed his "friend" in self-defense. The violence had erupted after Henley brought a girl to one of Corll's paint-sniffing orgies, driving the homosexual killer into a rage. Corll had threatened Elmer with a gun, then taunted his young friend when Henley managed to disarm him. Frightened for his life, Henley insisted that he shot Corll only to save himself. But, there was more. . . .

That afternoon, he led detectives to a rented boat shed in southwest Houston, leaving authorities to unearth seventeen victims from the earthen floor. A drive to Lake Sam Rayburn turned up four more graves, while six others were found on the beach at High Island, for a total of 27 dead. Henley insisted there were at least two more corpses in the boat shed, plus two more at High Island, but police called off the search, content to know that they had broken California's record in the Juan Corona case. (In *The Man with the Candy,* author Jack Olsen suggests that other victims might be buried around Corll's candy shop, but authorities show no interest in pursuing the case further.)

In custody, Brooks and Henley confessed their role in procuring victims for Corll through the years, with Brooks fingering Henley as the trigger man in at least one slaying. "Most of the killings that occurred after Wayne came into the picture involved all three of us," he told police. "Wayne seemed to enjoy causing pain."

Convicted of multiple murder in August 1974, Henley was sentenced to life imprisonment, with Brooks drawing an identical term in March 1975. A year later, Houston authorities announced that recent investigations of child pornography had linked other local pedophiles with Corll's murder ring, but no prosecutions were forthcoming. Elmer Henley's conviction was overturned on appeal in December 1978, based on the issue of pre-trial publicity, but he was convicted and sentenced a second time, in June 1979.

Corona, Juan Vallejo

A native of Mexico, born in 1934, Corona turned up in Yuba City, California, as a migrant worker in the early 1950s. Unlike most of his kind, he stayed on after the harvest, putting down roots and establishing a family, graduating from the role of picker in the fields to become a successful labor contractor. By his mid-thirties, Corona was known to ranchers throughout the county, supplying crews on demand. There was a bit of trouble during 1970, when a young Mexican was wounded—his scalp laid open by a machete—in the cafe run by Corona's homosexual brother, Natividad. Upon recovery, the victim filed suit against Natividad Corona, seeking $250,000 in damages, and the accused hacker fled back to Mexico, leaving the case unresolved. No one linked Juan with the crime; its violence scarcely seemed to touch his life.

And yet. . . .

On May 19, 1971, a Japanese farmer was touring his orchard when he noticed a fresh hole, roughly the size of a grave, excavated between two fruit trees. One of Corona's migrant crews was working nearby, and the farmer shrugged it off until that night, when he returned and found the hole filled in. Suspicious, he summoned deputies to the site next morning, and a bit of spade work revealed the fresh corpse of transient Kenneth Whitacre. The victim had been stabbed, his face and skull torn open by the blows of something like a cleaver or machete. Detectives logged the case as a sex crime, after finding pieces of gay literature in Whitacre's pocket.

Four days later, workers on a nearby ranch reported the discovery of a second grave. It yielded the remains of drifter Charles Fleming, but police were still working on his I.D. when they found the next burial site, and the next. In all, they spent nine days exhuming bodies from the orchard, counting twenty-five before the search was terminated on June 4. In Melford Sample's grave, deputies found two meat receipts dated May 21, signed with the name of "Juan V. Corona." On June 4, Joseph Maczak's remains would be discovered with two bank receipts, bearing the same signature. Some of the corpses were fresh, while others—like that of Donald Smith—had clearly been in the ground for months. (Medical examiners estimated that the first murders had occurred around February 1971.) Most of the victims were stabbed or hacked to death, with several bearing signs of homosexual assault. Four of the dead were ultimately unidentified; the rest were migrant workers, rootless drifters, with a sprinkling of skid row alcoholics. None of them had been reported missing by surviving relatives. The bank and meat receipts placed Juan Corona at the murder scenes, and he was held for trial. Defense attorneys tried to blame the murders on Natividad, a known homosexual given to fits of violence, but no one could document his presence in California during the murder spree. Jurors deliberated 45 hours before convicting Corona on all counts, in January 1973. A month later, he was sentenced to 25 consecutive terms of life imprisonment.

The case—which set an American record for individual murder convictions at the time—was not completed, yet. Reports issued in December 1973 linked Corona with the death of a twenty-sixth victim, but no new charges were filed. In May 1978, an appeals court ordered a new trial for Corona, finding his prior legal defense incompetent. The retrial was delayed by periods of psychiatric observation and a jailhouse stabbing in 1980, which cost Corona the sight in one eye. Convicted again in the spring of 1982, Corona was returned to prison on a new sentence of 25 life terms.

Costa, Antone Charles

Born in 1945, Costa was an infant when his father died in World War II. Around the age of seven, Costa told his mother that "a man" was entering his room by night, and he identified a photo of his father as the silent prowler. In November 1961, at age sixteen, he invaded a Somerville, Massachusetts, apartment, bending over the bed of a teenage girl before she woke and her screams drove him off. Three days later, he returned and tried to drag her down the stairs of her apartment house, but neighbors intervened. Convicted of burglary and assault on January 4, 1962, he drew a one-year suspended sentence, with three years probation.

Costa was married in April 1963, fathering three children before drugs complicated the relationship, producing bizarre and irresponsible behavior. In June 1966, he brought home two hippie girls—Bonnie Williams and Diane Federoff—with the announcement that he would be driving them to Pennsylvania, moving on alone from there to California. Later, Costa told police he drove the girls to Hayward, California, but they never got there. Costa surfaced at his home in Massachusetts, ten days later, and the girls are now believed to be his first known victims.

In August 1967, hiking in the Truro woods, near Provincetown, Costa shot a female acquaintance with an arrow, afterward apologizing for the "accident." By early 1968 his marriage was in shambles, and he drove to California in the latter days of January, settling briefly in San Francisco's free-swinging Haight-Ashbury district. Girlfriend Barbara Spaulding left her child with relatives and vanished on the day that Costa left for Massachusetts. She was never seen again, and homicide detectives now believe that Costa murdered her, as well.

Back home in Massachusetts, Costa burglarized a doctor's office on May 17, stealing various surgical instruments and drugs valued at $5,000. A week later, 18-year-old Sydney Monzon vanished from her home in Provincetown; her disappearance was reported to police on June 14. By August, Costa was divorced; his brand-new live-in lover, Susan Perry, lasted for a week before she disappeared, September 10. When questioned, Costa told his friends that she had "gone to Mexico."

In mid-September, Costa was arrested for driving with a suspended driver's license. Later, on the twenty-fifth, he was picked up for failure to support his wife and children, held in custody until November 8. Upon release, he started spending time and sharing drugs with Christine Gallant, another habitue of the "hip" scene. On the weekend of November 23, Gallant was found dead in her New York apartment, drowned in the bathtub after a barbiturate overdose.

On January 24, 1969, Patricia Walsh and Mary Anne Wysocki disappeared on a visit to Provincetown. Two weeks later, searchers found a woman's mutilated body at the Old Truro cemetery, identified as the last remains of Susan Perry. On March 4, the dismembered bodies of Walsh, Wysocki, and Sydney Monzon were found buried together, a mile and a half from the first grave site. Walsh and Wysocki had both been shot in the head, with hearts removed from all three victims; the remains bore human teeth marks, and the coroner discovered evidence of necrophilia.

Investigators learned that Walsh and Wysocki had met Antone Costa in Provincetown. Found in possession of their car, Costa produced a suspicious bill of sale, claiming he purchased the vehicle before the women "left for Canada." He was arrested on suspicion of murder after detectives learned that the burial site was Costa's private "garden," used for stashing drugs and growing marijuana.

In custody, the suspect changed his story several times, twice implicating innocent friends in the murders, repeatedly failing polygraph examinations. His first psychiatric exam, on March 31, resulted in the diagnosis of a "schizoid personality." Three months later, a second psychiatrist characterized Costa as "a modern-day 'Marquis de Sade' " and a "sexually dangerous man," capable of murder. The floodgates opened on July 12, 1969, when Costa finally confessed to the murder of Mary Wysocki.

Costa's trial opened on May 6, 1970, ending with his conviction on four counts of murder. Sentenced to life imprisonment on May 29, he began stocking his cell with books on ritual magic and the occult, including a copy of Anton LaVey's *Satanic Bible*. Four years later, on May 12, 1974, Costa was found hanging in his prison cell, a leather belt around his neck. The death was held to be a suicide.

Cottingham, Richard Francis

On December 2, 1979, New York City firemen responded to an alarm at a seedy hotel on West 42nd Street, not far from Times Square. They fought their way through smoky corridors to quench a blaze inside one room, discovering two women's bodies there. Stretched out on separate beds, the headless corpses also had their hands removed, legs doused with lighter fluid and set on fire. The missing parts were never found, but X-rays identified one victim as 22-year-Old Deedeh Goodarzi, a Kuwaiti immigrant who earned her living as a prostitute. Goodarzi's young companion in death was never identified.

The crime reminded homicide detectives of another unsolved case. Teenage hooker Helen Sikes had disappeared from Times Square in January, turning up in Queens, her throat slashed so deeply that she was nearly decapitated. Her severed legs were found a block away, laid side-by-side in ritual fashion, as if still attached to the body.

There were no leads in either case, and police were no closer to a suspect on May 5, 1980, when teenaged prostitute Valerie Street was found beaten and strangled, stuffed beneath a bed at a motel in Hasbrouck Heights, New Jersey. In addition to the savage beating, her breasts had been gnawed so violently that one nipple was nearly severed. Detectives recalled that a young nurse, Maryann Carr, had been brutally slain at the same motel on December 16, 1977, but the connections seemed tenuous, at best.

The similarities were obvious on May 15, when prostitute Jean Reyner was found stabbed to death in a 29th Street hotel near Times Square, her breasts severed, the body set afire. A week later, on May 22, officers were called back to the motel in Hasbrouck Heights, responding to reports of a woman screaming. They bagged a man emerging from the room, and went inside to find his teenage victim naked, handcuffed to the bed, hysterical from pain and fear. She had been beaten, raped and sodomized, forced to perform oral sex at knifepoint, after which her assailant slashed her with his blade, biting her breasts until they bled.

The prisoner, 33-year-old Richard Cottingham, made

an unlikely suspect at first glance. A respected family man from Lodi, New Jersey, he ran computers for a major health insurance firm. On the other hand, arresting officers had relieved him of handcuffs, a leather gag and two "slave" collars, a switchblade and replica pistol, plus several bottles of pills. A search of Cottingham's home turned up a bizarre "trophy room," containing personal effects from several of the murdered prostitutes.

Investigation of the suspect's background revealed two arrests for consorting with hookers in the early 1970s, with both cases dismissed. In April 1980, Cottingham's wife had filed for divorce, charging him with "extreme cruelty" and refusal to engage in marital sex since late 1976. The divorce affidavits further alleged that Cottingham was a habitual patron of gay bars and homosexual "spas" in Manhattan.

Despondent in custody, Cottingham smashed a lens of his spectacles and attempted suicide by slashing his wrists with the glass. Surviving that attempt and two others, he was held under $250,000 bond while detectives built their overwhelming case against him. In addition to multiple murder counts, Cottingham was linked with the brutal abduction and rape of three surviving victims—including two prostitutes and a young housewife—during 1978.

In May 1981, Cottingham was convicted on fifteen felony counts related to the murder of Valerie Street, drawing a sentence of 173 to 197 years in prison. A year later, conviction on second-degree murder charges in the death of Maryann Carr added another sentence of 20 years to life. In 1984, convicted on three counts of second-degree murder, involving Times Square prostitutes, Cottingham earned a final sentence of 75 years to life.

Dahmer, Jeffrey Lionel

Milwaukee born in 1960, Jeffrey Dahmer moved to Ohio with his family at age six. In 1968, he was sexually molested by a neighbor boy in rural Bath Township. Unreported at the time, the childhood incident may play a pivotal role in understanding Dahmer's subsequent crimes.

At 10, Dahmer was "experimenting" with dead animals, decapitating rodents, bleaching chicken bones with acid, nailing a dog's carcass to a tree and mounting its severed head on a stake. In June 1978, Jeffrey crossed the line from morbid "experimentation" to murder. His victim was hitchhiker Steven Hicks, whom Jeffrey took home for a drink and some laughs. When Hicks tried to leave, Dahmer crushed his skull with a barbell, strangled him to death, then dismembered and buried his corpse.

In 1982, he moved into his grandmother's house in West Allis, Wisconsin. That August, he logged an arrest for indecent exposure at the state fair. Identical charges were filed in September 1986, when two boys accused Dahmer of masturbating in public. Convicted of disorderly conduct, he received a one-year suspended sentence with orders for counseling.

On September 15, 1987, Steven Tuomi vanished in Milwaukee, the mystery unsolved until Dahmer confessed his murder in 1991. James Doxtator was the next to die, in January 1988, followed by Richard Guerrero on March 24. By September 1988, Jeffrey's odd hours and the stench of his "experiments" had become too much for his grandmother, and Dahmer was asked to move out. On September 25, he found an apartment on Milwaukee's North 25th Street.

The next day, Dahmer lured a Laotian boy to his flat, fondled him, and offered cash for a nude modeling session. Police were called, and Dahmer was charged with sexual assault. Convicted in January 1989, he remained free pending a formal sentencing scheduled for May. Meanwhile, on March 25, Dahmer slaughtered victim Anthony Sears.

Sentenced to one year in jail, Dahmer was released after 10 months. The death parade resumed with Edward Smith, in June 1990. July's victim was Raymond Smith. Ernest Miller and David Thomas were butchered in September. Dahmer bagged Curtis Straughter in February. Errol Lindsey joined the list in April, followed by Anthony Hughes in May.

Konerak Sinthasomphone was the brother of the youth Dahmer molested in 1988. Missing on May 26, 1991, he was next seen the following day, naked, dazed, and bleeding, when neighbors reported his plight to police. Officers questioned Dahmer, who described the boy as his adult homosexual lover, and since Konerak spoke no English, they returned the youth to Dahmer's custody . . . and to his death.

The juggernaut rolled on: Matt Turner killed on June 30; Jeremiah Weinberger on July 7; eight days later, Oliver Lacy; Joseph Brandehoft on July 19. Tracy Edwards was lucky, escaping on July 22 with handcuffs still dangling from one wrist. He flagged a squad car down and led the officers to Dahmer's home, where the dissected remains of 11 victims were found in acid vats and the refrigerator. By August 22, Dahmer was charged with a total of 15 murders. Dahmer has filed a plea of not guilty by reason of insanity, and psychiatric testing continues at this writing, with no end in sight.

Denke, Karl

A native of Munsterberg, Silesia—now Ziebice, Poland—Denke operated a rooming house in his hometown between 1918 and 1924. His tenants affectionately called him ''Papa,'' and Denke was also well-liked in the community at large, serving as the organ-blower for his local church. On the side, in three years time, he also murdered and devoured a minimum of thirty victims.

On December 21, 1924, one of Denke's tenants, a coachman by the name of Gabriel, heard cries for help which seemed to emanate from Denke's flat, downstairs. Afraid the landlord might be injured, Gabriel rushed down to help . . . and found a young man staggering along the corridor, blood streaming from his open scalp. Before he fell unconscious on the floor, the victim blurted out that ''Papa'' Denke had attacked him with an ax.

Police were summoned and arrested Denke, scouring his flat for evidence. They turned up identification papers for twelve traveling journeymen, plus assorted items of male clothing. In the kitchen, two large tubs held meat pickled in brine; with the assorted bones and pots of fat, detectives reckoned that it added up to thirty victims, more or less. In Denke's ledger, they found listed names and dates, with the respective weights of bodies he had pickled dating back to 1921.

According to the record, he had specialized in slaying beggars, tramps, and journeymen who seemed unlikely to be missed around the neighborhood.

No evidence of sexual assault was ever publicized in Denke's case, and homicide investigators were unable to explain his actions. Shortly after his arrest, the killer hanged himself with his suspenders, in his cell, permitting generations of historians to speculate in vain about his motives.

DeSalvo, Albert Henry

Born in Chelsea, Massachusetts, during 1931, DeSalvo was another product of a violent and abusive home. Frank DeSalvo beat his wife and children regularly, and was thrown in jail on two occasions prior to the divorce that split the family in 1944. Fleeing a record of teenage arrests for breaking and entering, Albert joined the army at age 17 and was stationed in Germany. He married a German girl and brought her back to the United States when he was transferred home.

Posted to Fort Dix, New Jersey, DeSalvo was charged with molesting a nine-year-old girl in January 1955, but the child's mother declined to press charges, and so he received an honorable discharge in 1956. At the same time, he experienced sexual problems with his wife, demanding intercourse five or six times a day, regarding her as "frigid" when she turned him down. Matters grew worse with the birth of their first child, in 1958, with the new shortage of cash driving DeSalvo back to a life of petty crime. Arrested twice for breaking and entering, he received suspended sentences each time.

During this same period, Massachusetts women began falling prey to the "Measuring Man," a smooth-talking impostor who posed as a talent scout for a modeling agency, wandering door-to-door in an endless search for "new talent." Once inside an apartment, the man would produce a measuring tape and proceed to record the tenant's "vital statistics," often fondling her intimately in the process. Some complained to the police, but many others didn't, and detectives noted the absence of any violent assault, ranking the case near the bottom of their priority list.

On March 17, 1960, Cambridge police arrested DeSalvo on suspicion of burglary, and he swiftly confessed to his role as the "Measuring Man." Charged with assault and battery, lewd conduct, and attempted breaking and entering, he was convicted only on the latter charge, sentenced to two years in prison. Paroled after eleven months, he was driven by sexual frustration to adopt a more aggressive, violent role. As the "Green Man"—so-called for his green work clothes—DeSalvo launched a two-year campaign of sexual assaults that claimed victims in Massachusetts, Connecticut, New Hampshire and Rhode Island. Police would later estimate that he had raped at least 300 women, while DeSalvo placed the total closer to 2,000. He once claimed a half-dozen victims in one day, spread over four towns, with two of the rapes unreported prior to his confession.

While police throughout New England sought the "Green Man," Boston homicide detectives were stalking an elusive killer, blamed for the deaths of eleven women between June 1962 and July 1964. In every case, the victims had been raped—sometimes with foreign objects—and their bodies laid out nude, as if on display for a pornographic snapshot. Death was always due to strangulation, though the killer sometimes also used a knife. The ligature—a stocking, pillow case, whatever—was inevitably left around the victim's neck, tied with an exaggerated, ornamental bow.

Anna Slessers, 55, had been the first to die, strangled with the cord of her bathrobe on June 14, 1962. A nylon stocking was used to kill 68-year-old Nina Nichols on June 30, and Helen Blake, age 65, was found the same day, a stocking and bra knotted around her neck. On August 19, 75-year-old Ida Irga was manually strangled in her home, "decorated" with a knotted pillow case, and 67-year-old

Jane Sullivan had been dead a week when she was found on August 20, strangled with her own stockings, slumped over the edge of the bathtub with her face submerged.

The killer seemed to break his pattern on December 5, 1962, murdering a 20-year-old black, Sophie Clark. Another shift was seen with 23-year-old Patricia Bissette, strangled on her bed and covered with a blanket to her chin, in place of the usual graphic display. With 23-year-old Beverly Samans, killed on May 6, 1963, the slayer used a knife for the first time, stabbing his victim 22 times before looping the traditional nylon stocking around her neck. Evelyn Corbin, 58, seemed to restore the pattern on September 8, strangled and violated by an "unnatural" assault, but the killer went back to young victims on November 23, strangling 23-year-old Joann Graff, leaving teethmarks in her breast. The final victim, 19-year-old Mary Sullivan, was found on January 4, 1964, strangled with a scarf, the shaft of a broomstick protruding from her vagina.

Ten months later, on November 3, DeSalvo was hauled in for questioning on rape charges, after one of the "Green Man's" victims gave police a description strongly resembling the "Measuring Man." DeSalvo's confession to a long series of rapes landed him in the Bridgewater State Hospital, committed for observation, and where he was befriended by George Nassar, a convicted murderer facing trial in his second robbery-slaying since 1948. Their private discussions were interspersed with visits from police, ultimately leading to DeSalvo's full confession in the "Boston strangler" crimes.

In his confession, Albert even tacked on two "new" victims, never previously linked by the authorities. One, 85-year-old Mary Mullen, was found dead at her home on June 28, 1962, her passing attributed to heart failure. DeSalvo claimed that Mullen had collapsed from shock when he invaded her apartment, whereupon he left her body on the couch without continuing the usual assault. Mary Brown, age 69, was stabbed and beaten in her home on March 9, 1963, again without a showing of the "strangler's knot."

It seemed like an open-and-shut case, but numerous

problems remained. The strangler's sole surviving victim, assaulted in February 1963, couldn't pick Albert out of a lineup, and neither could witnesses who sighted a suspect near the Graff and Sullivan murder scenes. Several detectives had focused their aim on another "prime suspect," fingered by psychic Peter Hurkos, but their man had voluntarily committed himself to an asylum soon after the last murder. And if Albert DeSalvo was driven by a mother-fixation, as psychiatrists claimed, why had he chosen young women as five of his last seven victims?

Some students of the case believe the answer may be found in Bridgewater, where killer George Nassar conferred with DeSalvo through long days and nights. It is possible, critics maintain, that Nassar might have been the strangler, briefing Albert on the details of his crimes in hope of sending authorities off on a wild goose chase. DeSalvo, already facing life imprisonment for countless rapes, admittedly struck a cash bargain with Nassar, whereby Nassar would pocket part of the outstanding reward for turning DeSalvo in, afterward passing on most of the cash to DeSalvo's wife. As a "clincher," the strangler's lone survivor favored Nassar as a suspect, rather than DeSalvo.

Be that as it may, DeSalvo never came to trial for homicide in Boston. Lawyer F. Lee Bailey managed to negotiate a deal in 1967, whereby Albert drew a term of life imprisonment for crimes committed as the "Green Man." Never charged in the Boston stranglings, he was stabbed to death by a fellow inmate at Walpole prison, in November 1973.

Drenth, Herman

A used furniture dealer from Clarksburg, West Virginia, Herman Drenth earned his real money through operation of a deadly matrimonial racket, spanning the United States in the 1920s and early '30s. Though legally married in Clarksburg, Drenth traveled widely in search of his victims, consoling his wife with reports of his "business trips" from Boston to Spokane, and all points in between. The "business," as police discovered during 1931, was bigamy and murder. Drenth attached himself to wealthy widows, married them, and brought them back to his "scientific laboratory," in the woods adjoining Clarksburg. There, his aging brides were gassed to death, with Herman pocketing their cash and selling off their other property.

A farmer living in the same vicinity complained to local officers about the noxious odors emanating from the "lab." Their search revealed two rooms: a killing chamber, where Drenth's victims had been bound, with lethal gas piped in; and an adjoining "operations room," where Drenth sat safe behind a plate glass window, gloating on their final agony. The killing chamber's floor was caked with blood, as Drenth had used a hammer on the three young children of his latest victim, Asta Buick Eicher, prior to gassing her as usual.

Arrested for the Eicher slayings and the murder of another widow, Dorothy Lemke of Worcester, Massachusetts, Drenth confessed after corpses were found in a ditch near the lab. He admitted deriving sexual pleasure from watching his victims die, commenting that, "It beat any cat house I was ever in."

The local press christened Drenth "America's worst bluebeard," and police speculated that he may have killed over fifty women, but the prisoner was uncooperative when it came to hunting corpses. "You got me on five," he reminded his jailers. "What good would fifty more do?" Taking his secret to the gallows, Drenth was hanged on March 18, 1932.

Drew, Carl H.

A Massachusetts pimp and self-styled Satanist, Drew used the trappings of his twisted religion to keep prostitutes in line, compelling their participation in cult rituals and threatening savage violence if they tried to reject his "protection." At his murder trial, in March 1981, several witnesses described Drew's role in a series of ritual gatherings held between October 1979 and February 1980. Declaring himself to be Satan, Drew would reportedly chant

and pray in "a different language," leading his flock
through the grisly steps of human sacrifice on at least two
occasions.

The first victim was Donna Levesque, of Fall River, her
mutilated body discovered on October 13, 1979. Witnesses
to that ritual murder included prostitutes Karen Marsden,
20, and Robin Murphy, 18. While Murphy was able to
tolerate the sadistic violence, gradually moving from the
role of an observer to that of a participant, Marsden was
repulsed and sought to break away from Drew's control.
On February 8, 1980, she was sacrificed at a cult gathering outside Westport, tortured by having her hair and fingernails ripped out, beaten over the head with stones before
Drew manually snapped her neck. Unsatisfied, the pimp
persuaded Robin Murphy to slash Marsden's throat, after
which he removed her head and the cultists kicked it
around like a football. Marsden's fingers were lopped off
in an effort to steal her rings, and Drew finished by raping
the headless corpse, carving an "X" on the chest and
smearing Marsden's blood on Murphy's forehead.

Fragments of Marsden's skull and scraps of her clothing
were found in the woods on April 13, 1980. No other trace
of her body has surfaced, but authorities identified the
meager remains by comparing bone fragments with skull
X-rays taken in 1978, when the victim was treated for a
sinus ailment. By that time, Robin Murphy had already
cracked under the strain of concealing two murders, and
she fingered Carl Drew as the killer. Pleading guilty to her
role in the Marsden sacrifice, Murphy accepted a life sentence and agreed to testify for the state, against Drew.

The 26-year-old Satanist's trial opened on March 2,
1981, and he was indicted for Donna Levesque's murder
the following day. In the meantime, his name had also
been mentioned in court proceedings against 43-year-old
Andre Maltais, convicted of murdering prostitute Barbara
Raposa, 19, in November 1979. Convicted of the Marsden
slaying on March 13, Drew was sentenced to life imprisonment. The investigation into his other crimes continues
at this writing.

Dudley, Kenneth E.
and Gwyn, Irene

On February 9, 1961, the body of a female child was found along Route 1, near Lawrenceville, Virginia. Indications of severe abuse included bruises, open sores, a healing fracture of the child's right leg. The cause of death was listed as a combination of exposure to the elements and malnutrition.

Suspicion quickly fell on Kenneth and Irene Dudley, stopped by a highway patrolman on February 6, not fifty yards from where the tiny corpse was found. The Dudleys had been traveling with several ragged children in their car, and a description was broadcast, leading to their arrest near Fuqua, North Carolina, on February 10. The next day, they were back in Brunswick County's jail, attempting to explain themselves to homicide investigators.

Interviews with two older daughters, in New York, revealed that Kenneth and Irene departed Syracuse in July 1958, with six children in their care. At the time of their arrest, only one—two-year-old Christine—was still alive. The other had been lost along a rambling trek across the continent and back again.

Authorities could chart the family's progress with a string of bodies. Claude had been the first to die, on November 19, 1958, still three months shy of his fourth birthday; his body, bound in canvas and a blanket, had been found near Lakeland, Florida. Norman Dudley, ten years old, had died December 23, 1959, with eight-year-old Charles following on Christmas day; their bodies, tied together in a blanket and canvas, were dropped off a bridge into Lake Pontchartrain, Louisiana, on January 1, 1960.

Three-year-old Deborrah Jane survived until May 21, 1960; her small corpse was wrapped in canvas, wedged into a cardboard box and dumped on a rubbish heap outside Jenkins, Kentucky. Carol Ann, age nine, was the last, her blanket-wrapped body discovered in a path of snow near Lawrenceville on February 9.

Investigation demonstrated that another Dudley child had been unearthed near Syracuse, New York, in 1946, resulting in Kenneth's imprisonment for improper burial. Dudley had served a year on that charge, but detectives never pressed the search for evidence of homicide.

In custody, statements from Irene Dudley documented a pattern of brutal abuse through the years. In fits of anger, Kenneth often beat the children over trivial offenses, sometimes binding them with ropes for a day or more at a time, resulting in loss of circulation to arms and legs. Once, Irene recalled, her husband slapped one of the girls for "moving a lot," and then thrust his fingers down the child's throat to silence her "hollering."

Above all else, the Dudley children finally fell prey to malnutrition and a general neglect. "Because we had no money," Irene told police, "at times the children were denied food, as punishment for misbehavior. At times, my husband and I ate while the children had nothing. We were better off than the children." Both defendants were confined for psychiatric observation pending trial.

Evans, Wesley Gareth

Slow-witted and hyperactive, Canadian Wesley Evans missed long months of schooling due to erratic behavior which made attendance impossible. Hit by a truck at age nine, he suffered severe head injuries that left him comatose for eight days, with temporary paralysis of his left side upon regaining consciousness. Released from the hospital after four months of therapy, Evans thereafter walked with a pronounced limp, communicating in slurred speech. Eighteen months later, he was burned over twenty percent of his body while playing with a cigarette lighter. He grew up obsessed with the notion that girls—and later, women—were laughing at his scars. In time, his hidden rage would reach a lethal boiling point.

On November 24, 1984, Lavonne Willems, age 27, of Vancouver, was found dead in a home she was watching for friends, then on vacation overseas. She had been murdered in the bedroom, stabbed a total of twenty-five times, her pants unbuckled and open at the waist. Detectives theorized a sexual motive, but they had no suspect in the case.

On March 31, 1985, realtor Beverly Seto, 39 hosted an open house for potential customers in Matsqui, British Columbia, a Vancouver suburb. When she failed to come home for supper, her husband dropped by the empty house and found her car outside, the door ajar. A light was burning in the kitchen, though the guests had long departed. Moving through the silent rooms, he found his wife in the bedroom, her throat slashed, skirt bunched up around her waist. The coroner reported Seto had been raped, then stabbed a minimum of twenty times.

In late July, police received a tip which named a young man from the Matsqui neighborhood as Seto's killer. He was held for questioning in early August 1985, but officers found nothing to connect him with the murder. Seeking further information on their suspect, they detained a friend, 21-year-old Wesley Evans, on marijuana charges, hoping they could pressure him for details of the suspect's movements. What they got instead, was a surprise confession to the crime.

In custody, their prisoner admitted killing Seto, and went on to offer details of the Willems murder. Homicide investigators checked their street maps, startled to discover Evans lived a short four blocks from the location of the Seto slaying, barely eight blocks from the house where Willems died. The opening remarks of Wesley's trial were heard on January 16, 1986; convicted two weeks later, he was sentenced to a term of life imprisonment, required to serve a minimum of twenty-five years before he would be eligible for parole.

Eyler, Larry

A native of Crawfordsville, Indiana, born December 21, 1952, Eyler was the youngest of four children born to parents who divorced while he was young. Dropping out of high school in his senior year, he worked odd jobs for a couple of years before earning his GED. Sporadic enrollment in college between 1974 and '78 left Eyler without

a degree, and he finally pulled up stakes, making the move
to Chicago.

Unknown to friends and relatives, Larry Eyler was a
young man at war within himself, struggling to cope with
homosexual tendencies which simultaneously fascinated
and repelled him. Like John Gacy and a host of others,
he would learn to take his sex where he could find it,
forcefully, and then eliminate the evidence of his abiding
shame.

On March 22, 1982, Jay Reynolds was found, stabbed
to death on the outskirts of Lexington, Kentucky. Nine
months later, on October 3, 14-year-old Delvoyd Baker
was strangled, his body dumped on the roadside north of
Indianapolis. Steven Crockett, 19, was the victim on October 23, stabbed 32 times with four wounds in the head,
discarded outside Lowell, Indiana. The killer moved into
Illinois on November 6, leaving Robert Foley in a field
northwest of Joliet.

Police were slow to see the pattern forming, unaware
that they had already spoken with one survivor. Drugged
and beaten near Lowell, Indiana, on November 4, 21-year-
old Craig Townsend had escaped from the hospital before
detectives completed their investigation of the unprovoked
assault.

The transient slayer celebrated Christmas 1982 by
dumping 25-year-old John Johnson's body in a field outside Belshaw, Indiana. Three days later, it was a double-
header, with 21-year-old John Roach discovered near
Belleville, and the trussed-up body of Steven Agan, a Terre
Haute native, discarded north of Newport, Indiana.

The grim toll continued to rise through the spring of
1983, with most of the action shifting to Illinois. By July
2, the body-count stood at twelve, with the latter victims
mutilated after death, a few disemboweled. Ralph Calise
made unlucky thirteen on August 31, dumped in a field
near Lake Forest, Illinois. He had been dead less than
twelve hours when he was discovered, bound with clothesline and surgical tape, stabbed 17 times, his pants pulled
down around his ankles.

On September 30, 1983, an Indiana highway patrolman
spotted a pickup truck parked along Interstate 65, with

two men moving toward a nearby stand of trees. One appeared to be bound, and the officer went to investigate, identifying Larry Eyler as the owner of the truck. His young companion accused Eyler of making homosexual propositions, then asking permission to tie him up. A search of the pickup revealed surgical tape, nylon clothesline, and a hunting knife stained with human blood. Forensics experts noted that the blood type matched Ralph Calise's, while tire tracks and imprints of Eyler's boots made a fair match with tracks from the field where Calise was discovered.

While the investigation continued, with Eyler still at liberty, the murders likewise kept pace. On October 4, 1983, 14-year-old Derrick Hansen was found dismembered, near Kenosha, Wisconsin. Eleven days later, a young "John Doe" was discovered near Rensselaer, Indiana. October 18 yielded four bodies in Newton County, dumped together at an abandoned farm; one victim had been decapitated, and all had their pants pulled down, indicating sexual motives in the slayings. Another "John Doe" was recovered on December 5, near Effingham, Illinois, and the body-count jumped again, two days later, when Richard Wayne and an unidentified male were found dead near Indianapolis.

By this time, police had focused their full attention on Larry Eyler. Craig Townsend had been traced to Chicago, after fleeing the Indiana hospital, and he grudgingly identified photographs of Eyler. Another survivor chimed in with similar testimony, but investigators wanted their man for homicide, and the circumstantial case was still incomplete.

Facing constant surveillance in Chicago, Eyler filed a civil suit against the Lake County sheriff's office, accusing officers of mounting a "psychological warfare" campaign to unhinge his mind. His claim for half a million dollars was denied, and as he left the courtroom, Eyler was arrested for the Ralph Calise murder, held in lieu of $1 million bond. Police were jubilant until a pretrial hearing on February 5, 1984, led to exclusion of all the evidence recovered from Eyler's truck. Released on bail, the killer went about his business while investigators scrambled to salvage their failing case.

On May 7, 1984, 22-year-old David Block was found murdered near Zion, Illinois, his wounds conforming to the pattern of his predecessors. Police got a break three months later, on August 21, when a janitor's skittish dog led his master to examine Eyler's garbage, in Chicago. Police were swiftly summoned to claim the remains of Danny Bridges, 15, a homosexual hustler whose dismembered body had been neatly bagged for disposal.

Eyler's arrogance had finally undone him. Experts noted that the Bridges mutilations were a carbon copy of the Derrick Hansen case, outside Kenosha, in October 1983. Convicted of the Bridges slaying on July 9, 1986, Eyler was sentenced to die. Investigations of his other murders are continuing, but there have been no further charges in the case.

Falling, Christine
Laverne Slaughter

Christine Falling was born at Perry, Florida, on March 12, 1963, the second child of a 65-year-old father and his 16-year-old wife. Reared in poverty, obese and dull-witted, she required regular doses of medication to control her epileptic seizures. As a child, she showed her ''love'' for cats by strangling them and dropping them from lethal heights in order to ''test their nine lives.'' At age nine, Christine and her sister were removed for a year to a children's refuge in Orlando, following domestic battles that resulted in police being summoned to their home.

In September 1977, at age 14, Christine was married to a man in his twenties. Their chaotic relationship lasted six weeks and was punctuated by violence, Christine once hurling a 25-pound stereo at her husband in the heat of battle. With the collapse of her marriage, Falling lapsed into a bizarre hypochondriac phase, logging 50 trips to the hospital in the space of two years. She complained of ailments ranging from ''red spots'' to vaginal bleeding and "snakebite," but physicians rarely found any treatable symptoms.

Rendered virtually unemployable by her appearance and mentality, Christine picked up spending money by baby-sitting for neighbors and relatives. On February 25, one of her charges—two-year-old Cassidy Johnson—was rushed to a doctor's office in Blountstown, tentatively diagnosed as suffering from encephalitis. The girl died on February 28, an autopsy listing cause of death as blunt trauma to the skull. Christine described the baby "passing out" and toppling from her crib, but she was unconvincing. One physician wrote a note to the police, advising them to check the babysitter out, but it was "lost" in transit and the case was closed.

Christine moved on to Lakeland, and two months after her arrival, four-year-old Jeffrey Davis "stopped breath-ing" in her care. An autopsy revealed symptoms of myocarditis, a heart inflammation rarely fatal in itself. Three days later, while the family attended Jeffrey's funeral, Falling was retained to sit with two-year-old Joseph Spring, a cousin of the dead boy. Joseph died in his crib that afternoon, while "napping," and physicians noted evidence of a viral infection, suggesting it might have killed Jeffrey, as well.

Christine was back in Perry—and in business—by July of 1981. She had received a clean bill of health from the doctors in Lakeland, but her bad luck was holding. She tried her hand at housekeeping, but 77-year-old William Swindle died in his kitchen her first day on the job. A short time later, Falling accompanied her stepsister to the doctor's office, where an eight-month-old niece, Jennifer Daniels, received some standard childhood vaccinations. Stopping by the market on her way home, the stepsister left Christine in the car with her child, returning to find that the baby had simply "stopped breathing."

Thus far, local physicians had sympathized with Chris-tine as an unfortunate "victim of circumstance," but their view changed on July 2, 1982, when ten-week-old Travis Coleman died in Falling's care. This time, an autopsy re-vealed internal ruptures, caused by suffocation, and Chris-tine was hauled in for questioning. In custody, she confessed to killing three of the children by means of "smotheration," pressing a blanket over their faces in response to disembodied voices chanting, "Kill the baby."

"The way I done it, I seen it done on TV shows," Christine explained. "I had my own way, though. Simple and easy. No one would hear them scream." Convicted on the basis of her own confession, she was sentenced to a term of life imprisonment, with no parole for the first 25 years.

Fernandez, Raymond Martinez and Beck, Martha

Hawaiian-born Raymond Fernandez was a self-styled Latin lover, who married twice and fathered an unknown number of children before turning to life as a bigamist, gigolo, and professional swindler. His targets were elderly spinsters and widows, selected from newspaper "personal" ads and the listings of various "lonely-hearts" clubs. One such advertisement, answered during 1947, brought Fernandez face-to-face with Martha Beck, a registered nurse and matron of a home for crippled children in Pensacola, Florida. Five years his junior, tipping the scales at 280 pounds, Beck swept Fernandez off his feet, delighting Raymond with her absolute approval of his larcenous life-style. They devised a scheme where Beck would pose as Raymond's sister, standing by to help while he bilked other women of their savings, joining him for kinky sex between engagements. Over two years time, they swindled scores of victims, killing off at least a dozen (some say 20) when confronted with resistance.

One of those who got the treatment was a widow, Delphine Dowling, 28, of Grand Rapids, Michigan. Easily the youngest of Raymond's victims, Mrs. Dowling allowed Fernandez and his "sister" to occupy her home, but she stalled the wedding until she was "sure of Raymond's affections." The delay blocked access to her cash, while making Martha jealous in her ring-side seat, compelled to watch as Raymond wooed their pigeon. Neighbors were suspicious when Mrs. Dowling and her two-year-old daughter vanished in January 1949, and police were summoned to investigate. Fernandez and Beck were still in residence when detectives arrived, cheerfully granting permission for a search of the house. Excavating a patch of fresh cement in the basement, officers unearthed two corpses, quickly arresting Fernandez and his ''sister'' on suspicion of murder.

In custody, the lovers cracked, confessing to a score of homicides. Fernandez admitted feeding Mrs. Dowling an overdose of sleeping pills, shooting her in the head for good measure, after which Beck had drowned two-year-old Rainelle Dowling in the bathtub. Accustomed to four-figure payoffs, Fernandez was disappointed with the $500 he picked up from Delphine Dowling. The take was hardly worth his time, and as he told detectives, ''I'm no average killer.''

The confessions seemed to bear him out. Jane Thompson had accompanied Raymond on a honeymoon in Spain, but she had not returned. Fernandez sold her relatives the story of a fatal (nonexistent) train wreck, moving in with Thompson's mother several weeks before she disappeared. Another victim, Myrtle Young, had joined Fernandez in Chicago during August 1948, where she reportedly ''croaked from overexertion'' after a weekend of non-stop sex. Janet Fay, age 66, was swindled by the pair in Albany, New York, after which Martha Beck brained her with a hammer, Fernandez finishing the job by strangulation with a scarf. Authorities recovered Fay's remains from a suburban cottage and indictments were returned, the prisoners delivered to New York since Michigan had no provision for capital punishment.

At their trial, beginning in July of 1949, the killers pled not guilty by reason of insanity. Jurors rejected the ploy, and on August 22 the ''lonely-hearts killers'' were sentenced to death. The Supreme Court rejected their appeals on January 2, 1951, and the executions were carried out at Sing Sing prison, on March 8.

Fish, Albert Howard

Born Hamilton Fish, in 1870, America's most notorious 20th-century cannibal was the product of a respected family living in Washington, D.C. A closer examination, however, reveals at least seven relatives with severe mental disorders in the two generations preceding Fish's birth, including two members of the family who died in institutions. Fish was five years old when his father died, and his mother placed him in an orphanage while she worked to support herself. Records describe young Fish as a problem child who "ran away every Saturday," persistently wetting the bed until his eleventh year. Graduating from public school at age 15, he began to call himself "Albert," discarding the hated first name which led classmates to tease him, calling him "Ham and Eggs."

As an adult, Fish worked odd jobs, making his way across country as an itinerant house painter and decorator. In 1898 he married a woman nine years his junior fathering six children before his wife ran away with a boarder named John Straube, in January 1917. She came back once, with Straube in tow, and Fish took her back on the condition that she send her lover away. Later, he discovered that his wife was keeping Straube in the attic, and she departed after a stormy argument, never to return.

By his own account, Fish committed his first murder in 1910, killing a man in Wilmington, Delaware, but his children marked the obvious change in Fish's behavior from the date of his wife's first departure. Apparently subject to hallucinations, he would shake his fist at the sky and repeatedly scream, "I am Christ!" Obsessed with sin, sacrifice, and atonement through pain, Fish encouraged his children and their friends to paddle him until his buttocks bled. On his own, he inserted numerous needles in his groin, losing track of some as they sank out of sight. (A prison X-ray revealed at least 29 separate needles, some eroded with time to mere fragments.) On other occasions, Fish would soak cotton balls in alcohol, insert them in his anus, and set them on fire. Frustrated by agony when he began slipping needles under his own fingernails, Fish lamented, "If only pain were not so painful!"

Though never divorced from his first wife, Fish married three more times, enjoying a sex life which court psychiatrists would describe as one of "unparalleled perversity." (In jail, authorities compiled a list of eighteen sexual perversions practiced by Fish, including coprophagia—the consumption of human excrement.) Tracing his sado-masochism back to the age of five or six, when he began to relish bare-bottom paddlings in the orphanage, Fish's obsession with pain was focused primarily on children. Ordered "by God" to castrate young boys, he impartially molested children of both sexes as he traveled around the country. Prosecutors confidently linked him with "at least 100" sexual attacks in 23 states, from New York to Wyoming, but Fish felt slighted by their estimate. "I have had children in every state," he declared, placing his own tally of victims closer to 400.

For all that, Fish was careless in his crimes, frequently losing jobs "because things about these children came out." Arrested eight times over the years, he served time for grand larceny, passing bad checks and violating parole or probation. Obscene letters were another of his passions, and Fish mailed off countless examples to strangers, their addresses obtained from matrimonial agencies or newspaper "lonely-hearts" columns.

In 1928, posing as "Mr. Howard," Fish befriended the Budd family in White Plains, New York. On June 3, while escorting 12-year-old Grace Budd to a mythical children's party, he took the child to an isolated cottage and there dismembered her body, saving several pieces for a stew which he consumed.

Two years later, with the Budd case still unsolved, Fish was confined to a psychiatric hospital for the first time. After two months of observation, he was discharged with a note reading: "Not insane; psychopathic personality; sexual type." In 1931, arresting Fish once more on a charge of mailing obscene letters, police found a well-used cat-o'-nine-tails in his room. He was released after two more weeks of observation in a psychiatric ward.

Compelled to gloat about his crimes, Fish sent a letter to the Budd family in 1934, breaking the news that Grace was dead, oddly emphasizing the fact that "she died a virgin.'' Traced by police through the letter, Fish readily confessed to other homicides, including children killed in 1919, 1927, and 1934.

Authorities disagreed on his ultimate body-count, detectives listing at least three more victims in New York City. Arrested for questioning in one case, Fish had been released because he "looked so innocent." On another occasion, a trolley conductor identified Fish as the man he saw with a small, sobbing boy on the day of the child's disappearance. A court psychiatrist suspected Albert of at least five murders, with New York detectives adding three more, and a justice of the New York Supreme Court was "reliably informed" of the killer's involvement in fifteen homicides.

At trial, the state was desperate to win a death penalty, overriding Fish's insanity defense with laughable psychiatric testimony. Speaking for the state, a battery of doctors declared, straight-faced, that "Coprophagia is a common sort of thing. We don't call people who do that mentally sick. A man who does that is socially perfectly all right. As far as his social status is concerned, he is supposed to be normal, because the State of New York Mental Hygiene Department also approves of that."

With Fish's rambling, obscene confessions in hand, the jury found him sane and guilty of premeditated murder. Sentenced to die, Fish was electrocuted at Sing Sing prison on January 16, 1936. It took two jolts before the chair, short-circuited by all the needles Fish had planted in his body, could complete its work.

"Four Pi Movement, The"

In 1969, while gathering material for a book on the Charles Manson case, journalist Ed Sanders encountered reports of a sinister Satanic cult alleged to practice human sacrifice in several parts of California, luring youthful members from college campuses throughout the western half of the United States. Calling itself the "Four Pi" or "Four P" movement, the cult originally boasted 55 members, of whom fifteen were middle-aged, the rest consisting of young men and women in their early twenties. The group's leader—dubbed the "Grand Chingon" or "Head Devil"—was said to be a wealthy California businessman of middle years, who exercised his power by compelling younger members of the cult to act as slaves and murder random targets on command. The central object of the cult was to promote "the total worship of evil."

Organized in Northern California during 1967, the Four Pi movement held its secret gatherings in the Santa Cruz mountains, south of San Francisco. Rituals were conducted on the basis of a stellar timetable, including the sacrifice of Doberman and German shepherd dogs. Beginning in June 1968, authorities in San Jose, Santa Cruz, and Los Gatos began recording discovery of canines, skinned and drained of blood without apparent motive. As the director of the Santa Cruz animal shelter told Sanders, "Whoever is doing this is a real expert with a knife. The skin is cut away without even marking the flesh. The really strange thing is that these dogs have been drained of blood."

If we accept the word of isolated witnesses, the missing blood was drunk by cultists in their ceremonies. So, according to reports, was human blood, obtained from sacrificial victims murdered on a dragon-festooned altar. Death was the result of stabbing with a custom-made six-bladed knife, designed with blades of varied length to penetrate a victim's stomach first, before the heart was skewered, causing death. Each sacrifice allegedly was climaxed by removal of the heart, which cultists then divided up among themselves to eat. The evidence of murder was incinerated in a portable crematorium, mounted in the back of a truck.

According to reports from self-styled members of the Four Pi cult, its victims were mainly hitchhikers, drifters and runaways, with an occasional volunteer from the ranks. One such, a young woman, reportedly went to her death with a smile in November 1968, near Boulder Creek, but even sacrifice of willing victims is a risky business, and the cult was said to mount patrols around its rural meeting places, using guards with automatic weapons and attack-trained dogs to guarantee privacy.

In early 1969, the cult reportedly moved southward, shifting operations to the O'Neil Park region of the Santa Ana Mountains, below Los Angeles. The move produced—or was occasioned by—a fractional dispute within the group, one segment striving to deemphasize Satanic ritual and concentrate wholeheartedly on kinky sex, while more traditional adherents clung to Lucifer and human sacrifice. The group apparently survived its schism and expanded nationwide, with author Maury Terry citing evidence of a thousand or more members across the country by 1979. One hotbed of activity appears to be New York, where 85 German shepherds and Dobermans were found skinned in the year between October 1976 and October 1977.

Along the way, the "Four Pi" movement has apparently rubbed shoulders with a number of notorious killers, feeding—or, perhaps, inspiring—their sadistic fantasies. Serial slayer Stanley Baker, jailed in Montana for eating the heart of one victim, confessed to other murders perpetrated on orders from the "Grand Chingon." Recruited from a college campus in Wyoming, Baker remained unrepentant in confinement, organizing fellow inmates into a Satanic coven of his own, but his testimony brought lawmen no closer to cracking the cult.

Charles Manson and his "family" reportedly had contact with the Four Pi movement, prior to making headlines in Los Angeles. Ed Sanders reports that some of Manson's followers referred to him—in Sanders' presence—as the "Grand Chingon," distinguished from the original article by his age and the fact that Manson was jailed while the real "Chingon" remains at large. Likewise, "family" hacker Susan Atkins has described the sacrifice of dogs by Manson's group, and searchers digging for the last remains of Manson victim Shorty Shea reported finding large numbers of chicken and animal bones at the family's campsite—a peculiar form of garbage for a group reputedly comprised of vegetarians.

Convicted killer, David Berkowitz—more famous as the "Son of Sam" who terrorized New York in 1976 and '77—has also professed membership in the Four Pi cult, revealing inside knowledge of a California homicide allegedly committed by the group. In 1979, Berkowitz smuggled a book on witchcraft out of his prison cell, with passages on Manson and the Four Pi movement underlined. One page bore a cryptic notation in the killer's own handwriting: "Arlis Perry. Hunted, stalked, and slain. Followed to California." As researched by Maury Terry, the Berkowitz note points directly to an unsolved murder committed at Stanford University in mid-October 1974.

On October 11 of that year, co-ed Arlis Perry was found in the campus chapel at Stanford, nude from the waist down, a long candle protruding from her vagina. Her blouse had been ripped open, and another candle stood between her breasts. Beaten and choked unconscious by her assailant, she was finally killed with an ice pick, buried in her skull behind the left ear. In subsequent conversations and correspondence, Berkowitz alleged that Perry was killed by Four Pi members as "a favor" to cultists in her hometown Bismarck, North Dakota, whom she had apparently offended in some way. Her slayer was named by Berkowitz as "Manson II," a professional killer "involved with the original Manson and the cult there in L.A."

Aside from participation in human and canine sacrifice, with the occasional gang-rape of teenage girls, Four Pi cultists also reportedly share a fascination with Nazi racist doctrines. One alleged member, named by Berkowitz, was Frederick Cowan, a neo-fascist from New Rochelle, New York, who was suspended from work after quarreling with his Jewish boss in February 1977. Turning up at the plant with a small arsenal on February 14, Cowan killed five persons and wounded two others before turning a gun on himself. Maury Terry has also linked cult activity with the unsolved case of the "Westchester Dart man," who wounded 23 women in New York's Westchester and Rockland Counties, between February 1975 and May 1976.

Despite the testimony of reputed Four Pi members, authorities have yet to build a case against the cult. Some suspects, named by witnesses, have died in "accidents" or "suicides" before they could be questioned by police. Another obstacle appears to be the use of code names, which prevent the cultists from identifying one another under questioning. The group itself relies on different names from place to place, with New York members meeting as "The Children," while Alabama hosts "The Children of the Light" (suspected of involvement in 25 murders since 1987). A faction called the "Black Cross" is said to operate as a kind of Satanic Murder Incorporated, fielding anonymous hit teams for cultists nationwide, disposing of defectors and offering pointers on the fine art of human sacrifice. If law enforcement spokesmen are correct, the cult is also deeply involved in white slavery, child pornography, and the international narcotics trade (See also: Baker, Stanley; Kogut, John; Manson, Charles; "Son of Sam").

Franklin, Joseph Paul

Born James Clayton Vaughn, Jr., in Mobile Alabama, Franklin was the eldest son of an alcoholic drifter who often abandoned his family for months or years at a stretch. Siblings remember that James Vaughn, Sr., would celebrate infrequent homecomings by beating his children, with James, Jr., absorbing the worst punishment. As a youth, Franklin went in for food fads and fringe religions, dropping out of high school after an accident left him with severely impaired eyesight.

The injury was a two-edged sword, exempting Franklin from military conscription, and he married in 1968, at an age when many young men were sweating out the draft lottery, fearful of the war in Vietnam. Soon after their wedding, Franklin's bride noted a change in his personality "like night and day." He began to beat her, emulating the father he hated, and on other occasions she would find him inexplicably weeping. Around the same time, their all-white neighborhood was racially integrated, and Franklin began to veer hard right, into the realm of pathological bigotry.

The next few years were marked by ugly racial incidents and sporadic arrests for carrying concealed weapons. Franklin was increasingly drawn to the American Nazi Party, lapsing into the segregationist movement full-time after his mother's death, in 1972. Moving to Atlanta, he joined the neo-fascist National States Rights Party, simultaneously holding membership in the local Ku Klux Klan. Franklin began insulting interracial couples in public, and on Labor Day 1976, he trailed one such couple to a dead-end street in Atlanta, spraying them with chemical Mace.

Around this time, Franklin legally changed his name, shedding the last links with his "normal" life. Federal prosecutors allege—and jurors have agreed—that he spent the year 1977 to 1980 wandering across the South and Midwest, employing 18 pseudonyms, changing cars and weapons frequently, dying his hair so often that it came close to falling out. Along the way, he killed some thirteen persons in a frenzied, one-man war against minorities.

According to the FBI, Franklin launched his campaign in the summer of 1977, bombing a Chattanooga synagogue on July 29. Nine days later, investigators say, he shot and killed Alphonse Manning and Toni Schwenn, an interracial couple, in Madison, Wisconsin. On October 8, Gerald Gordon was killed by sniper fire as he left a bar mitzvah in the St. Louis suburb of Richmond Heights.

Harold McIver, the black manager of a fast-food restaurant in Doraville, Georgia, was working the night shift when a sniper took his life on July 22, 1979. Three months later, in Oklahoma City, another interracial couple came under attack from the itinerant gunman. Jesse Taylor was hit three times with a high-powered rifle before he expired; a single round through the chest killed Marian Bresette as she ran to the aide of her common-law husband.

Franklin struck twice in Indianapolis during January 1980, killing black men with long-distance rifle fire in two separate attacks. On May 3, he allegedly killed a young white woman, Rebecca Bergstrom, dumping her body near Tomah, in central Wisconsin. On June 8 he surfaced in Cincinnati, bagging cousins Darrell Lane and Dante Brown from his sniper's perch on a nearby railroad trestle. A week later, in Johnstown, Pennsylvania, Franklin shot-gunned a black couple—Arthur Smothers and Kathleen Mikula—as they crossed a downtown bridge. On August 20, joggers Ted Fields and David Martin were cut down by rifle fire in Salt Lake City, Utah.

Arrested in September 1980 (and recaptured a month later, after escaping to Florida), Franklin faced a marathon series of state and federal trials, with mixed results. He was acquitted of the shooting which left civil rights leader Vernon Jordan critically injured in May 1980, but Utah juries found him guilty of murder and civil rights violations, handing down a sentence of life imprisonment. He also stands convicted of the Chattanooga bombing and the double murder in Wisconsin, described by prosecutors as "the closest thing to killing for sport."

Gacy, John Wayne, Jr.

John Gacy, Sr., was an alcoholic tyrant in his home, a crude exaggeration of the famous "Archie Bunker" character with every trace of humor wiped away. He took no pains to hide his disappointment with the son who bore his name, inflicting brutal beatings for the least offense, occasionally picking up the boy and hurling him across a room. In more pacific moments, he was satisfied to damn John, Jr., as a "sissy" who was "dumb and stupid," useless in the scheme of things. In time, the "sissy" portion of his groundless accusations would appear to be a self-fulfilling prophecy.

Chicago born in March 1942, Gacy grew up doubting his own masculinity, taking refuge from sports and other "manly" activities through precocious hypochondria. Struck on the head by a swing at age eleven, he suffered periodic blackouts for the next five years until their cause— a blood clot on his brain—was finally dissolved with medication. Deprived of one affliction, he developed—or imagined—another, settling on the symptoms of a heart ailment that seemed to come and go, depending on his mood.

After graduation from business college, Gacy became a shoe salesman, but he had his sights on better things. He married a coworker, whose parents owned a fried chicken restaurant in Waterloo, Iowa, and Gacy stepped into a ready-made role as the restaurant's manager. He was a whiz kid on the job, belying everything his father had to say about his intellect and drive, ascending to a post of admiration and respect among the local Jaycees. His wife and friends were absolutely unprepared for John's arrest, in May of 1968, on charges of coercing a young employee into homosexual acts spanning a period of months. Those accusations were still pending when Gacy hired a teenage thug to beat the prosecution's witness, and more charges were filed. Striking a bargain, Gacy pled guilty to sodomy, and the other felony counts were dismissed. Sentenced to ten years in prison, he proved himself a "model prisoner" and was released in eighteen months.

With the state's permission, Gacy moved back to Chicago, where he established himself as a successful building contractor. Divorced while in prison, he soon remarried, settling in a middle-class neighborhood where he was popular with his neighbors, the host of elaborate holiday theme parties. On the side, he was active in Democratic politics—once posing for photos with the wife of President Jimmy Carter—and as "Pogo the Clown," performing in full makeup at children's parties and charity benefits. Few of his new acquaintances knew anything about the Iowa arrest, and those who heard a rumor were assured that John had merely done some time for "dealing in a little porn."

On February 12, 1971, Gacy was charged with disorderly conduct in Chicago, on the complaint of a boy he attempted to rape. The accuser, a known homosexual, failed to appear in court for Gacy's hearing, and the charges were dismissed. Parole officers in Iowa were never notified of the arrest or accusations, and Gacy was formally discharged from parole on October 18, 1971.

By his own estimate, the first murder occurred less than three months later, on January 3, 1972. The victim, picked up at a bus terminal, remains unidentified, but his death was typical of Gacy's future approach. In searching for prey, Gacy sometimes fell back on young friends and employees, more often trolling the streets of Chicago for hustlers and runaways. Like the Hillside Strangler, he would sometimes flash a badge and gun, "arresting" his intended victim. Others were invited to the Gacy home for drinks, a game of pool, and John would show them "tricks" with "magic handcuffs," later hauling out the dildo and garrote. When he was finished, John would do the "rope trick"—strangulation—and his victim would be buried in a crawlspace underneath the house. In later years, as he ran out of space downstairs, he started dumping bodies in a nearby river.

Planting corpses in the crawlspace had its drawbacks, notably a rank, pervasive odor that the killer blamed on "sewer problems." Gacy's second wife was also in the way, her presence limiting his playtime to occasions when she left the house or traveled out of town, but when their marriage fell apart, in 1976, Gacy was able to accelerate his program of annihilation. Between April 6 and June 13, 1976, at least five boys were slaughtered at Gacy's home, and there seemed to be no end in sight. On October 25 of that year, he killed two victims at once, dumping their bodies into a common grave. As time went on, his targets ranged in age from nine to twenty, covering the social spectrum from middle-class teens to jailbirds and prostitutes.

Not all of Gacy's victims died. In December 1977, Robert Donnelly was abducted at gunpoint, tortured and sodomized with a dildo in Gacy's house of horror, then released. Three months later, 27-year-old Jeffrey Rignall was having a drink at Gacy's home when he was chloroformed and fastened to "the rack," a homemade torture device similar to one used by Dean Corll in Houston. Gacy spent several hours raping and whipping Rignall, applying the chloroform with such frequency that Rignall's liver suffered permanent damage. Regaining consciousness beside a lake in Lincoln Park, Rignall called police at once, but it was mid-July before they got around to charging Gacy with a misdemeanor. The case was still dragging on five months later, when Gacy was picked up on charges of multiple murder.

On December 12, 1978, Robert Piest disappeared from his job at a Chicago pharmacy. Gacy's construction firm had lately remodeled the store, and Piest had been offered a job with the crew, informing coworkers of his intention to meet "a contractor" on the night of his disappearance. Police dropped by to question Gacy at his home, and they immediately recognized the odor emanating from his crawlspace. Before they finished digging, Gacy's lot would yield 28 bodies, with five more recovered from rivers nearby. Of the 33 victims, nine would remain forever unidentified.

In custody, Gacy tried to blame his murderous activities on "Jack," an alter-ego (and, coincidentally, the alias he used when posing as a cop). Psychiatrists dismissed the ruse, and the defendant was convicted on all counts at his 1980 murder trial. Life sentences were handed down on 21 counts of murder, covering deaths that occurred before June 21, 1977, when Illinois reinstated capital punishment. In the case of twelve victims murdered between July 1977 and December 1978, Gacy was sentenced to die.

Gallego, Gerald Armand, Jr.

Gerald Gallego never met his father, but he had the old man's temper, all the same. Gerald, Sr., was serving time in San Quentin when his son was born, in 1946, and nine years later he became the first man to die in Mississippi's gas chamber, condemned for the murder of two police officers. Gerald, Jr., didn't know the difference, accepting his mother's fiction of an accidental death, but he would start to log his own arrests before the year was out. Minor scrapes climaxed with his incarceration, at age 13, for having sex with a six-year-old neighbor girl. By age 32, he had been married seven times—twice to the same woman—with several bigamous unions along the way. Outstanding warrants called for his arrest on charges that included incest, rape, and sodomy.

Gallego's latest wife, Charlene, would stand in striking contrast to her husband. A Sacramento native and the product of a solid, caring home, she somehow fell head-over-heels in love with Gerald, learning to accept his quirks and falling into line with fantasies that called for him to build a secret hideaway where hostage "sex slaves" would be kept to do his bidding.

On September 11, 1978, 17-year-old Rhonda Scheffler and a friend, 16-year-old Kippi Vaught, disappeared from

Sacramento, on the short walk to a local shopping center. Two days passed before their ravaged, battered bodies were recovered outside Baxter, 15 miles away. Both girls had been molested, bound and beaten with a tire iron, after which a single bullet had been fired through each one's skull.

On June 24, 1979, 14-year-old Brenda Judd and 13-year-old Sandra Colley vanished from the Washoe County fairgrounds, in Reno, Nevada. Neither girl was seen again, and both were listed as runaways until 1982, when Charlene Gallego's confession linked her husband with their abduction and murder.

Ten months later, on April 24, 1980, Karen Chipman and Stacey Redican disappeared from a Reno shopping mall, their remains discovered near Lovelock, Nevada, on July 27. Both girls had been sexually abused, then beaten to death with a blunt instrument.

Linda Aguilar, age 21, was four months pregnant when she disappeared from Port Orford, Oregon, on June 8, 1980. Relatives reported her missing on June 20, and her body was found two days later, in a shallow grave located south of Gold Beach. The victim's skull was shattered, her wrists and ankles bound with nylon cord, but an autopsy revealed sand in her nose, mouth, and throat, indicating that she was buried alive.

On July 17, 1980, 34-year-old Virginia Mochel was abducted from the parking lot of a West Sacramento tavern, where she worked as a barmaid. Her skeletal remains, still bound with nylon fishing line, were found outside of Clarksburg, California, on October 30. In the absence of other evidence, loops of cord around the neck were seen as proof of death by strangulation.

Craig Miller, 22, left a Sacramento fraternity dance with his date, 21-year-old Beth Sowers, around 1:30 a.m. on November 2, 1980. Moments later, friends observed them seated in a car outside, a rough-looking stranger sitting up front, on the passenger's side. One of Craig's friends was sliding behind the wheel, to make small talk, when Charlene Gallego appeared, slapping his face as she ordered him out of the car and sped away. Miller's frat brothers memorized the license plate, telling their story to police when Miller was found dead the next day, near Bass Lake. (Beth Sowers would not be found until November 22, shot three times and dumped in a Placer County ditch.)

Officers traced the vehicle to Charlene's parents, recording her flat denial of the incident. She also gave her name as "Mrs. Stephen Styles," a false identity Gallego had secured by stealing a policeman's I.D. card, using the vital information to request a "duplicate" birth certificate and driver's license for himself. Identified by Charlene's parents, Gallego skipped town with his wife, using Charlene to phone home for money on November 3. The next call came from Omaha, two weeks later, and federal agents were waiting when the suspects called for their money at Western Union, on November 17.

The killer team of man and wife hung tough for 18 months, but Charlene gave it up in mid-1982, turning state's evidence in return for a maximum sentence of sixteen and a half years in prison. Gallego's four-month trial in Sacramento, on charges of murdering Miller and Sowers, ended with his conviction and sentence of death in April 1983. Transferred to Nevada for trial in the Chipman and Redican murders, Gallego became the target of an unprecedented public subscription campaign, with California residents donating $23,000 to help defray the cost of his prosecution. Convicted on two more counts of murder, plus two of kidnapping, Gallego was sentenced to death a second time. At this writing, he awaits execution in Nevada.

Gein, Edward

Ed Gein may be America's most famous murderer, although his name is seldom heard and barely recognized today. Three decades have passed since he first made the headlines, but Gein is still with us, in spirit. His crimes inspired the movie *Psycho* and its sequels, spinning off in later years to terrify another generation as *The Texas Chainsaw Massacre*. (The latter film, billed as "a true story," changed literally everything except the grim decor of Gein's peculiar residence.) While other slayers have surpassed Gein's body-count and notoriety, America has never seen his equal in the field of mental aberration.

Gein was born August 8, 1906, at LaCrosse, Wisconsin, but his family soon moved to a farm outside Plainfield. His father held jobs as a tanner and carpenter when he wasn't working the farm, and Gein's mother emerged as the dominant parent, settling most family decisions on her own. Devoutly religious, she warned her two sons against premarital sex, but Gein recalled that she was "not as strong" in her opposition to masturbation. Ed's father died in 1940, and his brother Henry was lost four years later, while fighting a marsh fire. His mother suffered a stroke that same year, and a second one killed her in 1945, following an argument with one of her neighbors. Alone at last, Gein nailed her bedroom shut and set about "redecorating" in his own inimitable style.

From childhood, Gein had been ambiguous about his masculinity, considering amputation of his penis on several occasions. With Christine Jorgenson much in the headlines, Gein considered transsexual surgery, but the process was costly and frightening. There must be other ways, he thought, of "turning female" on a part-time basis.

Between 1950 and 1954, Gein haunted three local cemeteries, opening an estimated nine or ten graves in his nocturnal raids. He might recover whole corpses or settle for choice bits and pieces; a few bodies were later returned to their resting place, but Ed recalled that there were "not too many." Aided in the early days by "Gus," a simpleminded neighbor, Gein continued excavations on his own when his assistant died. At home, he used the ghoulish relics as domestic decorations. Skulls were mounted on the bedposts, severed skullcaps serving Gein as bowls. He fashioned hanging mobiles out of noses, lips, and labia, sporting a belt of nipples around the house. Human skin was variously utilized for lamp shades, the construction of waste baskets, and the upholstery of chairs.

The choicer bits were specially preserved for Gein to wear at home. For ceremonial occasions, such as dancing underneath the moon, he wore a human's scalp and face, a skinned-out "vest" complete with breasts, and female genitalia strapped above his own. By "putting on" another sex and personality, Gein seemed to find a measure of contentment, but his resurrection raids eventually failed to satisfy a deeper need.

On December 8, 1954, 51-year-old Mary Hogan disappeared from the tavern she managed in Pine Grove, Wisconsin. Authorities found a pool of blood on the floor, an overturned chair, and one spent cartridge from a .32-caliber pistol. Foul play was the obvious answer, and while deputies recall Ed Gein as a suspect in the case, no charges were filed at the time. (Three years later, the shell casing would be matched to a pistol found in Gein's home.)

On November 16, 1957, 58-year-old Bernice Worden disappeared from her Plainfield hardware store under strikingly similar circumstances. There was blood on the floor, a thin trail of it leading out back, where the victim's truck had last been seen. Worden's son recalled that Gein had asked his mother for a date, and on the day before she disappeared, Ed mentioned that he needed anti-freeze. A sales receipt for anti-freeze was found inside the store, and deputies went looking for their suspect. What they found would haunt them all for the remainder of their lives.

Inside a shed, behind Gein's house, the headless body of Bernice Worden hung from the rafters, gutted like a deer, the genitals carved out along with sundry bits of viscera. A tour of the cluttered house left searchers stunned. Worden's heart was found in a saucepan, on the stove, while her head had been turned into a macabre ornament, with twine attached to nails inserted in both ears. Her other organs occupied a box, shoved off to moulder in a corner. Deputies surveyed Gein's decorations and his "costumes," counting skins from ten skulls in one cardboard drum, taking hasty inventory of implements fashioned from human bones.

In custody, Gein readily confessed the Hogan and Worden murders, along with a series of unreported grave robberies. Confirmation of the latter was obtained by opening three graves: in one, the corpse was mutilated as described by Gein; the second held no corpse at all; a casket in the third showed pry-marks, but the body was intact, as Gein remembered.

On January 16, 1958, a judge found Gein insane and packed him off to Central State Hospital, at Waupun, Wisconsin. A decade later, Ed was ordered up for trial, with the proceedings held in mid-November 1968. Judge Robert Gollmar found Gein innocent by reason of insanity, and he returned to Waupun, where he died in 1984.

Gein willingly confessed the murders and was tried for one, but were there others? And, if so, how many?

Brother Henry was suggested, by Judge Gollmar, as a likely victim, inasmuch as there was no autopsy or investigation of his death. However that may be, there is a stronger case for murder in the disappearance of a man named Travis and his unnamed male companion, last seen at the time they hired Ed Gein to be their hunting guide. One victim's jacket was recovered from the woods near Plainfield, and while Gein professed to know the whereabouts of Travis's body—blaming his death on "a neighbor"—police never followed up on the case.

The search of Gein's home turned up two "fresh" vaginas, removed from young women, that could not be matched to existing cemetery records. Judge Gollmar suggested that one likely victim was Evelyn Hartley, abducted from LaCrosse on a night when Gein was visiting relatives, two blocks from her home. A pool of blood was found in the family garage after she vanished, with the trail disappearing at curbside. Mary Weckler was reported missing a short time later, from Jefferson, Wisconsin, with a white Ford seen in the area. When searchers scoured Gein's property, they found a white Ford sedan on the premises, though no one in Plainfield could ever recall Ed driving such a car. No other evidence exists to name Gein's victims, but if he did not dispose of Hartley and Weckler, he must have killed two other women, their names still unknown.

Glatman, Harvey Murray

Harvey Glatman was another random killer who selected victims from the want-ads. As a child, obsessed with ropes and bondage, Glatman had engaged in masochistic sessions where he hanged himself from rafters in the attic, gaining sexual release when he was on the verge of blacking out. A family physician counseled Harvey's parents that he would undoubtedly "grow out of it" if they could only find a way to "keep him busy." As an adolescent, Glatman turned to snatching purses from attractive girls, laughing at the "joke" before he gave their handbags back. In 1945, he tried to make a girl disrobe by threatening her with a cap gun; he was picked up by police, but fled immediately to New York when he was freed on bail. A robbery conviction there resulted in a five-year prison sentence. He was still receiving psychiatric treatment at the time of his release in 1951.

Apparently reformed, he settled in Los Angeles and opened up a small TV repairshop, with a sideline interest in photography. The former convict led a quiet bachelor life, avoiding social contact with the opposite sex for six long years, while inwardly he seethed with morbid lust. In late July of 1957, Glatman made a fateful house call and encountered model Judy Dull, nineteen. Explaining that he did some free-lance work for pulp detective magazines—"the typical bound and gagged stuff"—he persuaded Judy to accept a modeling assignment, at a fee of fifty dollars.

On the evening of August 1, Judy Dull arrived at Glatman's home prepared to model for the cover of a magazine, but Harvey had a rather different spread in mind. At gunpoint, Glatman raped his victim several times, then drove her to a lonely stretch of desert near the town of Indio, 125 miles east of Los Angeles. There, he photographed the sobbing woman in her underwear, strangled her with rope, and dug a shallow grave to hide her corpse.

Enlisting with a "lonely hearts" club, Glatman found his second victim, Shirley Bridgeford, during March of 1958. On their first and only date, he drove her to the desert east of San Diego, all the while attempting to impress her with his fabled skills as a photographer. Although she had come dressed for dinner in a formal supper club, Shirley let herself be talked into a set of bondage photographs, presumably for a detective magazine. When she was bound and helpless to resist, Glatman dropped his

act, assaulting her repeatedly and forcing her to pose for
photographs before he choked her with a length of rope
and left her corpse to rot behind a clump of cactus.

On July 23, Glatman read an advertisement placed by
Ruth Mercado, part-time stripper, who was seeking modeling assignments. Glatman summoned her to his apartment, where he met her with a pistol, raped her several
times, then drove her to the desert for a photo session and
the usual strangulation with his favorite rope.

Convinced that he had found a steady source of victims
in the classifieds, Glatman started placing advertisements
on his own. A number of young women telephoned or met
with Harvey, but became suspicious of his mannerisms
and declined to take the jobs he offered them. A fraction
less perceptive than the others, 28-year-old Loraine Vigil
was in Glatman's car, desert-bound along the Santa Ana
Freeway, when he pulled a pistol and demanded that she
shed her clothes. When she resisted, Harvey shot her in
the thigh, but then his would-be victim seized the pistol,
holding Glatman and his rope at bay until a lawman on
patrol drove by and noticed her predicament.

In custody, the want-ad killer readily confessed his
crimes, deriving pleasure from a recitation of the gruesome details. Glatman was convicted in a three-day trial,
condemned to die, and he rejected every effort of his lawyers to initiate appeals. "It's better this way," he explained. "I knew this is the way it would be." In August
1959, securely bound for one last time, Glatman breathed
the lethal fumes of cyanide in California's gas chamber,
at San Quentin.

Goode, Arthur Frederick III

A native of Hyattsville, Maryland, Arthur Goode was a
victim of borderline retardation who still wore his hair in
Little Lord Fauntleroy bangs at age 22. In his teens, Goode
began making sexual advances to younger boys, quickly
becoming notorious in his own neighborhood. Arrested
three times for indecent assaults upon minors, he was freed
each time when his parents posted bail.

In March 1975, Goode was arrested on five charges of sexual assault, stemming from his abuse of a 9-year-old boy. His parents raised $25,000 to spring him from jail, but Arthur wasn't finished yet. While out on bail, he molested an 11-year-old, escaping with five years probation on the condition that he undergo voluntary psychiatric treatment at Spring Grove State Hospital. The key word was "voluntary," and no one could stop him when Goode checked out of the hospital fifteen weeks later, catching a bus for his parents' new home in St. James City, Florida. Despite warnings and the issuance of a bench warrant for his arrest, no one bothered to go after Goode and bring him back.

On March 5, 1976, Goode lured 9-year-old Jason VerDow away from a school bus stop in Fort Myers, asking the child to help him "find something" in the woods nearby. "I told him he was going to die," Goode later confessed, "and described how I would kill him. I asked him if he had any last words, and he said, 'I love you,' and then I strangled him."

Police soon recovered the body, nude but for stockings, and Goode was twice questioned as a suspect in the case. Growing nervous, he bused back to Spring Grove and dropped in at the state hospital, spending five minutes there before fleeing, convinced that a receptionist was calling the police. (In fact, the staff professed to have no knowledge of the outstanding arrest warrants.)

Later that day, Goode picked up 10-year-old Billy Arthe, persuading the boy to join him in Washington, D.C., where they spent the next ten days touring the capital and sleeping in motels. Arthe was still with Goode, unharmed, on March 20, when they met Kenny Dawson, 11, and Goode talked the boy into joining them for a bus ride to Tysons Corner, Virginia. There, while hiking in the woods near town, Goode forced Dawson to undress, afterward strangling him with a belt while Billy Arthe looked on, horrified.

Days later, a Falls Church housewife recognized Billy Arthe from newspaper photographs and summoned police. As he was handcuffed, Goode complained, "You can't do nothing to me. I'm sick." A Maryland jury disagreed, finding him sane and guilty of murder, whereupon the court imposed a life sentence. Packed off to Florida after his trial, Goode was there convicted on a second murder count and sentenced to die in the electric chair.

Gossman, Klaus

German born in 1941, Klaus Gossman saw his father shot by American troops in the last days of World War II. He grew up obsessed with violence, and by age nineteen he was determined to become "death's agent." Dubbed the "Midday Murderer," Klaus planned his homicides meticulously, striking at noon, when the church bells of his native Nuremberg would cover the gunshots with their loud midday carillon.

Gossman was a student of theology in 1960, when he launched his new career in homicide. Striking off from the library one afternoon, he selected a strolling couple at random, shot them both as the bells began chiming for noon, and then calmly returned to his studies. Details of the murders were recorded in a diary, which also speaks of Gossman's strong desire to be a priest.

In 1962, Klaus robbed a bank in Ochenbruch—again at midday—gunning down the bank's director as he left. A few months later, in another bank, he shot and killed a porter picked at random. On March 29, 1963, he invaded a Nuremberg gunshop at noon, murdering the elderly proprietor and her 29-year-old son.

Gossman joined the army in December 1964, deserting four months later to escape the rigid discipline. His final victim was shot when he tried to snatch a customer's bag, in a Nuremberg department store, and he was captured at the scene. The name of actress Elke Sommer had been scratched along the barrel of his gun, and Gossman's diary detailed plans for her abduction. On conviction for the string of murders, he was jailed for life.

"Green River Killer, The"

America's most prolific unidentified killer is credited with 40 homicides around Seattle and Tacoma, Washington, in two years' time; another eight suspected victims are officially described as missing, since remains have not been found. Vaguely described as a white male in his late twenties or early thirties, the elusive killer draws his popular nickname from the fact that several victims were discarded in or near Washington's Green River. All of his victims were women, and many were prostitutes working the infamous "Sea-Tac Strip." At this writing, the slayer has claimed no new victims in Washington since autumn 1984, and authorities tend to believe that he has moved his hunting ground to Southern California.

The killer's first known victim, 16-year-old Leann Wilcox, from Tacoma, was found strangled in a field near Federal Way, eight miles south of Seattle, on January 21, 1982. The absence of a pattern in the case prevented homicide detectives from establishing connections with the string of later deaths, and nearly two years would elapse before Leann was finally acknowledged as a "Green River" victim, in November 1983. Likewise, number two, 36-year-old Amina Agisheff, was simply a missing person when she vanished on July 7, 1982, her skeletal remains recovered and identified in April 1984.

The first "official" victim, 16-year-old Wendy Coffield, was reported missing from her foster home on July 8, 1982, her body fished out of the Green River seven days later. On August 12, 23-year-old Deborah Bonner was dragged from the water, a half-mile upstream from where Coffield was found. Three days later, the Green River yielded three more victims, including 31-year-old Marcia Chapman, 17-year-old Cynthia Hinds, and 16-year-old Opal Mills.

Detectives realized they had a problem on their hands, and it was growing by the day. Two 17-year-olds, Karen Lee and Terri Milligan, went missing in late August (with Milligan's remains identified in April 1, 1984). Debra Estes, age 15, joined the missing list on September 14, followed by 19-year-old Mary Meehan a day later. (Their skeletal remains were found in May 1988 and November, 1983, respectively.) Gisele Lovvorn, age 17, became "official" victim number six when she was found September 25, two months after running away from home.

According to police, the six known dead had all been working prostitutes, but the killer also showed a taste for runaways and hitchhikers. Shawndra Summers, 17, disappeared on October 7, 1982, her remains identified by authorities in mid-August, 1982. Becky Marrero, a 20-year-old friend of Debra Estes, was last seen alive on December 2, 1982. Alma Smith, 19, picked up her last "john" in Seattle on March 3, 1983; her skeletal remains were found with Terri Milligan's on April 2, 1984. Two weeks later, 16-year-old Carrie Rois vanished from Seattle, her remains discovered almost two years later, on March 10, 1985. Kimi Pitsor, 16, joined the missing list on April 28.

The killer scored a double-header on May 8, 1983, picking off 21-year-old Carol Christenson in Seattle, dumping her body near Maple Valley, and then rebounding to snatch 16-year-old Joanne Hovland, shortly after her release from juvenile detention in the town of Everett. On May 5, he killed Martina Authorlee, 18, hiding her remains well enough that they would not be found until November 1984. Yvonne Antosh, a 19-year-old from Vancouver, British Columbia, vanished in Seattle on May 30, her decomposed remains identified October 18, 1983. On June 8, Constance Naon, a 20-year-old prostitute, was reported missing, her bones recovered in October. Four days later, on June 12, the killer found 27-year-old Kimberly Reames on the Sea-Tac Strip, her body discovered the next afternoon. April Buttram, 17, left home for the last time on August 4, 1983, and she remains among the missing.

Debbie Abernathy, 26, was the first victim in September, murdered on the fifth, her skeletal remains discovered on March 31, 1984. Nineteen-year-old Tracy Wilson was reported missing one week later, on September 12, and Maureen Feeney, another 19-year-old disappeared on September 29. (Her remains were found on May 3, 1986). October's victims included Kelly Ware, a 24-year-old hooker, and 25-year-old Mary Bello, from Enumclaw,

Washington. (Bello's remains were discovered a year and a day after her disappearance, on October 12, 1984.)

The killer took a break that autumn, returning to business as usual on February 6, 1984, with the murder of 16-year-old Mary West, abducted en route to the neighborhood market, her skull identified in September 1985. Patricia Osborn, a 19-year-old prostitute, had been reported missing by her family on January 24, and her name made the "Green River" victims list on February 11.

And the list kept growing, as investigators searched their files on missing women. Victims added with the benefit of hindsight included: Colleen Brockman, 15; Alma Smith, 18; Sandra Gabbert, 17; Cheryl Wyms, 18; Denise Bush, 24; Shirley Sherrill, 19; Marie Malvar, 18; Tammie Liles, 16; and Kelly McGuinness, 18. By April 1984, authorities had listed 24 known dead and 13 missing in the case, with 12 new skeletons unearthed since New Year's Day. By January 1986, the list of dead had grown to 34; it rose to 40 in the spring of 1988, with new discoveries, and there were still eight women unaccounted for.

If nothing else, police drew consolation from the fact their killer had apparently "retired," with no new victims missing in the past four years. Those hopes were dashed in August 1988, with the announcement of a link between the homicides in Washington and recent deaths in San Diego, California, dating back to June of 1985. Authorities could not agree upon the latest body-count—no less than ten; perhaps as many as 18—but all agreed the killer's move was "common knowledge." Be that as it may, new cases have provided no new leads or suspects, and the acknowledged slayer of some 48 to 66 women remains at large today. (See also: San Diego—Unsolved Murders)

Gretzler, Douglas
and Steelman, William Luther

A native of the Bronx, born in 1951, Doug Gretzler was drifting aimlessly around the country when he met 28-year-old Willie Steelman on October 11, 1973. Once com-

mitted to a mental institution, Steelman had compiled a
lengthy record of arrests around Lodi, California, serving
prison time on conviction of forgery. He recognized a kindred soul on sight, and soon the men became inseparable,
trolling the Southwest in their search for victims, stealing
to finance their travels and Steelman's heroin addiction.

On October 28, 1973, they invaded a house trailer near
Mesa, Arizona, binding 19-year-old Robert Robbins and
18-year-old Katherine Mestiter, then shooting both victims
to death. Drifting into Tucson, they killed 19-year-old Gil-
bert Sierra and dumped his body in the desert, doubling
back to murder Michael and Patricia Sandberg in their
Tucson apartment. On the Superstition Desert, Gretzler
and Steelman found victim number six, leaving his body
in the sleeping bag where he was shot to death. In Phoe-
nix, the killers abducted Michael Adshade and Ken Un-
rein, both 22, dumping their nude bodies in a creek bed
near Oakdale, California, rolling north in their stolen van.

Authorities in Arizona had already issued warrants for
Gretzler and Steelman by the time they reached Victor,
California, 40 miles south of Sacramento, on November
6. Walter and Joanne Parkin went bowling that night, leaving their two children—Lisa, 11, and Robert, 9—in the
care of 18-year-old neighbor Debra Earl. In the course of
the evening, Debra's parents dropped by to visit, along
with brother Richard and her fiancee, 20-year-old Mark
Lang. When the Parkins got home, they found a full
house—including two strangers with guns.

Carol Jenkins, a house guest of the Parkins, returned
from a date around 3 a.m. and went directly to bed, taking
the silent house for granted at that hour of the morning.
Near dawn, she was roused from sleep by two friends of
Mark Lang, who had spent the night trying to find him.
Jenkins started a search of her own, stopping short when
she found Walter and Joanne Parkin in the master bedroom, shot to death execution-style.

Deputies responding to the call found seven more bodies
jammed in the bedroom's walk-in closet. Victims
had been gagged with neckties, bound with nylon cord—
secured with as many as six knots in places—before they
were massacred. In all, medical examiners would remove

25 slugs from nine bodies, plus one stray from Bob Parkin's pillow.

Police published mug shots of Steelman, and Willie was recognized when he checked into a Sacramento hotel on November 8. Police descended on the scene and both gunmen were swiftly arrested, booked on nine charges of first-degree murder. Gretzler cracked under interrogation, directing police to the scattered bodies of other victims while Steelman kept silent, refusing to enter a plea on the charges. In June 1974, Gretzler pled guilty to nine counts of murder, while Steelman submitted his case to a judge and was promptly convicted. On July 8, both defendants were sentenced to life imprisonment without parole.

Grossmann, Georg Karl

Large and ugly, with a surly disposition, Grossmann was a sexual degenerate and sadist who included bestiality among his various perversions. Twenty-five arrests throughout his criminal career included three convictions for molesting children—one of whom was killed. Once employed as a butcher, Grossmann preferred to live by begging in the streets, invariably spending his receipts on sleazy prostitutes who nightly shared his bed. Protected by his rap sheet from the military draft in World War I, he soon devised a way to turn a profit on his appetites.

Before the outbreak of hostilities, Grossmann rented a squalid upstairs flat in the slums of Berlin, near the terminus of the Silesian railway. Sour and secretive, he was loathed by his neighbors but paid his rent on time, and the landlord left him alone. Grossmann's flat had been constructed with a separate entrance, and the other tenants seldom thought of him before the early morning hours, when he stumbled home from all-night drinking bouts with giggling prostitutes in tow.

He could afford the booze and women now, because he had devised another source of income. While the war and subsequent depression nearly ruined Germany, with famine a result of failure on the battlefield, Georg Grossmann peddled fresh meat in the streets. His neighbors might be starving, but the man upstairs was never phased by rationing or shortages.

In August 1921, the landlord was disturbed by sounds of violent struggle, emanating from the butcher's flat. Police were summoned, and they found a freshly murdered woman in the kitchen, trussed up like a hog for slaughter. Evidence recovered from the flat suggested Grossmann had dispatched at least three women in as many weeks; his diary and his statements to police revealed that he had used the women sexually, then sold their flesh as beef or pork, disposing of the "useless" remnants in a nearby river.

Grossmann's case inevitably called up recent memories of Karl Denke in Silesia, and newspapers dubbed it the case of the "bread and butter brides." (A "bride," in Germany, may either be a newly-married woman or a one-night stand.) Georg laughed when he was sentenced by the court to die and cheated justice, as had Denke, by hanging himself in his cell.

An interesting sidelight of the Grossmann case involves the search for Anastasia, the Russian grand duchess believed, by some, to have escaped the Marxist firing squad that killed her family. At one point, it was claimed that "Anastasia" was in fact a Polish peasant girl, Franziska Schamzkovski, but supporters of the would-be duchess countered that Schamzkovski had been killed by Grossmann during August 1920. Their authority—an entry in the killer's diary for "Sasnovski"—failed to silence critics of the would-be Anastasia.

Gunness, Belle

America's first "black widow" of the 20th century was born Brynhild Paulsdatter Storset, on November 11, 1859, in the fishing hamlet of Selbu, on Norway's west coast. The daughter of an unsuccessful merchant, Brynhild immigrated to the United States in 1881; three years later, she settled in Chicago, Americanizing her given name to "Belle" or "Bella." In 1884, at age 25, she married a Norwegian immigrant, Mads Sorenson.

The couple opened a confectioner's shop in 1896, but the business was wiped out by fire the following year. Belle told her insurance agents that a kerosene lamp had exploded, and the company paid off on her policy, although no lamp was found in the wreckage. The Sorensons used their found money to purchase a home, but fire leveled the house in 1898, bringing further insurance payments. Bad luck dogged the couple, and a second house burned down before they found a home that met their needs on Alma Street.

As everything Belle touched was soon reduced to ashes, so her family began to dwindle in the latter 1890s. Daughter Caroline, her oldest child, went first, in 1896. Two years later, Axel, her first son, was laid to rest. In each case, the children were diagnosed as victims of "acute colitis," demonstrating symptoms which—in hindsight—may have indicated they were poisoned.

On July 30, 1900, Mads Sorenson died at home, exhibiting the classic symptoms of strychnine poisoning. Belle admitted giving her husband "a powder," in an effort to "help his cold," but the family physician did not request an autopsy. With Mads under treatment for an enlarged heart, the death was automatically ascribed to natural causes.

The Widow Sorenson collected her insurance money and departed from Chicago, settling outside La Porte, Indiana, with three children under her wing. Two were her natural daughters: Myrtle, born in 1897, and Lucy, in 1899. The new addition, Jennie Olsen, was a foster daughter, passed along to Belle by parents who, apparently, were tired of dealing with the child.

In April 1902, Belle married a Norwegian farmer named Peter Gunness. Less durable than Sorenson before him, Gunness lasted only eight months. On December 16, 1902, he was killed when a heavy sausage grinder "fell" from its place on a shelf, fracturing his skull. A son, called Philip, was born of the brief union, in 1903, and Jennie Olsen vanished from the farm three years later. When neighbors inquired, Belle explained that her foster child had been sent "to a finishing school in California."

Widowed for the second time, with only children to

assist her on the farm, Belle started hiring drifters who would work a while and then, apparently, move on. She also started placing "lonely-hearts" ad in Norwegian-language newspapers throughout the Midwest, entertaining a series of prospective husbands at her farm. Somehow, none of them measured up to her standards . . . and none of them were ever seen again.

April 28, 1908, the Gunness homestead was leveled by fire. Searchers, digging through the rubble, found a quartet of incinerated bodies in the basement; three were clearly children, while the fourth—a woman's headless corpse, without a skull in evidence—was taken for the last remains of Mrs. Gunness. The local sheriff arrested handyman Ray Lamphere, employed by Belle from 1906 until his dismissal in February 1908, on charges of arson and murder.

The case became more complicated on May 5, when searchers started finding *other* bodies on the Gunness ranch. Dismembered, wrapped in gunny sacks and doused with lye, a few reduced to skeletons, the corpses told a graphic tale of wholesale slaughter spanning years. The final body-count has been a subject of enduring controversy. Without citing its source, the *Guinness Book of World Records* credited Belle with sixteen known victims and another twelve "possibles." The local coroner's report was more modest, listing—in addition to the basement bodies—ten male victims, two females, and an unspecified quantity of human bone fragments. Belle's suitors were buried together, in the muck of a hog pen, while her female victims had been planted in a nearby garden patch.

Only six of the victims were positively identified. Jennie Olsen was there, far removed from the mythical finishing school. Farm hands Eric Gurhold and Olaf Lindblom had ended their days in the hog pen, beside farmers John Moo, of Elbow Lake, Minnesota, and Ole Budsberg, of Iola, Wisconsin. Both of the latter had answered Belle's newspaper ads—and so, presumably, had their six anonymous companions in death. The single "Jane Doe," buried beside Jennie Olsen, is an anomaly, unexplained to this day.

A coroner's inquest was launched on April 29, and witness depositions taken through May 1 reflect a standard heading: "Over the dead body of Belle Gunness . . ." After May 5, with the discovery of new corpses, official documents began describing the headless woman as "an unidentified adult female," assuming that Belle might have faked her own death to escape from the scene. A futile search for the missing skull was launched on May 19, resulting in discovery of Belle's dental bridge, complete with anchor teeth attached. Ignoring the various unanswered questions, the coroner issued his final report on May 20, declaring that Belle Gunness had died "at the hands of persons unknown."

Ray Lamphere, from his cell, was adamant in claiming Belle was still alive. On April 28, he said, once Belle had set the house on fire, he drove her to the railway station at Stillwell, Indiana. Police initially took his story at face value, arresting an innocent widow, Flora Heerin, en route from Chicago to visit relatives in New York City. Hauled off the train at Syracuse and briefly detained as Belle Gunness, Mrs. Heerin retaliated in a lawsuit charging Syracuse police with false arrest.

Charged with four counts of murder and one count of arson, Ray Lamphere's case went to the jury in November 1908. On November 26, he was convicted on the arson charge alone, suggesting that the jurors felt Belle's death had not been proved "beyond a reasonable doubt." Surviving for two years in prison, Lamphere talked endlessly about the case, crediting Belle with 49 murders, netting more than $100,000 from her victims between 1903 and 1908. The basement victim, he contended, had been found in a saloon, hired for the evening, and murdered to serve as a stand-in. Belle had promised she would get in touch with Lamphere, after she was settled elsewhere, but it seemed that she had changed her plans.

The first reported sighting of a resurrected Belle was logged on April 29, six days before new bodies were discovered on the farm. Conductor Jesse Hurst was certain Mrs. Gunness went aboard his train at the Decatur, Indiana, station. She was bundled on a stretcher, Hurst recalled, and seemed quite ill.

Perhaps, but what are we to make of the reported sighting at La Porte, on April 30? While visiting Belle's closest friend, Almetta Hay, a local farmer claimed he saw the missing woman sitting down to coffee. When Almetta died, in 1916, neighbors picking through the litter in her crowded shack retrieved a woman's skull, wedged in between two mattresses. In spite of speculation that it might belong to the decapitated basement victim, the intriguing lead was not pursued.

More "sightings" were recorded through the years. In 1917, a childhood neighbor recognized Belle Gunness on admission, as a patient, to the South Bend hospital where he was working as a student nurse. He called police, but Belle had slipped away before detectives reached the scene. In 1931, a Los Angeles prosecutor wrote to La Porte's sheriff, claiming that murder defendant Esther Carlson—charged with poisoning 81-year-old August Lindstrom for his money—might be Mrs. Gunness. Carlson carried photographs of three children resembling Belle's, but La Porte could not afford to send its sheriff west in those Depression days, and the suspect died of tuberculosis before her trial, leaving the question forever open.

As late as 1935, subscribers to a magazine allegedly recognized Belle's photograph as the likeness of a whorehouse madam in Ohio. Confronting the old woman and addressing her as "Belle," one amateur detective was impressed by the vehemence of her reaction. Pursuing the matter through friends, he was urgently warned to let the matter rest . . . and so it has.

If Gunness did, in fact, survive her "death," she stands with Bela Kiss in that elite society of slayers who—although identified, with ample evidence to win convictions—manage to escape arrest and so live out their lives in anonymity. Her legacy is rumor, and a snatch of tawdry rhyme that reads, in part:

> There's red upon the Hoosier moon
> For Belle was strong and full of doom;
> And think of all those Norska men
> Who'll never see St. Paul again.

Haarmann, Fritz

Born October 25, 1879, in Hanover, Germany, Haarmann was the sixth child of a real-life odd couple. His father, a surly railroad fireman, was dubbed "Sulky Olle" by acquaintances; his mother, seven years her husband's senior, was an invalid. In early childhood, Fritz became his mother's pet and grew up hating his father, preferring dolls to the sports normally enjoyed by boys. Packed off to a military school at age sixteen, Haarmann was soon released when he showed symptoms of epilepsy. Back in Hanover, he was accused of molesting small children and was sent to an asylum for observation, but he escaped after six months in custody.

Thereafter, Haarmann earned his way through petty crimes, molesting children for amusement, on the side. Turning over a new leaf in 1900, he became engaged to a local girl but abandoned her for the army when she became pregnant. Honorably discharged in 1903, he returned to Hanover and successfully avoided his father's efforts to have him certified insane. A series of arrests followed, for burglary, con games, and picking pockets, before Haarmann's father set him up as proprietor of a fish-and-chips shop. Fritz promptly stole the business blind, but he was less successful when he preyed on strangers. Convicted of a warehouse burglary in 1914, he was sentenced to five years in prison. Upon parole, in 1918, he joined a Hanover smuggling ring and prospered, simultaneously working for police as an informer. On occasion, he would introduce himself to strangers as "Detective Haarmann."

Wartime Hanover was jammed with homeless refugees, and Haarmann had his pick of boys, enticing them with offers of a place to spend the night. Among the first was Friedel Rothe, age 17, whose parents learned that he had met "Detective Haarmann" just before he disappeared. Police searched Haarmann's flat, but came up empty. Six years later, he confessed that Friedel's head, wrapped in newspaper, was lying on the floor behind his stove while officers poked through his drawers and cupboards.

Late in 1918, Haarmann was sentenced to nine months

in prison on charges of indecency with a minor. On release, he found new quarters for himself, falling into company with 24-year-old Hans Grans, a homosexual pimp and petty thief. They became lovers and business associates, Haarmann adding new lines of used clothing and black market meat to the stolen items he sold for a living.

Together, Grans and Haarmann launched a wholesale scheme of homicide for fun and profit. Homeless boys were lured from the railway station, subsequently raped and killed by Haarmann (who informed police that his technique involved the biting of a victim's throat). The corpses were dismembered, sold as beef or pork, incriminating portions dropped into the River Leine. Grans took his pick of the discarded clothing prior to selling off the rest; one victim was reportedly disposed off after Grans expressed a wish to own his trousers.

Hanover police were strangely blind to Haarmann's murderous activities. On one occasion, a suspicious customer delivered some of Haarmann's meat to the authorities for testing, and the "experts" wrote it off as pork. "Detective Haarmann" further called attention to himself by visiting the parents of a boy named Keimes, found strangled in a Hanover canal, and subsequently told police that Grans had done the murder. Since the pimp was then incarcerated on another charge, police dismissed the tale and never bothered checking Haarmann's interest in the case.

On May 17, 1924, a human skull was found beside the Leine; another was unearthed May 29, two more on June 13, but Hanover authorities dismissed the matter as a "practical joke." Their attitude changed on July 24, when some children discovered a sack filled with human bones, including another skull, on the riverbank. Panic erupted, with newspapers reporting some 600 teenage boys missing in the past year alone. Dragging the Leine, police recovered more than 500 bones, accounting for an estimated twenty-seven victims.

By coincidence, Fritz Haarmann was arrested during this period and charged with another count of public indecency. A routine search of his flat revealed copious bloodstains, initially dismissed as a result of his unlicensed butcher's operation. Homicide detectives found their first hard evidence when parents of a missing boy identified a coat, now owned by the son of Haarmann's landlady.

In custody, the suspect suddenly decided to confess his crimes in gory detail. Asked the number of his victims, Fritz replied, "Thirty or forty, I don't remember exactly." Haarmann's trial opened on December 4 and lasted for two weeks, the defendant grandly puffing on cigars, complaining that there were too many women in the courtroom. Convicted of twenty-four murders and sentenced to die, Haarmann was decapitated on April 15, 1925. Grans, his accomplice, received a sentence of twelve years in prison.

Haigh, John George

A British slayer, Haigh was born in 1909, subjected by his parents to the strict regimen of the Plymouth Brethren, regarding all forms of amusement as sin. As a child, Haigh won a choral scholarship to Wakefield Grammer School, requiring his participation as a choir boy in Anglican services held at Wakefield cathedral. The contrast between those services and the drab Plymouth Brethren rituals confused him, allegedly inspiring bizarre visions of forests with trees spouting blood. Whatever the actual source, Haigh displayed early signs of hematomania, the obsession with blood haunting him throughout his life.

Briefly married in 1934, Haigh deserted his wife after serving his first jail term—for fraud—in November of that year. Before and during World War II, he chalked up numerous arrests for theft and minor swindles, completing his last prison term in 1943. Appearing to "go straight" at last, Haigh moved into the respectable Onslow Court Hotel, in South Kensington, and rented a nearby basement room for use in perfecting his "inventions." The makeshift lab was stocked with tools, a welding set—and a 40-gallon vat of sulfuric acid.

On September 9, 1944, Haigh lured a longtime acquaintance, Donald McSwann, to his basement workshop, killing his prey with a hammer, afterward slashing his throat for the purpose of drinking McSwann's blood. The dismembered remains were dissolved in Haigh's acid vat, with the resultant sludge later poured down a manhole. Taking over control of McSwann's nearby pinball arcade, Haigh told the dead man's parents that their son was hiding in Scotland, to avoid military conscription. Once a week he went to Scotland, mailing forged letters to the anxious couple, but their suspicions grew over time, even as Haigh's compulsive gambling devoured his stolen income.

On July 10, 1945, Haigh invited McSwann's parents to his lab, bludgeoned them both, and dissolved their remains in acid. Forged documents enabled him to usurp their estate, including five houses and a small fortune in securities, but gambling, poor investments and a lavish life-style left him strapped for cash again by February 1948.

Haigh's next customers were Archie and Rosalie Henderson, touring his new workshop at Crawley, south of London, when they were shot and slipped into an acid bath on February 12. Haigh later told police of sampling their blood, but he was rational enough to execute the forgeries that netted him $12,000 from the dead couple's estate.

A year later, in February 1949, 69-year-old Olivia Durand-Deacon approached "inventor" Haigh with her scheme for marketing artificial fingernails. Invited to the Crawley lab, she was there shot to death, with Haigh allegedly slitting her throat and quaffing a glass of blood before he consigned her to the acid vat. It took a week to finally dispose of her remains, and Haigh had little to show for his effort, selling off her jewelry for $250 to cover some outstanding debts.

Police responding to a missing person report were suspicious of Haigh's glib answers, his too-helpful attitude, and search warrants were obtained for his basement workshop. Searchers skimmed 28 pounds of human fat from the acid bath, along with bone fragments, dentures, gallstones, and a handbag belonging to Mrs. Durand-Deacon. In custody, Haigh confessed everything, playing up the vampirism angle in his bid for an insanity defense. He confessed two more murders—of victims called 'Mary'' and "Max"—committed solely in the pursuit of fresh blood, but some investigators dismissed the whole story as a theatrical ruse. (Haigh was also observed drinking his own urine in jail.)

Haigh's trial opened on July 18, 1949, with a defense psychiatrist branding him paranoid, describing his acts of vampirism as "pretty certain." Unimpressed, jurors voted him guilty and sane, the court imposing a sentence of death. Haigh was hanged at Wandsworth prison on August 6, 1949.

Harm, Teet

Born in Stockholm during 1953, Dr. Teet Harm was a criminal pathologist, renowned for helping the authorities discover evidence in local homicides. Unknown to the detectives he befriended, Harm was also a practicing vampire and cannibal, ultimately credited with slaughtering at least seven victims in late 1987 and early 1988.

According to investigators, Harm—a widower whose wife "committed suicide" in 1982—would cruise the Stockholm nightclubs in his search for female prey. Instead of winding up at Harm's apartment, the unlucky ladies were delivered to the morgue where Harm solved crimes by day, then murdered and dismembered on the operating table. An accomplice, Dr. Thomas Allgren, was occasionally called upon to join Harm in a feast of human flesh, though he apparently did not initiate the murder scheme.

Harm's final victim, model Katrina da Costa, was decapitated with a power saw in the presence of Harm's five-year-old daughter, the child later recreating the crime for police by plucking the head from a doll. Convicted of da Costa's murder in the spring of 1988, Harm and Allgren were committed for psychiatric evaluation, detectives estimating that at least six other slayings might be charged against them at a later time. With Harm's bizarre activities in mind, a new investigation has been opened in the death of his wife, Christine, found hanging in their bedroom six years prior to Harm's arrest.

Harvey, Donald

A homosexual and self-styled occultist, Don Harvey attached himself to the medical profession at age eighteen, working as an orderly at Marymount Hospital, in London, Kentucky, from May 1970 through March 1971. In 1987, Harvey would confess to killing off at least a dozen patients in his ten months on the job, smothering two with pillows and hooking ten others up to near-empty oxygen tanks, all in an effort to "ease their suffering." Arrested for burglary on March 31, he pled guilty to a reduced charge of petty theft the next day, escaping with a $50 fine. The judge recommended psychiatric treatment for "his troubled condition," but Harvey chose the air force instead, serving for ten months before he was prematurely discharged, in March 1972, on unspecified grounds.

Back home in Kentucky, Harvey was twice committed to the Veteran's Administration Medical Center in Lexington, from July 16 to August 25, and again from September 17 to October 17. His mother ascribed the committals to mental disorders, with Donald kept in restraints, and his lawyers would later refer to a bungled suicide attempt. The recipient of 21 electroshock-therapy treatments, Harvey emerged from the VA hospital with no visible improvement in his morbid condition.

Concealing his record, Harvey found work as a parttime nurse's aide at Cardinal Hill Hospital, in Lexington, between February and August 1973. In June, he added a second nursing job, at Lexington's Good Samaritan Hospital, remaining in that position through January 1974. Between August 1974 and September 1975, he worked first as a telephone operator in Lexington, moving on to a job as a clerk at St. Luke's Hospital in Fort Thomas, Kentucky. He kept his killing urge in check, somehow, but it became increasingly more difficult to manage, finally driving him away from home, across the border into Cincinnati.

From September 1975 through July 1985, Harvey held a variety of positions at the Cincinnati V.A. Medical Center, working as a nursing assistant, a housekeeping aide, a cardiac-catheterization technician, and an autopsy assistant. In the latter position, he sometimes stole tissue samples from the morgue, taking them home "for study." On the side, he murdered at least fifteen patients, supplementing his previous methods with an occasional dose of poison, once joking with ward nurses after a patient's death that "I got rid of that one for you." Nor were Harvey's victims limited to suffering patients. Fuming at neighbor Diane Alexander after a quarrel, he laced her beverage with hepatitis serum, killing her before the infection was diagnosed and treated by physicians.

On July 18, 1985, Harvey was caught leaving work with a suspicious satchel: inside, security guards found a .38-caliber pistol, hypodermic needles, surgical scissors and gloves, a cocaine spoon, two books of occult lore, and a biography of serial killer Charles Sobhraj. Cited by federal officers for bringing a weapon into the V.A. facility, Donald was fine $50 and forced to resign from his job.

Seven months later, in February 1986, Harvey was hired as a part-time nurse's aide at Cincinnati's Drake Memorial Hospital, later working his way up to a full-time position. In thirteen months, before his ultimate arrest, he murdered 23 more patients, disconnecting life-support equipment or injecting them with mixtures of arsenic, cyanide, and a petroleum-based cleanser. Outside of work, he sometimes practiced on his live-in lover, one Carl Hoeweler, poisoning Hoeweler after an argument, then nursing him back to health. Carl's parents were also poisoned, the father surviving, while Hoeweler's mother was killed.

On March 7, 1987, patient John Powell's death was ruled a murder, autopsy results placing lethal doses of cyanide in his system. Donald Harvey was arrested in April, charged with one count of aggravated murder, and held under $200,000 bond when he filed a plea of not guilty by reason of insanity. By August 11, he had confessed to a total of 33 slayings and bond was revoked two days later, with new charges filed.

As Harvey played the numbers game with prosecutors, adding victims to the tune of 52 in all, his mental state was questioned, psychiatric tests employed and scrutinized by experts. A spokesman for the Cincinnati prosecutor's office said, "This man is sane, competent, but is a compulsive killer. He builds up tension in his body, so he kills people.'' Harvey, for his part, insisted that most of the murders were ''mercy'' killings, admitting that some—including attacks on friends and acquaintance off the job—had been done ''out of spite.'' In televised interviews, Donald discussed his fascination with black magic, pointedly refusing to discuss his views on Satanism.

On August 18, 1987, Harvey pled guilty in Cincinnati on 24 counts of aggravated murder, four counts of attempted murder, and one count of felonious assault. A twenty-fifth guilty plea, four days later, earned him a total of four consecutive life sentences, barring parole for the first 80 years of his term. (For good measure, the court also levied $270,000 in fines against Harvey, with no realistic hope of collecting a penny.)

Moving on to Kentucky, Harvey confessed to a dozen Marymount slayings on September 7, 1987, entering a formal guilty plea on nine counts of murder in November. In breaking John Wayne Gacy's record for accumulated victims, Harvey earned another eight life terms plus twenty years, but he was still not finished. Back in Cincinnati during February 1988, he entered guilty pleas on three more homicides and three attempted murders, drawing three life sentences plus three terms of seven to 25 years on the latter charges.

Heidnik, Gary Michael

Gary Heidnik was two years old when his parents divorced, his mother charging her husband with ''gross neglect of duty.'' Two years later, her chronic alcoholism sent Gary and a younger brother back to live with their father, but the unstable pattern of Heidnik's life was already well established. Dropping out of high school in October 1961, he joined the army a month later and received medical training at Fort Sam Houston, in Texas. Heidnik was posted to a military hospital in West Germany during May 1962, but he was back in the States by October, committed to a Pennsylvania sanitarium for three months of psychiatric therapy. Honorably discharged from the military with a 100-percent disability rating, his records permanently sealed and classified, he received a monthly pension $1,355 from the government.

Over the next quarter-century, Heidnik was frequently committed to mental institutions at Morristown, Coatesville, and Honesdale, Pennsylvania, sometimes remaining for months at a time. He seemed to profit little from the therapy, professing ignorance about the details of his own condition. "They haven't given me the technical name," he told a judge in 1978, "but it's some kind of schizophrenia."

In February 1964, Heidnik signed up for a practical nursing program in Philadelphia, successfully completing twelve months of training and a six-month internship at Philadelphia General Hospital. By 1967, he had banked enough money from his job and government pension to purchase a three-story house, occupying one floor himself while he rented the others to tenants. On the side, he began hanging around the Elwyn Institute for the retarded, treating female inmates—usually black or Hispanic—to picnics, movies and shopping trips. The "dates" normally wound up at Heidnik's house, for sex, but if anyone objected, their complaints fell through the cracks and were ignored.

In 1971, Heidnik established the "United Church of the Ministries of God," drawing his eight-member congregation from the Elwyn Institute's clientele. His front yard became the repository for a derelict boat and four junk cars, but Gary dismissed the complaints of his neighbors with airy disdain. He preyed on black women for sex but despised their race otherwise, frequently lecturing friends on the imminence of an American "race war."

In autumn 1976, Heidnik barricaded himself in the basement of his home, armed with a rifle and handgun, daring his disgruntled tenants to deliver their complaints in person. One tried to climb through a window, and Gary shot him in the face, inflicting a superficial wound. Charges of aggravated assault were later dismissed, and Heidnik soon moved away, selling his house to a university professor. The new owner turned up collections of pornographic magazines, heaps of rotting garbage, and scores of spent .22-caliber cartridges in the attic. Down-stairs, in the cellar, he found an 18-inch hole in the con-crete floor, with the soil underneath excavated to a depth of three feet.

In 1977, Heidnik invested $35,000 in the stock market, building his fortune up to a half-million dollars over the next decade. He purchased a fleet of luxury cars—including a Rolls Royce, a Cadillac, a Lincoln Continental and a customized van—dodging legitimate taxes in the guise of a "bishop" in his nonexistent "church." He shared his home with an illiterate retarded woman, and she bore him a daughter in March 1978, the child later turning up in a foster home. On May 7 of that year, Heid-nik and his girlfriend drove to an institution in Harrisburg, picking up her sister for "a day's outing." At 34, their new companion had the IQ of a three-year-old, and she had been institutionalized for the past 20 years. Authori-ties found her in Heidnik's filthy basement room on May 17, returning her to the home, and Gary was arrested on June 6, charged with rape, kidnapping, deviate sexual intercourse, endangering, unlawful restraint, and interfer-ing with the custody of a committed person.

Hospitalized himself in August 1978, Heidnik was con-victed at trial three months later, drawing a sentence of three to seven years in prison. He served four years and four months of the time, dispatched to mental institutions on three occasions after suicide attempts—via pills, carbon monoxide, and by chewing a light bulb—before he was paroled in April 1983. In December 1984, Heidnik pur-chased his last house, on North Marshall Street in Phila-delphia, and put up a sign announcing the new location of his one-man "church." Around the same time, he be-friended Cyril Brown, a retarded black, employing Brown as a part-time handy man and general "gofer."

In October 1985, Heidnik married a 22-year-old Fili-pino woman, with whom he had corresponded over the past two years. Almost at once, he began bringing other women home for sexual liaisons, prompting his wife to flee their home in January 1986. She wound up in a shelter for battered women, complaining that Gary had frequently raped and assaulted her. Police booked Heidnik on charges of spousal rape, indecent assault and simple assault, while the courts handed down an injunction barring any form of harassment against his wife. Criminal charges were dropped in March, when the complainant failed to appear in court, but her affidavits remain, including descriptions of Heidnik performing with three female partners at once.

On Thanksgiving Day, 26-year-old Josephina Rivera left her boyfriend's apartment following a birthday celebration, bound to do some shopping. A part-time prostitute, she readily accepted Heidnik's offer of $20 for sex and accompanied him to his house, where he choked her unconscious and shackled her to the bed. Later, she was transferred to the basement, dumped in a pit with a weighted board over the hole. In captivity, Rivera was raped daily by Heidnik, surviving on a diet of bread and water, with an occasional "treat" in the form of dog food or biscuits.

In early December, Heidnik bagged his second captive in Sandra Lindsay, a 25-year-old retarded friend of Cyril Brown. Chained to a beam in the basement, she was subjected to the regimen of torture, rape, and rancid food, Heidnik dividing his time between the two prisoners. Lisa Thomas, 19, was abducted at Christmas, with 18-year-old Jacqueline Askins joining the harem in January. Heidnik began playing the women off against each other, encouraging them to inform on acts of disobedience. Punishments included beatings and electric shocks, with the occasional refinement of a screwdriver jammed into a victim's ears. In his reflective moments, Heidnik regaled them with plans for collecting ten prisoners, fathering as many children as possible before he died.

In February 1987, Sandra Lindsay died after several days of hanging in chains from the rafters. Heidnik and Rivera bore the corpse upstairs, where it was placed in a tub and dismembered with a power saw. Lindsay's replacement was 23-year-old Deborah Dudley, kidnapped in March, but she proved uncooperative, and Heidnik killed her on March 19, hooking electrical wires to her chains while she stood in a pit filled with water. Dudley spent two days in a freezer before Heidnik and Josephina Rivera drove to the

Whaton State Forest, near Camden, New Jersey, dumping her corpse in the woods on March 22.

Two days later, Rivera escaped from the basement prison, seeking refuge at her boyfriend's home. He called police, and raiders swept through Heidnik's house on March 25, finding bedroom walls papered with currency, the kitchen decorated with pennies, Susan Lindsay's chopped-up remains stored in a freezer nearby. The basement was a bona fide chamber of horrors, with three malnourished women chained to the plumbing, nude from the waist down. Foul-smelling pits in the floor had served as their sleeping quarters, and neighbors belatedly recalled a persistent odor of burning flesh emanating from Heidnik's abode. Human flesh was retrieved from the drains, and searchers made the drive to New Jersey that afternoon, recovering Deborah Dudley's remains.

Held in lieu of $4 million bond, Heidnik was hospitalized in April, after trying to hang himself in a jail shower stall. Defense attorneys sought to prove their client insane, suggesting that he had been used for military LSD experiments during the 1960s, but jurors rejected the argument, convicting Heidnik of double murder on July 1, 1988. (Other charges included six counts of kidnapping, five counts of rape, four counts of aggravated assault, and one count of deviate sexual intercourse.) On July 3, the defendant was sentenced to die.

On December 31, 1988, Heidnik attempted suicide in his prison cell by swallowing an overdose of Thorazine, an anti-psychotic drug. A guard found him unconscious on New Year's morning, and he remains comatose at this writing.

Hein, Juergen

A native of Berlin, Hein was the oldest of eight children born to an alcoholic tailor and his mentally retarded wife. Departing from his troubled home as soon as he was legally of age, Hein carried with him years of pent-up rage, a stunted sexuality that later found its outlet through sadistic violence. Hein married Edith Dzillak in Berlin; she bore two children, but Hein's second bid at family life proved no more stable than the first. On March 3, 1967, a domestic argument turned savage and his wife was strangled in their home. Convicted of manslaughter in November, Hein was sentenced to eight years in prison; he served only five, and was freed on parole November 24, 1972. A waiter's job and lodgings, in the Neukoelln district of Berlin, were waiting for him, courtesy of German rehabilitation officers.

On April 4, 1973, six-year-old Sonja Kleber disappeared while walking home from school in the Neukoelln district. Strollers in a wooded park discovered her that night, unconscious, naked, hemorrhaging from her vagina. She survived to offer the police a clear description of her rapist, leading officers to the address where she had been attacked. They picked up tenant Juergen Hein for questioning, and he confessed to the assault. Returned to prison on a violation of parole, with ten years added for the rape, he was released again in mid-July of 1985.

Berlin was too restrictive for him now, with the authorities alert to his propensity for violent sex. Around October 30, he moved to Baden-Baden in West Germany, a few miles east of Strasbourg, France. The morning of October 31, he stopped 50-year-old Elvira Kaszuba on the street outside her home, inviting her to dine with him that evening. She accepted, smitten with the young man's charm, and they grew intimate within the next few days. Elvira let him have a key to her apartment, and he came to visit her each night. The evening of November 6, he cooked their supper there, then disemboweled Kaszuba with a hunting knife and stuffed her body in a closet.

Five days later, police in Baden-Baden filed a missing person report in the name of Theresia Hoog, age 55. Hoog's son had found her missing from the home they shared that morning, and he got no answer when he called her closest friend, Elvira Kaszuba. Alarmed, the young man noted that his mother's car was also missing. She had gone for rheumatism treatments at a local clinic on the evening of November 10; it now appeared the widow never made it home.

Detectives visited the Black Forest Clinic, where a nurse

remembered seeing Mrs. Hoog the night before. She had arrived on schedule for her treatment, but was called away beforehand, by a man whom clinic workers readily described. Theresia's missing car was not outside the clinic, and its license number was relayed to street patrolmen, with composite sketches of a suspect sought for questioning.

That afternoon, a traffic officer discovered the elusive car, parked out in front of an apartment house. He was retreating toward a call box, to report, when he observed a man resembling the suspect sketch emerging from the house. The suspect, Juergen Hein, was taken into custody without resistance as he slipped a key into the door latch on the driver's side.

Aware of Juergen's record, officers began to search the building. In a second-floor apartment, they discovered Mrs. Hoog, stripped naked and spread-eagle on the bed, her wrists and ankles tethered to the bed posts, tape wound tight around her head and face. Her breasts and genitals were bloody, marked with superficial cuts that indicated that she had been tortured with a hunting knife that lay beside her on the bloodstained sheets.

Theresia Hoog survived her painful injuries, describing how her captor lured her from the clinic with a story that her friend, Elvira Kaszuba, had been gravely injured in "an accident." At knifepoint, he had lashed her to the bed, assaulted her repeatedly and tortured her with superficial cuts, apparently intending to return and finish her at leisure when he came back from the errand that resulted in his apprehension on the street below.

Concerned detectives went to see Kaszuba at her flat, and found her mutilated body in the closet. Seeking information from the building's manager, Ruth Tschantscher, 48, police found she had also fallen victim to the killer. Strangled, stripped, and slashed, her body had lain undiscovered in the bathroom for eleven days.

In custody, Hein readily confessed his crimes. Ruth Tschantscher's son, had been a former cellmate in Berlin; he had performed the introductions, once suggesting Hein might look his mother up in Baden-Baden, if he ever needed lodgings, and the rest was history. On June 27,

1986, Hein was convicted of double murder, consigned to prison on two consecutive life sentences. In theory, he would never walk the streets in search of human prey again.

Heirens, William

On the surface, William Heirens seemed to have every advantage. Born in 1928, he was the son of affluent parents in the Chicago suburb of Lincolnwood. His family weathered the Great Depression without serious difficulty, and if Heirens had any problems, they sprang from within. At age thirteen, he observed a couple in the act of making love and told his mother, receiving the sage advice that "All sex is dirty. If you touch anyone, you get a disease." In later years, while necking with a girlfriend, Heirens spontaneously burst into tears, vomiting in the girl's presence and fleeing the scene in abject humiliation. His adolescent frustration began to find other outlets, with Heirens dressing in women's garments, achieving climax as he leafed through a scrapbook filled with photos of Hitler and other ranking Nazis.

In 1942, Heirens was arrested for bringing a loaded pistol to school. His parents were stunned when police came calling, turning up a rifle and three more pistols behind the refrigerator, four more weapons hidden on the roof. A judge agreed to grant probation, on condition that William be sent to a youth facility at Peru, Indiana. Returning home after three years "in school," he was bright enough to enroll at the University of Chicago, as a sophomore, skipping over the usual freshman classes. At the same time, he was honing his skills as a housebreaker, finding sexual release through burglary and the risk of invading strange dwellings.

On June 3, 1945, Heirens was looting the Chicago apartment of Josephine Ross when his victim woke and caught him in the act. Attacking ruthlessly, he cut her throat and stabbed her several times, relenting at the sight of blood and trying hopelessly to bind her neck with bandages. That done, he spent two hours at the scene, wandering aimlessly from room to room as he enjoyed multiple orgasms.

Four months later, on October 5, he was surprised while prowling the apartment of an army nurse, Lieutenant Evelyn Peterson. Heirens decked her and fled, leaving fingerprints behind, but police failed to match them with the records from his earlier arrest.

On December 10, 1945, 33-year-old Frances Brown emerged from her bathroom to find Heirens rifling her purse. As she began to scream, he shot her twice, then fetched a kitchen knife to finish off the job.

Dragging his victim into the bathroom, Heirens tried in vain to wash her blood away, then left her draped across the tub, half-covered with a housecoat. On the mirror, in his victim's lipstick, Heirens wrote: "For Heaven's sake catch me before I kill more. I cannot control myself."

A month later, on January 7, 1946, he invaded the bedroom of six-year-old Suzanne Degnan, abducting the child and leaving a written demand for $20,000 ransom as a ruse, to baffle the police. Retreating to a nearby basement, Heirens murdered the child and dismembered her remains with a hunting knife, wrapping the pieces in paper and dropping them into storm drains as he roamed the streets in early morning darkness.

The case was still unsolved on June 26, when police answered a prowler call on Chicago's north side. Confronted with uniforms, Heirens drew a pistol and squeezed the trigger twice, his weapon misfiring each time. Undaunted, he began to grapple with the officers, struggling fiercely until he was cracked on the head with a flower pot.

In jail, the teenage killer blamed his crimes on an alter-ego, "George Murman"—short for Murder Man. Despite a plea of innocent by reason of insanity, Heirens was convicted of triple murder in September 1946 and sentenced to three consecutive life terms. A federal judge ordered Heirens' release in April 1983, citing his alleged "rehabilitation," but the ruling was overturned on appeal by the prosecution, in February 1984. At this writing, he remains in prison, still convinced of George Murman's existence. "To me, he is very real," Heirens says. "He exists. A couple of times I had talks with him. I wrote lots of notes to him, which I kept.''

Hofmann, Kuno

Born in 1931, Kuno Hofmann suffered a traumatic childhood, beaten so severely by his alcoholic father that he lost the powers of speech and hearing. Imprisoned for nine years on theft charges, he emerged with an obsession for self-improvement via the occult "sciences." Hofmann read widely on Satanism and black magic, focusing compulsively on rituals involving necrophilia and vampirism.

In April 1971, police and morgue attendants across Germany began comparing notes on a series of bizarre grave robberies. At least five bodies were exhumed and gnawed upon, with evidence of sex attempted in the case of female corpses. Seeking fresher victims, Hofmann later shot and killed three victims, drinking blood from each and pausing to molest the lifeless bodies.

In May 1972, a morgue attendant surprised Hofmann in the act of kissing a cadaver. Kuno drew a pistol, but his shot went wild, and the surviving witness offered a description to police. Arrested in the dragnet, Hofmann readily confessed and drew a term of life imprisonment for murder. As a parting shot, while waiting for his transfer to a federal penitentiary, he pestered jailers with requests for one last sip of virgin's blood.

Honka, Fritz

At five foot five, Fritz Honka was extremely sensitive about his height. He liked his women shorter, and he also liked them toothless, to alleviate his fears of mutilation during oral sex. He found relief with aging prostitutes from Hamburg's red light district, killing at least four of them in his small attic room between 1971 and late '74.

Disposal was a problem, given Honka's size and basic laziness. He chose to keep the bodies in his flat, and fortified himself with alcohol against the stench. When neigh-

bors griped about unpleasant smells, Fritz doused the place
with quarts of cheap deodorant. In January 1975, he
torched the flat, but firemen noticed mummified remains
among the ashes and police were called. In custody, Fritz
said he killed the women after they mocked his preference
for oral sex over "straight" intercourse. He was sentenced
to life imprisonment, the maximum possible under German law.

Hurd, Steven Craig

A barbiturate addict and native of Southern California,
born in 1950, by the age of 20 Hurd had organized a small
Satanic cult in Orange County, recruiting three teenage
boys and a 31-year-old woman as his devoted followers.
From time to time, as cash ran short, they lived like trolls,
in highway culverts, dropping pills and raiding garbage
cans for food. When they grew tired of chanting and dismembering small animals, they looked around for larger
game, a greater "kick," and found it in the form of human sacrifice. On two consecutive nights, in June 1970,
the cultists murdered a gas station attendant and a teacher,
mutilating their victims after death in honor of Lucifer.

Their second victim, 31-year-old Florence Brown, was
stopped at the intersection of Interstate 5 and Sand Canyon
Boulevard when the killers piled into her station wagon on
June 4, abducting her to an orange grove near the campus
of U.S. Irvine. There, Brown was stabbed repeatedly with
a long knife, her right arm severed, heart and lungs removed as sacrificial offerings. The pitiful remains were
found by hikers on June 17, in a shallow grave near the
village of El Cariso, a half-mile east of the Orange County
line. So grisly were the mutilations that a sheriff's officer
advised the press, "We have some kind of nut on our
hands."

Upon arrest, Hurd told authorities that he had planned
to use Brown's car to visit San Francisco and meet the
presiding "Head Devil." Hurd's attorney rejected any
connection to Anton LaVey's Church of Satan, a sentiment
LaVey was quick to echo from his base in San Francisco,

but it made no difference in the end. Diagnosed as legally insane, Hurd was confined to Atascadero State Hospital, where he continues to report the periodic visits of "Father Satan." His teenage disciples were referred to the California juvenile system for "rehabilitation."

Husereau, Philip

The accidental death of Philip Husereau, on February 18, 1988, was no more curious or twisted than the drifter's life. Police in Rochester, New York, report that Husereau was suffocated while engaged in masturbation, with his head inside a plastic bag of nitrous oxide "laughing gas." Next day, his sister told authorities of Husereau's confessions in the deaths of five successive girlfriends, during 1983 and '84. His victims included Phyllis Weathers, a cocktail waitress and topless dancer whose body was found on a vacant lot in Las Vegas, Nevada, on August 10, 1984. According to Husereau's confession, kept secret by his sister while he lived, the murders occurred during sex, when Husereau lost control of himself and strangled his partners or beat them to death.

Jones, Sydney

Hanged for murder in the yard of the Jefferson County jail, in Birmingham, Alabama, on June 25, 1915, Syd Jones left a note in his cell confessing to thirteen separate homicides. Eleven of his victims were reportedly black men; the two whites were described as a Nebraska deputy sheriff and a brakeman on the Mobile & Ohio railroad. The letter ended on a wistful note. "I'm sorry I missed Richard Moore Sept. 12, 1912," Jones wrote. "Just one more would have made an even number."

Judy, Steven

The product of a broken home, Steven Judy grew up nursing memories of violent arguments between his parents. Later, when a foster family provided him with loving care, it was apparently too late; the violence of his early years had taken root and twisted something in his personality.

At twelve, he visited a neighbor's home, pretending to have cookies for sale. Upon discovering that the young housewife was home alone, Judy forced her into the bedroom, raped her at knifepoint, and stabbed her forty-one times, finishing off his assault with a hatchet. His victim survived after brain surgery and testified against Judy, earning him a nine-month period of treatment in a mental institution. Therapy proved ineffective, and at age eighteen he was convicted of beating a woman in Chicago, spending twenty months in jail. Later, in Indianapolis, he abducted a young woman and forced her to drive into the countryside, but she managed to leap from the car and escape on foot. A kidnapping charge put him back in prison for a year.

On April 28, 1979, a group of mushroom hunters found a woman's naked body floating in White Lick Creek, outside Indianapolis. Further downstream, the bodies of three small children—two boys and a girl—were also found in the water. The woman had been raped and strangled; her children had drowned when they fell—or were thrown—into the creek.

A bank book found nearby identified the adult victim as 20-year-old Terry Chasteen. Her boyfriend told police that she left home around seven o'clock that morning, taking her children to their babysitter before she reported for work at a local department store. None of them had made it to their destination.

Public appeals for information brought reports of a distinctive red-and-silver pickup truck, observed near the murder scene. Detectives traced it to a building site, where its owner, 22-year-old Steven Judy, was employed as a bricklayer. Arrested at the home of his foster parents, Judy described how he had tricked Terry Chasteen into stopping her car, then disabled the engine while "checking under the hood." She had accepted his offer of a ride to the nearest filling station, but he took her to the murder site instead, not far from where his previous victim had escaped two years earlier. Chasteen's three children were sent for a walk while he raped her, strangling his victim when she began to scream. The woman's children returned at the sound of her cries, and Judy threw them in the creek, where all three drowned.

At trial, the unrepentant Judy told assembled jurors, "You had better put me to death, because next time it might be one of you or your daughter." They took him at his word, and on February 16, 1980, he was sentenced to die in the electric chair.

Resisting all appeals on his behalf, Judy steadfastly fought for the right to die on schedule. While awaiting execution, he regaled authorities with tales of other homicides, across the country. He had killed so many women, Judy said, that he could not remember all his victims, but there was a "string of bodies" spanning Indiana, Illinois, Louisiana, Texas, Florida. Despite investigation, sketchy details kept police from verifying any of his claims before he met his fate on March 8, 1981.

Kallinger, Joseph

Born December 11, 1936, in Philadelphia, Kallinger was surrendered for adoption as an infant, finding a home with Austrian immigrants Stephen and Anna Kallinger in October 1938. His childhood was bizarre, to say the least, marked by parental abuse in the form of floggings with a cat-o'-nine-tails, beatings with a hammer, and repeated threats of emasculation. In the summer of 1944, Kallinger was sexually abused at knifepoint by a gang of older boys, prompting subsequent episodes in which he masturbated while clenching a knife in his fist.

Kallinger married his first wife at age 17, the stormy relationship producing ten children before she abandoned their home for another man in September 1956. A year later, Joseph was hospitalized with a suspected brain lesion, but tests revealed only a "psychopathological nervous disorder." Married a second time in April 1958, Kallinger soon torched his own home for amusement, reaping the fringe benefit of $1,600 from fire insurance. Committed to a state hospital in July 1959, following a suicide attempt, Kallinger would set fire to the family's second home on four separate occasions—twice in May 1963, once in August 1965, and once in October 1967.

By 1972, the Kallingers had six children at home, including two from his failed first marriage. On January 23 of that year, Joseph branded his oldest daughter's thigh with a hot iron, as punishment for running away. Arrested a week later, he was found incompetent for trial and held for 60 days psychological examination, ultimately ruled fit for trial in June. Conviction on child abuse charges earned him four years probation, with a provision for mandatory psychiatric treatment.

By mid-1974, Kallinger was reportedly hallucinating constantly, holding animated discussions with a disembodied head (dubbed "Charlie") and receiving personal "orders from God." The divine orders included demands that Kallinger murder young boys and sever their genitals, an urge that he confided to his son, 13-year-old Michael, on June 26. When Joe requested Michael's help, the boy responded with enthusiasm: "Glad to do it, Dad!" Eleven days later, they murdered Jose Collazo, a Puerto Rican youth, in Philadelphia, first torturing their victim and cutting off his penis.

Kallinger next set his sights on one of his own children, Joseph, Jr. In his first attempt, Joe tried to make the boy back off a cliff, cartoon-style, while posing for photographs. Failing in that, he took both boys along on a July 25 arson run, bungling an attempt to trap Joe Junior in a burning trailer. Finally, three days later, Kallinger and Michael drowned their victim at a demolition site, the body recovered by authorities on August 9, 1974. Questioned as a suspect in the murder, Kallinger was not arrested due to lack of evidence.

That autumn, the father-son team began ranging farther afield in their search for victims. On November 22, they burglarized a house in Lindenwold, New Jersey, but no one was home. At their second stop, victim Joan Carty was tied to her bed and sexually abused by Joe Kallinger. Eleven days later, in Susquehanna Township, Pennsylvania, five hostages were bound and robbed at knifepoint, the Kallingers making off with $20,000 in cash and jewelry after slashing one victim's breast. Striking in Homeland, Maryland—a Baltimore suburb—father and son held Pamela Jaske captive in her home, forcing her to fellate Joseph at gunpoint. On January 6, the ritual was repeated in Dumont, New Jersey, with victim Mary Rudolph.

Two days later, on January 8, Kallinger and son invaded a home at Leonia, New Jersey, holding eight captives at gunpoint while they ransacked the house. Nurse Maria Fasching was stabbed to death for refusing Joe's order to bite off a male victim's penis, but Kallinger got careless during the getaway, discarding a bloody shirt near the scene. Officers traced the shirt to its owner, and the Kallingers were arrested on January 17 by a joint raiding party of federal and state authorities. (Two months later, Michael Kallinger was ruled delinquent but "salvageable," with murder charges dismissed in return for his guilty plea on two counts of robbery. He was placed on probation until his twenty-fifth birthday, in December 1982.)

Joe Kallinger's first trial, in Pennsylvania, ended with a hung jury in June 1975. Three months later, at his retrial, he was convicted on nine felony counts, sentenced to prison for 30 to 80 years by a judge who called him "an evil man . . . utterly vile and depraved." Convicted of the New Jersey murder in October 1976, Kallinger received a mandatory life sentence, to run consecutively with his time in Pennsylvania.

Kallinger's outbursts have continued in prison, with Joseph setting himself on fire in March 1977. A month later, he assaulted a fellow inmate before lighting a fire on his cell block. In March 1978, he slashed another convict's throat in an unprovoked attack, but his victim managed to survive. As recently as 1988, in television interviews, Kallinger expressed his continuing desire to slaughter every person on earth, after which he hopes to commit suicide and "become God."

Kearney, Patrick Wayne

On July 5, 1977, authorities in Riverside, California, announced the confessions of two male suspects in a series of grisly "trash bag" murders, thought to include fifteen victims in five different counties since 1973. The suspects, Patrick Kearney and David Douglas Hill, were charged in only two cases—both victims slain in March 1977—but that day Kearney led detectives to six alleged dumping sites in Imperial County. Evidence recovered from Kearney's home, where Hill resided as a live-in lover, included fibers matched to those on several corpses and a bloody hacksaw, used in the dismemberment of certain victims.

The California "trash bag" case officially began on April 13, 1975, when the mutilated remains of Albert Rivera, age 21, were discovered near San Juan Capistrano. By November, six bodies had been found in Los Angeles, Orange, Riverside and San Diego Counties. The discovery of two more victims in March 1977 raised the body-count to eight, and by that time police had their pattern. All the identified victims had homosexual backgrounds; each was found nude, shot in the head with a similar weapon; several were dismembered or otherwise mutilated, their remains tied up in identical plastic garbage bags.

The final victim was 17-year-old John LaMay, last seen by his parents on March 13, when he left home to visit "Dave." Police entered the case five days later, after LaMay's dismembered remains were found beside a highway, south of Corona. Friends of the victim identified "Dave" as David Hill, supplying homicide detectives with an address. Warrants were issued for Hill and his roommate, but the lovers remained at large until July 1, when they entered the Riverside County sheriff's office, pointed to their posters on the wall, and smilingly announced, "That's us."

A high school dropout from Lubbock, Texas, David Hill joined the army in 1960 but was soon discharged on diagnosis of an unspecified personality disorder. Back in Lubbock, he married his high school sweetheart, but the romance was short-lived. In 1962, he met Patrick Kearney, stationed with the air force in Texas, and their attraction was mutual. Hill divorced his wife in 1966 and moved to California with Kearney a year later. They were living together in Culver City, a Los Angeles suburb, when the long string of murders began. (The first victim, known only as "George," was buried behind Kearney's Culver City duplex in September 1968; detectives, following the killer's directions, unearthed his skeleton in July 1977.)

On July 14, Patrick Kearney was formally indicted on two counts of murder, including that of John LaMay. David Hill was released the same day, his charges dismissed as Kearney shouldered full responsibility in the slayings, telling police that he killed because "it excited him and gave him a feeling of dominance." By July 15, Kearney had signed confessions to twenty-eight murders, with twelve of the cases confirmed by police. On December 21, he pled guilty on three counts of first-degree murder, receiving a sentence of life imprisonment.

Prosecutors launched the new year by charging Kearney with another eighteen counts of murder in February 1978. Nine of those charges disposed of the first dozen victims in Kearney's confessions; the others included two children, ages five and eight, along with four victims whose bodies were never recovered. On February 21, Kearney pled guilty on all counts, receiving another life sentence. If his original confessions were truthful, at least seven victims remain unidentified.

Kelbach, Walter and Lance, Myron

Walter Kelbach, 28, and 25-year-old Myron Lance had many things in common. Both were veterans of prison and aggressive homosexuals, each given to abuse of drugs and alcohol. Above all else, they shared a fondness for inflicting pain—and, ultimately, death—on fellow human beings. In December 1966, their twisted passion claimed five lives in Salt Lake City, Utah, touching off a local reign of terror.

On December 17, hopped up on pills and wine, the duo stopped for gas at a service station where 18-year-old Stephen Shea was working the night shift alone. Impulsively, the "customers" drew weapons, robbing Shea of $147, forcing him into the back of their station wagon and driving him into the desert. There, Shea was ordered to strip, and was raped by both Kelbach and Lance. Afterward, a coin was tossed to see who would receive the "honor" of eliminating Shea. The winner—Kelbach—plunged a knife into his victim's chest five times and left the body lying on a lonely desert road.

Repeating their performance on the eighteenth of December, Lance and Kelbach kidnapped Michael Holtz, the night attendant at another Salt Lake City filling station. Raped by both of his abductors, Holtz was forced to watch while coins were tossed to choose his executioner. Lance won, this time, and stabbed his victim once in the heart with the same stiletto used on Stephen Shea.

December 21. The killers changed their *modus operandi*, flagging down a taxi driver named Grant Strong, directing him to Salt Lake City's airport. On the way, Strong stopped off at the taxi barn to tell his supervisor that he didn't trust his latest fares. It was decided Strong should click his microphone transmitter switch in case of any trouble, and he flashed the signal moments later, after Kelbach drew a gun and pressed it to his skull, demanding money. Strong surrendered all cash on hand—nine dollars—but his captors were not seriously interested in robbery. Police and fellow cabbies were converging on the scene when Kelbach put a bullet through his victim's brain. "I just pulled the trigger and blood flew everywhere," he later told an NBC reporter. "Oh boy! I never seen so much blood!"

Police found Strong a short time later, lying dead inside his cab. By that time, Lance and Kelbach had arrived at Lolly's Tavern, near the airport, acting casual as they perused the bar for further victims. Kelbach tinkered with a pinball game while Lance walked up behind a patron, 47-year-old James Sizemore, and coolly shot him in the head, immediately ordering the manager to empty out his till. Pocketing $300 from the cash register, Lance and Kelbach turned their pistols on the bartender and his four surviving customers; Fred Lillie and Beverly Mace were killed where they stood, three other human targets feigning death until the manic marksmen took their leave.

As Lance and Kelbach left, the manager retrieved a pistol from behind the bar and opened fire; he scored no hits, but panicked his assailants, and they fled on foot. Retrieving their car, both gunmen were captured at a roadblock several hours later. Convicted on five counts of murder, Kelbach and Lance were sentenced to death, their penalties commuted to life imprisonment after the U.S. Supreme Court ruled the death penalty unconstitutional.

As lifers, Lance and Kelbach are theoretically eligible for parole. It is a prospect that concerns the residents of Utah, and the common fear was spread from coast to coast in 1972, after Kelbach was tapped for an interview by NBC News, on a televised program entitled *Thou Shalt Not Kill*. "I haven't any feelings toward the victims," Walter told his audience of millions, grinning for the camera. "I don't mind people getting hurt because I just like to watch it."

Kelly, Kieron

An Irish native, born in 1928, Kelly migrated to London at age 25, working odd jobs and spending most of his money on liquor while launching a one-man war against "poofters." He slaughtered an uncertain number of gays over the next three decades, clearly recalling five victims at his arrest in 1983. Considering that he had killed those five in eight years time—and two within a three-month period preceding his incarceration—it is possible that Kelly murdered dozens in his thirty years at large.

Kelly's first known victim, elderly panhandler Hector Fisher, was found in a Clapham churchyard on Christmas Day 1975, stabbed repeatedly about the head and neck. Last seen alive on Christmas Eve, Fisher had been loitering with several men dressed up as "Father Christmas." Homicide investigators grilled a dozen suspects in the case—including Kieron Kelly—but they found no evidence that would support a murder charge.

Eighteen months later, on June 2, 1977, 68-year-old

Maurice Weighly was found dead in Soho, his face and
genitals mutilated, the neck of a broken bottle thrust up
his rectum. Constables found Kelly and another transient
in the neighborhood, with bloodstains on their clothing,
and Kelly was charged with the murder, his companion
describing the crime in grisly detail. Six months passed
before the trial, and Kelly was acquitted after his lawyer
branded the state's key witness an alcoholic, "blind
drunk" at the time of the murder. (The witness subsequently vanished and was never seen again. In 1983, Kieron Kelly confessed to his murder.)

In May 1983, an elderly panhandler was pushed onto
the tracks at London's Kensington Station, saved when the
driver managed to stop his train in time. Witnesses fingered Kelly in the attack, prompting his arrest on charges
of attempted murder, but jurors failed to reach a verdict
in his first trial, and he was acquitted the second time
around.

By August 4, Kelly was back in jail, charged with robbery and public drunkenness. Locked in the drunk tank
with transients, he crushed the skull of inmate William
Boyd, finishing his victim off with a garrote fashioned
from stockings and shoelaces. When tea was delivered next
morning, Kelly's surviving cellmate begged for protection, ignoring dire threats in his eagerness to testify.

Under close interrogation, Kelly confessed to five remembered slayings. William Boyd aside, he now admitted
killing Hector Fisher and Maurice Weighly, protected from
further charges in the later case by his previous acquittal.
Other victims included the missing witness from his first
murder trial, and an elderly transient, shoved beneath a
train days after the Kensington Station attack. Authorities
confirmed a fatal "accident" at Oval Station on the date
in question, but they had no firm corroborating evidence.
Convicted of the Fisher homicide in June 1984, Kelly was
sentenced to life imprisonment. A few days later, he received an identical term for William Boyd's murder, departing the courtroom with a cheerful "Happy Christmas
to you all!"

Kemper, Edmund Emil III

The product of a broken and abusive home, belittled by a shrewish mother who occasionally locked him in the basement when he failed to meet her standards of behavior, Edmund Kemper grew up timid and resentful, nursing a perception of his own inadequacy that gave rise to morbid fantasies of death and mutilation. As a child, he often played a "game" in which his sisters took the part of executioners, with Kemper as their victim, writhing in imaginary death throes when they "threw the switch." Preoccupied with visions of decapitation and dismemberment, he cut the head and hands off of his sister's doll—a *modus operandi* that he would repeat, as an adult, with human victims.

Before the age of ten, Kemper graduated to living targets, burying the family cat alive and subsequently cutting off its head, returning with the gruesome trophy to his room, where it was placed on proud display. Despite his tender age, he brooded over fantasies of love and sex, with violence playing an inevitable role. Unable to express affection in a normal way, he showed the warning signals of a latent necrophile. One afternoon, discussing Edmund's childish crush upon a grade-school teacher, Kemper's sister asked him why he did not simply kiss the woman. Kemper answered, dead-pan, "If I kiss her, I would have to kill her first." A second family cat fell victim to his urges, this one hacked with a machete, pieces of the carcass hidden in his closet until they were accidentally discovered by his mother.

Branding her son "a real weirdo," Kemper's mother first packed him off to live with her estranged husband, and then—after running away—the boy was delivered to his paternal grandparents, residing on a remote California ranch. There, in August 1963, fourteen-year-old Kemper shot his grandmother with a .22-caliber rifle, afterward stabbing her body repeatedly with a kitchen knife. When his grandfather came home, Kemper shot the old man as well, leaving him dead in the yard.

Interrogated by authorities, Kemper could only say that "I just wondered how it would feel to shoot Grandma."

He regretted not stripping her corpse, and this statement, along with the motiveless violence displayed in his actions, got Kemper committed to the state's maximum-security hospital at Atascadero. In 1969, a 21-year-old behemoth grown to six-foot-nine and some 300 pounds, Kemper was paroled to his mother's custody over the objections of the state psychiatrists.

During Kemper's enforced absence, his mother had settled in Santa Cruz, a college town whose population boasted thousands of attractive co-eds. For the next two years, through 1970 and '71, Kemper bided his time, holding odd jobs and cruising the highways in his leisure time, picking up dozens of young female hitchhikers, refining his approach, his "line," until, he knew that he could put them totally at ease. Some evenings, he would frequent a saloon patronized by off-duty policemen, rubbing shoulders with the law and soaking up their tales of crime, becoming friendly with a number of detectives who would later be assigned to track him down.

On May 7, 1972, Kemper picked up two 18-year-old roommates from Fresno State College, Mary Ann Pesce and Anita Luchessa. Driving them to a secluded cul-de-sac, he stabbed both girls to death, then took their bodies home and hid them in his room. Delighted with his "trophies," Kemper took Polaroid snapshots, dissected the corpses, and sexually assaulted various organs before finally tiring of the game. Bundling the remains into plastic bags, he buried the truncated bodies in the Santa Cruz mountains, tossing the heads into a roadside ravine.

Four months later, on September 14, Kemper offered a ride to 15-year-old Aiko Koo. Suffocating her with his large hands, Kemper raped her corpse on the spot and then carried it home for dissection. Koo's severed head was resting in the trunk of Kemper's car next morning, when he met with state psychiatrists and they pronounced him "safe," recommending that his juvenile record be sealed for Kemper's future protection. Following the interview, he buried Koo's remains near a religious camp located in the mountains.

Another four months passed before the "Co-ed Killer" struck again, on January 9, 1973. Picking up student Cindy

Schall, Kemper forced her into the trunk of his car at gunpoint, then shot her to death. Driving back to his mother's house, he carried the corpse to his room, and there had sex with it in his bed. Afterward, Kemper dissected Schall's body in the bathtub, bagging the remains and tossing them over a cliff, into the sea. Schall's head was buried in the back yard of his mother's home.

By this time, various remains of Kemper's victims had been found and officers were on the case. Apparently none of them had the least suspicion that their friend, Ed Kemper, was the man they sought, and some felt comfortable enough in Kemper's company to brief him on the progress of their homicide investigation. Smiling, often springing for the next round, Kemper was all ears.

On February 5, 1973, Kemper picked up Rosalind Thorpe, 23, and another hitchhiker, Alice Lin. Both young women were shot to death in the car, then stacked in the trunk like so much excess luggage. Driving home, Kemper ate dinner and waited for his mother to retire before stepping outside and decapitating both corpses as they lay in the trunk. Unsatisfied, he carried Lin's body inside and sexually assaulted it on the floor. Returning to the car, he chopped her hands off as a casual afterthought.

With spring's arrival, Kemper's frenzy escalated, coming back full circle to his home and family. He toyed with the idea of killing everybody on his block, as "a demonstration to the authorities," but finally dismissed the notion. Instead, on Easter weekend, Kemper turned upon his mother, hammering her skull in as she slept. Decapitating her, he raped the headless corpse, then jammed her severed larynx down the garbage disposal. ("This seemed appropriate," he told police, "as much as she'd bitched and screamed and yelled at me over so many years.") Her head was propped on the mantle for use as a dart board.

Still not sated, Kemper telephoned a friend of his mother's, Sally Hallett, and invited her over for a "surprise" dinner in his mother's honor. Upon her arrival, Kemper clubbed her over the head, strangled her to death, and then decapitated her. The headless body was deposited in his bed, while he wandered off to sleep in his mother's room.

On Easter Sunday, Kemper started driving east, with no

destination in mind. He got as far as Colorado before pulling over to a roadside telephone booth and calling police in Santa Cruz. Several attempts were necessary before his friends would accept his confession, and local officers were dispatched to make the arrest while Kemper waited patiently in his car.

In his detailed confessions, Kemper admitted slicing flesh from the legs of at least two victims, cooking it in a macaroni casserole and devouring it as a means of "possessing" his prey. He also acknowledged removing teeth, along with bits of hair and skin from his victims, retaining them as grisly keepsakes, trophies of the hunt. Described as sane by state psychiatrists, Kemper was convicted on eight counts of murder. Asked what punishment he considered fitting for his crimes, the defendant replied, "Death by torture." Instead, he was sentenced to life imprisonment, with the possibility of parole.

Kiss, Bela

A family man and amateur astrologer, Hungarian Bela Kiss began his career as a serial murderer relatively late in life. In February 1912, at forty years of age, Kiss moved to the village of Czinkota with his wife Marie, some fifteen years his junior. Within a matter of weeks, Marie had found herself a lover, one Paul Bikari, and in December 1912, Kiss sadly told his neighbors that the couple had run off together, leaving him alone. In place of his wife, Kiss hired an elderly housekeeper. She, in turn, learned to ignore the parade of women who came to spend time with Czinkota's newly-eligible bachelor.

Around this same time, Kiss began collecting large metal drums, informing the curious village constable that they were filled with gasoline, expected to be scarce with the approach of war in Europe. Budapest authorities, meanwhile, were seeking information on the disappearance of two widows, named Schmeidak and Varga, who had not made contact with their friends or relatives for several weeks. Both women had been last seen in the company of a man named Hoffmann, dwelling near the Mar-

garet Bridge in Budapest, but he had also disappeared
without a trace. Czinkota's constable was generally aware
of the investigation, but he saw no reason to connect Herr
Hoffmann with the quiet, unassuming Bela Kiss.

In November 1914, Kiss was drafted into military service, leaving for the front as soon as he was sworn into
the ranks and issued gear. Another eighteen months would
pass before officials in Czinkota were informed that Kiss
had died in combat, one more grim statistic for the casualty rosters in that bloody spring of 1916. He was forgotten
by the townsfolk until June, when soldiers visited Czinkota in a search for stockpiled gasoline.

The village constable remembered Kiss, his cache of
metal drums, and led a squad of soldiers to the dead man's
home. Inside the house, searchers turned up seven drums
. . . but they contained no gasoline. Instead, each drum
contained the naked body of a woman, strangled and preserved in alcohol. The drawers of Kiss's bureau overflowed with cards and letters from women responding to
newspaper advertisements, purchased by Kiss in the name
of Hoffmann, a self-described "lonely widower seeking
female companionship."

Czinkota's constable recalled that there had been more
drums—and many more, at that. A search of the surrounding countryside revealed another seventeen, each with a
pickled corpse inside. Authorities from Budapest identified the missing widows, and Marie Kiss occupied another
drum; her lover, Paul Bikari, was the only male among
the twenty-four recovered victims.

Homicide detectives theorized that Bela Kiss had slain
his wife and her clandestine lover in a jealous rage, disposing of their bodies in a fashion that—he thought—
eliminated any possibility of subsequent discovery. The
crime apparently unleashed some hidden mania, and Kiss
had spent the next two years pursuing lonely women with
a passion, bilking several of their savings prior to strangling them and sealing them inside of makeshift funeral
vaults. It was a grisly case, but Kiss had gone to face a
higher court.

Or had he?

In the spring of 1919, Kiss was sighted on the Margaret

Bridge in Budapest, "Herr Hoffmann's" pre-war stomping grounds. Police investigation proved that Kiss had switched his papers with a battlefield fatality, assuming the dead man's identity to make good his escape. That knowledge brought detectives no closer to their man, however, for Kiss had slipped the net again.

The futile search went on. In 1924, a deserter from the French Foreign Legion told officers of the Surete about a fellow legionnaire who entertained the troops with tales of his proficiency with the garrote. The soldier's name was Hofman, and he matched descriptions of Bela Kiss, but the lead was another dead end. By the time Hungarian police were informed, Legionnaire "Hofman" had also deserted, vanishing without a trace.

In 1932, a New York homicide detective, Henry Oswald, was convinced that he had sighted Bela Kiss, emerging from the Times Square subway station. Nicknamed "Camera Eye" by colleagues, after his uncanny memory for faces, Oswald was unshakable in his belief that Kiss—who would have been approaching 70—was living somewhere in New York. Unfortunately, Times Square crowds prevented Oswald from pursuing Kiss, and he could only watch in helpless rage as his intended quarry disappeared.

In 1936, a rumor spread that Kiss was working as a janitor, in some apartment buildings on Sixth Avenue. Again, he managed to evade police, and there the trail grew cold. Whatever finally became of Bela Kiss, if he was ever in New York at all, remains a mystery, beyond solution with the passage of a full half-century. In Hungary, he is remembered as the one who got away.

Kogut, John

In 1984 and early 1985, Long Island was the scene of several rapes and murders aimed at teenage girls, with evidence suggesting that the crimes had been committed by a mobile group including three or more young men. Police have solved one case, with indications that the perpetrators—and unknown accomplices—may be responsible for other slayings in the area. New evidence, secured by newsman Maury Terry, further indicates the possible involvement of a devil-worship cult with ties to other lethal groups in New York City and in California.

The first Long Island victim was 15-year-old Kelly Morrissey, who vanished on the short walk home from a popular teenage hangout, on June 12, 1984. Five months later, on November 11, a friend of the missing girl—Theresa Fusco—was forced into a van after leaving a skating rink in Lynbrook, one mile from the spot where Morrissey disappeared. Fusco's body, beaten, strangled, and raped by at least three men, was found on December 5, realizing the worst fears of her family and friends.

John Kogut, a 21-year-old high school dropout and unemployed landscaper, was jailed on charges of burglary and disorderly conduct when police began asking him questions about the Fusco homicide. Cracking under interrogation, he confessed to the crime, naming two accomplices, and was formally charged with the murder on March 26, 1985. Kelly Morrissey was still missing, but her diary contained entries describing at least one date with Kogut prior to her disappearance.

Eight hours after the announcement of Kogut's arrest, 19-year-old Jacqueline Martarella was reported missing from Oceanside, a short four miles from the scene of Theresa Fusco's abduction. Kogut was obviously innocent in that case, but his alleged accomplices were still at large, and police were already collecting evidence of Kogut's alleged participation in a Satanic cult that favored the rape of young virgins as a form of "sacrifice." Kogut's friends informed police that he had once burned the mark of an inverted cross of his arm, and acquaintances of Theresa Fusco recalled her discussions of a Satanic coven reportedly active in the Long Beach-Oceanside area.

On April 22, Martarella's raped and strangled corpse was found beside a golf course at Lawrence, Long Island, Visiting the scene, journalist Maury Terry reported discovery of a "cult sign" linked with Satanists in Queens and Yonkers, who allegedly participated in the infamous "Son of Sam" murders in 1976 and '77. Not far from the dump site, searchers discovered an abandoned root cellar, its walls festooned with cult symbols and slogans. Outside, some articles of clothing were found, described by Jacqueline Martarella's parents as "very similar" to items she wore on the night of her disappearance.

John Kogut steadfastly refused to discuss the cult angle, while freely admitting his role in the rape and strangulation of Theresa Fusco. After she was raped, he said, the girl had threatened to inform police, whereupon one of Kogut's associates handed him a rope, with instructions to "Do what you gotta do." On May 9, 1985, authorities went public with their theory that a gang of twelve associates was linked with three known murders and at least four rapes in which the victims had survived. By June 21, suspects John Restivo, 26, and Dennis Halstead, 30, were in custody on charges of first-degree rape and second-degree murder in the Fusco case. Kogut was convicted and sentenced to life in May 1986, with Restivo and Halstead joining him later that year. (Prior to Kogut's trial, a teen-age friend—Bob Fletcher—who had testified to Kogut's Satanism and involvement in pornography "committed suicide" in Rosedale, Queens. Police have been unable to explain the disappearance of the weapon that he used to shoot himself.)

Kraft, Randy Steven

Shortly after 1 a.m. on May 14, 1983, highway patrol officers in Orange County, California, stopped a weaving motorist suspected of intoxication. The driver Randy Kraft, immediately left his vehicle, all smiles as he approached the cruiser to conduct his business. Growing more suspicious by the moment, officers walked Kraft back to his car, where they found Terry Gambrel, a 25-year-old Marine, slumped dead in the passenger's seat. He had been strangled with a belt, and Kraft was booked on suspicion of murder, held in lieu of $250,000 bail.

A background check on Kraft revealed a 1966 arrest for lewd conduct in Huntington Beach, with charges dismissed. He graduated from college a year later, with a degree in economics, and spent a year in the air force before he was discharged on grounds related to homosex-

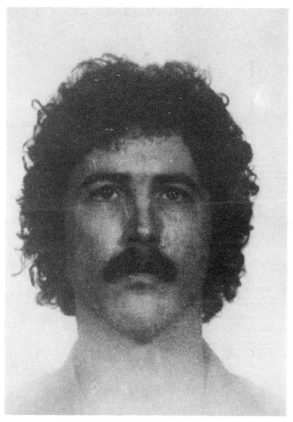

Kenneth Bianchi

(Courtesy of The Los Angeles County Sheriff's Department)

Lawrence Bittaker

(Courtesy of The Los
Angeles County
Sheriff's Department)

Roy Norris

(Courtesy of The Los
Angeles County
Sheriff's Department)

Theodore Robert Bundy

(Courtesy of The Federal Bureau of Investigation)

Carroll Edward Cole (right)

with the author on the afternoon before
Cole's execution in Nevada, December 1985.
(Courtesy of Michael Newton)

Alton Coleman

(Courtesy of The
Federal Bureau of
Investigation)

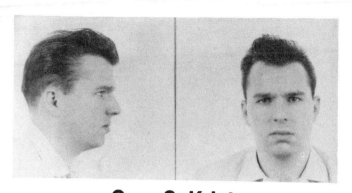

Gary S. Krist

(Courtesy of The Federal Bureau of Investigation)

Ruth Eisemann-Schier

(Courtesy of The Federal Bureau of Investigation)

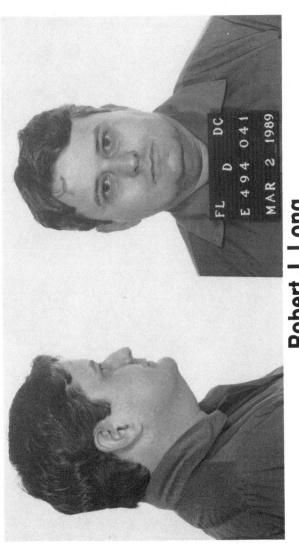

Robert J. Long

(Courtesy of The Florida Department of Corrections)

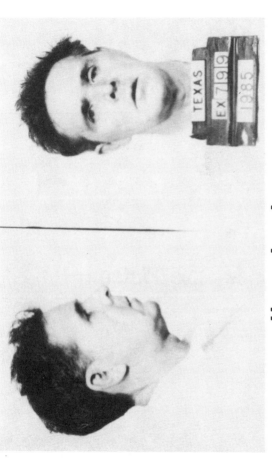

Henry Lee Lucas

(Courtesy of The Texas Department of Corrections)

Charles Manson

(Courtesy of The
Los Angeles County
Sheriff's Department)

Charles "Tex" Watson

(Courtesy of The Los
Angeles County
Sheriff's Department)

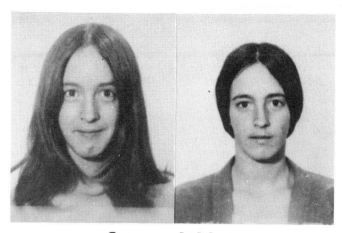

Susan Atkins

(Courtesy of The Los Angeles County Sheriff's Department)

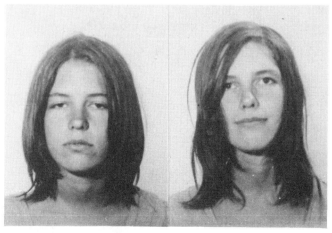

Leslie Van Houten

(Courtesy of The Los Angeles County Sheriff's Department)

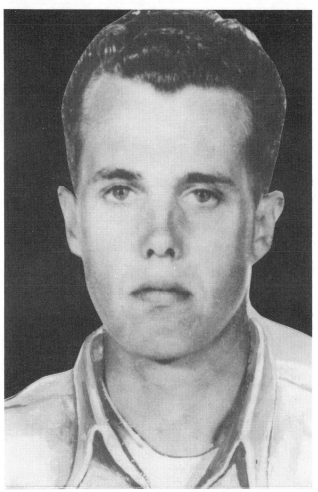

Hugh Bion Morse

(Courtesy of The Federal Bureau of Investigation)

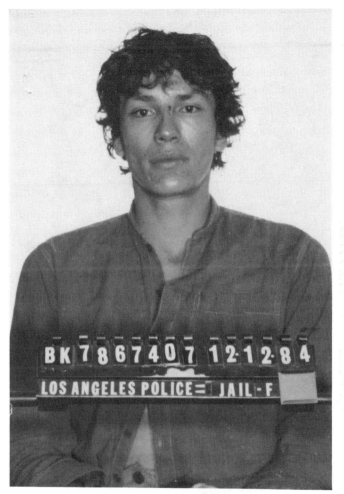

Richard Ramirez

(Courtesy of The Los Angeles County Sheriff's Department)

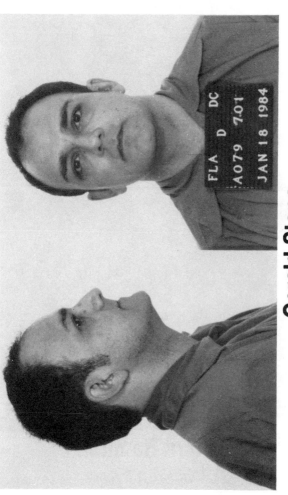

Gerald Stano

(Courtesy of The Florida Department of Corrections)

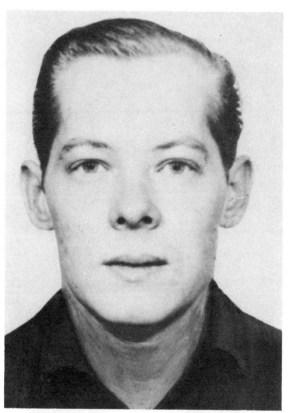

Richard Lee Tingler, Jr.

(Courtesy of The Federal Bureau of Investigation)

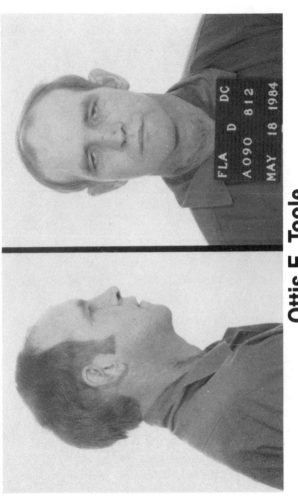

Ottis E. Toole

(Courtesy of The Florida Department of Corrections)

Coral Eugene Watts

(Courtesy of The Texas Department of Corrections)

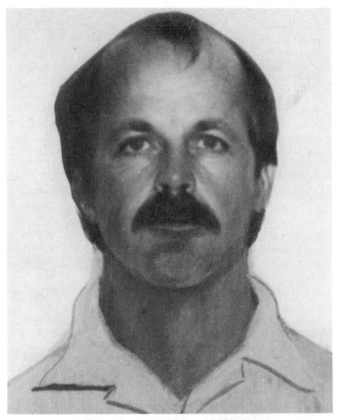

Christopher Wilder

(Courtesy of The Federal Bureau of Investigation)

ual behavior. In 1975, Kraft was arrested in Long Beach for lewd conduct with another man; on conviction, he spent five days in jail and paid a $125 fine.

The search of Kraft's impounded auto turned up forty-seven color photographs depicting several young men, some of them naked, some apparently unconscious—or worse. A briefcase in the trunk contained a notebook, filled with more than sixty cryptic messages in some personal code. A tour of Kraft's home uncovered further evidence, convincing the authorities they had a most prolific killer on their hands, Kraft's photographs depicted three young men whose deaths were still unsolved in Southern California. Robert Loggins, a teenaged Marine, had been found dead in September 1980; now, police examined snapshots of his naked body, stretched out on a couch recovered from Kraft's home. Roger De Vaul, age 20, was last seen alive while hitchhiking with a friend, Geoffrey Nelson, on February 12, 1983. Nelson's body was found in Garden Grove that afternoon; De Vaul's had turned up the following day. Eric Church, another chronic hitch-hiker, was found dead in Orange County on March 27, 1983.

And the body-count kept growing. Fibers from a rug in Kraft's garage matched those recovered from the corpse of Scott Hughes, 18, discarded beside the Riverside Freeway in April 1978. Personal items recovered from Kraft's home included property stolen from three murder victims in Oregon, plus two items belonging to a man found dead near Grand Rapids, Michigan, in December 1982. Investigators learned that Kraft had worked for a Santa Monica-based aerospace firm between June 1980 and January 1983, visiting company offices in Oregon and Michigan at the times of unsolved murders in both states.

As names were added to the list of victims, prosecutors cracked the code in Kraft's notebook. Thus, "2 in 1 Hitch" referred to the double murder of Nelson and De Vaul. "Marine Carson" was a reference to Richard Keith, a young marine last seen in Carson, California, whose strangled body was found in Laguna Hills in June 1978. "Jail Out" described the case of Ronald Young, found stabbed in Irvine, hours after his release from the Orange

County jail on June 11, 1978. ''Parking Lot'' recalled memories of an eight-year-old case, in which Keith Crotwell had vanished on March 26, 1975. Fishermen found his severed head, days later, off the coast of Long Beach, and his skeleton was finally recovered in October. Kraft was briefly questioned in the case, and while he copped to meeting Crotwell *in a parking lot* the day he vanished, officers did not consider him a suspect in the crime.

The list went on and on, with each notation matched against another unsolved homicide. A prosecutor working on the case told newsmen, ''What we have here is a true score-card killer.''

By August 1983, Kraft was charged with six counts of murder. A month later, the tally stood at sixteen homicides, eleven counts of sodomy, nine counts of sexual mutilation and three counts of robbery. In January 1984, prosecutors filed written notice of their intent to prove twenty-one additional murders, spanning twelve years and three states, during the penalty phase of Kraft's trial. Jury selection finally began in July 1988, with prospective jurors advised that the trial might last a year or more.

Krist, Gary Steven

Gary Krist launched his criminal career at age fourteen, with the theft of a boat. A year later he stole a car, and at sixteen he was committed to the Utah State Industrial School, at Ogden, for a year. Krist entered confinement on June 2, 1961, but soon escaped; he was recaptured in Idaho on July 29, 1961. At age eighteen, he was sentenced to the state vocational school at Tracy, California, on conviction for two auto thefts in the vicinity of Oakland. Released on December 4, 1964, he was next arrested on January 6, 1966, after stealing two cars from a sales lot in San Mateo, California. Convicted of auto theft on May 20, 1966, he drew a term of six months to five years in state prison. Krist escaped from custody on November 11, 1966, and was still at large two years later, when he graduated to the big time.

On December 17, 1968, 20-year-old Barbara Jane

Mackle, a student at Emory College in Atlanta, was spending the night with her mother in a suburban motel. Recovering from influenza, Barbara had left her dormitory in consideration of her roommates, and her mother had flown in from Florida to nurse her through the illness. While the treatment might have seemed extravagant, it fit the Mackle life-style; Barbara's father was a millionaire land developer and personal friend of President-elect Richard Nixon.

The women weren't expecting visitors that morning, in the pre-dawn hours, when Krist and female accomplice Ruth Eisemann-Schier forced their way into the room at gunpoint. Barbara's mother, bound and chloroformed, was left behind; the ailing girl was driven twenty miles northeast of town and buried in a box that had been fitted with an air pump, food and water, and a battery-powered lamp. Their dirty work complete, the kidnappers drove back to Florida, waiting for the news to break.

A ransom note, buried in the Mackles' front yard at Coral Gables, Florida, demanded $500,000 ransom in old $20 bills. The family followed orders, running a specified ad in a Miami newspaper on December 18, waiting nervously for instructions on the ransom's delivery. The drop was arranged for December 19, on a causeway leading to uninhabited Fair Isle, in Biscayne Bay. Losing his way in the darkness, Robert Mackle arrived an hour late at the drop point, but Krist confirmed the pay-off via telephone, circling back to pick up the suitcase. He barely had the bag in hand, when a policeman on routine patrol mistook Krist for a burglar, giving chase. The kidnapper escaped on foot, but clues from his abandoned vehicle identified both suspects for the FBI.

At half-past midnight on December 20, a phone call to the Bureau's office in Atlanta gave directions to the site where Barbara Mackle had been buried. Exhumed after 83 hours, she was found alive and well. Arrest warrants for Gary Krist and Ruth Eisemann-Schier were issued the same day, and their names were simultaneously added to the "Ten Most Wanted" list.

In flight, Krist had used some of the ransom money to purchase a boat, planning to escape by water. A Coast

Guard helicopter spoiled his plan, trailing him until Krist abandoned his craft on Hog Island, in Charleston Harbor. Captured by Sheriff Richard McLeod on December 22, the fugitive was held in lieu of $500,000 bail. On January 3, Krist and his accomplice were indicted on state charges of kidnapping with ransom, a capital crime in Georgia.

In custody, awaiting trial, Krist startled jailers with confessions to a string of previously unsolved murders. According to the prisoner, his first victim was a 65-year-old hermit, with whom Krist had a homosexual relationship at age fourteen, while living in Pelican, Alaska. He had killed the man, Krist said, by tripping him while they were walking on a bridge across a deep ravine. Investigators verified a case, identical to Krist's description, that had previously been described as death by accident.

At nineteen, Krist asserted, he had killed a girl near San Diego, strangling and beating her to death, concealing her body under a pile or rocks. Local officers confirmed the discovery of Helen Crow's body on October 3, 1964, with a coroner's estimate of death occurring six to eight weeks earlier. At that time, Krist was under lock and key at Tracy, California; his knowledge of the graphic details in the case remains a mystery.

A third homicide, reported by Krist, was committed in 1961, shortly after his escape from confinement in Utah. According to Gary's confession, he picked up a homosexual, described as a "sissy," and later killed his victim in a violent fit of rage. The body had been dumped near Wendover, Utah, where local officers confirmed discovery of a skeleton on July 27, 1967. The coroner's vague estimate of death, some three to five years earlier, roughly corresponds with Krist's period of freedom from custody.

Despite allusions to a fourth murder, Krist refrained from offering any details. Convicted of kidnapping on 26, 1969, he was sentenced to a term of life imprisonment in Georgia. At this writing, there are no plans to prosecute murder charges in Utah or Alaska.

Kroll, Joachim

A nomadic German sex killer, Kroll lived in the vicinity of Duisburg, filling his bachelor apartment with electronic gadgets and inflatable sex dolls, frequently strangling the latter with one hand while he masturbated with the other. Too nervous and shy for sex with conscious partners, he turned to rape and murder at age 22, killing so often over the next two decades that he lost count of his victims. In the 1960s, Kroll tried cannibalism on a whim, enjoying it so much that he kept up the practice, stalking "tender" victims in an effort to reduce his grocery bills.

Kroll's first remembered victim was 19-year-old Irmgard Strehl, raped and murdered in a barn near the village of Walstedde, during February 1955. Twelve-year-old Erika Schuletter was the next to die, raped and strangled at Kirchhellen in 1956. Three years later and miles away, he killed Klara Jesmer in the woods near Rheinhausen, on June 17, 1959. Sixteen-year-old Manuela Knodt was raped and murdered near Bredeney, south of Essen, with slices cut from her buttocks and thighs in the first slaying attributed to the man police would dub the "Ruhr Hunter."

On April 23, 1962, 13-year-old Petra Giese was raped and killed at Rees, near Walsum, both buttocks sliced off, along with her left forearm and hand. The Hunter was still stalking Walsum on June 4, when 13-year-old Monica Tafel vanished on her way to school. Searchers found her body in a nearby rye field, steaks carved from her buttocks and the back of her thighs.

Kroll sometimes changed his pattern, in an effort to confuse police. No meat was taken when he murdered 12-year-old Barbara Bruder, in Burscheid, during 1962. In August 1965, at Grossenbaum, he crept up on a pair of young lovers, stabbing a tire on their car, then fatally knifing the driver, Hermann Schmitz, when he stepped out to investigate the noise. In Marl, he raped and murdered Ursula Roling on September 13, 1966, rebounding three months later to kill five-year-old Ilona Harke at Wuppertal, slicing steaks from her buttocks and shoulders.

Kroll's luck nearly ran out in 1967, when he settled briefly in Grafenhausen, befriending local children who began to call him "Uncle." Luring a 10-year-old girl into a nearby field one afternoon, he promised to "show her a rabbit" but produced obscene photos instead, hoping the child might become sexually aroused. Instead, she was horrified, bolting for safety as Kroll made a grab for her throat, and he fled Grafenhausen the same day, before police could begin asking troublesome questions.

On July 12, 1969, he invaded the home of 61-year-old Maria Hettgen, in Hueckeswagen, strangling her to death and raping her corpse in the front hall. Reverting to children on May 21, 1970, Kroll waylaid 13-year-old Jutta Ranh in Breitscheid, discarding her strangled body after he had satisfied his lust. In 1976, 10-year-old Karin Toepfer was raped and strangled on her way to school, in Dinslaken Voerde.

Kroll's arrogance defeated him in July 1976, when he claimed the next victim in his own neighborhood of Laar, a Duisburg suburb. Four-year-old Marion Ketter was reported missing from a nearby playground, and police were asking questions door-to-door when they heard a curious story from one of Kroll's neighbors. According to their witness, Kroll had warned him that the upstairs toilet in their block of flats was clogged "with guts." A plumber quickly verified the statement, flushing a child's lungs and other organs out of the pipe, and detectives went calling on Kroll. In his apartment, they discovered plastic bags of human flesh stored in the freezer; on the stove, a tiny hand was boiling in a pot with carrots and potatoes.

Convinced that they had bagged the Hunter, officers were stunned by Kroll's long-running litany of rape and murder. He remembered fourteen victims, but he really couldn't say if there were more, a circumstance that left detectives free to speculate upon his final body-count. With capital punishment abolished in Germany after World War II, Kroll received the maximum possible sentence of life imprisonment.

Kurten, Peter

Born in Koln-Mulheim, Germany, in 1883, Peter Kurten was the product of a violent, abusive childhood. Thirteen members of his family existed in a single room, devoid of privacy, the atmosphere heavily charged with sexual tension. Kurten's father, a brutal alcoholic, frequently compelled his wife to strip for sex in front of the assembled children, and he later went to prison for attempting to rape his own daughter. Peter likewise molested his sisters on occasion, and he was further influenced by a sadistic dog-catcher who lived in the same building. As a child, Kurten frequently watched this man torture his dogs, and was instructed in the art of masturbating animals for sport.

Kurten claimed his first murders at age nine, when he pushed a playmate from a raft on the banks of the Rhine. A second boy jumped in to help the first, and Kurten managed to push them both under the raft, where they drowned. As in the case of Carroll Edward Cole, a half-century later, these youthful murders were dismissed by the authorities as "accidental deaths."

Around age twelve, Kurten moved with his family to Dusseldorf. Already twisted in his view of sexuality, he masturbated compulsively, attempting intercourse with his sisters and various schoolgirls. From age thirteen, he also practiced bestiality with sheep, pigs, and goats, deriving special satisfaction when he stabbed sheep to death during intercourse.

In his early teens, Kurten ran away from home to live as a nomadic robber, choosing girls and women as his prey. Back home in Dusseldorf at age sixteen, he briefly worked as an apprentice moulder, but his master proved abusive and Kurten absconded with cash from the till, settling in Coblenz with a prostitute who thrived on violence and perversion. Kurten logged his first arrest in Coblenz—one of seventeen indictments that would land him in jail for a total of twenty-seven years. Released in 1899, he learned his parents had divorced, and Kurten promptly moved in with another masochistic hooker twice his age.

Kurten claimed his first adult murder in November 1899, strangling a girl during sex in the Grafenberger Wald, outside Dusseldorf, but no body was found and his victim may well have survived. He was jailed twice for fraud in 1900, then received another two years for attempting to shoot a girl with a rifle. Theft charges kept him behind bars until 1904, where he occupied his time with fantasies of violent sex and vengeance on society.

Drafted by the military on release from prison, Kurten soon deserted. He had started setting fires by this time, drawing sensual excitement from the flames. His targets normally were barns and hayricks, torched in hopes that sleeping tramps might be burned up alive. Sentenced to seven years on a theft charge, in 1905, Kurten later claimed to have poisoned several inmates in the prison hospital. On release, in 1912, he raped a servant girl, and shortly after that was found accosting women in a local restaurant. A waiter tried to intervene, and Kurten drove him off with pistol fire, earning another year in prison for his trouble.

On May 25, 1913, Kurten broke into a pub in Koln-Mulheim while the owners were away. Creeping up to their quarters, he found their 13-year-old daughter, Christine Klein, asleep in bed. He cut her throat and penetrated her vagina with his fingers, taking time to drop a handkerchief with his initials at the scene, but luck was with him. The victim's father, Peter Klein, had recently quarreled with his brother Otto, the latter threatening to do something Klein "would remember all his life." Otto Klein was indicted and tried for the murder, finally cleared for lack of evidence, while Kurten followed the proceedings with amusement.

Stepping up his schedule, Kurten found another sleeping victim but was frightened off by members of her family. In separate incidents, he struck a man and woman with a hatchet, reaching climax at the sight of blood. He also torched another hayrick and attempted strangulation of two women, prior to drawing eight more years in jail on unrelated charges.

Freed in 1921, he moved to Altenburg, informing new acquaintances that he had been a prisoner of war in Russia. Kurten met his future wife in Altenburg, a woman who had served five years in jail for shooting her fiancee.

She initially rejected his proposals, but agreed to marry Kurten when he threatened her with murder.

Settling down to a peculiar version of domestic bliss, Kurten endured a "normal" life for several years before he had a relapse and was charged with sexually assaulting servant girls on two occasions. Moving back to Dusseldorf in 1925, he was delighted by a blood-red sunset on the night of his arrival. He was ready to begin his final reign of terror.

Based upon his subsequent confessions, Kurten bore responsibility, by 1928, in four attempted strangulations—all of women—and a rash of fires that claimed two homes and fifteen other targets. Still, he did not hit his stride until the early weeks of 1929. On February 3, he stabbed a woman twenty-four times and left her lying in the street, but she recovered after months of care. Ten days later, Kurten scored his first fatality at Flingern, stabbing a mechanic twenty times and leaving him for dead.

On March 9, eight-year-old Rose Ohliger was found at a construction site in Dusseldorf; she had been raped, stabbed thirteen times, and efforts had been made to burn the corpse with paraffin. Comparing notes, detectives found their last three victims had been marked by stab wounds in the temples, but the choice of targets—first a woman, then a man, and now a child—apparently ruled out a pattern in the case.

In April 1929, police picked up a simple-minded transient for assaulting local women, but they found no evidence connecting him with homicide and he was sent to an asylum. Kurten rested from his labors, meanwhile, dallying with servant girls at home and "playfully" attempting strangulation during sex. Returning with a vengeance during August, Kurten later claimed that he had choked a woman by the name of "Ann" and dumped her body in the river, but no trace of her was ever found. Before the month was out, three other victims—one a man—were stabbed in hit-and-run attacks in Dusseldorf, but all survived. On August 24, two children—Gertrude Hamacher, age five, and Louise Lenzen, age 14—were found dead near their homes, both strangled, with their throats cut. One day later, Gertrude Schulte was accosted on her way to see the fair, at Neuss. Confronted with a crude demand for sex, she said that she would rather die. ''Well, die then,'' Kurten answered, stabbing Gertrude several times before he fled. She lived and gave police a fair description of her would-be rapist, but detectives still rejected the suggestion of a single man behind their recent crime wave.

Kurten tried to strangle three more women in September, hurling one victim into the river for good measure, but all survived. Ida Reuter was less fortunate, her skull crushed with a hammer near the end of the month. Another hammer victim, Elizabeth Dirries, was killed at Grafenbery, October 12. On the twenty-fifth, two more women were bludgeoned in separate attacks, but both recovered from their wounds.

Five-year-old Gertrude Alberman was reported missing in Dusseldorf on November 7, her body recovered two days later, after Kurten sent directions to a local newspaper. The child had been strangled, then stabbed thirty-six times for good measure. Following directions in Kurten's letter, police also unearthed the remains of Maria Hahn, stabbed to death and buried in mid-August. Stabbed twenty times, Hahn had also been raped after death.

Kurten's luck ran out on May 14, 1930, when he picked up Maria Budlick and took her home for a meal, thereafter strolling through the woods with sex and strangulation on his mind. Maria fought him off, and Kurten unaccountably released her after she assured him that she had forgotten his address. Police were summoned and, in custody, their suspect launched a marathon confession that would send him to his death.

Kurten's trial opened on April 13, 1931, and ended eight days later. Jurors needed only ninety minutes to convict him on nine counts of murder, sternly rejecting Kurten's insanity defense. Sentenced to death by decapitation, Kurten informed a psychiatrist that his greatest thrill of all time would be hearing the blood spurt from his own severed neck. He went to the guillotine, all smiles, on July 2, 1931.

Kuznetsof

Described by Soviet reporters as a leader of the "Volga pirates," cruel Kuznetsof stood accused, in 1929, of some 200 crimes, including six known homicides in which his relatives were normally selected as the victims. Unrepentant to the end, he chilled and titillated Russian audiences with his philosophical approach to murder, offering decisive proof that differences in politics have little bearing on the bestial side of man.

The first three victims charged against Kuznetsof were his uncle, his aunt, and their lodger, an invalid soldier. According to Kuznetsof's own description of the crime, the triple murder grew out of resentment toward his uncle. "When I went away," the killer said, "he stole my property. He offered to give it back, but I thought buried men cannot bear witness, so I shot him, with his wife and lodger."

Next, Kuznetsof killed his infant daughter, whom he had regarded as a nuisance. "You cannot make a good plank out of rotten wood," he decided, "so she was better off dead." When his grieving wife called Kuznetsof a murderer, he threw her in the Volga River, "because flowing streams wash away sorrow." A second wife was also murdered, after Kuznetsof adopted a full-time criminal career. "She knew too much," he told assembled journalists, "but in the grave all knowledge ends."

Asked if he believed he could escape detection for his crime, Kuznetsof said, "Of course not. My exploits became famous as soon as done. We criminals have our ways of communication faster than your telegraph, but the more and quicker they know us, the more they fear us." On conviction for his crimes, Kuznetsof was immediately executed by a firing squad.

Lake, Leonard
and Ng, Charles Chitat

A native of San Francisco, Leonard Lake was born July 20, 1946. His mother sought to teach pride in the human body by encouraging Lake to photograph nude girls, including his sisters and cousins, but the "pride" soon developed into a precocious obsession with pornography. In adolescence, Lake extorted sexual favors from his sister, in return for protection from the violent outbursts of a younger brother, Donald. By his teens, Leonard displayed a fascination with the concept of collecting "slaves." Lake joined the Marine Corps in 1966 and served a noncombatant tour in Vietnam, as a radar operator. He also underwent two years of psychiatric therapy at Camp Pendleton, for unspecified mental problems, before his ultimate discharge in 1971.

Back in civilian life, Lake moved to San Jose and was married, developing a local reputation as a gun buff, "survivalist," and sex freak. His favorite high was filming bondage scenes, including female partners other than his wife, and they were soon divorced. In 1980, Lake was charged with grand theft, after ripping off building materials from a construction site, but he got off easy with one year's probation. Married a second time in August 1981, he moved with his wife to a communal ranch in Ukiah, California, where a "renaissance" life-style was practiced—complete with medieval costumes and surgical alteration of young goats to produce "unicorns." A few months after his arrival in Ukiah, Lake met Charles Ng.

Hong Kong born, in 1961, Charles Chitat Ng was the son of wealthy Chinese parents. Forever in trouble, Ng was expelled from school in England, where he was caught stealing from his fellow students. A subsequent shoplifting arrest drove him to California, where he joined the Marine Corps after a hit-and-run incident, falsely listing his place of birth as Bloomington, Indiana. An expert martial artist and self-styled "ninja warrior" who was "born to fight," Ng talked incessantly of violence to his fellow leathernecks. In October 1979, he led two accomplices in stealing $11,000 worth of automatic weapons from a Marine arsenal in Hawaii and found himself under arrest. During psychiatric evaluation, Ng boasted of "assassinating" someone in California, but he never got around to naming the victim. He escaped from custody before his trial, and was listed as a deserter when he answered Lake's ad in a war gamer's magazine, in 1981.

The two men hit it off at once, in spite of Lake's racism, which seemed to encompass only blacks and Hispanics. They began collecting automatic weapons from illegal sources, and a team of federal agents raided the Ukiah ranch in April 1982, arresting Lake and Ng for firearms violations. Released on $6,000 bond, Lake promptly went into hiding, using a variety of pseudonyms as he drifted around northern California. His second wife divorced him after the arrest, but they remained on friendly terms. As a fugitive, Ng was denied bail, and he struck a bargain with military prosecutors in August, pleading guilty to theft in return for a promise that he would serve no more than three years of a 14-year sentence. Confined to the military stockade at Leavenworth federal penitentiary, Ng was paroled after 18 months, avoiding deportation with a reference to the phony birthplace shown on his enlistment papers. On release from prison, he returned to California and again teamed up with Leonard Lake.

By that time, Lake had settled on two and a half acres of woodland near Wilseyville, in Calaveras County, enlisting the help of neighbors to construct a fortified bunker beside his cabin, stockpiling illegal weapons and stolen video equipment. His every thought was recorded in various diaries, including details of "Operation Miranda," entailing collection of sex slaves to serve his needs after a nuclear holocaust. On the subject of females, Lake wrote: "God meant women for cooking, cleaning house and sex. And when they are not in use, they should be locked up." An oft-repeated motto in the diaries advised, "If you love something, let it go. If it doesn't come back, hunt it down and kill it." On February 25, 1984, shortly before his reunion with Ng, Lake described his life as "Mostly dull day-to-day routine still with death in my pocket and fantasy my major goal." If authorities are correct, the first death in Lake's pocket may have claimed brother Donald, reported missing by their mother—and never seen again—after he went to visit Lake in July 1983.

On June 2, 1985, employees of a lumberyard in South San Francisco called police to report a peculiar shoplifting incident. An Oriental man had walked out of the store with a $75 vice, placed it in the trunk of a Honda auto parked nearby, and then escaped on foot before they could detain him. The car was still outside, and officers found a bearded white man at the wheel. He cheerfully produced a driver's license in the name of ''Robin Stapley,'' but he bore no resemblance to its photograph. A brief examination of the trunk turned up the stolen vice, along with a silencer-equipped .22-caliber pistol. Booked on theft and weapons charges, ''Stapley'' evaded questions for several hours, then asked for a drink of water, gulping a cyanide capsule removed from a secret compartment in his belt buckle. He was comatose on arrival at the hospital, where he would linger on life-support machines over the next four days, before he was finally pronounced dead on June 6.

A fingerprint comparison identified ''Stapley'' as Leonard Lake, but the driver's license was not a forgery. Its original owner was also the founder of San Diego's Guardian Angels chapter—and he had not been seen at home for several weeks. The Honda's license plate was registered to Lake, but the vehicle was not. Its owner of record, 39-year-old Paul Cosner, was a San Francisco car dealer who had disappeared in November 1984, after leaving home to sell the car to ''a weird guy.''

Lake's auto registration led detectives to the property in Wilseyville, where they discovered weapons, torture devices, and Leonard's voluminous diaries. Serial numbers on Lake's video equipment traced ownership to Harvey Dubs, a San Francisco photographer reported missing from home—along with his wife Deborah and infant son, Sean—on July 25, 1984. As detectives soon learned, the equipment had been used to produce ghoulish ''home movies'' of young women being stripped and threatened, raped and tortured, at least one of them mutilated so savagely she must have died as a result. Lake and Ng were the principal stars of the snuff tapes, but one of their "leading ladies" was quickly identified as the missing Deborah Dubs.

Another reluctant "actress" was Brenda O'Connor, who once occupied the cabin adjacent to Lake's with her husband, Lonnie Bond, and their infant son, Lonnie, Jr. They had known Lake as "Charles Gunnar," an alias lifted from the best man at Lake's second wedding and another missing person, last seen alive in 1983. O'Connor was afraid of "Gunnar," telling friends that she had seen him plant a woman's body in the woods, but rather than inform police, her husband had invited a friend—Guardian Angel Robin Stapely—to share their quarters and offer personal protection. All four had disappeared in May of 1985.

Another snuff-tape victim, 18-year-old Kathleen Allen, made the acquaintance of Lake and Ng through her boyfriend, 23-year-old Mike Carroll. Carroll had served time with Ng at Leavenworth and later came west to join him in various shady enterprises. Allen abandoned her job in a supermarket after Lake informed her that Carroll had been shot and wounded "near Lake Tahoe," offering to show her where he was. Her final paycheck had been mailed to Lake's address in Wilseyville.

Aside from videocassettes, authorities retrieved numerous still photos from Lake's bunker, including snapshots of Leonard in long "witchy" robes, and photos of 21 young women captured in various stages of undress. Six were finally identified and found alive; the other 15 have remained elusive, despite publication of the photographs, and police suspect that most or all of them were murdered on the death ranch.

Gradually, the search moved outward from Lake's bunker, into the surrounding woods. A vehicle abandoned near the cabin was registered to another missing person, Sunnyvale photographer Jeffrey Askern, and police soon had a fair idea of what had happened to Lake's vanishing acquaintances. On June 8, portions of four human skeletons were unearthed near the bunker, with a fifth victim—and numerous charred bone fragments, including infant's teeth—discovered on June 13. Number six was turned up five days later, and was first to be identified. A 34-year-old drifter, Randy Jacobson was last seen alive in October

1984, when he left his San Francisco rooming house to visit Lake and sell his van. Two of Jacobson's neighbors, 26-year-old Cheryl Okoro and 38-year-old Maurice Wok, were also on the missing list, linked to the Wilseyville killers by personal contacts and cryptic entries in Lake's diary.

Three more skeletons were sorted out of scattered fragments on June 26, and authorities declared that Lake and Ng were linked with the disappearance of at least 25 persons. One of those was Mike Carroll, who reportedly agreed to dress in "sissy" clothes and lure gays for Ng to kill, then died himself when Charlie tired of the game. Donald Giuletti, a 36-year-old disc jockey in San Francisco, had offered oral sex through published advertisements, and one of the callers was a young Oriental who shot Giuletti to death in July 1984, critically wounding his roommate at the same time. Lake's wife recalled that Ng had boasted of shooting two homosexuals, and the survivor readily identified Ng's mugshot as a likeness of the gunman.

Two other friends of Ng—and occasional co-workers at a Bay Area warehouse—were also on the missing list. Clifford Parenteau, age 24, had vanished after winning $400 on a Superbowl bet, telling associates that he was going "to the country" to spend the money with Ng. A short time later, 25-year-old Jeffrey Gerald dropped from sight after he agreed to help Ng move some furniture. Neither man was seen again, and Ng is formally charged with their deaths, in two of twelve first-degree murder counts filed against him. Other victims named in the indictment include Mike Carroll and Kathleen Allen, Lonnie Bond and family, Robin Stapley, Don Giuletti, and three members of the Dubs family. Ng is also charged as an accessory to murder in the disappearance of Paul Cosner. (Remains of Stapley and Lonnie Bond were found in a common grave on July 9, bringing the official body-count to 12 known victims.)

On July 6, 1985, Ng was arrested while shoplifting food from a market in Calgary, Alberta. A security guard was shot in the hand before Ng was subdued. Charges of attempted murder were reduced to aggravated assault, robbery, and illegal use of a weapon, with Ng sentenced to four and a half years imprisonment upon conviction.

On November 29, 1988, a Canadian judge ruled that Ng should be extradited to the United States for trial on 19 of 25 charges filed against him in California. Ng's appeal of the decision was rejected on August 31, 1989.

Lang, Donald

An illiterate deaf mute, Lang was charged with his first murder—of a Chicago woman—in 1965. Ruled unfit for trial on grounds that he could not participate in his defense, he was confined in a mental institution until 1971, when the state supreme court decreed that he must either be tried or released. Back on the street, Lang was charged with killing another Chicago woman in 1972, this time convicted and sentenced to prison for life. The conviction was overturned on appeal, since Lang could not communicate with his attorneys, and he was remanded into custody of the state mental health department. Despite his highly-publicized escape, in March of 1982, a Chicago judge granted Lang permission to leave the hospital grounds a month later, for purposes of learning sign language and meeting with other deaf patients. The court acknowledged that Lang was "potentially dangerous," but ruled that "a reasonable risk" should be taken to help him develop emotionally.

LeGrand, Devernon

A New York native, born in 1925, LeGrand was arrested on charges of kidnapping, assault, and firearms possession in 1965. Three years later, police accused him of snatching a 23-year-old woman from her home, assaulting and raping her before she managed to escape. Neither case was prosecuted, but in 1975, LeGrand was convicted of bribery and sexual misconduct with a 17-year-old girl. That same year, along with his 20-year-old son Noconda, LeGrand was convicted of kidnapping and rape; he drew a sentence of five to 15 years in prison, while his son got off "easy" with an eight-year prison term.

Such conduct is not unheard of in New York City, but it is peculiar for the leader of a church. A self-styled holy man, LeGrand had organized St. John's Pentecostal Church of Our Lord a decade earlier, putting down roots in the Crown Heights district of Brooklyn. His headquarters, a four-story townhouse, was occupied by eleven "nuns" and their 47 children, many of them fathered by LeGrand. According to police, LeGrand did most of his recruiting by seduction, impregnating young women, then threatening them or their children if they refused to beg for money on the streets. His black-clad "nuns" were often seen around Grand Central Station, and others had been jailed on misdemeanor charges in New Jersey. It was within the Crown Heights "chapel" that LeGrand had raped his final victim, during August 1974, and authorities suspected that sexual assault was only the tip of the iceberg.

In 1966, LeGrand's "church" had purchased a 58-acre spread in the Catskills, near White Sulphur Springs, converting the place to a summer retreat for the faithful. Over the next eight years, state police received steady complaints from the neighbors, alleging child abuse and health violations, wild parties and indiscriminate gunfire. Children from the camp roamed freely through the countryside, begging and stealing, while horses were cruelly beaten and left to starve. Authorities raided the camp in October 1968, seizing drug paraphernalia, photographing clogged toilets and general squalor, but LeGrand's troop returned each summer, without fail, immune to public opinion.

Church members Gladys Stewart, 16, and her sister Yvonne, 18, had testified for the prosecution in LeGrand's bribery trial, but they were missing when the D.A. sought to use their testimony in the later rape case. Informants said the girls were dead, dismembered in the Brooklyn "church," with their remains transported to the Catskills for disposal. State police dug up the ranch in mid-December 1975, but they came away empty-handed. Three months later, on March 6, assorted bones and bits of cartilage were found in Briscoe Lake, and Brooklyn raiding parties turned up human bloodstains in the Crown Heights townhouse.

By April, state police were confident that Devernon LeGrand had murdered a dozen or more victims, dumping some of them in Briscoe Lake. The list included three wives, two of LeGrand's step-children, the Stewart sisters, and two male employees of his "church." In May 1976, LeGrand was indicted on four counts of murder, including the Stewarts and two of his wives, slain in 1963 and 1970, respectively. The "reverend's" son, 26-year-old Steven LeGrand, was also charged with murdering the Stewart sisters, plus two men employed by his father as pimps. Father and son were convicted together in the Stewart case, on May 7, 1977, and both drew prison terms of 25 years to life.

Leonski, Edward Joseph

A self-described "Dr. Jekyll and Mr. Hyde," Leonski was a U.S. Army private stationed in Australia during World War II, convicted and sentenced to die for strangling three women in Melbourne. The first victim was Ivy McLeod, found dead on the night of May 2, 1942, after leaving a tavern for home. A week later, Pauline Thompson was murdered in similar fashion, with Gladys Hosking joining the list on May 28. A fourth woman was also accosted, but the killer unaccountably left her alone when she threatened to call the police.

Suspicion focused on American servicemen after an Australian sentry reported sighting a GI in blood-stained clothing on May 28. Troops in Melbourne were assembled on parade, for inspection, and the sentry picked Leonski from the lineup. Under questioning, the stocky Texan made a full confession, telling his interrogators of a twisted fascination with the female voice. "That's why I choked those ladies," he explained. "It was to get their voices." Pauline Thompson had sung for Leonski on their last date, and he recalled that "Her voice was sweet and soft, and I could feel myself going mad about it."

Dubbed the "Singing Strangler" in the press, Leonski filed a plea of not guilty by reason of insanity. Convicted at his court martial and sentenced to die for his crimes, the defendant was hanged on November 9, 1942.

Long, Robert Joseph

Born October 14, 1953, at Kenova, West Virginia, Long may be the classic case of someone "destined" to become a random killer. With other members of his family, he suffered from a genetic disorder characterized by an extra "X" chromosome, causing his glands to produce abnormal amounts of estrogen in puberty, with the result that his breasts began to enlarge. Surgery removed six pounds of excess tissue from his chest, but the resultant gender confusion remained, perhaps exacerbated by his mother, who shared Long's bed until he reached the age of 13 years. (Long's mother, twice divorced, denies his allegations that he watched her entertain numerous male "visitors" in their one-bedroom apartment.)

Aside from genetic and family problems, Long also suffered a series of grievous head injuries beginning at age five, when he was knocked unconscious in a fall from a swing, one eyelid skewered by a stick. The following year, he was thrown from his bicycle, crashing head-first into a parked car, with injuries including loss of several teeth and a severe concussion. At age seven, he fell from a pony onto his head, remaining dizzy and nauseous for several weeks after the accident.

At age 13, Long met the girl who would become his wife and simultaneously gave up sleeping with his mother. Various accounts agree that he was dominated by his girlfriend almost from the moment of their meeting, but his mother kept her hand in, too, the females in his life apparently cooperating rather than competing.

Long enlisted in the army prior to marriage, and he crashed a motorcycle six months later, shattering his helmet with the impact of his skull on asphalt. Convalescing in the hospital, he was alternately stricken by blinding headaches and unpredictable violent rages, discovering a new obsession with sex. While still in a cast, Long masturbated five times a day to relieve himself, continuing the practice at home despite twice-daily intercourse with his wife. Still, it was not enough, and soon he began to search for other prey.

Between 1980 and 1983, Long terrorized the Florida communities of Miami, Ocala and Fort Lauderdale as the "Classified Ad Rapist," preying on housewives in midday attacks. Dropping by while their husbands were working, Long typically produced a knife, bound his victims, raped them violently, and robbed their homes before he fled. Convicted of rape in November 1981, Long was cleared on appeal through discovery of "witnesses" alleging the victim's consent, and so the attacks continued, with murder shortly added to his list of crimes.

Unlike the 50 women raped by Long, his murder victims were selected from the ranks of prostitutes or other women whom he viewed as "tramps." Between May and November 1984, he strangled, stabbed and shot at least nine victims, with a tenth suspected by police but never charged against him. In early November, he snatched a 17-year-old girl off the street and raped her, sparing her life when she described acts of incest performed by her father. In releasing a victim capable of describing him and his car, Long sealed his own fate, but police were too slow to save victim Kim Swann, murdered two days later in a final frenzy.

Arrested on November 17, 1984, Long was charged with nine counts of first-degree murder, plus felony counts of abduction, rape, and sexual assault on his surviving victim. Convicted at his trial in early 1985, he was sentenced to die.

Lopez, Pedro Alonzo

Pedro Lopez was the seventh child of thirteen, born in squalor to a prostitute in the village of Tolima, Colombia. Exiled from the family hovel at age eight, after his mother caught him fondling a younger sister, Pedro was picked up on the streets by a pedophile who offered food, a place to stay. Instead, the boy was taken into a deserted building and there sodomized, a trauma that apparently did lethal damage to his already-twisted psyche.

Homeless, terrified of strangers, Pedro slept in alleyways and empty village market stalls, drifting from town to town and living hand-to-mouth on the streets. In Bogota, an American family took Lopez in, providing him with free room and board, enrolling him in a day school for orphans. At age twelve, Pedro ran away after stealing money from the school, his flight allegedly precipitated by a teacher's sexual advances.

Six years passed before the future "Monster of the Andes" left another mark on public records, this time charged and sent to prison for the theft of an automobile. On his second day behind bars, 18-year-old Lopez was gang-raped by four older inmates, a risk run by young men in jails the world over. Instead of reporting the crime, Lopez fashioned himself a crude knife and went out for revenge, killing three of his assailants in the next two weeks. Authorities described the homicides as self-defense, and tacked a token two years onto Pedro's standing sentence.

On release from prison, Lopez started stalking young girls with a vengeance; by 1978, the killer estimated he had raped and slain at least 100 in Peru. His specialty appeared to be abducting children from Indian tribes, but the technique backfired when he was captured by a group of Ayachucos, in northern Peru, while attempting to kidnap a nine-year-old girl. Lopez was beaten by his captors, stripped and tortured. The Ayachucos were prepared to bury him alive, when a female American missionary intervened, convincing Pedro's captors that they should deliver him to the police. They grudgingly agreed, and Lopez was deported within days, Peruvian authorities declining to waste valuable time on Indian complaints.

Once more at liberty, Lopez began traveling widely through Colombia and Ecuador, selecting victims with impunity. A sudden rash of missing girls in three adjacent nations was ascribed to the activity of slavery or prostitution rings, but the authorities had no firm evidence, no suspects, prior to April 1980, when a flash flood near Ambato, Ecuador, uncovered bodies of four vanished children. Days later, Carvina Poveda observed Lopez leaving the Plaza Rosa marketplace with her 12-year-old daughter, Maria. Summoning help, she pursued him, and Lopez was captured by townspeople, held for police, who began to suspect that they might have a madman in custody.

In the face of Pedro's continuing silence, police tried a different stratagem. Dressing a priest, Father Cordoba Gudino, in prison garb, they placed him in a cell with Lopez, leaving Gudino to win the suspect's confidence, swapping stories of real or imagined crimes late into the evening. At length, when the padre had heard enough, Lopez was confronted with the evidence of his own admissions and he broke down, making a full confession. Liaison with authorities in Peru and Colombia substantiated parts of the prisoner's grisly, almost incredible story.

According to Pedro's best estimate, he had murdered at least 110 girls in Ecuador, perhaps 100 in Colombia, and "many more than 100" in Peru. "I like the girls in Ecuador," he told police. "They are more gentle and trusting, more innocent. They are not as suspicious of strangers as Colombian girls."

In the course of his confession, Lopez made an effort to invest his crimes with philosophical trappings. "I lost my innocence at age eight," he told interrogators, "so I decided to do the same to as many young girls as I could." Trolling village markets for selected targets with "a certain look of innocence," Lopez first raped his victims, then stared into their eyes as he strangled them, deriving sadistic pleasure from watching them die. Hunting by daylight, so darkness could not hide their death throes, Lopez allegedly sought out one victim immediately after another, his bloodlust becoming insatiable over time.

Police were initially skeptical of their suspect's grandiose claims, but doubts evaporated after Lopez led detectives to 53 graves in the vicinity of Ambato, standing by in irons as they unearthed the remains of girls aged eight to twelve. At 28 other sites, searchers came up empty in the wake of raids by predatory animals, but the police were now convinced. Originally charged with 53 murders, Lopez saw the ante boosted to 110 as a result of his detailed confessions. As Major Victor Lascano, director of the Ambato prison, explained: "If someone confesses to 53 you find and hundreds more you don't, you tend to believe what he says." Lascano also told reporters, in response to questions, that "I think his estimate of 300 is very low, because in the beginning he cooperated with us and took us each day to three or four hidden corpses. But then he tired, changed his mind, and stopped helping."

The change of heart occurred too late to let the "Monster of the Andes" off the hook. Convicted of murder in Ecuador, Lopez was sentenced to life imprisonment—a penalty that normally amounts to 16 years in custody. With time for good behavior, Lopez could be eligible for parole in 1990, but Colombia is waiting to receive him . . . and the penalty for murder there is death by firing squad.

Lucas, Henry Lee

America's most controversial murderer was born August 23, 1936, at Blacksburg, Virginia. The Lucas family home was a two-room, dirt-floor cabin in the woods outside of town, where Henry's alcoholic parents brewed bootleg whiskey, his mother doing occasional turns as the neighborhood prostitute. Viola Lucas ran her family with a rod of iron, while husband Anderson Lucas—dubbed "No Legs" after his drunken encounter with a freight train—dragged himself around the house and tried to drown his personal humiliation in a nonstop flow of liquor.

The Lucas brood consisted of nine children, but several were farmed out to relatives, institutions, and foster homes over the years. Henry was one of those "lucky" enough to remain with his parents, and mother Viola appears to have hated the child from the moment of birth, seizing every opportunity to make his life a living hell on earth. Both Anderson and Henry were the targets of her violent outbursts, man and boy alike enduring wicked beatings, forced to witness the parade of strangers who were called upon to share Viola's bed. Sickened by one such episode, Anderson Lucas dragged himself outside to spend a night in the snow, there contracting a fatal case of pneumonia.

Henry survived, after a fashion, but his mother's cruelty seemed to know no bounds. When Lucas entered school, in 1943, she curled his stringy hair in ringlets, dressed him as a girl, and sent him off to class that way. Barefoot until a kindly teacher bought him shoes, Henry was beaten at home for accepting the gift. If Henry found a pet, his mother killed it, and he came to understand that life—like sex—was cheap. When Henry's eye was gashed, reportedly while playing with a knife, Viola let him suffer until doctors had to surgically remove the withered orb, replacing it with glass. On one occasion, after he was beaten with a piece of lumber, Henry lay semi-conscious for three days before Viola's live-in lover—"Uncle Bernie"—took him to a local hospital for treatment.

Bernie also introduced the boy to bestiality, teaching Henry to kill various animals after they were raped and tortured. At age 15, anxious to try sex with a human being, Lucas picked up a girl near Lynchburg, strangled her when she resisted his clumsy advances, and buried her corpse in the woods near Harrisburg, Virginia. (The March 1951 disappearance of 17-year-old Laura Burnley would remain unsolved for three decades, until Lucas confessed the murder in 1983.)

In June 1954, a series of burglaries around Richmond earned Lucas a six-year prison term. He walked away from a road gang on September 14, 1957, and authorities tracked him to his half-sister's home, in Tecumseh, Michigan, three months later. A second escape attempt, in December 1957, saw Lucas recaptured the same day, and he was discharged from prison on September 2, 1959.

Back in Tecumseh, Henry was furious when his 74-year-old mother turned up on the doorstep, nagging him incessantly with her demands that he return to Blacksburg. Both of them were drinking on the night of January 11, 1960, when she struck him with a broom and Henry struck back with a knife, leaving her dead on the floor. Arrested five days later, in Toledo, Ohio, Lucas confessed to the murder and boasted of raping his mother's corpse, a detail he later retracted as "something I made up." Convicted in March 1960, he drew a term of 20 to 40 years in prison. Two months later, he was transferred to Ionia's state hospital for the criminally insane, where he remained until April 1966. Paroled on June 3, 1970, Lucas went back to Tecumseh and moved in with relatives.

In December 1971, Henry was booked on a charge of molesting two teenaged girls. The charge was reduced to simple kidnapping at his trial, and Lucas went back to the state pen at Jackson. Paroled in August 1975, over his own objections, Henry found brief employment at a Pennsylvania mushroom farm, then married Betty Crawford—the widow of a cousin—in December 1975. Three months later, they moved to Port Deposit, Maryland, and Betty divorced him in the summer of 1977, charging that Lucas molested her daughters by a previous marriage.

Meanwhile, according to Henry's confessions, he had already launched a career of random murder, traveling and killing as the spirit moved him, claiming victims in Maryland and farther afield. In late 1976, he met 29-year-old Ottis Toole at a Jacksonville, Florida, soup kitchen. The homosexual Toole was an arsonist and serial killer in his own right, and they hit it off immediately, swapping grisly tales of their adventures in homicide. Over the next six and a half years, Lucas and Toole were fast friends, occasional lovers and frequent traveling companions, taking their murderous act on the road.

A bachelor once again by 1978, Lucas moved in with Toole's family in Jacksonville. There, he met Toole's niece and nephew, Frieda and Frank Powell, falling slowly in love with the ten-year-old girl who called herself Becky. In 1979, Lucas and Toole were hired by a Jacksonville roofing company, Southeast Color Coat, but they often missed work as they answered the call of the highway. Two years later, after Toole's mother and sister died a few months apart, Becky and Frank were placed in juvenile homes. Lucas helped spring them both, and they made a quartet on the road, Frank Powell witnessing deeds that would drive him into a mental institution by 1983.

Authorities came looking for Becky Powell in January 1982, and she fled westward with Lucas. In Hemet, California, they met Jack and O'Bere Smart, spending four months with the couple as house guests and hired hands, refinishing furniture to earn their keep. In May, O'Bere

Smart had a brainstorm, dispatching Lucas and Powell to care for her 80-year-old mother, Kate Rich, in Ringgold, Texas.

Henry and Becky arrived on May 14, spending four days with Rich and cashing two $50 checks on her bank account before relatives booted them out of the house. Thumbing their way out of town, they were picked up by Ruben Moore and invited to join his religious commune—the All People's House of Prayer—near Stoneburg, Texas. Becky grew homesick in August, and they set off, hitchhiking, on August 23. Camped out that night, in Denton County, they began to quarrel. Becky made the grave mistake of slapping Lucas, and he stabbed her on the spot, dismembering her corpse and scattering its parts around the desert.

Back in Stoneburg the next morning, Lucas explained that Becky had "run off" with a truck driver. Kate Rich dropped from sight three weeks later, on September 16, and police grew suspicious when Lucas left town the next day, his car found abandoned in Needles, California, on September 21. An arsonist burned Rich's home on October 17, and deputies were waiting when Lucas surfaced in Stoneburg the following day. Held on a fugitive warrant from Maryland, he was released when authorities there dropped pending charges of auto theft.

Chafing under sporadic surveillance, Lucas huddled with Ruben Moore on June 4, 1983, declaring an intent to "clear his name" by finding Powell and Rich, wherever they might be. He left a pistol with Moore, for safekeeping, and rolled out of town in a wheezing old junker. Four days later, Moore was summoned to fetch him from San Juan, New Mexico, where his car had given up the ghost. Returning to Stoneburg on June 11, Lucas was jailed as an ex-con possessing a handgun. Four nights later, he summoned the jailer, pressing his face to the bars of his cage as he whispered, "I've done some bad things."

Over the next 18 months, Lucas confessed to a seemingly endless series of murders, bumping his estimated body-count from 75 to 100, then from 150 to 360, tossing in murders by friends and associates to reach a total "way over 500." Ottis Toole, then serving time on a Florida arson charge, was implicated in many of the crimes, and Toole chimed in with more confessions of his own. Some of the crimes, said Lucas, were committed under orders from a nationwide Satanic cult, the "Hand of Death," that he had joined at Toole's request. Toole sometimes ate the flesh of victims they had killed, but Lucas abstained. His reason: "I don't like barbecue sauce."

Detectives from around the country gathered in Monroe, Louisiana, in October 1983, comparing notes and going home convinced that Toole and Lucas were responsible for at least 69 murders. A second conference at Monroe, in January 1984, raised the total to 81. By March 1985, police in 20 states had "cleared" 90 murders for Lucas alone, plus another 108 committed with Toole as an accomplice. Henry stood convicted in nine deaths—including a Texas death sentence on one of the unsolved "I-35 murders"—and he was formally charged with 30 others across the country. Dozens of officers visited Lucas in jail, and he also toured the country under guard, visiting crime scenes, providing details from memory. A California tour, in August 1984, "cleared" 14 unsolved cases. Five months later, in New Orleans, Lucas solved five more. In the first week of April 1985, he led a caravan across the state of Georgia, closing the books on ten murders.

Lucas was barely home from that trip when the storm broke, on April 15. Writing for the Dallas *Times-Herald*, journalist Hugh Aynesworth prepared a series of headline articles, blasting the "massive hoax" that Lucas had perpetrated, misleading homicide investigators and the public, sometimes with connivance from the officers themselves. According to Aynesworth, over-zealous detectives had prompted Lucas with vital bits of information, coaching him through his confessions, deliberately ignoring evidence that placed him miles away from various murder scenes at the crucial moment. From jail, Lucas joined in by recanting his statements across the board. Aside from his mother, he claimed to have slain only two victims—Powell and Rich—in his life. By April 23, he was denying *those* crimes, despite the fact that he led police to Becky's grave, while Rich's bones had been recovered from his stove, at Stoneburg.

From the beginning, officers had been aware of Henry's penchant for exaggeration. One of his first alleged victims, a Virginia schoolteacher, was found alive and well by police. Some of his statements were clearly absurd, including confessions to murders in Spain and Japan, plus delivery of poison to the People's Temple cultists in Guyana. On the other hand, there were also problems with Henry's retraction. Soon after the Aynesworth story broke, Lucas smuggled a letter to authors Jerry Potter and Joel Norris, claiming that he had been drugged and forced to recant. A local minister, close to Lucas since his 1983 "conversion," produced a tape recording of Henry's voice, warning listeners not to believe the new stories emerging from prison.

The most curious part about Henry's new tale was the role of Hugh Aynesworth, himself. In his newspaper series, Aynesworth claimed to have known of the "hoax"—hearing the scheme from Henry's own lips—since October 1983. A month later, on November 9, Aynesworth signed a contract to write Henry's biography. In September 1984, he appeared on the CBS-TV "Nightwatch" program, offering no objections as videotapes of the Lucas confessions were aired. As late as February 1985, Aynesworth published a Lucas interview in *Penthouse* magazine, prompting Henry with leading remarks about Lucas "killing furiously" and claiming victims "all over the country" in the 1970s. Through it all, the *Times-Herald* maintained stony silence, allowing the "hoax" to proceed, while dozens (or hundreds) of killers remained free on the basis of Henry's "false" confessions.

In retrospect, the Aynesworth series smells strongly of sour grapes. A clue to the author's motive is found in his first article, with a passing reference to the fact that Lucas had signed an exclusive publishing contract—with a Waco used-car dealer—shortly after his June 1983 arrest. The prior existence of that contract scuttled Aynesworth's deal, concocted five months later, and prevented him from winning fame as Lucas's biographer. The next best thing, perhaps, would be to foul the waters and prevent competitors from publishing a book about the case. (It is worth noting that Aynesworth omits all mention of his own contract with Lucas, while listing various authors who tried to "cash in" on the "hoax.")

Aynesworth produced an elaborate time-line to support his "fraud" story, comparing Henry's "known movements" with various crimes to discredit police, but the final product is riddled with flaws. Aynesworth rules out numerous murders by placing the Lucas-Toole meeting in 1979, while both killers and numerous independent witnesses describe an earlier meeting, in late 1976. (In fact, Lucas was living with Toole's family in 1978, a year before Aynesworth's acknowledged "first meeting.") The reporter cites pay records from Southeast Color Coat to prove that the killers seldom left Jacksonville, but office manager Eileen Knight recalls that they would often "come and go." (At the same time, Aynesworth places Lucas in West Virginia while he was working in Florida, the same error of which he accuses police.) According to Aynesworth, Lucas spent "all the time" between January and March 1978 with girlfriend Rhonda Knuckles, never leaving her side, but his version ignores the testimony of a surviving witness, tailed by Lucas across 200 miles of Colorado and New Mexico in February of that year. The woman remembers Henry's face—and she recorded his license number for police—but her story is lost in Aynesworth's account. At one point, Aynesworth is so anxious to clear Henry's name that he lists one victim twice on the time-line, murdered on two occasions, four days apart, in July 1981.

Authorities reacted in various ways to Henry's turnaround. Arkansas filed new murder charges against him on April 23, eight days after his change of heart, and other jurisdictions remain unimpressed by his belated pleas of innocence. In Marrero, Louisiana, relatives of victim Ruth Kaiser point out that Lucas confessed to stealing a stereo after he killed the 79-year-old woman: a theft that was never reported and therefore could not have been "leaked" by police. As they recalled, "He described things we had forgotten about, details that never appeared in the paper and that we never put in a police report."

Investigator Jim Lawson, of the Scotts Bluff County sheriff's office, in Nebraska, questioned Lucas in September 1984, regarding the February 1978 murder of schoolteacher Stella McLean. "I purposely tried to trick him several times during the interview," Lawson said, "but to no avail. We even tried to 'feed' him another homicide from our area to see if he was confessing to anything and everything in an effort to build a name for himself, but he denied any participation in the crime."

Commander J.T. Duff, intelligence chief for the Georgia Bureau of Investigation, describes Henry's April 1985 tour thus: "Lucas was not provided with any information or directions to any of the crime scenes, but gave the information to law enforcement. When a crime scene was encountered, Lucas voluntarily and freely gave details that only the perpetrator would have known."

By November 1985, police in 18 states had reopened 90 "Lucas cases," but what of the other 108? And what of the telephone conversation between Lucas, in Texas, and Toole, in Florida, monitored by police in November 1983? At the time, Henry and Ottis had not seen or spoken to each other in at least seven months, deprived of any chance to work up a script, but their dialogue lends chilling support to the later confessions.

LUCAS: Ottis, I don't want you to think I'm doing this as a revenge.

TOOLE: No. I don't want you to hold anything back about me.

LUCAS: See, we got so many of them, Ottis. We got to turn up the bodies. Now, this boy and girl, I don't know anything about.

TOOLE: Well, maybe that's the two I killed my own self. Just like that Mexican that wasn't going to let me out of the house. I took an ax and chopped him all up. What made me—I been meaning to ask you. That time when I cooked some of those people. Why'd I do that?

LUCAS: I think it was just the hands doing it. I know a lot of the things we done, in human sight, are impossible to believe.

Indeed. And yet, the victims *were* dispatched, if not by Toole and Lucas, then by someone else. The truth may never be revealed, but in the meantime, Henry's jailers are convinced of his involvement in at least 100 homicides. (See also: Toole, Ottis)

Lupo, Michael

A former choir boy in his native Italy, Lupo discovered his homosexual tendencies while serving with an elite military unit in the early 1970s. Commando training taught him how to kill bare-handed, and he took the lessons with him when he moved to London, in 1975. Starting out as a hairdresser, Lupo worked his way up to ownership of a styling boutique, buying himself a $300,000 home in Roland Gardens, South Kensington. Along the way, he boasted of liaisons with some 4,000 male lovers, recording the intimate details in numerous journals. The payoff for promiscuity arrived in March 1986, with a positive diagnosis of AIDS, after which Lupo apparently ran amok, indulging his taste for sadomasochism in a violent campaign of revenge against the gay community.

On March 15, 1986, 37-year-old James Burns was prowling leather bars in search of a companion for the night, undeterred by his own diagnosis of AIDS two weeks earlier. Vagrants found his body in a London basement, mutilated with a razor, sodomized and smeared with excrement, his tongue bitten off in the frenzied attack that took his life. Three weeks later, on the afternoon of April 5, AIDS victim Anthony Connolly was found by children playing in a railroad shed, his body slashed and smeared with human offal in a carbon-copy homicide.

Lupo was leaving a gay bar, the night of April 18, when he met an elderly tramp on Hungerford Bridge and something inside of him suddenly "screamed out at the world." Assaulting the stranger, Lupo kicked him in the groin and strangled him on the spot, afterward dumping his body into the Thames. The following day, Lupo met Mark Leyland at Charing Cross, and the men made their way to a public restroom for sex. Once there, Leyland changed his mind, whereupon Lupo produced an iron bar and attacked him. Escaping with his life, Leyland reported the incident as a mugging, later telling the truth to police after Lupo's arrest. (He has since disappeared.) Victim Damien McCluskey was last seen alive, in a Kensington tavern, on April 24, 1986. His body, strangled, raped, and mutilated with a razor, was discovered some time later in a basement flat.

On the night of May 7, Lupo picked up another gay partner, attempting to strangle him with a black nylon stocking, but once more his prey escaped. This time, police received a full report, the victim touring gay bars with an escort to identify the culprit, finally spotting Lupo on the night of May 15. A search of Lupo's home revealed one room converted to a modern torture chamber, and his confiscated diaries were reported to contain the names of many prominent connections. Convicted at his trial in July 1987, Lupo received four life sentences and two terms of seven years each (for attempted murder), with the judge's assurance that in his case, "life meant life." At this writing, Interpol is doublechecking mutilation deaths in Amsterdam, West Berlin, Hamburg, Los Angeles and New York City, seeking connections with Lupo and his various trips abroad.

MacDonald, William

On June 4, 1961, Australian detectives were summoned to the Sydney Domain Baths, where a man's nude, mutilated body had been found beneath the dressing sheds. The victim, Alfred Greenfield, had been stabbed a minimum of 30 times, his genitals hacked off, and homicide investigators pegged the crime as a homosexual assault. Their suspicions were confirmed when the killer left his second victim, William Cobbin, stabbed repeatedly and mutilated in a public restroom at Moore Park.

Investigators were scouring homosexual hangouts, searching for possible witnesses, when a third victim was savaged in suburban Darlinghurst, on March 31, 1962. Frank Mclean was still alive when found, but he died from his wounds a short time later, without providing a description of his killer.

In mid-November, merchants in suburban Concord filed complaints of rancid odors emanating from a shop purchased by William MacDonald two weeks earlier. The new tenant had not been seen since November 4, and searchers were convinced that he had fallen victim to the "Sidney Mutilator" when they found a naked, butchered corpse concealed beneath the shop. The latest victim had been stabbed 41 times, his genitals slashed, but a new twist was added to the case when police examined clothing found beside the body, tracing a laundry mark back to its source. In time, the victim was identified as an Irishman, Patrick Hackett, and the search for William MacDonald resumed.

On April 22, 1963, a former co-worker sighted MacDonald on a Sydney street. A month later, he was traced to his new job, in a Melbourne railway station, where he had been hired as "David Allan." Under questioning, MacDonald confessed his identity along with the series of murders, blaming the crimes on an irresistible compulsion. Traumatized by a homosexual rape in his teens, the slayer was driven to seek revenge against gays selected at random. Sentenced to life on conviction of murder, MacDonald was later transferred to the Morriset Home for the Criminally Insane.

Mackay, Patrick David

Born September 25, 1952, in Middlesex, England, Mackay was the son of a violent, alcoholic father who once kicked his pregnant wife in the stomach while she was carrying Patrick. Ten years old when his father died, Mackay had already established his reputation as a bully, thief, and liar. As a child, he tortured his pets, including cats and rabbits, once roasting a tortoise alive, and his preoccupation with death was manifested in habitual fondling of dead birds. Hauled into juvenile court for setting a Catholic church on fire, Mackay was let off with probation. At thirteen, he was committed to a mental hospital for the first time, after trashing the furniture at home, and assaulting his mother and sisters. Though large for his age—topping six feet in his early teens—Mackay insisted on taking a doll to bed in his hospital room.

By age 15, Mackay had compiled a long record of violent offenses, including the attempted strangulation of his mother and a near-fatal assault on a younger neighborhood boy. Diagnosed by one psychiatrist as a "cold, psychopathic killer," Mackay was released from the asylum a second time against staff recommendations, moving in with two aunts. Drinking heavily and dabbling in drugs, he later tried to strangle one of the women in a drunken rage. On the side, Mackay developed a fascination with Nazism, decorating his bedroom with World War II photos and fixing himself a stormtrooper's uniform. In public, he began to call himself "Franklin Bollvolt the First," imagining himself as a world dictator.

In 1973, Mackay was befriended by a Catholic priest, 63-year-old Father Anthony Crean. He repaid the priest's kindness by burglarizing Crean's home, cashing a stolen check, escaping with a $50 fine on conviction of theft. Police dismissed him as a petty criminal, and they would recognize their grave mistake too late to save an estimated dozen lives.

In July 1973, Mackay killed Heidi Mnilk, an au pair girl, by hurling her from a train near New Cross. That same month, victim Mary Hynes was beaten to death in her Kentish Town apartment. In January 1974, Stephanie Britton and her four-year-old grandson were stabbed to death at Hadley Green, in Hertfordshire. A few days later, Mackay tossed an aging vagrant to his death from Hungerford Bridge. In February 1974, he invaded the Chelsea home of Isabella Griffiths, strangling her to death and plunging a kitchen knife into her stomach. The rash of "unconnected" slayings would be solved with Mackay's confessions, in 1975, but none of the crimes were ever charged against him.

By early 1974, Mackay was living with friends in Finchley, north London, proclaiming himself possessed by demons. Ejected from the house for his bizarre activities, he tried to rob the dwelling out of spite and drew six months in jail on conviction of burglary. By autumn, he had settled into a career of purse-snatching and mugging the elderly, chalking up three more homicides in the process. At Finsbury Park, he bludgeoned a 62-year-old tobacconist to death with a piece of lead pipe. Sarah Rodwell, age 92, was beaten to death on her doorstep in Hackney, robbed of a $10 Christmas bonus. In Southend, cafe proprietress Ivy Davies was slain with an ax.

By March 1975, Mackay was out of control. On March 10, he strangled Adele Price, an elderly widow, in her London apartment. Eleven days later, he invaded the home of Father Crean, in Gravesend, splitting the priest's skull with an ax, stabbing the body repeatedly for good measure. Arrested two days later, he was charged with Crean's murder, convicted, and sentenced to life.

"Mad Butcher of Kingsbury Run, The"

The gully known as Kingsbury Run lies like a scar across the face of downtown Cleveland, Ohio. Sixty feet deep in places, the ancient creek bed is lined with 30-odd pairs of railroad tracks serving local factories and distant cities, bearing cargo to Pittsburgh, Chicago, or Youngstown, whisking commuters to posh bedroom communities like Shaker Heights. During the Depression, Kingsbury Run was also a favorite camp site for hobos, and a playground for children with time on their hands. In the latter 1930s, it became the focal point of America's most fascinating murder mystery—a puzzle that endures to this day—though, in fact, the case had its origins elsewhere, on the shores of Lake Erie.

On September 5, 1934, a driftwood hunter found the lower portion of a woman's torso buried in the sand at Euclid Beach, eight miles east of downtown Cleveland. The victim's legs were severed at the knees, her skin discolored by the application of a chemical preservative. A coroner extrapolated height and age from the pathetic evidence available, but victim number one did not resemble any of Cleveland's known missing women. She was never

identified, police adding insult to injury by their stubborn
refusal to count her as an "official" victim once a pattern
of crime became apparent.

A year later, on September 23, 1935, boys playing in
Kingsbury Run found two headless male bodies, nude but
for stockings worn by the younger victim. Both had been
emasculated, and their severed heads were found nearby.
The older victim, unidentified, had died at least five days
before the younger, and his skin possessed a reddish tinge
from treatment with a chemical preservative. The younger
man, identified as 29-year-old Edward Andrassy, was a
bisexual ex-convict with a long record of petty arrests in
Cleveland. Retraction of the neck muscles on both corpses
pointed to decapitation as the cause of death.

On January 26, 1936, a Cleveland butcher was alerted
to the presence of "some meat in a basket," behind his
shop. Investigating, he was stunned to find two human
thighs, one arm, and the lower half of a woman's torso.
The upper torso, lower legs and missing arm were found
behind a vacant house on February 7, several blocks away,
but fingerprints had already identified the victim as Florence Polillo, a 41-year-old prostitute. Her severed head
was never found.

Four months later, on June 5, two boys found the severed head of a man in Kingsbury Run, a mile from the
spot where Andrassy and his nameless companion were
found in September 1935. Railroad workers found the
matching body on June 6, but the victim number five remained anonymous, despite publication of numerous distinctive tattoos. His fingerprints were not on file in
Cleveland, and he had not been reported missing.

On July 22, 1936, the naked, headless body of an unknown man was found beside Big Creek, in the suburb of
Brooklyn, across town from Kingsbury Run. The only victim slain on Cleveland's southwest side, this new "John
Doe" would also be the only victim killed where he was
found. Decomposition foiled all efforts to identify the
corpse.

A hobo spotted number seven—or, a portion of him—
in Kingsbury Run, on September 10, 1936. The dismembered remains were floating in a stagnant pond, and police

divers were called to retrieve two halves of a torso, plus the lower legs and thighs. The severed head, along with arms and genitals, was never found. Decapitation had not been the cause of death, but medical examiners could not identify another cause.

Soon after the discovery of victim number seven, Detectives Peter Merylo and Martin Zalewski were assigned to the "torso" case full-time. Over the next two years, they investigated hundreds of leads, cleared scores of innocent suspects, jailed dozens of perverts and fugitives— all without bagging their man. The press, meanwhile, ran banner headlines on the futile search for Cleveland's "Mad Butcher," speculating endlessly on motives, the identity of victims, and the killer's supposed surgical skill.

On February 23, 1937, the upper half of a woman's torso was found at Euclid Beach, almost precisely where the first (and unacknowledged) victim was discovered in September 1934. The lower trunk was found in Lake Erie, off East 30th Street, on May 5, while the head, arms, and legs remained forever missing.

On June 6, the skeleton of a black woman—missing one rib, plus the bones of arms and legs—was found beneath the Lorain-Carnegie Bridge. The victim was decapitated, and Coroner Samuel Gerber placed her death some time in early June of 1936. In April 1938, the son of Rose Wallace "identified" his mother's remains on the basis of dental work, but problems remained. Wallace had disappeared in August 1936, two months after the victim's estimated date of death, and her Cincinnati dentist was also deceased, his files destroyed, rendering positive identification impossible. Detective Merylo accepted the shaky I.D., but it brought him no closer to the arrest of a suspect.

Exactly one month after number nine was found, the lower torso of a man was sighted in the Cuyahoga River, underneath the Third Street Bridge. Police retrieved the upper trunk and severed thighs that afternoon, and other pieces surfaced in the days to come. By July 14, authorities had everything except the nameless victim's head, and that was never found.

On April 8, 1938, a woman's lower left leg was fished

out of the Cuyahoga, behind Public Square. The missing left foot, both thighs, and two halves of the torso were hauled ashore, wrapped in burlap, on May 2, but the victim's head, right leg, and arms remained at large.

The last "official" victims—male and female, killed at different times—were found on August 16, 1938, by workmen at a lakeside rubbish dump. The new "John Doe" was nothing but a skeleton, decapitated in familiar style, missing two ribs, plus both hands and feet. Murdered no later than February 1938, he might have died as early as December 1937. The female victim was cut into nine pieces, but all were accounted for. She had been killed some time between February and April 1938, her identity forever disguised by advanced decomposition.

In January 1939, the Cleveland *Press* reprinted this letter mailed from Los Angeles:

Chief of Police Matowitz:

You can rest easy now, as I have come to sunny California for the winter. I felt bad operating on those people, but science must advance. I shall astound the medical profession, a man with only a D.C.

What did their lives mean in comparison to hundreds of sick and disease-twisted bodies? Just laboratory guinea pigs found on any public street. No one missed them when I failed. My last case was successful. I know now the feeling of Pasteur, Thoreau and other pioneers.

Right now I have a volunteer who will absolutely prove my theory. They call me mad and a butcher, but the truth will out.

I have failed but once here. The body has not been found and never will be, but the head, minus the features, is buried on Century Boulevard, between Western and Crenshaw. I feel it my duty to dispose of the bodies as I do. It is God's will not to let them suffer. (Signed) "X"

No buried heads were found in Los Angeles, and the manhunt shifted back to Cleveland. On July 5, 1939, sheriff's deputies arrested a Slavic immigrant, 52-year-old

Frank Dolezal, and launched a marathon interrogation of their suspect. Dolezal eventually confessed to murdering Andrassy and Polillo, fumbling numerous details that were "corrected" in later "confessions." He later retracted his statements, charging detectives with third-degree tactics, and suspicious stains found in his flat were identified as animal blood. On August 24, Dolezal "hanged himself" in his cell, suspended from a wall hook shorter than he was, and the autopsy revealed four ribs broken by beatings in jail. Today, no one regards him seriously as a suspect in the "torso" case.

On May 3, 1940, three male corpses were discovered in abandoned box cars at McKees Rocks, Pennsylvania, outside Pittsburgh. All had been decapitated, and the heads were missing; one was otherwise intact, while two had been dissected at the hips and shoulders. Killed in the cars where they lay, the men had been dead from three to six months, and all three bodies had been scorched by fire. The most "complete" victim was identified as 30-year-old James Nicholson, a homosexual ex-convict from Wisconsin. The killer had carved the word "NAZI" on Nicholson's chest, inverting the "Z" by accident or design. Authorities unanimously blamed the crimes on Cleveland's butcher, tracing movements of the box cars to pinpoint the murders in Youngstown, Ohio, during December 1939.

In *4 Against the Mob,* journalist Oscar Fraley contends that Eliot Ness—then Cleveland's director of public safety—not only identified the Butcher in 1938, but also brought him to a semblance of justice. Dubbed "Gaylord Sundheim," in defense against libel suits, the suspect was described as a homosexual pre-med student and member of a prominent Cleveland family. Interrogated by Ness in autumn 1938, "Sundheim" escaped prosecution by committing himself to a mental hospital where he died around 1940 or '41. In the interim, he tormented Ness with a barrage of obscene, menacing notes, that terminated with his death.

The tale deserves consideration, inasmuch as Ness preserved the "greeting cards"—all carefully anonymous—and they are viewable in Cleveland archives. But, do taunting notes provide a viable solution in the torso murders? Why did experts on the case insist the Butcher claimed three victims in December 1939, when "Sundheim" had been out of circulation for a year or more? If Ness was certain of the killer's whereabouts, why did he allow "suspect" Frank Dolezal to be abused (and possibly murdered) by sheriff's officers in 1939? If the case was solved in 1938, why did Detective Merylo pursue the Butcher into retirement, blaming his elusive quarry for 50-odd murders by 1947? Tantalizing as it is, the Fraley story falls apart on close examination, failing every test of common sense.

There is a grisly post script to the Butcher's story. On July 23, 1950, a man's headless body, emasculated and dismembered, was found in a Cleveland lumber yard, a few miles from Kingsbury Run. The missing head turned up four days later, and the victim was identified as Robert Robertson. Coroner Samuel Gerber, responsible for handling most of the Butcher's "official" victims, reported that "The work resembles exactly that of the torso murderer."

In retrospect, it is clear that the headhunter murdered at least 16 victims between 1934 and 1939. He may have slaughtered the 1950 victim, as well, and speculation links the Butcher with a series of decapitation murders around New Castle, Pennsylvania, between 1925 and 1939. No firm connections were established in that case, and the number of New Castle victims has been widely inflated by sensational journalists, but the crimes were committed in close proximity to rail lines serving Cleveland and Youngstown. None of the New Castle victims were ever identified, and the identity of their killer—like the whereabouts of the Butcher's eight trophy heads—remains a mystery.

Manson, Charles Milles

Born "no name Maddox" in Cincinnati, Ohio, on November 12, 1934, Manson was the illegitimate son of Kathleen Maddox, a 16-year-old prostitute. His surname was derived from one of Kathleen's many lovers, whom she briefly married, but it signified no blood connection. During 1936, Kathleen filed a paternity suit against one "Colonel Scott," of Ashland, Kentucky, winning the grand monthly sum of five dollars for the support of "Charles Milles Manson." Scott instantly defaulted on the judgment, and he died in 1954, without acknowledging his son.

In 1939, Kathleen and her brother were sentenced to five years in prison for robbing a West Virginia gas station. Charles was packed off to live with a strictly religious aunt and her sadistic husband, who constantly berated the boy as a "sissy," dressing him in girl's clothing for his first day of school in an effort to help Manson "act like a man." Paroled in 1942, Maddox reclaimed her son, but she was clearly unsuited to motherhood. An alcoholic tramp who brought home lovers of both sexes, Kathleen frequently left Charles with neighbors "for an hour," then disappeared for days or weeks on end, leaving relatives to track the boy down. On one occasion, she reportedly gave Charles to a barmaid, in payment for a pitcher of beer.

By 1947, Kathleen was seeking a foster home for her son, but none was available. Charles wound up in the Gibault School for Boys, in Terre Haute, Indiana, but fled after ten months, rejoining his mother. She still didn't want him, and so Manson took to living on the streets, making his way by theft. Arrested in Indiana, he escaped from the local juvenile center after one day's confinement. Recaptured and sent to Father Flanagan's Boy's Town, he lasted four days before his next escape, fleeing in a stolen car to visit relatives in Illinois. He pulled more robberies en route and on arrival, leading to another bust at age 13. Confined for three years in a reform school at Plainfield, Indiana, Manson recalls sadistic abuse by older boys and guards alike. If we may trust his memory, at least one guard incited other boys to rape and torture Manson, while the officer stood by and masturbated on the sidelines.

In February 1951, Manson and two other inmates escaped from the Plainfield "school," fleeing westward in a series of stolen cars. Arrested in Beaver, Utah, Manson was sentenced to federal time for driving hot cars across state lines. Starting off in a minimum-security establishment, Manson assaulted another inmate in January 1952, holding a razor blade to the boy's throat and sodomizing him. Reclassified as "dangerous," Manson was transferred to a tougher lockup, logging eight major disciplinary infractions—including three homosexual assaults—by August 1952. He was moved to the Chilicothe, Ohio, reformatory a month later, and suddenly turned over a new leaf, becoming a "model" prisoner almost overnight. The cunning act was rewarded by parole in May 1954.

Arrested a second time for driving hot cars interstate, in September 1955, Manson got off easy with five years probation. He celebrated by skipping a court date in Florida, on pending charges of auto theft, and his probation was promptly revoked. Picked up in Indianapolis on March 14, 1956, he was sent to the federal prison at Terminal Island, California, winning parole on September 30, 1958. Seven months later, on May 1, 1959, he was jailed in Los Angeles, on charges of forging and cashing stolen U.S. Treasury checks. Once more, he escaped with probation, swiftly revoked with his April 1960 arrest for pimping and transporting whores interstate. Entering the lock-up at McNeil Island, Manson listed his religion as "Scientologist"; his IQ was tested at 121. Paroled on March 21, 1967, over his own objections, Manson was drawn to San Francisco and the teeming Haight-Ashbury district.

It was the "Summer of Love," when thousands of young people flocked to the banner of drugs and "flower power," heeding Timothy Leary's advice to "tune in, turn on, drop out." The streets and crash-pads overflowed with teenage runaways and drifters, seeking insight on the world and on themselves. Behind the scenes, a minor army of manipulators—gurus, outlaw bikers, pushers, pimps and Satanists—stood ready to squeeze a grim profit from the Age of Aquarius.

In San Francisco, Manson displayed a surprising charisma, attracting young drop-outs of both sexes, drawn from all strata of white society. Some, like Mary Brunner, were college graduates. Others, like Susan Atkins and Robert Beausoleil, were involved with Satanic cults. Most were hopelessly confused about their lives, adopting Manson as a combination mentor, father-figure, lover, Christ incarnate, and the self-styled "God of Fuck." They drifted up and down the state in fluctuating numbers, with the "family" topping fifty members at its peak. From Mendocino and the Haight to Hollywood, Los Angeles, Death Valley, Manson's nomads followed their leader as the Summer of Love became a nightmare. Along the way, they rubbed shoulders with the Church of Satan, the Process Church of Final Judgment (worshipping Satan, Lucifer and Jehovah simultaneously), the Circe Order of Dog Blood, and—some say—the homicidal "Four Pi Movement." Manson grew obsessed with death and "Helter Skelter," his interpretation of a Beatles song predicting race war in America. In Manson's view, once "blackie" had been driven to a point of violence, helpless whites would be annihilated, leaving Manson and his family to rule the roost.

On October 13, 1968, two women were found beaten and strangled to death near Ukiah, California. One, Nancy Warren, was the pregnant wife of a highway patrol officer. The other victim, Clida Delaney, was Warren's 64-year-old grandmother. The murders were ritualistic in nature, with 36 leather thongs wrapped around each victim's throat, and several members of the Manson "family"— including two later convicted of unrelated murders—were visiting Ukiah at the time.

Two months later, on December 30, 17-year-old Marina Habe was abducted outside her West Hollywood home, her body recovered on New Year's Day, with multiple stab wounds in the neck and chest. Investigators learned that Habe was friendly with various "family" members, and police believe her ties with the Manson group led directly to her death.

On May 27, 1969, 64-year-old Darwin Scott—the brother of Manson's alleged father—was hacked to death in his Ashland, Kentucky, apartment, pinned to the floor by a long butcher knife. Manson was out of touch with his California parole officer between May 22 and June 18, 1969, and an unidentified "LSD preacher from California" set up shop with several young women, in nearby Huntington, around the same time.

On July 17, 1969, 16-year-old Mark Walts disappeared while hitchhiking from Chatsworth, California, to the pier at Santa Monica, to do some fishing. His battered body, shot three times and possibly run over by a car, was found next morning in Topanga Canyon. Walts was a frequent visitor to Manson's commune at the Spahn movie ranch, and the dead boy's brother publicly accused Manson of the murder, though no charges were filed.

Around the time of Walts' death, a "Jane Doe" corpse was discovered near Castaic, northeast of the Spahn ranch, tentatively identified from articles of clothing as Susan Scott, a "family" member once arrested with a group of Manson girls in Mendocino. Scott was living at the ranch when she dropped out of sight, and while the Castaic corpse remains technically unidentified, Susan has not been seen again.

In the month between July 27 and August 26, 1969, Manson's tribe slaughtered at least nine persons in Southern California. Musician Gary Hinman was the first to die, hacked to death in retaliation for a drug deal gone sour, "political" graffiti scrawled at the scene in his blood, as Manson tried to blame the crime on "blackie." On August 9, a Manson hit team raided the home of movie director Roman Polanski, slaughtering Polanski's wife—pregnant actress Sharon Tate—and four of her guests: Abigail Folger, Jay Sebring, Voytek Frykowski, and Steven Parent. The following night, Manson's "creepy crawlers" killed and mutilated another couple, Leno and Rosemary LaBianca, in their Los Angeles home.

An atmosphere of general panic gripped affluent L.A., the grisly crimes demonstrating that no one was safe. On August 16, sheriff's deputies raided the Spahn ranch, arresting Manson and company on various drug-related charges, but Charles was back on the street by August 26. That night, he directed the murder and dismemberment of movie stuntman Donald "Shorty" Shea, a hanger-on who "knew too much" and was suspected of discussing family business with people.

Ironically, Manson's downfall came about through a relatively petty crime. On the night of September 18-19, 1969, members of the family burned a piece of road-grading equipment that was "obstructing" one of their desert dune buggy routes. Arson investigators traced the evidence to Manson, and he was arrested again on October 12. A day later, Susan Atkins was picked up in Ontario, California, and she soon confided details of the Tate-LaBianca murders to cellmates in Los Angeles. Sweeping indictments followed, but even Manson's removal from circulation could not halt the violence.

On November 5, 1969, family member John Haught—alias "Zero"—was shot and killed while "playing Russian roulette" in Venice, California. Eleven days later, another "Jane Doe"—tentatively identified as family associate Sherry Cooper—was found near the site where Marina Habe's body had been discovered in 1968. On November 21, Scientologists James Sharp, 15, and Doreen Gaul, 19, were found dead in a Los Angeles alley, stabbed more than 50 times each with a long-bladed knife. Investigators learned that Gaul had been a girlfriend of Bruce Davis, a family member subsequently convicted of first-degree murder in L.A.

And Manson's arm was long. Joel Pugh, husband of Mansonite Sandra Good, flew to London in late 1968, accompanied by Bruce Davis. Their mission included the sale of some rare coins and the establishment of connections with Satanic orders in Britain. Davis returned to the United States in April 1969, but Pugh lingered on, and his body was found in a London hotel room on December 1, his throat slit with razor blades, his blood used to inscribe "backwards writing" and "comic book drawings" on a nearby mirror.

Charged with the seven Tate-LaBianca murders, Manson and three of his female disciples—Susan Atkins, Patricia Krenwinkel, and Leslie Van Houten—went to trial in June 1970. The defense rested its case on November 19, and attorney Ronald Hughes disappeared eight days later, after he was driven to Sespe Hot Springs by two family associates called "James" and "Lauren." The lawyer's decomposing corpse was found in Sespe Creek five months later, around the time Manson's death sentence was announced, and positive identification was confirmed through dental X-rays.

Prosecutor Vincent Bugliosi believes that he has traced the fate of "James" and "Lauren," suspected of guilty knowledge in Hughes's death. On November 8, 1972, hikers found the body of 26-year-old James Willett, shotgunned and decapitated, in a shallow grave near Guerneville, California. Three days later, Willett's station wagon was spotted outside a house in Stockton, and police arrested two members of the Aryan Brotherhood inside, along with three Manson women. Lauren Willett, wife of James, was buried in the basement, and an initial tale of "Russian roulette" was dropped in April 1973, when four of the suspects pled guilty to murder charges.

Meanwhile, the Manson trials continued in Los Angeles. Trigger man Charles "Tex" Watson was convicted and sentenced to die for the Tate-LaBianca murders in 1971. During August of that year, six family members—including original disciple Mary Brunner—tried to steal 140 weapons from a Hawthorne gunshop, planning to break Manson out of jail, but they were captured in a shootout with police. All were subsequently convicted, and Brunner was also sentenced for participation in the Hinman murder. Robert Beausoleil and Susan Atkins picked up additional death sentences for that slaying, while Manson, Bruce Davis, and Steve Grogan were convicted in both the Hinman and Shea murders. Various death sentences were overturned by the U.S. Supreme Court in 1972, and all of the family hackers are now technically eligible for parole.

In Manson's absence, Lynette "Squeaky" Fromme held the family reins, corresponding with Charlie in prison and spreading his gospel on the streets, forging new alliances with sundry cults and racist groups. In September 1975, she tried to assassinate President Gerald Ford, but her pistol misfired, and Squeaky was sentenced to life imprisonment. Family remnants survive to the present day, and members have been linked with groups promoting child pornography and sexual abuse, as well as rumored human sacrifice.

Maxwell, Bobby Joe

Los Angeles police were still recovering from jibes about the "Skid Row Slasher" case when transients in their city started falling prey to yet another random slayer. Knives were favored once again, and there was a suggestion of familiar ritual about the murders, with the name of Satan scrawled in blood, on cardboard, near one victim's body. Newsmen dubbed their latest maniac the "Skid Row Stabber," to avoid confusion, and before his ultimate arrest, he proved himself as lethally prolific as his predecessor.

Jesse Martinez, age 50, was the stabber's first victim, found in a skid row parking lot on the morning of October 23, 1978. Five days later, 32-year-old Jose Cortez was knifed to death in an alley, followed by 46-year-old Bruce Drake on October 30, J.P. Henderson, age 65, was found sprawled on a sidewalk, in the predawn hours of November 4. Five days later, taking a leaf from the old Slasher's book, 39-year-old David Jones was killed on a walkway of L.A.'s Central Library. Francisco Rodriguez, 57, and 36-year-old Frank Reed were both found in parking lots, killed on November 11 and 12, respectively. The second victim in a double-header on November 12, 49-year-old Augustine Luna was stabbed to death behind a building on South Main Street. Jimmie White Buffalo, a 34-year-old Indian, became the ninth victim five days later, stabbed repeatedly in the upper torso with a long-bladed knife, his body dumped in a parking lot.

Thus far, the Stabber's victims had been claimed within an area of fifteen blocks, and there were no survivors. That changed on November 20, when transients Jose Ramirez, 27, and Ricardo Seja, 24, were wounded in separate attacks, detectives admitting a "strong likelihood" of the Stabber's involvement. If they needed a motive, it could be found on the wall of a downtown bus station: "I'm Luther. I kill winos to put them out of their misery." On Thanksgiving Day, 45-year-old derelict Frank Garcia was stabbed to death on a bench in City Hall Plaza, less than 200 feet from the entrance of L.A. police headquarters. A latent palmprint was recovered from the bench, but it was useless to authorities without a suspect for comparison.

Two months later, 34-year-old Bobby Maxwell was arrested while standing over a skid row derelict, clutching a ten-inch dagger in his hand. Pleading guilty on misdemeanor weapons charges, he was sentenced to 60 days in jail while police pressed their investigation of the most promising suspect to date. A Tennessee native, Maxwell had served time for robbery in the Volunteer State, and cellmates recalled his devotion to Satan—whom Maxwell called "Luther." A search of his flat turned up knives compatible with nine of the Stabber slayings, and Maxwell's palm print matched the latent print recovered from the bench where Frank Garcia died. Charged with ten counts of murder and five counts of robbery in May 1979, Maxwell smilingly confided to another prisoner that he had killed the derelicts in order "to obtain souls for Satan."

Legal wrangling delayed Maxwell's trial until January 1984, and testimony took another seven months, leaving jurors divided in their opinions of his guilt. On July 12, Maxwell was convicted of murdering Frank Garcia and David Jones; he was also acquitted of three murder counts, with jurors failing to reach a decision on five homicides. In Bobby's case, two did the trick, and he received a term of life imprisonment.

McCrary Family, The

On June 16, 1972, a Santa Barbara police officer was shot and wounded by a gunman fleeing the scene of an $11,000 supermarket robbery. Witnesses recalled the license number of the bandit's car, and it was traced to an address in suburban Goleta, occupied by 47-year-old Sherman McCrary, his wife Carolyn, and their 19-year-old son Danny. Evidence pointed to McCrary's son-in-law, 38-year-old Raymond Carl Taylor, as the trigger man in the robbery, and he was arrested days later, at his mother's home in Athens, Texas.

In custody, Taylor and Sherman McCrary pled guilty to

three local robberies—the others netting $23,000 and $12,000, respectively—and they were handed prison terms of five years to life. Carolyn McCrary, son Danny and daughter Ginger Taylor each drew nine months for harboring fugitives, but investigators soon realized they were only glimpsing the tip of a sinister iceberg. Between August 1971 and February 1972, the nomadic McCrarys were finally linked with a total of 22 kidnap-murders, ranging from Florida to Southern California.

Alcoholic Sherman McCrary blamed his first Texas robberies on a back injury, resulting in chronic unemployment. Later, he recruited son-in-law Carl Taylor for the "family business," with both men spending time in jail on charges of robbery, burglary, and forgery. When the heat got too strong around Athens, Texas, they pulled up stakes and started drifting in August 1971, settling in Goleta eight months later, using the proceeds from various holdups to purchase a home in the middle-class suburb.

Their first known victim was 17-year-old Sheri Martin, kidnapped from Salt Lake City in August 12, 1971, after a bakery holdup that netted the family $200. Martin's body was found a month later, near Wendover, Nevada, where she had been raped and shot to death by her abductors.

On August 20, the McCrary's invaded Denver, looting a suburban shop and snatching employee Leeora Looney. Three days later and 200 miles away, her naked, violated body was discovered by police. She had been executed with the same .32-caliber weapon used to kill Sheri Martin in Nevada.

The same pistol was used in Lubbock, Texas, on September 28, when the McCrarys robbed a restaurant at closing time, abducting waitress Elizabeth Perryman. Her skeleton and scattered clothes were found by a farmer on December 19, her identity confirmed from dental records.

On October 17, Forrest and Jena Covey disappeared from their grocery store in Mesquite, Texas, the shop looted for money and cartons of cigarettes. Three days later, 16-year-old Susan Shaw was abducted from a bakery two blocks away, her ravaged body pulled from a nearby lake on October 24. The Coveys were found that same day, bound and shot with the familiar .32-caliber pistol in a barn near Quinlan, Texas.

The McCrary men and Raymond Taylor were indicted for Leeora Looney's murder, and forensic evidence established firm connections with eleven other deaths. FBI evaluation of the family's normal *modus operandi* made the killers suspect in at least ten other cases, most involving victims who were raped, but Carolyn McCrary and her daughter saw no reason to complain. "I love my husband very much," Ginger told interviewers from jail, "and it never occurred to me to do anything other than to stay with him."

Mengel, Alex J.

On the evening of February 24, 1985, Westchester County police officer Gary Stymiloski notified headquarters that he was making a routine traffic stop in Yonkers, New York. Moments later, after spotting shotgun shells in the car, Stymiloski radioed for support. Reinforcements arrived in time to find him dying, in his cruiser, with a single bullet in his brain.

The suspect vehicle was found abandoned in the Bronx and traced to Alex Mengel, age 30, an immigrant from Guyana who entered the United States in November 1976. A tool and die maker by trade, Mengel had logged one arrest—for assaulting his ex-wife—in 1984. Investigators learned that Mengel was returning from a weekend's shooting in the Catskills, traveling with friends, when Stymiloski flagged him down for speeding. Two of his companions, held in custody as material witnesses, agreed that the shooting was senseless and unprovoked, leading to issuance of a murder warrant on February 27.

Three days later, in Toronto, local officers spotted Mengel outside a shopping mall. The fugitive crashed his car into a wall while trying to escape, then swerved into a dead-end street where he was cornered and arrested. The stolen vehicle was registered to Beverly Capone, an IBM computer programmer reported missing by her family, in Mount Vernon, New York, on February 26. Two pistols and a woman's scalp were found inside the car; ballistics tests established that one of the guns had been used to kill Officer Stymiloski in Yonkers.

On March 4, while Mengel fought extradition from Canada, New York state police found items belonging to Beverly Capone in a Catskills summer cabin near Durham. Eleven days later, the woman's remains were discovered in heavy woods a half-mile from the cabin; she had been stabbed once in the chest, her scalp and the skin of her face sliced away by her killer. Tissue samples from the body made a positive match with the scalp recovered from Capone's car in Toronto.

With the new evidence in hand, authorities linked Mengel with the attempted abduction of a 13-year-old girl in Skaneateles, New York, southwest of Syracuse, on February 27. The child was delivering papers when a stranger, wearing lipstick and an ill-fitting wig, tried to snatch her off the street. Escaping without injury, she agreed with detectives that the "wig" might just as well have been a woman's scalp.

On March 26, Canadian authorities ordered Mengel's deportation to New York as an illegal alien with insufficient money to support himself. Two days later, a grand jury in Westchester County indicted Mengel for first-degree murder in the slaying of Officer Stymiloski. Greene County followed suit on April 8, charging the prisoner with second-degree murder in the case of Beverly Capone.

On April 26, returning under guard from his arraignment in Greene County, Mengel tried to escape from his state police escort on the Taconic State Parkway. Undaunted by handcuffs and chains, he grappled with one guard, seizing the officer's sidearm, and was killed by the driver before he could squeeze off a shot.

Miller, John Lawrence

A native of Los Angeles, born in 1942, Miller was convicted of auto theft and confined to a California reform school at age 15. His parents paid a visit to the school on November 11, 1957, and were allowed to take John home for Sunday dinner, but he slipped away from them that night and disappeared. Next morning, 22-month-old Laura Wetzel was found beaten to death in her crib, at the family home in Rolling Hills. Neighbors identified Miller as the boy who threatened them with a gun the previous night, and he was arrested in Reno on November 15, driving a car stolen from Redondo Beach.

Miller confessed to the crime, telling police, "I wanted to know how it would feel . . . but I'm sorry about it now, of course." Convicted of murder, he spent 17 years in prison before his parole, in August 1975. Two months later, on October 23, Miller shot both his parents at their home, in Long Beach. His father survived long enough to reach a neighbor's house, and Miller was soon arrested, convicted of double murder and sentenced to life imprisonment.

"Missing and Dead Case"
—El Paso, TX

El Paso, like so many other cities in America, has seen its share of runaways in recent years. With drugs and broken homes, the promise of excitement to be found in other cities, other states, uncounted teens have fled their homes and schools to search for fame and fortune on the road. A few make good, some wander back in time, but nearly all leave tokens of themselves behind, some indication of their motive for departure. During 1987, though, a rash of disappearances around El Paso baffled parents and police as normal, well-adjusted girls and women dropped from sight, without a trace.

Fourteen-year-old Marjorie Knox was the first to go, reported missing from nearby Chaparral, New Mexico, on February 14, 1987. Three weeks later, on March 7, 13-year-old Melissa Alaniz vanished from El Paso, police noting that both girls had parents working at the Rockwell plant, outside of town. Desiree Wheatly, 15, disappeared in El Paso on June 7, last seen in the company of a man with heavily-tattooed arms.

Three days later, Karen Baker's disappearance seemed to break the pattern. At 20, she was a legal adult, but police learned that her mother worked in the same Rockwell plant, with a nodding acquaintance to Marjorie Knox. Was there some hidden link between the missing girls, thus far unknown to the police?

On June 28, 19-year-old Cheryl Vasquez-Dismukes vanished from El Paso, followed on July 3 by 17-year-old Angela Frausto. Maria Casio, age 24, was staying with friends when she failed to come home on the night of August 19. They reported her missing next day, and her car was found on August 21, without a trace of the missing woman. On August 28, 14-year-old Dawn Smith left her El Paso home, promising to "keep in touch," and abruptly dropped out of sight.

On September 4, utility workers unearthed Maria Casio's remains in the desert northwest of El Paso. Police were summoned to the scene, and they soon found Karen Baker buried in a shallow grave 100 yards away. With no obvious wounds on either body, the cause of death for both victims was listed as "apparent strangulation." On October 20, 1987, hikers found the remains of Desiree Wheatly and Dawn Smith within a mile of the other grave sites. Two weeks later, desert prospectors found Angela Frausto in a nearby shallow grave. Marjorie Knox, Melissa Alaniz and Cheryl Vasquez-Dismukes are still missing, but all are now presumed dead by authorities.

Police, meanwhile, have focused their attention on a suspect in the case. On September 19, 1987, an El Paso prostitute complained to police that one of her "tricks" had driven her into the desert, near the grave sites, where he pulled a knife and threatened her before she fled on foot. Another hooker, raped some weeks before, came forward after the report was published, both women remarking on their assailant's numerous tattoos. A search of police tattoo files led to the October 22 arrest of David Leonard Wood, an ex-convict with a history of violence against females. Born in 1957, Wood logged his first arrest at 19, for the attempted rape of a 12-year-old girl. In court, he pled guilty to a reduced charge of indecency with a minor and spent three years in prison, paroled in January

1980. Four months later, he raped a 13-year-old stranger and a 19-year-old acquaintance, the latter mistake earning him concurrent prison terms of 20 years on each charge. He was paroled again in January 1987, days before El Paso's string of deaths and disappearances began.

Wood denies any involvement in the spate of murders, and he has never been charged in the case. (Conviction of kidnapping and rape, in March 1988, has returned him to prison with a new 50-year sentence.) In the absence of an indictment, authorities note that Woods—and his tattoos—perfectly match descriptions of the man last seen with Desiree Wheatly in June 1987. He was also seen riding a motorcycle with Karen Baker, several months before she died, and witnesses have placed Woods at a local convenience store where Cheryl Vasquez-Dismukes was last seen alive on June 28. (Wood admits hearing "rumors" that Cheryl's family suspected him of her murder, and claims he "went searching" for her, all in vain.) Finally, friends of Wood have identified photos of Maria Casio and Dawn Smith as friends of the suspect, a claim Wood dismisses as simple "mistaken identity."

Hanging tough in the face of mounting suspicion, Wood granted an interview to local journalists in March 1988, prior to his sentencing on the kidnap and rape charges. Avoiding the question of guilt or innocence, he harped on the killer's apparent carelessness in disposing of victims. "If I am going to kill somebody," he declared, "I'm going to put them 15 feet under, up in the mountains, where the coyotes can't get to them."

Mitchell, Roy

On May 7, 1922, William Driskell, a cotton buyer and part-time deputy constable in Waco, Texas, was axed to death in his own garage, robbed of his pistol, his watch, and a ring. It seemed to be a clear-cut case of robbery gone wrong, but homicide investigators had no clues, and they were getting nowhere when the killer struck again.

Harvey Bolton, 21 years old, was parking with his girl-friend outside Waco, on May 25, when a black man emerged from some nearby bushes, brandishing a pistol. The gunman shot Bolton three times, killing him instantly, then dragged the woman out and raped her on the ground. Next day, the victim fingered Jesse Thomas as her rapist, and he was shot to death by the young woman's father, his body carried downtown and publicly burned by a lunch mob. Unfortunately for Thomas—and for Waco—the woman had made a mistake, deceived by her own hysteria and a conviction that "all blacks look alike."

On November 20, 19-year-old Grady Skipworth was parked near "Lover's Leap," in Cameron Park, with his girlfriend, Naomi Boucher. Suddenly, a black man rushed at their car from the darkness, killing Skipworth with a shotgun blast to the head, dragging his body out of the car and tossing it over the cliff. The killer returned, wrestling Naomi from the vehicle and pushing her over the precipice, but a tree broke her fall, and she survived with only superficial injuries. Once more, an innocent black was accused, but Waco had learned its lesson. An all-white jury acquitted the suspect, despite Boucher's identification, and he was released in a storm of applause from the court.

On January 10, 1923, a black gunman leaped onto the running board of a car passing through Cameron Park, jabbing a shotgun through the passenger's window, but he was knocked to the ground without firing a shot. He left behind a checkered cap, delivered to police as evidence, but nearly three weeks would elapse before its owner was identified.

Meanwhile, on January 20, W.E. Holt and Ethel Denecamp were parked five miles from Waco when a gunman materialized out of the shadows, killing Holt with a shot to the head, beating Denecamp to death and dumping her body in a nearby field. Their car was recovered in Waco next morning, abandoned by the killer on a city street.

Detectives got their break when a witness identified the checkered cap's owner as 30-year-old Roy Mitchell, a Louisiana native currently living in Waco. Mitchell was arrested January 30, on a gambling charge, and a search of his home turned up William Driskell's handgun and holster, along with a watch stolen from Grady Skipworth. After three days in jail, Mitchell confessed to five murders, recanting the statement before his trial in March 1923. Convicted on all counts and sentenced to die, he was hanged on July 30, 1923, before a cheering crowd of 8,000 spectators.

"Monster of Florence, The"

The countryside surrounding Florence, Italy, has long been favored as a prime vacation spot for campers, hikers, nature-lovers. In the summer months, warm breezes, starry skies, and rolling meadows make the area a perfect trysting spot for lovers, honeymooners, couples seeking to rekindle a romantic flame in their relationships. In recent years, however, Florence has acquired a different sort of reputation on the side, as the selected hunting ground of a sadistic killer who prefers to prey on couples, randomly selecting victims for a yearly sacrifice of blood. Two decades after the commencement of the terror, homicide detectives have no suspect, no substantial clues.

The Florence slayer's first appearance was recorded on August 21, 1968, when Barbara Locci and her adulterous lover, Antonio Lo Bianco, were shot to death as they lay in the front seat of an automobile, parked beside a rural lane. In the back seat, the dead woman's six-year-old son slept through the murder undisturbed, suggesting that the killer may have used a silencer. Despite the lack of any solid evidence, the crime appeared routine to local homicide investigators, and Locci's husband was convicted in a hasty trial. Six years elapsed before his innocence was proven, as the killer struck again.

The second set of victims, slain in September 1974, were shot with the same .22-caliber Beretta automatic pistol used in 1968; once more, the gunman used distinctive copper-jacketed Winchester bullets, manufactured in Australia during the 1950s. Unlike the first crime, however, this time the female victim was sexually mutilated after death, a grim addition that became the Florence slayer's trademark.

Another long hiatus in the murders followed, broken in June and October 1981, when two more couples were killed with the same Beretta automatic. Mutilation of female victims remained a trademark of the killer. Stefani Pettini, killed on June 6, was stabbed over 300 times, a severed grape vine thrust into one of her wounds. Susanna Cambi, killed October 23, had her genitals sliced away like Carmela De Nuccio in 1974.

Each year since 1981, the faceless hunter has returned to kill one couple camped or parked within a 19-mile radius of Florence, shooting both victims before savaging the women with a knife. The pattern has been broken only once, in 1983, when two West German men were shot while sleeping in a camper, killed by the familiar trademark bullets fired at point-blank range. Police believe the long blond hair of one young man confused the killer, making him believe one of the victims was a woman.

Recreation of the ''Monster's'' crimes reveals a striking similarity in every case. Each of the double murders has occurred on moonless nights, between the hours of 10 o'clock and midnight. In each case, police believe the man was murdered first, the woman subsequently shot and mutilated as the killer exorcised his private frenzy. Fingerprint examinations of the murder scenes indicate the gunman typically wears rubber surgical gloves, and homicide detectives freely admit they have no leads in the baffling case. As described by Francisco Fleury, the district attorney in charge of the investigation, ''The man could be your respectable next-door neighbor, a man above suspicion.'' Like so much else about the crimes, the six- and seven-year delays between the first three sets of homicides are unexplained.

Investigators thought they had a solid lead in 1985, when two French tourists camping in a tent were murdered on September 8. The woman's body had been slashed at least 100 times, her left breast severed in the killer's frenzy. On the morning that the bodies were discovered, a copper-jacketed Winchester bullet was found on the sidewalk in front of a hospital close by the murder site. The hospital's proximity, together with evidence of surgical gloves and a scalpel employed in the crimes, led detectives to question members of the hospital staff, but no suspects were identified. Next day, police received an envelope addressed with letters clipped from a newspaper; inside, they found a portion of the murdered woman's genitalia, a mocking gift from their elusive quarry.

Three movies have been made, so far, about the "Monster" and his crimes, ranging from a pornographic feature to a documentary. One film was in production in September 1985, and members of the crew rushed to the latest murder site, shooting new scenes to up-date their story. Police, meanwhile, are fearful that increased publicity may prompt the killer to become more active, or encourage "copycats" to emulate his crimes. For now, the faceless hunter seems content to keep his schedule, striking once a year, when summer brings the tourists back to Florence and his prey is readily available.

"Moonlight Murderer, The"

America was still recovering from the trauma of World War II and the euphoria of V-J Day when headlines focused national attention on the town of Texarkana, straddling the Texas-Arkansas border. There, between March 23 and May 4, 1946, an unknown slayer claimed at least five victims, surfacing at three-week intervals to murder when the moon was full. His rampage brought hysteria to Texarkana and environs, causing citizens to fortify their homes or flee the town entirely, sparking incidents of violence when a paperboy or salesman were mistaken for a lethal prowler in the night. Despite four decades of investigation and production of a feature film about the case, it stands officially unsolved today, the so-called "phantom gunman" still at large.

The killer's first attack, unrecognized for several weeks, took place on February 23. Jimmy Hollis, age 24, was parked with his 19-year-old girlfriend, Mary Larey, on a lonely road near Texarkana, when a tall masked man approached their car with gun in hand. He ordered Hollis from the car and clubbed him to the ground, next turning on Larey and raping her with his gun barrel to the point that she begged him to kill her. Instead, he slugged her with the gun and turned back toward Hollis, allowing the young woman to escape on foot. Both victims managed to survive their ordeal, but the gunman would not be so lax a second time.

On March 23, 1946, 29-year-old Richard Griffin and 17-year-old Polly Ann Moore were killed on a lonely Texarkana lover's lane. Both victims were shot in the back of the head, Griffin kneeling underneath the dash board while his girlfriend sprawled in the back seat, but a blood-soaked patch of earth some 20 feet away suggested they had died outside the car. Both bodies were fully clothed, and recent reports deny any evidence of sexual assault, but contemporary rumors featured mention of sexual abuse, torture, and mutilation inflicted on Polly Moore.

Precisely three weeks later, on April 13, 17-year-old Paul Martin and 15-year-old Betty Jo Booker were ambushed in Spring Lake Park, following a late dance at the local VFW hall. Martin's lifeless body, shot four times, was found beside a rural highway on the morning of April 14, Booker's corpse discovered six hours later and a mile away, shot in the face and heart. Again, the tales of fiendish torture spread through Texarkana, though a crop of modern journalists reject them as untrue.

The fanfare of publicity, complete with Texas Rangers on patrol and homicide detectives staked out in the guise of teenage lovers, cause the killer to adopt a new technique for what was said to be his last attack. On May 4, 1946, 36-year-old Virgil Starks was shot through the window of his farmhouse, ten miles from Texarkana, as he read his evening paper after supper. Emerging from a bedroom at the sound of breaking glass, his wife was wounded twice before she managed to escape and summon help from neighbors. In her absence, the intruder prowled from room to room, leaving bloody footprints behind as he fled, dropping an untraceable flashlight in the bushes outside. Tracking dogs were hurried to the scene, but they lost their man at the point where he entered his car and drove off.

Two days after the Starks attack, with Texarkana living in a state of siege, a man's mangled body was found on the railroad tracks north of town. While some reporters have suggested that he may have been the killer, capping off his murder spree with suicide, a coroner's report from May 7, 1946, reveals that victim Earl McSpadden had been stabbed to death before his body was dumped on the tracks, suffering further mutilation when a train passed over at 5:30 a.m. Today, it seems more likely that McSpadden was another victim of the "Moonlight Murderer," dispatched in an attempt to end the manhunt with a simulated suicide.

Arkansas state trooper Max Tackett claiming to have captured the killer in the summer of 1946, basing his case on disjointed remarks from a convicted car thief and an inadmissible statement from the suspect's wife. At least one FBI agent also fingered the thief, later sentenced to life on unrelated charges, as a prime suspect in the murders, but he was never charged. If he *was* the killer, that fact somehow managed to elude Captain M.T. Gonzaullas, in charge of the Texas Rangers' investigation at Texarkana. As late as 1973, Gonzaullas listed the "moonlight" murders as his most baffling case, vowing that he would never stop hunting the killer as long as he lived. Today, the ranger captain is no longer with us, and the case remains unsolved.

Morris, Raymond Leslie

Born at Walsall, England, during August 1929, Raymond Morris possessed good looks and above-average intelligence. He dabbled in poetry and photography, impressing acquaintances with the fact that he never lost his temper, shifting from sunny charm to icy stoicism in an instant. Married at nineteen, Morris frightened his wife with abrupt changes of mood, displaying cold fury when she balked at his spontaneous demands for sex. They separated nine years later, Morris withholding support payments until she agreed to visit him once or twice a week, bending over a table so that he could take her in the "animal position." By the time he married for the second time, the violent side of Raymond's nature had apparently evaporated, leaving him the perfect husband. But, in fact, his silent rage had merely been diverted from the home front to another area.

On September 8, 1965, six-year-old Margaret Reynolds vanished en route to her school, in the Birmingham suburb of Aston. No trace of her had been discovered by December 30, when five-year-old Diane Tift disappeared on the short walk between her home and her grandmother's house, in nearby Bromwich. On January 12, 1966, a workman spotted a child's body in a field near Cannock Chase, a few miles to the north; when the small corpse was moved, a second body was discovered underneath, pressed into the soft earth. The search for Margaret Reynolds and Diane Tift was over.

On August 14, 1966, ten-year-old Jane Taylor went for a ride on her bicycle in Mobberly, south of the Cannock Chase region, and disappeared forever. Two months later, in October, Morris was accused of taking two girls into his Walsall apartment, leading them to separate rooms, and afterward undressing each. Because neither girl could corroborate the other's testimony, charges were eventually dismissed.

On August 19, 1967, Christine Darby, age 7, was playing with friends in Walsall, when a man pulled his car to the curb and asked directions to Caldmore Green. Christine climbed in the car, her playmates startled as the driver soared off in the wrong direction. Five days later, searchers found her violated body in a field; she had been killed by suffocation, probably by hands pressed tight across her nose and mouth.

Descriptions of the suspect car led homicide detectives to question various locals, including Raymond Morris, suspect in the prior molestation case. The matter was reluctantly abandoned after Raymond's wife confirmed that he had joined her in a shopping expedition on the day Christine was killed. On November 4, Morris tried, unsuccessfully, to abduct ten-year-old Margaret Aulton in Walsall. This time, a neighbor saw his license plate, and he was taken into custody. A search of his apartment turned up pornographic photos of his niece, the latter evidence persuading Raymond's wife to testify against him. At trial, with her admission that the shopping alibi had been a fabrication, Morris was convicted and received a term of life imprisonment.

Morse, Hugh Bion

Born in Kansas City during January 1930, Hugh Morse was the product of a forced marriage, abandoned by his father in infancy. He grew up in a harsh, abusive home, completely dominated by a grandmother who brutalized her daughter and grandson with total impartiality. When Hugh was four years old, a hammer blow from grandma scarred his face for life; another time, she slaughtered his pet mice after Morse went to a movie without her permission. It comes as no surprise that he informed police in later years, "I can't remember being happy at any time since I was born." In adolescence and adulthood, Morse was tortured by a mix of awe and hatred for the women who had ruled his early life. The end result was sexual ambivalence and violence, the trademarks of a classic serial murderer.

Escaping from his home environment, Morse enlisted in the Marine Corps, but he soon ran into conflict with the law. Arrested the first time in May 1951, for indecent exposure and assaulting a woman in Wilmington, North Carolina, he left the service seven months later with a dishonorable discharge. More arrests followed, in Los Angeles, during 1953 and '54, with Morse serving six months on a burglary conviction. In 1955, charged with trying to molest two eight-year-old girls in Fairfield, California, he was committed to Atascadero state hospital for therapy. Released as "cured" in January 1957, he was picked up for sex crimes in Burbank four months later.

A pattern had begun to form in Morse's criminal behavior. Prowling residential neighborhoods by night, he entered houses and apartments, creeping up on girls and women in their beds. Briefly settled in Spokane, Washington, Morse tried his hand at marriage, but it didn't take. On November 7, 1959, he raped and murdered Glorie Brie, age 28, in her Spokane home. His second known victim, on September 26, 1960, was 69-year-old Blanche Boggs.

Two weeks later, on October 10, Beverly Myers was attacked in her home, but managed to survive her wounds.

On October 28, 1960, Morse broke into the home of his estranged wife, attempting to strangle her before he was interrupted and forced to flee. A federal warrant was issued, charging unlawful flight to avoid prosecution for burglary and attempted murder. Morse was added to the FBI's "Ten Most Wanted" list on August 29, 1961.

By that time, there were other victims, all unknown to federal agents who were stalking Morse. He raped at least two women in Atlanta, Georgia, in the spring of 1961; arrested on a charge of voyeurism there, he paid $200 bail and walked away, amused that officers had failed to recognize his WANTED poster hanging in the jailhouse.

On July 11, 1961, Morse entered Bobbi Ann Landini's home in Birmingham, choking her unconscious and beating her to death with a length of pipe. Moving north, he attacked Mildred Chasteen in her Dayton apartment on August 2, stabbing her several times and leaving her for dead. Morse drifted into St. Paul, Minnesota, on August 15, posing as "Darwin Corman" when he rented a room, acquiring odd jobs at a car wash, a gas station, a hotel kitchen. On September 18, he raped and strangled Carol Ronan in her home, five blocks from his rooming house. A few days later, Morse lured a six-year-old girl into an alley, where she was molested.

Published photographs of Morse, meanwhile, were turning heads around St. Paul, and phones were ringing at the local office of the FBI. On August 29, a flying squad of agents called on Morse at home, arresting him without struggle. Searchers found a knife, a straightedge razor, and a loaded pistol in his room.

Pleading guilty to the Ronan case, Morse received a double life sentence in December 1961, on charges of second-degree murder and first-degree burglary. As late as January 1964, he was attempting suicide in jail, without success. In the event he is paroled, the states of Washington and Alabama are prepared to level other murder charges, guaranteeing Morse will never be at liberty to kill again.

Moseley, Winston

The stabbing death of barmaid Catherine "Kitty" Genovese, outside her Queens apartment house on March 13, 1964, was neither startling nor unusual for New York. What made the case a *cause celebre* were the reactions of an estimated thirty-seven witnesses who watched the victim grapple with her killer, over half an hour in three separate attacks, before they called police. When questioned by authorities and newsmen, neighbors voiced the sentiment that has become a grim refrain from major cities everywhere: "I didn't want to get involved."

On April 2, Winston Moseley, a 29-year-old business machine operator, confessed to the murders of Catherine Genovese and two other female victims in Queens. The first, Barbara Kralik, 15, was stabbed in her home on July 20, 1963. Moseley's second victim, housewife Ann Johnson, was shot and then burned to death on February 29, two weeks before the Genovese attack made headlines in New York.

Moseley's defense attorney announced plans to plead his client "guilty by reason of insanity," but there were problems with the prosecution's case. Another suspect, 10-year-old Alvin Mitchell, was already charged with the Kralik slaying, and prosecutors refused to cancel his trial on the basis of Moseley's confession. True, they also had a "confession" from Mitchell, but it was less than persuasive; their suspect "didn't remember" stabbing Kralik, but he thought he might have punched her several times.

On June 11, 1964, Moseley was convicted of first-degree murder in the Genovese case; four days later, announcement of his death sentence was greeted by applause from courtroom spectators. Alvin Mitchell went to trial later that month, with Moseley repeating his confessions from the witness stand on June 23, and jurors were unable to reach a verdict in the case.

Mullin, Herbert

Born in Salinas, California, in April 1947, Mullin was the son of Catholic parents, reared by his devout mother in an atmosphere that his own father regarded as oppressively religious. Still, Herbert seemed normal through his teens, participating in high school athletics and winning the class vote of confidence as "most likely to succeed." The June 1965 death of Mullin's best friend, in a car crash, appeared to change everything, producing a sudden and startling shift in Herb's personality. His bedroom was transformed into a shrine, with furniture arranged around the dead boy's photograph, and Mullin warned his girlfriend that he might be turning gay.

By February 1969, Mullin seemed obsessed with eastern religions, his family noting that he had become "more and more unrealistic" in daily behavior. A month later, they persuaded him to enter a mental institution, but he refused to cooperate with psychiatrists and was released after six weeks. October found him in the depths of full-blown paranoid schizophrenia, exacerbated by continuing use of marijuana and LSD. Mullin heard "voices," commanding him to shave his head or burn his penis with a cigarette, and he obeyed their every order. Briefly returned to the hospital, he began writing letters to dozens of total strangers, signing them, "a human sacrifice, Herb Mullin." An ill-advised visit to Hawaii, in June 1970, resulted in Mullin's commitment to a mental institution there. Back in Santa Cruz, his odd behavior led to conflicts with police, and his problems were not erased by fifteen months of hiding out in cheap San Francisco hotels. By the time he came home again, in September 1972, the disembodied voices were commanding him to kill.

On October 13, 1972, while driving aimlessly through the Santa Cruz mountains, Mullin spotted elderly transient Lawrence White. Pulling his car to the side of the road, Mullin asked White to help him with some "engine trouble," then beat the old man to death with a baseball bat and left his body where it lay. Eleven days later, he picked up co-ed Mary Guilfoyle, stabbed her in the heart, then disemboweled her, scattering her organs on the shoulder of a lonely road, where skeletal remains were found in February 1973. On November 2, Mullin spoke too freely in the confessional at St. Mary's Church, fatally stabbing Father Henry Tomei in a bid to protect himself from exposure.

Mullin's crimes coincidentally overlapped with those of serial slayer Edmund Kemper, earning Santa Cruz an unwelcome reputation as "Murderville, USA." By November 1972, Herbert was hearing brand-new voices, emanating from prospective victims, begging him to kill them. He bought a pistol in December and resumed the hunt.

On January 25, 1973, Mullin went looking for Jim Gianera, the man who had "turned him on" to marijuana years earlier. Herb now regarded that act as part of a plot to destroy his mind, and he meant to avenge himself. Calling at Gianera's old address, he received new directions from 29-year-old Kathy Francis. Moving on, he found Gianera at home, shot the man to death, then knifed and shot Gianera's wife for good measure. From there, Mullin doubled back to kill Kathy Francis and her two small sons, shooting all three as they lay in bed.

On February 6, Mullin was hiking in a nearby state park, when he met four teenage campers. Approaching the boys with casual conversation, he whipped out his gun and killed all four in a burst of rapid fire, before they could react or flee. A week later, driving through Santa Cruz, Mullin pulled to the curb and fatally shot Fred Perez, while the old man was working in his garden. This time, neighbors saw his license plate, and Mullin was arrested by patrolmen moments later.

In custody, Mullin confessed to his crimes, maintaining that the homicides were necessary to prevent catastrophic earthquakes from destroying California. Charged and convicted in ten of the murders (omitting White, Guilfoyle, and Tomei), Mullin was sentenced to life imprisonment. He will be eligible for parole in the year 2020 A.D.

"Murder Alley"—
Kenosha, Wisconsin

Kenosha's "murder alley" is an unpaved strip of land running south from 64th Street, between 20th and 21st Avenues. Two blocks away, the downtown business district bustles with activity, but residents along the alley live with daily apprehension that is more akin to an excursion through the Twilight Zone.

"There's something strange out by that alley," Coroner Thomas Dorff told the press in February 1981. "Sort of a 'Bermuda Triangle of murder,' I'd say. What seems to be going on is unexplainable." Lieutenant Rudy Blotz, of the Kenosha Police Department, was equally direct, branding the alley "a jinx or something."

The "happenings" include a string of seven grisly homicides between 1967 and 1981, their savagery baffling locals who remark on Kenosha's relative freedom from violent crime. Three of the cases have been solved, unrelated to one another, but the grim geographical coincidence has authorities shaking their heads in confusion.

The first "alley" murder occurred on February 9, 1967, when 17-year-old Mary Kaldenburg left her home, on 64th Street, to purchase a bottle of pop from the corner drugstore. Four days later, officers discovered her corpse in the back of a 1948 hearse, parked at the city auto pound a mile from her house. Fully clothed except for her shoes, which were removed and placed near the body, Mary had been stabbed twelve times in the neck, chest, forehead and back. The case remains unsolved.

Eleven years later, on January 30, 1978, Jerald Burnett, 52, was found sprawled in a snowbank near his home, at the mouth of the alley. He had been beaten to death with a tire iron, killed in what police described as a robbery. Suspect Steven Gross has been convicted and imprisoned for the crime.

On May 27, 1979, 80-year-old Herman Bosman was found beaten to death in his burning home, on the alley's east side. Authorities speculate that the fire was set to destroy evidence of the murder, which remains unsolved at this writing.

A month later, on June 23, Alice Alzner, age 18, was unearthed in a rose garden adjoining the alley. A jury convicted the property owner, 23-year-old Thomas Holt, of raping the victim and strangling her with her own brassiere. Holt was sentenced to die.

On January 26, 1981, news of a triple murder rocked the neighborhood's fragile peace. Victims Alice Eaton, John Amann, and Raphael Petrucci were found dead in Eaton's home, adjoining the alley. Her grandson, Robert McRoberts, was arrested and charged with the slayings.

Science fiction? Mere coincidence? Whichever, local officers and residents along the alley keep their personal opinions to themselves, agreeing only that "there's something going on out there."

Nance, Wayne

An independent truck driver from Missoula, Montana, Wayne Nance had been known as a "weirdo" since his teens, when he boasted of worshipping Satan and once used a hot coathanger to brand himself with Satanic symbols. By age thirty, Nance appeared to have worked through most of his adolescent problems, impressing his employers and acquaintances as something of an "average guy."

On the night of September 4, 1986, Nance turned up at the Missoula home of a female store manager, for whom he sometimes delivered furniture. Meeting her husband outside, Nance clubbed him with a piece of wood, invading the house and drawing a pistol as he forced the woman upstairs, tying her to a bed. Doubling back, Nance dragged her husband to the basement and was binding him to a post when the man regained consciousness. Drawing a knife, Nance plunged it into the victim's chest and left him for dead.

While Nance went back upstairs to rape his female victim, the wounded husband freed himself and found a rifle he kept in the basement. Nance met him on the stairs, gun in hand, and both men were wounded in the exchange of shots. Attacking despite his injuries, the husband broke his rifle stock on Nance's skull, then seized the pistol and dispatched Nance with a bullet to the brain.

The would-be killer's bind-and-slash technique reminded local officers of an unsolved case dating from 1974. Housewife Donna Pounds had been raped and murdered in her Missoula home by persons unknown, twelve years before the bungled crime that left Nance dead. Their suspect, then eighteen, had been a friend of Pounds's son, but officers had not suspected Nance of personal involvement in the case.

A search of Nance's home turned up a hunting knife and small ceramic statue stolen from the home of Michael and Theresa Shook, in nearby Hamilton, Montana, after they were murdered in December 1985. Their killer also tried to burn the house while children slept upstairs, but neighbors had arrived before the fire had time to spread.

The body-count for Nance was three and climbing. Female hairs recovered from his camper had been treated with a dye that matched the tresses of a "Jane Doe" corpse unearthed outside Missoula in December 1984. In those days, Nance was working as a bouncer in a local bar, and witnesses recalled a youthful female drifter who had shared his lodgings—and abruptly disappeared—in autumn of that year. Detectives also feel that Nance may be connected with the death of a Seattle runaway, found buried near Missoula during March of 1980. With the suspect permanently silent, we may never know how many other crimes "weird" Wayne committed in the years before he pushed his luck too far.

Neelley, Alvin and Judith Ann

Al Neelley couldn't get along with women. His first marriage was a violent debacle, marked by savage beatings, and he once served time for shooting his wife in the back with a pistol. Defense attorneys claim that wife number two received the same kind of treatment, and worse, transforming her into a virtual slave, but Alvin tells another story, describing Judith Ann as his murderous soul-mate, the "brains" behind most of the dozen-odd murders he later confessed.

From 1979 to 1982, they roamed a tri-state hunting ground including Alabama, Tennessee, and Georgia, working odd jobs when they had to, surviving for the most part on proceeds from con games and worthless checks. Alvin was 27, and Judith a mere 16, where they were arrested for armed robbery in 1980. Both did time, and Judith bore their twins in prison, counting down the days until she could rejoin her husband on the road. Upon release, Al found work in a gas station, staying long enough to get his hands on $1,800 from the till and using it to buy two cars, equipped with CB radios. Alvin became "The Nightrider," while Judith billed herself as "Lady Sundance." If new acquaintances missed the point, she was quick to enlighten them: "You know, like *Butch Cassidy and the Sundance Kid*."

When robbery and swindles palled, they turned to murder for the hell of it. Alvin would later blame Judith for most of the crimes, fingering her for eight to fifteen homicides, committed in her alleged role as procurer and "enforcer" for an interstate white-slave ring. Judith, for her part, counters that she acted only under orders from her husband, luring women for Alvin to rape and abuse, participating in their murders under Alvin's standing threat against her children. Police accept the body-count of fifteen victims as a reasonable figure, though they've come up short on verified remains.

The first documented victim was 13-year-old Lisa Millican, abducted on September 25, 1982, from a shopping mall in Rome, Georgia. A resident of Cedartown's home for neglected children, Lisa was enjoying a day's outing when she met Judith Neelley and was lured into Alvin's clutches. The couple held her prisoner for several days, repeatedly molesting her in seedy motel rooms while their own children looked on. Tiring of the game, Judith tried injecting their victim with drain cleaner, but she kept hitting muscle instead of the vein, reducing Lisa's flesh to what a coroner would call "the consistency of anchovy paste." Still Lisa lived, in agony, and she was driven to

Alabama's Little River Canyon, finished off with bullets after more injections failed to do the job. Back in Rome, Judith made several calls to police, directing them to the body, apparently unaware that her voice was being recorded for posterity.

A short time later, 26-year-old John Hancock and his fiancee, 23-year-old Janice Chatman, were walking down a street in Rome when a flashy car stopped at the curb. Incredibly, when total stranger Judith Neelley asked them to a party, both agreed, climbing into her car for a drive into the nearby woods. Alvin joined them there, but Hancock later fingered Judith as the one who shot him in the back, before both killers turned on Janice Chatman. Hancock would survive, and on a hunch, detectives had him listen to recordings of their unknown suspect in the Millican case. Without a trace of hesitation, Hancock recognized the voice.

The case might still have gone unsolved, if Al and Judith had not been arrested on a bad check rap in Murfreesboro, Tennessee. While still in custody, Judith was recognized from photographs as the woman responsible for recent threats against the Youth Development Center in Rome, an institution where she had once spent time (and, allegedly, suffered from sexual abuse). Recordings of threatening phone calls were matched against police logs in the Millican murder, and John Hancock quickly identified the Neelleys as his assailants. In custody, Alvin gave directions to a site in Chattanooga County, where Janice Chatman's body was recovered. She had been shot to death—by Judith—after both kidnappers took turns sexually abusing her in a nearby motel room.

With marathon confessions in progress, Al Neelley pled guilty to murder and aggravated assault in Georgia, receiving two life sentences. Only Judith would be tried in Alabama, for Lisa Millican's death, and before trial she continued a family tradition by giving birth to her third child in jail. Jurors in the Millican case convicted Judith, recommending life imprisonment, but a judge exercised his option to ignore the recommendation, imposing a sentence of death.

Nelson, Earle Leonard

Born in Philadelphia on May 12, 1897, Nelson was orphaned at nine months of age when his mother died of advanced venereal disease. Raised by an aunt whose religious zeal bordered on fanaticism, he was described as "quiet and morbid" during early childhood. At age ten, while playing in the street, he was struck by a trolley and dragged fifty feet; the accident left him comatose for six days, with a hole in his temple, resulting in headaches and dizziness that grew progressively worse. Near the end of his life, Nelson suffered from pain so severe he was sometimes unable to walk.

Aside from headaches, there were other side-affects from Nelson's accident. His moods grew more oppressive, broken up by manic periods in which he took to walking on his hands or lifting heavy chairs with his teeth. He read the Bible compulsively, underlining numerous passages, but also shocked his aunt by talking "smut" and spying on his female cousin as she stripped for bed. When not preoccupied with voyeurism or the scriptures, Nelson spent his time in basements, relishing the solitude and darkness.

On May 21, 1918, Earle was charged with dragging a neighborhood girl into one of those basements, attempting to rape her. In court, it was revealed that Nelson had been called for military service and rejected as insane by the Naval Hospital Board, but he was convicted regardless and sentenced to two years on a penal farm. His third escape attempt was finally successful, on December 4, and Nelson would remain at large until the spring of 1921.

On August 12, 1919, posing as "Roger Wilson," Earle married a young schoolteacher. Their relationship was short-lived, with Nelson's sexual perversions and obsessive jealousy driving his wife to the point of a nervous breakdown after six months. He called upon her in the hospital, and there attempted to molest her in her bed, before the staff responded to her screams and drove him off. Arrested as a fugitive, he staged another break from prison in November 1923.

The next two years of Nelson's life are lost, but sometime in the interim between his flight and reappearance,

Nelson made the move from rape to homicide. In sixteen months, from February 1926 to June 1927, he claimed at least twenty-two victims, preying chiefly on widows and spinsters who took in a mild-mannered boarder, impressed by his manners, his smile and the Bible he carried.

On February 20, 1926, Earle rented rooms from Clara Newman, 60, in San Francisco; she was strangled and raped the same day. Following the identical murder of 60-year-old Laura Beale, in San Jose, newsmen began writing stories about "the Dark Strangler," but their suspect remained elusive.

On June 10, Nelson was back in San Francisco, where he raped and strangled Lilian St. Mary, 63, stuffing her body under a bed. Mrs. George Russell was the next to die, in Santa Barbara, on June 26. On August 16, Mary Nesbit suffered an identical fate in Oakland.

California had become too hot for Nelson, and he sought a change of scene, selecting Portland, Oregon, at random. On October 19, Beata Withers, 35, was raped and strangled, her remains deposited inside a trunk. The next day, Nelson killed Virginia Grant and left her corpse behind the furnace in a house that she had advertised for rent. October 21 found Nelson in the company of Mable Fluke; her body, strangled with a scarf, was found inside the attic of her home.

Police in Portland finally identified their man, but finding him was something else, entirely. (Interviews, conducted with his aunt, recalled tales of Earle's handwalking exploits, leading to his being christened "the Gorilla Murderer.") Nelson struck again in San Francisco on November 18, strangling the wife of William Edmonds. On November 24, he strangled Blanche Myers in Oregon City, tucking her body beneath a bed in her rooming house.

As police dragnets rendered the West Coast uninhabitable, Nelson moved eastward, hitchhiking and riding the rails. In Council Bluffs, Iowa, on December 23, he killed Mrs. John Beard, another landlady. Settling in Kansas City for Christmas, he strangled 23-year-old Bonnie Pace, rebounding on December 28 with the double murder of Germania Harpin and her eight-month-old child.

On April 27, 1927, Nelson strangled Mary McConnell,

age 60, in his hometown Philadelphia. A month later, in Buffalo, New York, the victim was Jenny Randolph, 35. Moving on to Detroit, he murdered landlady Minnie May and one of her tenants, Mrs. M.C. Atworthy, on June 1. Two days later, he strangled Mary Sietsom, 27, in Chicago.

Nelson feared police were closing in on him by now, and made a move to save himself that ultimately brought him to the gallows. Crossing the border into Winnipeg, Canada, he rented a room on June 8, 1927, and strangled Lola Cowan, 14-year-old daughter of his neighboring tenants, the same day. On June 9, housewife Emily Patterson was found bludgeoned and raped in her home, her body hidden underneath a bed.

Hoping to cash in on his last crime, Nelson stole some clothing and resold it at a Winnipeg second-hand shop. Spending his cash on a haircut, he aroused further suspicion when the barber noticed dried blood in his hair. Recognized from his wanted poster in a local post office, Nelson was picked up and jailed at Killarney; he escaped after picking the lock on his cell with a nail file, but he was recaptured twelve hours later, as he tried to slip out of town.

Nelson's trial in the murder of Emily Patterson opened in Winnipeg on November 1, 1927. Only two witnesses— his aunt and former wife—were called by the defense in support of Nelson's insanity plea. Convicted and sentenced to die, he was hanged on January 13, 1928. Before the trap was sprung, he told spectators, "I am innocent. I stand innocent before God and man. I forgive those who have wronged me and ask forgiveness of those I have injured. God have mercy!"

In addition to his twenty-two known murders, Nelson was the leading suspect in a triple murder in Newark, New Jersey, during 1926. The victims included Rose Valentine and Margaret Stanton, both strangled, along with Laura Tidor, shot to death when she attempted to defend them from their killer.

Nilsen, Dennis

Born in Scotland on November 23, 1945, Nilsen seldom saw his Norwegian father, who preferred strong drink and travel to the quiet life at home. Nilsen's parents were divorced when he was four years old, and his mother soon remarried. Joining the army in 1961, Nilsen remained in uniform until 1972. Upon discharge, he moved to London and became a policeman, moving on from there through a series of government jobs. A closet homosexual who holds the standing British record for serial murders, Nilsen would not kill for sex, like Dean Corll and John Gacy in the United States. Rather, his crimes appear to be the product of sheer loneliness, coupled with a morbid fascination for death. Keeping remains of his victims on hand for months at a time, Nilsen was (in the words of biographer Brian Masters) literally "killing for company."

Nilsen's loneliness was held at bay through 1976 and early 1977 by the presence of a live-in companion ten years his junior. While they apparently never had sex, the younger man provided Nilsen with friendship and someone to talk to, sharing the daily grind of cooking, housework, and so forth. Nilsen was stricken by his roommate's departure, in May 1977, and the pressures of a solitary life gradually mounted to the detonation point.

Nilsen's first victim, in December 1978, was an anonymous Irish youth whom he brought home and strangled with a necktie. Dennis later masturbated over the corpse, storing it beneath his floorboards until August 1979, when it was cremated in an outdoor bonfire. In November 1979, Nilsen tried to strangle Andrew Ho, a young Chinese, but Ho escaped and summoned the police. Confronted with a former colleague, officers accepted Nilsen's story of attempted robbery by Ho and let the matter drop. A few days later, on December 3, Nilsen strangled Canadian Kenneth Ockendon with an electric cord and dissected his body, flushing parts down the toilet while most of the butchered remains were stashed under his floor.

In May 1980, Nilsen murdered 19-year-old Martyn Duffey, hiding his corpse with the fragmentary Ockendon remains. That summer, 26-year-old Billy Sutherland joined the growing crowd, followed shortly by a victim who might have been Mexican or Filipino. "I can't remember the details," Nilsen said later. "It's academic. I put him under the floorboards."

Memories were vague on the next five victims, their names unknown, identified only by some physical trait or quirk of behavior that stuck in Nilsen's mind. A young Irishman and a malnourished transient were brought home in swift succession, strangled to death in Nilsen's flat. Number eight was cut into three pieces, his remains hidden beneath the floor for two days before they were burned in another garden bonfire. Number nine was a young Scot, and his successor an unruly "Billy Sutherland type." Number eleven was a tough-talking skinhead, notable for the tattoo of a dotted line around his neck, with the instructions "Cut Here." Nilsen did, and the young man was incinerated on a bonfire during May of 1981.

In September of that year, Nilsen found epileptic Malcolm Barlow slumped against his garden wall and phoned for an ambulance. Barlow came back to see Nilsen the next day, on his release from the hospital, and it proved a fatal mistake. A month later, when Nilsen found new lodgings, he cleaned house with one last bonfire, the blaze leaving police with no evidence of twelve murders spanning almost three years.

A month after settling in his new apartment, on November 25, 1981, Nilsen attempted to strangle Paul Nobbs with a necktie. Nobbs survived the attack, which took place as he slept, but he made no report to police. The next victim, John Howlett, fought bitterly for his life, forcing Nilsen to drown him in the bathtub when strangulation proved ineffective. Howlett's remains were hacked up in the tub, then boiled down in a kettle before they were flushed through the drains.

In May 1982, Nilsen tried to drown Carl Stottor in his bathtub, changing his mind in midstream, persuading Stottor the assault had been intended to "revive" him after he had nearly suffocated in his sleeping bag. Next day, while walking in the woods, Nilsen crept up behind Stottor and clubbed him to the ground, but again Stottor survived, shrugging off the attack and filing no complaint until after Nilsen was jailed for multiple murder.

Number fourteen was alcoholic Graham Allen, killed and dissected in Nilsen's flat, portions of his body bagged and stored in the cupboard, while others were boiled and flushed down the toilet. A local "punk" named Stephen Sinclair was the last to die, murdered on February 1, 1983, portions of his body flushed down the toilet a week later.

It was finally too much for the plumbing, and Nilsen— like Joachim Kroll before him—was betrayed by his pipes. Tenants of Nilsen's apartment building summoned a plumber to clear out the lines, and his discovery of human flesh brought police to the scene. In custody, Nilsen freely confessed his crimes and was sentenced to life imprisonment. Asked about the motive for his murders, he replied, "Well, enjoying it is as good a reason as any."

Northcott, Gordon Stewart

Canadian born in 1908, Northcott would later claim that his father sodomized him at age ten. The old man finished his life in a lunatic asylum, and one of Northcott's paternal uncles died years later, in San Quentin, while serving a life term for murder. A homosexual sadist in the mold of Dean Corll and John Gacy, by age 21, Northcott was living on a poultry ranch near Riverdale, California, sharing quarters with his mother and a 15-year-old nephew, Sanford Clark.

For years, Northcott mixed business with pleasure in Riverside, abducting boys and hiding them out on his ranch, renting his victims to wealthy Southern California pedophiles. When he tired of the boys, they were shot or brained with an ax, their flesh dissolved with quick lime and their bones transported to the desert for disposal. Only one was ever found—a headless, teenage Mexican, discovered near La Puente during February 1928—but homicide detectives identified three other victims. Walter Collins disappeared from home on March 10, 1928, and Northcott's mother was convicted of his death, but evidence suggests that she was acting under orders from her son.

Twelve-year-old Lewis Winslow and his brother Nelson, 10, vanished from Pomona on May 16, 1928, and Northcott was later condemned for their murders, despite the absence of bodies.

Gordon might have gone on raping and killing indefinitely, but in the summer of 1928, he visited the district attorney's office, complaining about a neighbor's "profane and violent" behavior. The outbursts reportedly upset his nephew, who was "training for the priesthood" by tending chickens at age 15. Under investigation, the neighbor recalled seeing Gordon beat Clark on occasion, and he urged detectives to "find out what goes on" at Northcott's ranch.

Immigration officials struck first, taking Clark into custody on a complaint from his Canadian parents, and the boy regaled authorities with tales of murder, pointing out newly-excavated "grave sites" on the ranch. Detectives dug up blood-soaked earth, unearthing human ankle bones and fingers on September 17. They also found a blood-stained ax and hatchet on the premises, that Clark said had been used on human prey, as well as chickens.

Northcott fled to Canada, but he was captured there and extradited back to Riverside. His mother claimed responsibility for slaying Walter Collins, but Clark fingered Gordon as the actual killer. Convicted on three counts of murder, including the Winslow brothers and the anonymous Mexican, Northcott was sentenced to death. Spared by her sex, his mother received a life sentence in the Collins case.

Marking time at San Quentin, Northcott alternated between protestations of innocence and detailed confessions to the murder of "18 or 19, maybe 20" victims. A pathological liar who cherished the spotlight, he several times offered to point out remains of more victims, always reneging at the last moment. (Northcott also named several of his wealthy "customers" at the ranch, but their identities were never published.) Warden Duffy recalled his conversations with Northcott as "a lurid account of mass murder, sodomy, oral copulation, and torture so vivid it made my flesh creep."

Northcott mounted the gallows on October 2, 1930, fi-

nally quailing in the face of death. Before the trap was
sprung, he screamed, "A prayer! Please, say a prayer for
me!" His mother subsequently died in prison, of old age.

Olson, Clifford Robert

A native of Vancouver, British Columbia, born on New
Years 1940, Olson spent most of his life in trouble with
the police. Remembered as a bully in school, he logged
94 separate arrests in the quarter-century between 1957
and 1981, serving time on charges that ranged from fraud
to armed robbery and sexual assault. In prison, Olson was
known as a homosexual rapist and sometime informer,
once coaching fellow inmate Gary Marcoux in writing a
detailed confession to the rape and mutilation-murder of a
nine-year-old girl, then surfacing as a prosecution witness
at the trial where the letters were used to convict Marcoux.
Back on the street, Olson kept up his role as a police stool
pigeon, moving in with the mother of his illegitimate son.

In November 1980, 12-year-old Christine Weller was
abducted from home in the Vancouver suburb of Surrey,
her mutilated body found in the woods, south of town, on
Christmas Day. Colleen Daignault, age 13, vanished from
Surrey on April 16, and 16-year-old Darren Johnsrud was
abducted from a Vancouver shopping mall less than a week
later, found dead on May 2, his skull shattered by heavy
blows.

Olson finally got around to marrying his girlfriend on
May 15, 1981, and 16-year-old Sandra Wolfsteiner disappeared four days later, while hitchhiking through suburban
Langley. On June 21, 13-year-old Ada Court was reported
missing at Coquitlam, when she failed to return home from
a babysitting job. Judy Kozma, 14, disappeared on July 9,
her mutilated body recovered from Lake Weaver, near Ag-
assiz in the Frazer Valley, on July 25.

By that time, Olson was already considered a suspect
in the various deaths and disappearances, his name first
mentioned at a law enforcement conference on July 15.
Despite sporadic surveillance of their man, police were
unable to prevent him from claiming four more victims in

the last week of July. Fifteen-year-old Raymond King disappeared from New Westminster on July 23, his body recovered from the shore of Lake Weaver two weeks later. On July 25, 18-year-old Sigrun Arnd was abducted and killed while thumbing rides near Vancouver, her remains finally identified through dental charts. Terri Carson vanished from the same Surrey housing complex where Christine Weller had lived, her corpse joining a list of those recovered from Lake Weaver. On July 30, 17-year-old Louise Chartrand disappeared while hitchhiking at Maple Ridge.

Officers trailing Olson arrested him days later, after he picked up two female hitchhikers on Vancouver Island. The girls were unharmed, but a search of his van turned up an address book, containing the name of Judy Kozma. Formally charged with her murder six days later, Olson started dealing with the prosecution, striking a bargain that would net his wife and child $10,000 per victim, in return for information on four known murders and directions to the six outstanding bodies. Olson made good on his part of the controversial deal, and the money was paid on schedule. On January 11, 1982, he pled guilty to eleven counts of murder and was sentenced to eleven concurrent life terms.

Panzram, Carl

A son of Prussian immigrants, born at Warren, Minnesota, in 1891, Panzram logged his first arrest at age eight, for drunk and disorderly conduct. Three years later, a series of robberies landed him in reform school, and he set the place on fire at age 12, causing an estimated $100,000 damage. Paroled to his mother's custody in 1906, he ran away from home soon afterward. Life on the road meant more conflict with the law, and Panzram spent time in various juvenile institutions. He volunteered for the army while drunk, but could not adapt to the discipline. Court-martialed for theft of government property in April 1907, he served 37 months in Leavenworth before his release from prison—and military service—in 1910. Upon discharge, Panzram described himself as "the spirit of meanness personified."

Back in civilian life, Panzram launched a career of robbery and indiscriminate murder spanning two continents. After one big score, he hired a yacht and lured several sailors out with promises of liquor; once on board, the men were drugged and raped, then murdered, their bodies dumped into the sea. In Portuguese West Africa, Panzram hired eight blacks to help him hunt for crocodiles, then killed them, sodomized their corpses, and fed them to the hungry reptiles. Back in New York, he strangled a Kingston woman on June 16, 1923, "for the fun it gave me."

Five years later, on August 16, 1928, Panzram was arrested following a series of burglaries in Washington, D.C. Conviction earned him 20 years in Leavenworth, where he promised to kill the first man who "crossed" him. His victim, selected without apparent motive, was Robert Warnke, a civilian laundry foreman. Panzram crushed his skull on June 20, 1929, and was promptly sentenced to hang.

From death row, the killer wrote, "In my lifetime I have murdered 21 human beings, I have committed thousands of burglaries, robberies, larcenies, arsons and last but not least I have committed sodomy on more than 1,000 male human beings. For all these things I am not in the least bit sorry." When opponents of capital punishment fought for his life, Panzram responded with venomous letters. "I wish you all had one neck," he wrote, "and I had my hands on it." Mounting the scaffold on September 5, 1930, he seemed eager for death. "Hurry it up, you bastard," he snapped at the executioner. "I could hang a dozen men while you're fooling around."

Peete, Louise

Born Lofie Louise Preslar, in Bienville, Louisiana, one of America's leading "black widows" was the daughter of a socially prominent newspaper publisher. She attended the best private schools in New Orleans, where she became notorious for her sexual escapades. Expelled by a posh finishing school, Louise went home to Bienville and settled down to the business of pleasure.

In 1903, she married Henry Bosley, a traveling salesman, joining him on the road. Working Dallas, Texas, in the summer of 1906, Henry caught his wife in bed with a local oilman and, grief-stricken, killed himself two days later. Louise sold Henry's belongings and moved to Shreveport, where she worked as a prostitute until she could afford a trip to Boston.

The dramatic change of scene meant little to Louise. Her trade was still the same, and as a hooker making house calls, she became a favorite with the local gentry. On the side, she also pilfered jewelry from the absent wives of wealthy clients, selling off the pieces that she did not choose to keep herself. In time, she pushed her luck too far and was discovered. Threatened with exposure, she retired to Waco, Texas, where she wooed and won Joe Appel, wildcat oil man, best known for the diamonds that studded his rings, belt buckle—even the buttons of his clothing.

One week after Joe first met Louise, he was discovered dead, a bullet in his skull, his diamonds missing. Called before a special grand jury, Louise admitted shooting Appel down—in "self-defense." The oil man tried to rape her, she maintained, and she was forced to act accordingly. The missing jewels forgotten, members of the jury openly applauded as they set her free.

By 1913, running out of luck and ready cash in Dallas, Louise married local hotel clerk Harry Faurote. It was primarily a marriage of convenience—hers—and flagrant adultery on the part of his bride soon drove Faurote to hang himself in the hotel basement.

In 1915, moving on to Denver, Louise married Richard Peete, a door-to-door salesman. She bore him a daughter in 1916, but Peete's meager income did not measure up to her standards, and she took off alone, for Los Angeles, in 1920. There, while shopping for a house to rent, Louise met mining executive Jacob Denton. Denton had a house to rent, but he was soon persuaded to retain the property himself, acquiring Louise as a live-in companion. After several weeks of torrid sex, Louise asked Denton to marry her, but he refused. It was a fatal error.

Smiling through rejection, Louise ordered Denton's caretaker to dump a ton of earth in the basement, where she planned to "raise mushrooms"—Denton's favorite delicacy—as a treat for her lover. No mushrooms had sprouted by the time Denton disappeared, on May 30, 1920, but Louise had numerous explanations for curious callers. First, she told all comers that her man had quarreled with "a Spanish-looking woman," who became enraged and chopped his arm off with a sword. Although he managed to survive, she said, poor Jacob was embarrassed by his handicap, and so had gone into seclusion! Pressed by Denton's lawyer, she revised the story to incorporate an amputated leg; the missing businessman was scheduled to return once he was comfortable with an artificial limb.

Incredibly, these tales kept everyone at bay for several months, while "Mrs. Denton" threw a string of lavish parties in her absent lover's home. It was September by the time that Denton's lawyer grew suspicious, calling on police to search the house. An hour's spade work turned up Denton's body in the basement, with a bullet in his head. Detectives started hunting for Louise, and traced her back to Denver, where she had resumed a life of wedded bliss with Richard Peete.

Convicted of a murder charge in January 1921, Louise was sentenced to a term of life imprisonment. In the beginning, husband Richard corresponded faithfully, but absence failed to make Louise's heart grow fonder of the man she left behind. In 1924, when several of his letters went unanswered, Peete committed suicide.

San Quentin's warden, Clinton Duffy, once described Louise Peete as projecting "an air of innocent sweetness which masked a heart of ice." It was reported that she liked to boast about the lovers she had driven to their deaths, and she especially cherished Richard's suicide, as proof that even prison walls could not contain her fatal charm. In 1933, Louise was transferred from San Quentin to the prison at Tehachapi, and six years later, on her tenth attempt to win parole, she was released from custody.

Her ultimate release was due, in no small part, to intercession from a social worker, Margaret Logan, and her husband Arthur. Paroled to the care of a Mrs. Latham, in Los Angeles, Louise was allowed to take the name "Anna Lee," after her favorite movie star. She found employment at a servicemen's canteen in World War II; in 1942, an elderly female co-worker vanished inexplicably, her home discovered in a state of disarray. Detectives called on "Anna Lee," the missing woman's closest friend, and they were told the woman had died of injuries sustained in a fall. In what may only be described as monumental negligence, they bought the story, never bothering to check out "Anna's" background or obtain a death certificate.

The kindly Mrs. Latham died in 1943, and Louise was paroled to the Logans. she married elderly bank manager Lee Judson in May 1944, and on May 30, Margaret Logan vanished without a trace, Louise telling Margaret's aged husband that his wife was in the hospital, unable to receive visitors. By late June, Louise had persuaded the authorities that Arthur Logan was insane; he was committed to a state hospital, where he died six months later. With typical lack of feeling, Louise donated his body to a medical school for dissection.

Louise moved into the Logan home with Judson, but all was not well in the household. In short order, her husband discovered a bullet hole in one wall, a suspicious mound of earth in the garden, and an insurance policy naming Louise as Margaret Logan's sole beneficiary. Still he said nothing, and it remained for Louise, herself, to unravel the web of deception.

By December 1944, Louise's parole officer had grown suspicious of the regular reports, submitted over Margaret Logan's shaky signature, that contained such glowing praise for their charge. Police invaded the Logan home shortly before Christmas, prompting Lee Judson to voice his suspicions at last. Margaret Logan's body was unearthed in the garden, whereupon Louise offered another of her patented fables. In this story, decrepit Arthur Logan had gone suddenly insane, beating his wife to death in a maniacal rage. Terrified of attracting suspicion due to her background, Louise had buried the corpse and stalled for a month before having Arthur committed to an asylum.

Louise was charged with Margaret Logan's murder, her husband booked as an accessory. Acquitted on January 12, 1945, Judson took his own life the next day, leaping from the thirteenth floor of a Los Angeles office building. Louise, it was observed, seemed pleased with his reaction to their separation. Convicted of first-degree murder by a jury that included eleven women, Louise was this time sentenced to die. Her appeals failed, and she was executed in San Quentin's gas chamber on April 11, 1947.

Petoit, Marcel

A Frenchman, born in 1897, Petoit first demonstrated criminal tendencies in public school, by stealing from classmates. He later moved on to looting mail boxes, and during military service, in 1917, he stole drugs from an army dispensary for sale to street addicts, at black market prices. Discharged with a pension and free treatment for psychoneurosis, Petoit went on to obtain a medical degree, despite spending part of his time as a student in an asylum. In 1928, he was elected mayor of Villanueve, while practicing medicine there, but his term was cut short by Petoit's conviction of theft in 1930.

That same year, one of Petoit's patients—a Madame Debauve—was robbed and murdered in her home. Gossip blamed the doctor, but his chief accuser—another patient—was soon silenced by sudden death. A woman who accused Petoit of actively encouraging her daughter's drug addiction disappeared without a trace, but things were getting hot in Villanueve, and the good doctor struck off in search of friendlier climate.

In Paris, he was convicted of shoplifting, discharged on the condition that he seek psychiatric therapy. As World War II began, Petoit was convicted of drug trafficking, alleged to be an addict himself, but the court released him after payment of a small fine. By early 1941, with Nazi occupation troops controlling France, he had devised a get-rich scheme that mirrored elements of Hitler's "final solution to the Jewish question."

Petoit bought a house on Rue Lesueur, in Paris, contracting for special modifications that were completed in September 1941. The revisions included raising garden walls, to block his neighbors' view, and construction of a triangular, windowless death chamber inside the house. As the war dragged on, Petoit made a fortune by posing as a member of the French resistance movement, offering to help Jews and other fugitives flee the country. Clients arrived at his house after dark, receiving an injection to guard against "foreign disease," and Petoit then led them to the chamber, watching their death throes through a hatch in one wall. Arrested by Gestapo agents in May 1943, on suspicion of aiding escapees, Petoit was released seven months later, when Nazis recognized a kindred spirit.

On March 11, 1944, neighbors complained of rancid smoke pouring from Petoit's chimney, and police found the chimney on fire, with no one at home. Firemen broke into the house and found 27 corpses in the basement, most in various stages of dismemberment. Held on suspicion of murder, Petoit was released after telling police that the dead men were Nazis, executed by the French resistance.

The doctor dropped out of sight in August 1944, when Paris was liberated, but two months later he fired off a letter to the press, claiming the Gestapo had tried to frame him by dumping corpses at his home. The renewed investigation climaxed with Petoit's arrest on November 2, 1944, and while his rap sheet had mysteriously disappeared in Villenueve, authorities had ample evidence in hand. Charged with 27 murders, Petoit admitted 63 killings at his trial, in March 1946, describing various homicides as the patriotic acts of a resistance fighter. The total may well have been higher, as one of Petoit's statements referred to 150 "liquidations," and 86 dissected bodies were pulled from the Seine, between 1941 and '43. Finally convicted of 26 counts, Petoit was guillotined on May 26, 1946.

Pleil, Rudolf

Rudolf Pleil made an unlikely-looking monster. Fat and jovial, he radiated charm and a disarming sense of humor, worming his way into the confidence of the women who became his victims. None would see the darker side in time to save themselves, but it existed all the same, concealed within a man who called himself Germany's "champion death-maker." As Pleil once explained, "Every man has his passion. Some prefer whist. I prefer killing people."

His taste for blood surfaced early in life, when Pleil tortured and killed a cat at age seven. Later, as a teenage soldier during World War II, he had an opportunity to witness victims stripped and starved to death by the Gestapo, recalling the grisly spectacle as "my finest sexual experience."

In March 1946, Pleil claimed his first human victim, braining Eva Miehe with an ax and dumping her body in a canal. Others would follow, through 1946 and early 1947, with Pleil impersonating a policeman, offering to escort female refugees across the frontier from East Germany into the western zone. Instead of sanctuary, they found death, invariably raped by Pleil, then killed and mutilated as he tried his hand with hatchets, hammers, knives and stones. In 1947, he was charged with manslaughter and sentenced to twelve years in prison after impulsively axing a salesman to death. Marking time in his cell, he prepared a diary titled *Mein Kampf,* signing it "by Rudolf Pleil, death dealer (retired)."

The killer's hopes for freedom were demolished when a lone survivor of his murder spree, Frau Lydia Schmidt, identified Pleil as the man who bludgeoned her and then did "indescribable things" to her prostrate body. Police launched a full-scale investigation, ultimately charging Pleil with nine rape-slayings. Five of the victims were never identified, but detectives did name two accomplices. At his trial in Brunswick, in November 1950, Pleil would share the dock with 36-year-old Karl Hoffman, charged in six slayings, and 22-year-old Konrad Schuessler, linked with two murders and one bungled attempt.

Pleil's behavior was bizarre and arrogant throughout the trial. Whenever prosecutors made a reference to his estimated body-count, he interrupted them indignantly. "It is 25," he insisted. "I had 25 victims but they can find only nine bodies. You underrate me. I am Germany's greatest killer. I put others, both here and abroad, to shame.''

Pleil angrily denied that any of his victims had been killed for purposes of robbery, maintaining that the random slaughter had been ''necessary for my sexual satisfaction.'' ''What I did is not such a great harm,'' he declared, ''with all these surplus women nowadays. Anyway, I had a good time.''

Convicted across the board, all three defendants were sentenced to life imprisonment. Pleil passed his time by writing to authorities and offering the whereabouts of new remains, in exchange for an ''airing'' to visit the scene of his crimes. On one occasion, he wrote to the mayor of a town, offering his services as a hangman; his credentials for the job could be determined by examining an old well on the city's outskirts—where authorities retrieved a woman's strangled corpse.

In time, Pleil tired of the sadistic game and made good on his promise that ''I'll hang myself one day.'' In February 1958, a jailer found him dangling in his cell, the final victim of his own desire to kill.

Pommerenke, Heinrich

Dubbed ''the Beast of the Black Forest'' by sensational journalists, Pommerenke was born at Mecklenburg in West Germany, in the village of Bentwich, near Rostock. Driven by violent sexual appetites and frustrated by his own introversion, he boasted of seducing his first girl at age ten. By fifteen, he was waiting outside local dance halls, knocking girls down and attempting to rape them before he was driven away by their screams. Fearing prosecution on a sex charge, he fled from Germany to Switzerland in 1953, but was deported after serving time in a Swiss jail. From 1955 to 1957, he lived in Hamburg, committing at least seven rapes before he was jailed on a robbery charge. A year later, in Austria, he assaulted two English tourists, but the women were saved when bystanders intervened.

Pommerenke killed his first woman in the spring of 1959, after sitting through a screening of *The Ten Com-*

mandments. Disgusted by scenes of women dancing around the golden calf, he decided that females were the root of all worldly evil. Exiting the theater intent on "teaching them a lesson," he met 18-year-old Hilde Knothe in a nearby park, raped her there, and finished his lesson by slashing her throat with a razor.

On June 1, 1959, Pommerenke assaulted 21-year-old Dagmar Klimek on a German train, pushing her off and leaping after her, stabbing his victim to death as she lay beside the tracks. A week later, he strangled 16-year-old Rita Waltersbacher, afterward raping the body.

While sex remained the root of his problem, Pommerenke also dabbled in other crimes, including burglary and robbery, with the latter leading to his ultimate arrest. In the summer of 1960, he accidentally left a parcel containing his pistol at a local tailor's shop, and the gun was delivered to police, who matched it with the bullets fired in a recent bank robbery. On arrest, Pommerenke was charged with ten sex murders, 20 rapes, and 35 other felonies, all of which he freely confessed.

According to his testimony, racy films made Heinrich feel so tense that he "had to do something to a woman." He had initially intended killing seven, but the game got out of hand and he could not restrain himself. On October 22, 1960, he drew six life terms in prison, amounting to a minimum term of 140 years behind bars.

Popova, Madame

A prolific poisoner who undertook her work as much from sympathy as for the minor fees she charged, Madame Popova was an advocate of women's liberation long before the cause was recognized. A native of Samara, Russia, she was so distressed by the travail of peasant wives held "captive" by their brutish husbands that she volunteered an inexpensive, lethal remedy. For thirty years before her ultimate arrest, in March 1909, she ran a small disposal service for her female neighbors, picking up spare change and executing her commissions with dispatch. A client, suddenly remorseful, turned her in to the police, and Ma-

dame Popova confessed to "liberating" some 300 wives
in her career. In custody, she boasted of the fact that she
"did excellent work in freeing unhappy wives from their
tyrants." In her own defense, Madame Popova told her
captors she had never killed a woman. Czarist soldiers
saved her from a mob that sought to burn her at the stake,
and she was unrepentant as she stood before the firing
squad.

Puente, Dorothea Montalvo

Born in 1959 and raised in an orphanage, Dorothea Puente claimed a total of four marriages, from which police
were able to document two divorces. Her only child, a
daughter, was put up for adoption at birth, finally meeting
her mother—whom she described as a woman with "no
real personality"—in 1986. Eight years earlier, Puente had
been diagnosed as suffering from "chronic undifferen-
tiated schizophrenia," a condition that sometimes produces delusions. Neighbors recall her fascination with
acting, including boasts of non-existent starring roles as
"the evil woman" in various feature films. On the side,
Puente billed herself as a "holistic doctor," but she earned
her income, after 1978, from operation of a boarding house
in Sacramento, California.

In 1982, Puente was convicted of drugging and robbing
strangers she met in various taverns, serving two and a
half years in prison before she returned to her rooming
house. She spent hours working in the garden, and neighbors described her as "very protective of her lawn." As
one told reporters, "If somebody walked on her lawn,
she'd cuss at them in language that would make a sailor
blush."

In 1986, Puente approached social worker Peggy Nickerson with an offer of quality lodgings for elderly persons
on fixed incomes. Referring to Puente as "the best the
system had to offer," Nickerson sent her 19 clients over
the next two years, growing concerned when some of them
dropped out of sight. In May 1988, when neighbors complained of a sickly-sweet smell in her yard, Puente blamed

the aroma on applications of "fish emulsion." "We couldn't stand it," one resident recalled. "There was a sick smell in the air, and there were a lot of flies in the area."

On November 7, 1988, police dropped by the rooming house to check on tenant Bert Montoya, last seen in August. Briefly satisfied with Puente's explanation—that Montoya had gone home to Mexico—officers returned with shovels five days later, after Peggy Nickerson reported one of her clients as missing.

The first corpse was unearthed November 11, with two more recovered the following day. Puente disappeared that afternoon, before she could be taken into custody, and officers kept digging in her absence. By November 14, police had seven bodies in hand, and tenant John McCauley, 59, was charged as an accomplice in the murders. (He was later freed, for lack of evidence.) Detectives shook their heads in wonder as they realized that they were only blocks away from where another clutch of corpses had been excavated, at the home of killer Morris Solomon, in April 1987.

No more bodies were discovered at the rooming house, but officers believed there might be other victims, all the same. "We are getting a large number of calls from people with relatives who have stayed here," a police spokesman announced. "There are a lot more than seven names." In fact, as many as 25 former tenants were missing, and police had no I.D. on any of the seven corpses. (At least one had been decapitated, feet and hands removed, to prevent identification.) Detectives believe Puente murdered her tenants in a scheme to obtain their Social Security checks.

On November 17, Puente was traced to Los Angeles, fingered by a new acquaintance she met in a bar. Introducing herself as "Donna Johansson," she displayed an unusual interest in the man's disability income, offering to move in with him and "fix Thanksgiving dinner" on short acquaintance. Held without bond, she faces indictment on seven counts of murder, and the investigation continues.

By December 10, 1988, Sacramento authorities had identified four of the victims unearthed at the Puente rooming house. Fingerprints and x-rays indicated that the four were 55-year-old Ben Fink, 52-year-old Alvaro Montoya, 65-year-old Dorothy Miller, and 65-year-old Vera Martin. One male victim and two females from the rooming house remain unidentified at this writing, while police have added an eighth victim—a middle-aged male, found January 1, 1986, in a wooden box beside the Sacramento River—to the list of Puente's victims. On December 11, authorities charged 46-year-old Ismael Carrasco Florez as an accessory to murder in the 1986 case, alleging that he built the box and aided Puente in disposing of the body.

Putt, George Howard

It may be fairly said that George Putt had two strikes against him from the moment of his birth. His father was a petty criminal and drifter, frequently away from home and brutal to his children when in residence. One of his numerous arrests, on June 4, 1946, involved a charge of cruelty to a minor; his victim, George—still shy of three months old—had been severely beaten with a leather strap.

Putt's family moved repeatedly throughout the latter 1940s and the early 1950s. In January 1947, George was dropped off with a family friend in Tupelo, Mississippi, where he remained, without word from his parents, for the next year. In 1954, when both his parents went to jail for forgery, Putt and his six siblings were sent to live with their grandparents in Richmond, Virginia. Putt and an elder brother were arrested in November 1957, after shooting out a neighbor's windows with a stolen air rifle. Fed up, his grandparents sent George and four of his brothers to a rural orphan's school, where fundamentalist religion was enforced with frequent beatings.

Putt handled discipline poorly. With a brother, Clifford, he twice ran away from the school, and was rewarded with expulsion on his second failed attempt. Returned to the custody of his grandparents, George was packed off to the Richmond Home for Boys. Kicked in the forehead during a football game, Putt was knocked unconscious for ''many minutes,'' and may have sustained permanent damage. In months to come, Putt began sleepwalking with his eyes open, suffering blackouts that alternated with violent seizures, throwing furniture and ripping towel racks from the walls, professing amnesia after the fact.

The summer after his injury, Richmond police arrested George for attacking two young girls, one of whom was stripped naked and forced to suck his penis. Arrested at his grandparents' home, he was delivered to juvenile authorities. Psychological tests revealed Putt's "morbid preoccupation with blood and gore," a fact that led authorities to consider placing George in a mental institution. Terrified by the prospect, he fled from custody one night, clad only in his undershorts, teaming up with brother Clifford for several days before he was recaptured.

Diagnosed as a "sociopathic personality," created by "almost unbelievable physical and emotional deprivation," Putt was ruled fit for trial on a sodomy charge. He escaped from custody again, on December 22, 1961; two weeks later, he abducted a 30-year-old Richmond woman at knifepoint, robbed her of $35, and raped her. A warrant was issued for his arrest, but George fled Virginia, hoping to locate his father somewhere in Mexico. On January 13, 1962, he kidnapped a woman from Laredo, Texas, at gunpoint, forcing her to drive him out of town, escaping on foot when she deliberately crashed her car.

Two days later, Putt climbed through the window of a Laredo apartment, abducting the female tenant by threatening to kill her children if she failed to cooperate. George was driving the woman out of town in her own car when he spotted a police van and crashed, fleeing on foot. Captured the next day, as he emerged from a local theater, he spent thirteen months in the Webb County jail.

Transferred to the Terrace School, in Laredo, on February 28, 1963, Putt escaped in October, was recaptured and sent to the more secure Hilltop School, where he passed his eighteenth birthday. In June 1964, following exposure of his plan to kidnap the school's librarian and escape in her car, Putt was transferred to an "adjustment center." Diagnosed as possessing the "earmarks of a psychopath in his makeup," he was shipped on from there to the maximum-security juvenile lockup at Gatesville. A

1965 report termed him psychotic, but it made no difference in the end; Putt was routinely discharged from custody on his twenty-first birthday, in 1967.

Returning to Tupelo, where his grandparents now lived, George found work as a hospital orderly. A few days later, he was fired for stealing $100 from a nurse's handbag, but he escaped prosecution by repaying the money. From Tupelo, he moved back to his native New Orleans, and was there charged with stealing a checkbook from a room at the Roosevelt Hotel. On May 5, 1967, he was picked up for pilfering $46 from the till of a local cafe, but the owner declined to prosecute when his money was recovered from Putt's stocking.

In the fall of 1967, Putt married a Mississippi woman, insisting on six to eight bouts of intercourse every night, although he rarely climaxed. In public, he erupted into violent fits of jealousy whenever his wife spoke to another man, including co-workers, and by 1968 his violence was not confined to his marriage.

On October 16, 1968, police in Memphis, Tennessee, arrested Putt after he forced his way into a black woman's car and began beating her with his fists. Settling in Jackson, Mississippi, with his brother Clifford and their wives, Putt tried to rape his mother-in-law on three separate occasions in early 1969. Police believe he committed his first murder in Jackson, shortly after the third rape attempt, when a socially-prominent bachelor was slain on April 27, 1969. Rumored to participate in homosexual affairs, the victim was stabbed fifteen times at his home, a short distance from the gas station where Putt was employed. George was never charged in the crime, but authorities remain convinced of his involvement.

Putt and his wife moved back to Memphis in the summer of 1969, and George launched a one-man reign of terror shortly after their arrival. On August 14, Roy and Bernalyn Dumas were found dead in their home, the woman spread-eagle on her bed, gagged, wrists and ankles bound to the bedposts. Both victims had been bludgeoned and strangled; Bernalyn Dumas had also been raped, her anus and vagina afterward mutilated with a pair of surgical scissors. Saliva samples taken at the scene revealed a blood type different from that of the victims.

On August 25, Leila Jackson, an 80-year-old widow, was found strangled in her home, a nylon stocking tied around her neck, genitals mutilated with a butcher knife. Four days later, Glenda Harden, 21, was abducted and murdered in Riverside Park, stabbed fourteen times as she lay helpless, with her hands bound behind her back. Discovery of her body on August 30 touched off a panic in Memphis, as police scrambled to identify the killer.

On September 9, an anonymous caller fingered George Putt as a suspect in the crimes, but detectives were still muddling through other leads two days later, when the slayer struck again. Mary Pickens was ambushed inside her apartment, returning from work, and stabbed nineteen times by a man who wielded his knife with desperate speed. Neighbors heard her screams and called police, providing officers with the description of a young man spotted running from the scene. The suspect led patrolmen and civilians on a wild, winding chase before two officers ran down George Putt, his clothing smeared with blood, and took him into custody. Before the day was out, he had confessed to all five homicides, and thereby sealed his fate.

Convicted of the Pickens murder on October 27, 1970, Putt was sentenced to die, his punishment altered to a term of 99 years when the Supreme Court struck down the death penalty in 1972. A double conviction in the Dumas case, during April 1973, added 398 years to his term, making George a local record-holder, with accumulated prison time of 497 years. Unable to contain his mirth, Putt giggled as the judge pronounced his sentence.

Ramirez, Richard

Los Angeles is the serial murder capital of the world. It takes a special "twist" to capture headlines in a city where, by autumn 1983, five random slayers were reportedly at large and acting independently of one another. In the summer months of 1985, reporters found their twist and filled front pages with reports of the sinister "Night Stalker," a sadistic home-invader with a preference for unlocked windows and a taste for savage mutilation. As the story broke, the Stalker had three weeks of freedom left, but he was bent on making every moment count, and he would claim a minimum of 16 lives before the bitter end.

Unrecognized, the terror had begun a full year earlier, with the murder of a 79-year-old woman at her home in suburban Glassell Park, in June 1984. Police lifted fingerprints from a window screen at the site, but without a suspect the clue led them nowhere.

By February 1985, police had two more murders on their hands, but they were keeping details to themselves. They saw no link, at first, with the abduction of a six-year-old Montabello girl, snatched from a bus stop near her school and carried away in a laundry bag, sexually abused before she was dropped off in Silver Lake on February 25. Two weeks later, on March 11, a nine-year-old girl was kidnapped from her bedroom in Monterey Park, raped by her abductor, and dumped in Elysian Park.

The Stalker reverted from child molestation to murder on March 17, shooting 34-year-old Dayle Okazaki to death in her Rosemead condominium, wounding roommate Maria Hernandez before he fled. Hernandez provided police with their first description of a long-faced intruder, notable for his curly hair, bulging eyes, and wide-spaced, rotting teeth.

Another victim on March 17 was 30-year-old Tsa Lian Yu, ambushed near her home in Monterey Park, dragged from her car and shot several times by the attacker. She was pronounced dead the following day, and her killer celebrated his new score by abducting an Eagle Rock girl from her home on the night of March 20, sexually abusing her before he let her go.

The action moved to Whittier on March 27, with 64-year-old Vincent Zazzara beaten to death in his home. Zazzara's wife, 44-year-old Maxine, was fatally stabbed in the same attack, her eyes carved out and carried from the house by her assailant. The Zazzaras had been dead two days before their bodies were discovered, on March 29, and homicide detectives launched a futile search for clues.

On May 14, 65-year-old William Doi was shot in the head by a man who invaded his home, in Monterey Park. Dying, he staggered to the telephone and dialed an emergency number before he collapsed, thus saving his wife from a lethal assault by the Stalker. Two weeks later, on May 29, 84-year-old Mabel Bell and her invalid sister, 81-year-old Florence Lang, were savagely beaten in their Monrovia home. The Stalker paused to ink Satanic pentagrams on Bell's body, drawing more on the walls before he departed. Found by a gardener on June 2, Lang would survive her injuries, but Mable Bell was pronounced dead on July 15.

In the meantime, the Night Stalker seemed intent on running up his score. On June 27, 32-year-old Patty Higgins was killed in her home at Arcadia, her throat slashed, and 77-year-old Mary Cannon was slain in identical style, less than two miles away, on July 2. Five days later, 61-year-old Joyce Nelson was beaten to death at her home, in Monterey Park. The killer struck twice on July 20, first invading a Sun Valley home where he killed 32-year-old Chainarong Khovanath, beating and raping the dead man's wife, battering their eight-year-old son before escaping with $30,000 worth of cash and jewelry. A short time later, Max Kneiding, 69, and his wife Lela, 66, were shot to death in their home, in Glendale.

Police were still maintaining silence on the subject of their latest maniac-at-large, but they began to feel the heat on August 6, after 38-year-old Christopher Petersen and his wife Virginia, 27, were critically wounded by gunshots in their Northridge home. Descriptions matched the Stalker, and he struck again on August 8, shooting 35-year-old Elyas Abowath dead in his Diamond Bar home, brutally beating the victim's wife. That night, authorities announced their manhunt for a killer linked with half a dozen recent homicides, a toll that nearly tripled in the next three weeks, with fresh assaults and new evaluation of outstanding cases.

On August 17, the Stalker deserted his normal hunting ground, gunning down 66-year-old Peter Pan at his home in San Francisco. Pan's wife was shot and beaten, but she managed to survive her wounds, identifying suspect sketches of the homicidal prowler.

By August 22, police had credited the Stalker with a total of 14 murders in California. Three weeks later, in Mission Viejo, he wounded 29-year-old Bill Carns with a shot to the head, then raped his fiancee before escaping in a stolen car. The vehicle was recovered on August 28, complete with a clear set of fingerprints belonging to Richard Ramirez, a 25-year-old drifter from Texas whose L.A. rap sheet included numerous arrests for traffic and drug violations. Acquaintances described Ramirez as an ardent Satanist and long-time drug abuser, obsessed with the mock-Satanic rock band AC/DC. According to reports, Ramirez had adopted one of the group's songs—"Night Prowler"—as his personal anthem, playing it repeatedly, sometimes for hours on end.

An all-points bulletin was issued for Ramirez on August 30, his mug shots broadcast on TV, and he was captured by civilians in East Los Angeles the following day, mobbed and beaten as he tried to steal a car. Police arrived in time to save his life, and by September 29, Ramirez was facing a total of 68 felony charges, including 14 counts of murder and 22 counts of sexual assault. (One of the murder counts was dropped prior to trial, but eight new felonies—including two more rapes and one attempted murder—were added to the list in December 1985.)

A sister of Ramirez told the press he wanted to plead guilty, a desire reportedly frustrated by his attorneys, but the suspect made no public display of repentance. Sporting a pentagram on the palm of one hand, Ramirez waved to photographers and shouted "Hail Satan!" during a preliminary court appearance. Back in jail, he told a fellow inmate, "I've killed 20 people, man. I love all that blood." Jury selection in the case began on July 22, 1988, with Ramirez convicted of 13 murders and 30 felonies on September 20, 1989.

Rath, Thomas

On October 30, 1981, 18-year-old Britta Schilling vanished while hitchhiking home from a disco near Bremen,
in West Germany. Her naked, ravaged body—bearing 27
stab wounds and the marks of torture prior to death—was
found November 6, discarded on the Devil's Moor, a
hundred-square-mile area of marshland north of Bremen.

Three days after Schilling's body was recovered, a 17-
year-old girl was thumbing her way home from school
when a young, handsome man picked her up. Instead of
dropping her at home, he drove her to the moors, where
she was raped and turned out naked in the marsh, her
clothing scattered on the road to delay a report of the
crime. Police saw a pattern forming on December 3, when
a 20-year-old woman was raped in similar fashion, and
they began reexamining the Schilling case, for possible
connections. Heike Schnier, age 20, was reported missing
when she failed to show for work in Bremen, on February 9, 1982, and her body—stabbed 36 times—was recovered from the Devil's Moor on March 24. On May 22,
18-year-old Angele Marks disappeared while thumbing
rides in Bremen; seven months would pass before her skeletal remains were found, together with her clothes and
handbag, on the moors.

The killer switched back to simple rape in July, assaulting two more teenaged girls before he dropped out of sight
for nearly a year. On June 6, 1983, he abducted a 17-year-
old at knifepoint, forcing her to perform oral sex before
she was released.

Twenty-year-old Martina Volkmann was hitchhiking
from Vahr, a Bremen suburb, to Hamburg when she met
her killer on December 26, 1983. Her body was found the
same day, stabbed more than 100 times, with traces of
semen found in her mouth. On January 4, 1984, the stalker
abducted another teenage victim, forcing her to fellate him,
and he repeated the process with a 20-year-old a month
later. The victim selected on March 8, an 18-year-old,
proved more clever. Requesting a smoke before sex, she
mashed the lit cigarette in her attacker's face and leaped
from the car, memorizing his license number as the rapist

drove away. Police traced the plates to 24-year-old Thomas Rath, a noncommissioned officer in the West German army, and he confessed after brief interrogation. Rath was sentenced to life imprisonment on April 26, 1985, with a provision for psychiatric therapy in jail.

Rees, Melvin David

A Maryland native, born in 1933, Rees attended the state university at age 20, dropping out before graduation to pursue a career in music. On March 12, 1955, he was arrested on charges of assaulting a 36-year-old woman, dragging her into his car when she refused to enter voluntarily, but the case was dropped when his victim refused to press charges. Melvin's friends ignored the incident, if they were even conscious of it, viewing Rees as mild-mannered and intelligent, a talented artist who played the piano, guitar, clarinet and saxophone with equal skill. He had a taste for modern jazz, and his employment often took him on the road.

On June 26, 1957, Margaret Harold was parked with her date—a young army sergeant—on a lonely lover's lane near Annapolis, Maryland, when a green Chrysler pulled up in front of their car. A tall, thin-faced man approached, identified himself as the property's caretaker, then produced a gun and climbed into the back seat. He demanded money from the couple, shooting Margaret in the head when she indignantly refused. Her date escaped on foot and called police, returning with an escort to discover that her body had been raped in death.

Nearby, the search team found a building made of cinder blocks, a basement window broken, and they crept inside. The inner walls were covered with a mix of pornographic photos and morgue shots of dead women; the only "normal" photo was a college yearbook picture that depicted Wanda Tipton, a 1955 graduate from the University of Maryland. Under questioning, she denied knowing anyone who fit the killer's description.

On January 11, 1959, a family of four disappeared while out for a drive near Apple Grove, Virginia. A relative found their abandoned car later that day, but no trace remained of Carroll Jackson, his wife Mildred, or their two daughters, five-year-old Susan and 18-month-old Janet. While police were beating the bushes in vain, a young couple reported that they had been forced off the road by an old blue Chevy that morning. The strange driver had climbed out, approaching their car, at which time they made good their escape.

Two months later, on March 4, Carroll Jackson's body was discovered by two men whose car had bogged down in the mud near Fredericksburg, Virginia. Homicide detectives found the victim's hands bound with a necktie, a single bullet in his head. When they removed his body from the roadside ditch, another corpse was found beneath it. Janet Jackson had been thrown into the ditch alive and literally suffocated by her father's weight.

On March 21, hunters stumbled across a grave site in Maryland, not far from the spot where Margaret Harold was murdered in 1957. The bodies of Mildred and Susan Jackson were unearthed by investigators, both bearing signs of sexual assault and savage beatings with a blunt instrument. A stocking was knotted around Mildred's neck, but she had not been strangled, police speculating that the tourniquet had been applied to coerce her participation in oral sex. A quarter-mile away, manhunters found a run-down shack with "fresh" tire tracks outside, a button from Mildred Jackson's dress lying on the floor within.

The case was still unsolved in May, when homicide detectives received an anonymous letter from Norfolk, naming Rees as the killer. A background search revealed his link to the University of Maryland—and a former close relationship with Wanda Tipton—but solid evidence was scarce, and no one seemed to know the traveling musician's whereabouts. In early 1960, the anonymous informant came forward with a recent letter from Rees, describing his latest job at a music store in West Memphis, Arkansas. FBI agents made the collar, and a search of the Rees home in Hyattsville turned up an instrument case with a pistol inside, plus various notes describing assorted sadistic acts. One such was clipped to a newspaper photo of Mildred Jackson. Ir read, in part: "Caught on a lonely road . . . Drove to a select area and killed husband and baby. Now the mother and daughter were all mine . . .''

Maryland officers finally linked Rees to four other sex-slayings. Schoolgirls Mary Shomette, 16, and Ann Ryan, 14, had each been raped and killed in College Park, near the University of Maryland, while 18-year-old Mary Fellers and 16-year-old Shelby Venable had been fished out of area rivers. Rees was not indicted in their deaths, but prosecutors felt they had enough to keep him off the streets, regardless. Convicted of Margaret Harold's murder, in Baltimore, Rees was sentenced to life imprisonment, then handed over to Virginia authorities for trial. Upon conviction of multiple murder in that state, he was sentenced to death and executed in 1961.

Reldan, Robert R.

Between August 1974 and November 1975, residents of northern New Jersey were alarmed by a series of random, brutal homicides that claimed the lives of eight young women, perpetrated by a man who liked to pick his victims off in pairs. He would resort to solitary targets in a pinch, however, and he kept authorities off-balance by continually altering his methods—suffocating, strangulation, gunshots—on a whim.

The first to die were 17-year-old Mary Pryor and 16-year-old Lorraine Kelly, reported missing from North Bergen on August 10, 1974. The girls were last seen on August 9, when they left Pryor's home to do some shopping, and police believe they were hitchhiking when they met their killer that afternoon. Their bodies, raped and smothered, were recovered from a wooded area near Montvale, four days later.

On December 13, 1974, 14-year-old Doreen Carlucci and 15-year-old Joanne Delardo vanished from a church youth center in Woodbridge, their bodies discovered two weeks later, in Manalapan Township. Beaten and strangled, one victim was completely nude when found, the other dressed only in shoes and a sweater. The killer's garrote, an electrical extension cord, was knotted tight around Carlucci's neck.

The first solitary victim, 26-year-old Susan Reynes, disappeared from her home in Haworth, New Jersey, on October 6, 1975. Eight days later, in Demarest, 22-year-old Susan Reeve vanished without a trace on the short walk home from her bus stop, after work. Both were still missing when 15-year-olds Denise Evans and Carolyn Hedgepeth disappeared from home in Wilmington, Delaware, on October 24, their bodies—shot execution-style—recovered in Salem County, New Jersey, the following day. On October 27 and 28, the remains of victims Reynes and Reeve were found, seven miles apart, in a wooded region of Rockland County, New York, just north of the New Jersey state line. Searchers were led to one corpse by an arrow, scratched on a highway embankment above the name "Reeve." Autopsies revealed that both women were strangled.

On October 31, 1975, police arrested 35-year-old Robert Reldan in Closter, New Jersey, on a charge of attempted burglary. A resident of Tenafly, Reldan was convicted of raping a woman at Teaneck, in 1967, serving three years in prison before he was paroled. Five months later, in 1971, he assaulted another woman in a hospital parking lot, pulling a knife on her moments after his latest therapy session. Convicted a second time, he emerged as a "model graduate" of Rahway prison's rehabilitation program for sex offenders. Authorities were so impressed with Reldan's progress that they chose him for a television interview with David Frost, aired shortly before his parole in May 1975.

Held without bond on the burglary charge, Reldan was questioned about the murders of Reeve and Reynes, but on November 2, homicide detectives publicly announced that he was "not considered a suspect" in the slayings. They had changed their tune by January 1976, but another full year elapsed before Reldan's indictment on two counts of murder, in January 1977. Four months later, on April 21, he was charged with plotting to arrange the deaths of a wealthy aunt and her boyfriend, hoping to expedite a hoped-for inheritance. A Bergen County detective, posing as a hit man, twice visited Reldan at Trenton state prison, where he was serving three years on the burglary charge, and their conversations were secretly recorded as evidence. Convicted of conspiracy in June 1978, Reldan drew a term of 20 to 50 years in prison, but the worst was yet to come.

Reldan's first murder trial ended with a hung jury, in June 1979, and a retrial was scheduled for October. On October 15, Reldan used a smuggled key to unlock his handcuffs, sprayed his guards with chemical Mace, and escaped from the courthouse in Hackensack. He was recaptured hours later, at a hospital in Tuxedo, New York, after crashing his stolen getaway car into a ditch. The trial resumed next day, despite the anonymous mailing of $100 bribes to several jurors, and Reldan was convicted of two murders on October 17. He remains a suspect in six other homicides, although no further charges have been filed.

Renczi, Vera

Born to affluent parents at Bucharest, in the early 1900s, Vera Renczi had already displayed a precocious interest in sex by age ten, when her family moved to Berkerekul. At age 15, she was found in the dormitory of a boy's school at midnight, and Vera afterward eloped with several lovers, coming home each time when she grew bored with their attentions. It was fine for Vera to desert a paramour, but none must ever try to turn the tables, as she had begun to demonstrate possessiveness that bordered on the pathological.

Vera's first husband was a wealthy businessman, many years her senior, and she bore a son before he disappeared one day, without a trace. Declaring that her man had left without a word of explanation, Vera passed a year in mourning, finally reporting "news" of her husband's recent death in a car crash.

Vera soon remarried, to a younger man, but he was flagrantly unfaithful, vanishing a few months later on what Vera described as "a long journey." Another year passed before she announced the receipt of a letter, penned by her spouse, declaring his intent of leaving her forever.

Vera Renczi would not wed again, but she had many lovers—32 in all—as years went by. They never seemed to stay around for long, and none were ever seen again once they "abandoned" Vera, but she always had an explanation for her neighbors . . . and another lover waiting in the wings. Police became involved when Vera's latest was reported missing by the wife he left at home; a search of Renczi's basement turned up 35 zinc coffins, with the bodies of her missing husbands, son, and lovers tucked away inside.

Detained on murder charges, Vera made a full confession, stating that she killed her husbands and her lovers off with arsenic when they began to stray, sometimes arranging for a romantic "last supper" to climax a tryst. Her son's demise had been a different story, brought about by threats of blackmail when he stumbled on the basement crypt by accident. Some evenings, Vera said, she liked to sit among the coffins in an armchair and enjoy the company of her adoring beaus. Convicted on the basis of her own confession, Vera drew a term of life and subsequently died in prison.

Robinson, Alonzo

Born to poverty in Cleveland, Mississippi, Robinson was arrested by hometown authorities in 1918, on charges of mailing obscene letters to local women. He escaped from custody en route to jail, and made his getaway despite a bullet in the shoulder. Eight years later, when decapitated women's bodies started turning up around Michigan City, police suspected Robinson—alias "James Coyner"—of multiple murder. Four severed heads were found at a house he once occupied, in Ferndale, Michigan, but Robinson had moved on by that time, convicted and sentenced to prison for grave-robbing in Indiana. Interrogated by Michigan authorities in jail, Robinson played dumb, and the existing evidence proved insufficient to support a murder charge.

Paroled in July 1934, Robinson—as "Coyner"—returned to Cleveland, Mississippi, and picked up his old hobby of writing obscene letters. One was mailed to an Indianapolis woman, the incorrect address identical to a recent misprint in an Indianapolis newspaper. Postal inspectors were still scouring the paper's subscription list when Robinson claimed two more victims, close to home.

On December 8, 1934, Aurelius Turner and his wife were shot to death in Cleveland, the woman's body mutilated with chunks of flesh sliced off and carried away by the killer. A month later, federal authorities traced poison-pen artist "James Coyner" to a post office box in Shaw, Mississippi, and officers were waiting when he came to get his mail on January 12, 1935. Robinson went for his .38, but the deputies were faster, and he surrendered in the face of superior firepower. A search of his pockets and lodgings revealed more obscene letters, a packet of human hair in Turner's color, and strips of human flesh, salted and cured like beef jerky.

In custody, Robinson freely confessed to the murders; he also admitted ownership of the heads found in Michigan, but claimed they were trophies secured during various grave-robbing expeditions. The prisoner offered no motive for his actions, but as the local newspaper proclaimed, Robinson "admitted that he was a sex pervert, which is considered to be the underlying cause for the crime."

Rozier, Robert

A star football player at UC Berkeley, Rozier was drafted by the St. Louis Cardinals but quit the team after playing two games as a pro. He moved on to the Canadian Football League, then signed up briefly with the Oakland Raiders, but his will to win had disappeared somewhere along the way. Cut from the squad, Rozier drifted around the country for several years before joining the black-supremacist Hebrew Israelite sect in 1981. The cult had been founded a year earlier, by Eulon Mitchell, Jr.—alias Yahweh ben Yahweh—who billed himself as the son of

God incarnate. As a new recruit, Rozier adopted the name of "Neriah Israel."

Trouble was already dogging Rozier's footsteps, with Canadian authorities investigating $50,000 worth of bad checks passed in his CFL days, but the worst was yet to come. In 1981, the Yaweh sect was linked with the murder of two ex-members in Florida, and cultists were suspected of firebombing homes in Delray Beach, after residents clashed with Yaweh recruiters. By 1986, authorities estimated that there were 300 active cult members in Miami and Dade County, with other groups springing up nationwide.

In November 1986, Rozier was arrested on multiple murder charges in Miami, linked with the October 30 shooting deaths of Rudolph Broussard and Anthony Brown. (Rozier listed his age as "404 years" on the arrest report.) The victims had staunchly resisted cult efforts to take over their apartment complex, but other crimes charged against Rozier had no such obvious motives. Detectives reported that Rozier's fingerprints had been found at the scene of two random murders where transients were killed, their ears sliced off, and press releases linked him with at least five murders in Miami and environs. At this writing, authorities in St. Louis and New York City are studying Rozier's possible involvement in other unsolved homicides. He has been sentenced to 22 years in Florida.

Ruzicka, James

In and out of juvenile facilities and prisons from the age of nine, James Ruzicka was the product of an abusive home who compounded his problem with abuse of LSD, cocaine, mescaline and heroin. He first practiced bestiality as a child, soon progressing to the molestation of young girls. In 1973, at age 23, he was convicted of raping two Washington women at knifepoint. Pronounced a sexual psychopath by the court, he received a ten-year prison sentence, suspended on condition that he join a sex-offender rehabilitation program at Western State Hospital, near Tacoma.

Ruzicka jumped at the chance to escape prison time, and soon advanced to the position of trusty, escorting other patients to their work stations outside the hospital's maximum-security wing. Administrators thought enough of Ruzicka to grant him a 48-hour furlough, from which he never returned. Making tracks for Seattle, the fugitive moved in with his ex-wife and her new husband, living rent-free for a time before striking off on his own.

In the four weeks after his flight from Tacoma, Ruzicka murdered two girls in Seattle. Nancy Kinghammer, 16, and Penny Haddenham, 14, were both abducted from their homes by night, with Penny's corpse recovered first. Investigators found her hanging from a tree, just off the West Seattle Expressway; an autopsy determined that she had been raped, then strangled, before her body was strung up.

Nancy Kinghammer surfaced a month later, her half-naked body concealed beneath trash in a vacant lot used as a dumping ground. Some towels were wrapped around the decomposing corpse; together with a knife, found near the scene, they would be traced by homicide detectives to the home of Ruzicka's ex-wife.

By that time, Ruzicka had been arrested in Beaverton, Oregon, for the brutal rape of a 13-year-old girl. "I asked her if she wanted to ball," he told police, "and she didn't say 'no,' so I figured she wouldn't mind." Sentenced to prison on that charge, Ruzicka later confessed to the murders in Washington and was extradited for trial. Convicted on all counts, he received two consecutive life terms, to be served following completion of his Oregon sentence. (Authorities in Oregon have reportedly ordered a series of hormone injections for Ruzicka, designed to reduce his libido.)

San Diego, CA—Unsolved Murders

In August 1988, authorities from Washington and San Diego issued an announcement that at least ten unsolved murders, logged since June of 1985, were "definitely" linked with other homicides committed near Seattle and

Tacoma by the elusive "Green River Killer." One detective referred to the connection as "common knowledge," and some investigators placed the body-count a good deal higher. Lt. Bill Baxter, head of the San Diego Sheriff's Homicide Department, declared that at least ten—and no more than twelve—women had been murdered by one man over the past three years. Detective Tom Streed, leading the investigation, was inclined to think the killer's death toll might have reached eighteen. Whatever their opinion, all concerned agreed upon ten victims in the case.

The first to die had been 22-year-old Donna Gentile, last seen alive on June 22, 1985. Her naked, strangled body was recovered three days later, in the neighborhood of Mount Laguna, rocks and gravel packed inside her mouth and throat.

The second victim was a young "Jane Doe," her body badly decomposed when hikers found it near a rural creek, head lodged beneath a tree limb, on July 22, 1986. Nearby, authorities found clothing and a wedding ring believed to be the victim's, but the evidence has not provided any clue to her identity.

Theresa Brewer, 26 years old, was next to face the killer's wrath. Bound in a fetal position and "probably strangled," her body was found on August 3, 1986, identified three days later from a comparison of dental records.

On April 23, 1987, a group of illegal immigrants discovered the nude, decomposing remains of Rosmarie Ritter, age 29. Despite a ruling of death due to methamphetamine poisoning, she is listed as one of the murderer's "definite" victims. Two months later, on June 22, 32-year-old Anna Varela was found in Pine Valley, by joggers who nearly stumbled over her naked, strangled corpse.

Sally Moorman-Field, a 19-year-old prostitute and drug abuser, joined the list on September 20, 1987, stripped and strangled prior to her discovery by bicyclists. The cause of death was undetermined five days later, when the decomposed remains of Sara Gedalecia, a 36-year-old transient, were discovered at Alpine. Likewise, on October 19, the authorities could list no cause of death for

24-year-old Diana Moffitt, but dismemberment of her skeleton placed her on the victims list.

Another "Jane Doe" victim, found at Rancho Bernardo on April 13, 1988, had been dead for a week when her body was discovered, the cause of death once again undetermined. Melissa Sandoval, a 20-year-old junkie prostitute, was last seen alive on May 21, climbing into the car of an unidentified "trick." Her strangled body was recovered eight days later, within thirty yards of the previous dump site at Rancho Bernardo.

At this writing, police appear no closer to solution of the homicides in Washington or San Diego County. If their statements on a link between the crimes are accurate, the nomadic "Green River" killer may hold a new record for American serial murders, with a minimum toll of 56 known victims.

[See also: "Green River Killer"]

Sarmento, William

On November 4, 1987, nine-year-old Frankie Barnes was reported missing when he failed to return from a neighborhood bike ride in Providence, Rhode Island. His bicycle was found two weeks later, concealed in tall grass near an abandoned brewery, less than a half-mile from his home.

A month later, on December 14, six-year-old Jason Wolf vanished in Providence, after his mother sent him out to retrieve the daily mail. Teenagers found his body on December 21, two miles from home, discarded in some brush near Mashapaug Pond. An autopsy revealed the cause of death as blows to the head, inflicted with a blunt instrument. Police were still puzzling over the case five days later, when they received an anonymous note in the mail. It read:

You will find the little boy by a wooden cross near Tongue Pond. I didn't want to do it. Satan ordered me to. I hope you will kill me, cops, because I don't know why I killed the children.

Following the note's instructions, searchers found Frankie Barnes on the northern shoreline of Tongue Pond, his body gashed by multiple stab wounds. An examination of the envelope revealed faint impressions of a man's name, followed by the phrase: "Catch me if you can, ha, ha, ha." Police called on the suspect, and he suggested his name might have been used by an enemy, William Sarmento, who had recently tried to seduce the man's girlfriend.

Police were familiar with the 21-year-old Sarmento. In 1985, he pled guilty to assaulting a neighborhood dog catcher and was sentenced to one year's probation. Three days later, he was picked up again, on charges of assault with a dangerous weapon, and he served 20 days in jail for violating his probation. Residents of Frankie Barnes's neighborhood recalled seeing Sarmento in the vicinity, and investigation disclosed that Sarmento was a childhood acquaintance of Jason Wolf's mother.

Detectives held a press conference on December 29, 1987, naming Sarmento as their primary suspect in two murders. Later that day, he was seen ducking into a cellar and police were summoned to make the arrest. Held without bond pending psychiatric evaluation, Sarmento is rumored to have confessed to both homicides.

Schaefer, Gerard John

A homicidal ex-policeman from Oakland Park, Florida, dubbed the "Sex Beast" by local newsmen, Schaefer was theoretically linked with the murders of at least 20 persons after the jewelry, teeth, and clothing of several victims were recovered from a trunk in the attic of his mother's home. The public defender's office was unable to prevent Schaefer's conviction and imprisonment on first-degree murder charges, but the killer took it in stride. When Schaefer's wife divorced him and became engaged to his defense attorney, he gave the couple his blessing, requesting that the same lawyer continue to handle his case through forthcoming appeals.

Schmid, Charles Howard

Born in Tucson in 1942, Schmid was the pampered only child of parents who ran a local rest home, indulging their son's every whim on the side. A pathological braggart and liar, he wore cowboy boots stuffed with paper and crushed beer cans to increase his small stature, explaining the resultant limp as an injury sustained while fighting members of the Mafia. On graduation from high school, Schmid began dyeing his hair jet black, applied layers of cosmetics, and designed a phony mole to make his face "look meaner." In spite of his bizarre appearance, he became a hero to a quasi-cult of disaffected local youth, with various teenage girls competing for his affection.

Boozing it up with friends Mary French and John Saunders on the night of May 31, 1964, Schmid suddenly announced, "I want to kill a girl tonight. I think I can get away with it." His chosen victim was 15-year-old Alleen Rowe, lured from home to a stretch of desert near the local golf course, where Schmid raped her, beat her to death with a stone, and planted her corpse in a shallow grave.

Over the next year, Schmid became romantically involved with Gretchen Fritz, a possessive 17-year-old whose clinging ways eventually grated on Schmid's nerves. On the night of August 11, 1965, Schmid strangled Gretchen and her sister, 13-year-old Wendy Fritz, at his home, afterward dumping their bodies in the desert. Unable to contain himself, he boasted of the crime to friend Richard Bruns, driving Bruns out to look at the bodies, enlisting his help for a hasty burial.

The murders were an open secret, shared by scores of Tucson teens, but no one notified police or parents. Schmid was questioned by a pair of hoodlum types, allegedly employed to find the missing sisters, but he claimed that they had run away to California. Backing up his story, Schmid drove to San Diego, where he was arrested for impersonating an FBI agent, "questioning" girls at the beach. Back home in Tucson, Schmid was married in September, proposing to his 15-year-old bride after a blind date, but his facade was cracking, his behavior growing even more erratic. Richard Bruns believed his own girlfriend might be Schmid's next target, and he finally phoned the police on November 11, leading to Schmid's arrest.

Exposure of the crimes stunned Tucson, with revelations of teenage drinking, drug abuse and sex, plus dabbling in the occult. Dubbed the "Pied Piper of Tucson," Schmid was sentenced to die for killing the Fritz sisters; a guilty plea to second-degree murder in the case of Alleen Rowe earned him a sentence of 50 years to life. The death sentence was commuted to life imprisonment six years later, when the U.S. Supreme Court declared capital punishment unconstitutional.

On November 11, 1972, Schmid escaped from prison in the company of triple-murderer Raymond Hudgens. The fugitives held four hostages at a ranch near Tempe, then split up, and both were recaptured within days. On March 20, 1975, Schmid was stabbed 20 times in a prison brawl, and he died from his wounds ten days later.

Sellers, Sean

Born in 1969, Sellers was 18 months old when his parents divorced. A year later, in 1972, he was left with relatives while his mother hit the road, seeking work. By 1976, she had remarried—to auto mechanic Paul Bellofatto—but they still traveled widely on jobs, and young Sean spent most of his time with aunts and uncles, developing a painful sense of rejection along the way. By age 12, he was actively studying Satanism, immersed in the dark fantasy world of "Dungeons and Dragons." Frequent moves increased his sense of isolation, and a 1983 reunion with his mother and stepfather scarcely improved matters. Dumped with an aunt at Okmulgee, Oklahoma, in March 1984, Sellers plunged deeper into his occult studies, drinking the blood of fellow teenage cultists and using it to write his own personal "dedication to Satan."

Sean's family was reunited in the fall of 1984, in Oklahoma City, but the brooding 15-year-old was already over the edge. In February 1985, Sellers used his own blood to write: "I renounce God, I renounce Christ. I will serve only Satan . . . Hail Satan." Discovery of his occult interests led to angry scenes with Paul Bellofatto, Sean's step-father telling the troubled boy, "You don't exist!"

On September 8, 1985, Sellers and another teenage Satanist invaded a local convenience store, Sean fatally shooting a clerk—Richard Bower—who had once refused to sell them beer. In his own words, the murder "opened a new portal" for Sellers, and he "plunged into Satanism with everything I had."

A few months later, in the middle of the night, he crept into the master bedroom of his family home, executing his mother and Bellofatto with his step-father's own pistol. Sellers contrived to "find" the bodies the next day, but his friends were suspicious, and his accomplice in the Bower homicide eventually turned state's evidence to save himself. Convicted on three counts of murder in September 1986, Sellers was sentenced to die, becoming the youngest inmate on Oklahoma's death row.

Sims, Mitchell Carlton
and Padgett, Ruby Carolyn

A drifter from South Carolina, 25-year-old Mitchell Sims liked to call himself "a human ashtray," amusing his friends by stubbing out cigarettes on his bare chest. Self-mutilation was only one of his pastimes, however, and Sims also cultivated a deep interest in the occult. Along the way, he found time for Ruby Padgett, five years his junior, and developed a bizarre, abiding hatred for the nationwide chain of Domino's Pizza restaurants.

The latter quirk may have been rooted in his own employment with the chain, which had been terminated in the fall of 1985. On December 3, 1985, Sims invaded the Domino's restaurant in Wanahan, South Carolina, where he had recently worked, holding two employees at gunpoint and torturing both before he shot them, execution-style. One victim was killed outright; the other—hit four times—managed to reach a police station, naming Sims as the gunman before he collapsed.

The charge was double murder when his second victim

died, a week later, but Sims and Padgett were already settled in Glendale, California, lining up their next crime. On December 10, Sims ordered a Domino's pizza delivered to his motel room. Upon arrival, deliveryman John Harrington was stripped, gagged with a washcloth, and drowned in the bathtub. Sims wore the dead man's uniform when he returned to the restaurant, looted its safe, and left two employees locked in the freezer, bound in such a way that they were forced to stand on tip-toe to avoid hanging themselves.

This time, both victims managed to escape, and they identified a photograph of Sims as their assailant. Domino's offered a $100,000 reward for his arrest, but once again, the bird had flown.

By December 11, Sims and Padgett were hiding in Las Vegas, where he registered as "Jeff Richardson" at a cheap motel. Harrington's stolen pickup was recovered from the parking lot of a casino on December 21, and mass publicity resulted in the arrest of both suspects on Christmas morning. (An unemployed iron worker had taken the couple home for drinks before seeing their published photographs, after which he promptly turned them in for the reward.)

Sims and Padgett waived extradition to California, there pleading innocent to all counts in the Glendale robbery and murder. Fearful of execution in South Carolina, they resisted extradition to their home state, and California's governor agreed in February 1986, asserting Glendale's priority in placing the killers on trial. Mitchell Sims was convicted of Harrington's murder on May 20, 1987, and a month later his jury recommended the death penalty. On September 11, 1987, he was formally sentenced to die in the gas chamber at San Quentin.

Smith, Harold Glenn

On August 14, 1985, police in Houston were summoned to the Rest Haven Cemetery, where the custodian had found a young man's mutilated body. Identified as 19-year-old Dennis Medler, the victim had been savagely tortured before death, beaten and slashed with knives, one eye gouged from its socket, his hair burned down to the scalp and his teeth hammered out.

Death apparently had been produced by strangulation and/or loss of blood. The victim had no record with police, but an investigation soon revealed that he was known to pal around with local teenage Satanists. The mutilation of his body—and his murder in a cemetery—smacked of ritual, and deputies pursued the lead, interrogating members of the cult whom they were able to identify.

One girl informed detectives that her boyfriend was responsible for killing another victim, 16-year-old Wayne Schubert, shot to death some time before the Medler slaying. She reported that the killer showed her Schubert's bullet-riddled body, in his pickup truck, one afternoon when he dropped by her house to visit. He had seemed particularly proud of his achievement, which presumably endeared him to the Prince of Darkness.

Around the same time, police interviewed a 25-year-old motorist who had survived a brutal slashing at the hands of teenage hitchhikers. Under questioning, one of the repentant suspects fingered his companion, the slasher, as a Satanist and follower of "high priest" Harold Smith, a 19-year-old loser who achieved new status with his peers by means of mumbo-jumbo. Smith allegedly had driven the informant to a Houston flat where 25-year-old Ronald Monahan lay dead on the floor, his stabbing initially dismissed by police as a simple burglary gone sour. A witness to the Medler slaying, the informant named three other cultists who participated in the crime with Smith.

Before police could bag their suspects, a fourth murder was added to the list, a young "Jane Doe" found shot to death outside of Houston. Her death was theoretically linked to the cult by tattoos—including an inverted pentagram and the numerals "666"—discovered on her body by authorities. No charges have been filed in that case, though police believe the girl may have intended to defect, her death insuring silence to protect the cult.

In January 1986 authorities arrested Smith, two other teenage boys and a 16-year-old girl, charging all four with the murder of Dennis Medler. Jurors deliberated for 45 minutes before convicting Smith of first-degree murder, on August 13, 1986, and he was sentenced to life imprisonment, with an additional $10,000 fine.

Smith, Stephen Richard

A policeman turned homicidal vigilante in San Antonio, Texas, Stephen Smith was not exposed until his death, at the hands of a one-time friend and former patrol partner. The shooting of one police officer by another is guaranteed to rate headlines, but initial reports paled in comparison to statements from Smith's killer, charging that he had been forced to kill in self-defense, thereby preventing scheduled acts of murder meant to launch a local reign of terror.

By the date of his death, on August 18, 1986, Stephen Smith was already skating on thin ice as a guardian of law and order. In March, he had been indicted on charges of brutality stemming from the arrest of a shoplifting suspect on August 7, 1985. According to eyewitnesses, Smith had assaulted the 27-year-old subject without provocation, beating him to the ground, afterward brawling with bystanders who sought to intervene and help his victim. The incident was not Smith's first encounter with an allegation of excessive force; suspended after his indictment, by August 1986 he was a peace officer in name only.

Furious at his superiors for their "lack of support," Smith allegedly planned to assassinate Bexar County's district attorney, Sam Millsap, along with various high-ranking members of the police department. A search of Smith's home, after his death, revealed an arsenal of eighteen pistols, five shotguns, six rifles, and at least 100,000 rounds of ammunition. In retrospect, he was also suspected as the author of recent anonymous letters, mailed to newspapers and public officials, accusing department leaders of child molestation and other crimes.

Completely unhinged by the evening of August 17, 1986, Smith quarreled bitterly with his wife, and she called on a mutual friend, Patrolman Farrell Tucker, for help. Tucker visited Smith's apartment, where he was informed—by

Smith's wife—of the murder schemes in progress. He was also told that Mrs. Smith had seen her husband, while off duty, beat and murder several persons he suspected of criminal activity. (Smith was already suspect in the December 1982 slaying of Terrnell Folsom, gunned down by persons unknown while breaking into a parked car, but there was insufficient evidence for an indictment.)

On August 18, Tucker warned Smith's alleged targets of their potential danger. That night, wearing a concealed microphone and hidden pistol, Tucker met with Smith to hear his former partner's story. Rather than denying anything, Smith drew a .45 and threatened Tucker's life. Smith's momentary hesitation granted Tucker time to reach his gun, and five shots fired at point-blank range eliminated Smith as any kind of threat.

In retrospect, authorities believe that Stephen Smith was probably responsible for a 1983 sniper attack on the home of Deputy Police Chief Robert Heuck, as well as the 1985 firebombing of Police Chief Frank Hoyack's residence. Investigations are continuing in an attempt to trace the other victims mentioned by Smith's wife.

Smith, William Scott

A high school dropout and unemployed fry cook, William Smith was convicted on charges of "menacing" in 1978, at Silverton, Oregon. That same year, a second-degree burglary conviction, in nearby Salem, earned him a one-year suspended sentence. In 1979, Smith and another man were accused of second-degree sexual assault on an adult female victim; Smith was acquitted of the charge, while his companion went to jail. Authorities in Boise, Idaho, convicted Smith of indecent exposure during 1981, and a year later he was questioned by Ada County sheriff's officers in the unsolved murder of 14-year-old Lisa Chambers.

Things were getting hot in Idaho, and Smith returned to Salem, Oregon, where he felt more at home. On February 19, 1984, Rebecca Darling, 21, disappeared from her job on the graveyard shift at an all-night convenience store. A customer had seen her on the job around 3:20 a.m., but she was missing thirty minutes later, when another early shopper found the store deserted. Darling's decomposed remains were found March 25, concealed in brush along the Little Pudding River, six miles northeast of town. Nude from the waist up, she had been strangled with a piece of rope, hands bound behind her back.

On April 7, 1984, police responded to reports of an abandoned car and traced it back to 18-year-old co-ed Katherine Redmond, who had borrowed the wheels from her roommate after a campus frat party. Last seen alive around 2:15 a.m., Redmond was found on April 11, her nude body discarded four miles from the spot where Rebecca Darling was discovered. Death had been induced by "traumatic asphyxiation," her vagina lacerated with some unknown foreign object.

Witnesses reported sightings of a late-1960s Pontiac station wagon in the area where Redmond's car was recovered, around the time she must have met her killer. Another Salem resident reported being bumped by a similar car, days earlier; the hulking driver had invited her to leave her car and "check the damage," but he soon lost interest when she countered with suggestions that they both drive to a nearby gas station.

By April 18, police were focusing on William Smith as their primary suspect. He owned the right kind of car, and in the early hours of April 7, he had called a tow truck to rescue him from a ditch near the place where Katherine Redmond's car was found. Before detectives had a chance to move against their man, he was incarcerated for 180 days after pleading guilty to a series of obscene and threatening phone calls.

On April 26, 1984, Smith was arraigned on two counts of first-degree murder in Salem. (Police saw no links between Smith and five other unsolved homicides that had plagued Salem since 1981.) Waiving his right to a jury trial in July, Smith was convicted on all counts by the presiding judge, drawing two consecutive terms of life imprisonment. He must complete a minimum of forty years before he is considered for parole.

Sobhraj, Charles Gurmukh

Born Hotchand Bhawnani Gurmukh Sobhraj, in April 1944, Asia's premier serial slayer was the illegitimate son of a Vietnamese peasant girl and a wealthy Indian merchant living in Saigon. Soon after his birth, Sobhraj's father married an Indian woman in Poona, and his mother retaliated by wedding a French military officer when Sobhraj was four years old. The land of Indochina was in turmoil at the time, with French colonial troops fighting a hopeless rear-guard action against Viet Minh communist rebels, and Hotchand Sobhraj witnessed countless acts of violence before his step-father took the family to France in 1953.

Sobhraj hated Europe and the Catholic boarding school in Paris where he soon became the butt of racial jokes and insults. (The school's lasting mark was a name change—to "Charles"—after Sobhraj's clever impersonation of comedian Charlie Chaplin.) At first, he expressed his displeasure through tantrums and persistent bed-wetting, twice running away to Saigon in his teens. Sobhraj's father sent him back each time, but finally agreed to pay his passage for a trial visit home. The ticket never came, and Sobhraj turned to robbery, landing briefly in jail on his second try. He finally reached Vietnam on his own, but the family reunion was tense, and Sobhraj was soon packed off to live with relatives in India after wrecking his father's car. When he turned up in Saigon again, uninvited, Charles's father threw in the towel, sending him back to France.

In Paris, Charles was locked up twice for auto theft, emerging from jail the second time with a short-lived desire to "go straight." He married, found a job, but the straight life quickly palled. Jailed again for writing forged checks on his sister's account, Charles was freed when she dropped the charges. He continued bouncing checks thereafter, saving up some 30,000 francs before he took his wife to Bombay, setting up shop as an international con man and smuggler, specializing in the theft of passports from American and European tourists. Arrested for a jewel robbery in Delhi, Charles was granted bail in spite of an escape attempt. He fled at once to Kabul, in Afghanistan, where he was jailed for auto theft and lesser charges. Another escape brought him back to France, where he kidnapped his infant daughter from his mother-in-law, leaving the woman drugged and locked in a hotel room.

Sobhraj's first known murder victim was a Pakistani chauffeur named Habib, hired by Charles and a female companion in September 1972, for a drive between Rawalpindi and Peshawar. Along the way, for reasons unknown, Charles injected Habib with a drug that took his life, then dumped the driver's body in a river. Warrants were issued for suspect "Damon Seaman," but another year would pass before Sobhraj was finally identified.

Arresting him was something else. In November 1973, Sobhraj was in Istanbul, teaming up with his brother Guy to drug and rob wealthy tourists. Both were arrested in Greece, but Charles managed another escape, leaving his brother in jail as he fled back to India. In Delhi, he entered the heroin trade, gaining a foothold in the cut-throat business with inside information procured—under drugs and torture—from a local pusher whom Sobhraj later killed.

Murder seemed to come easier each time. In October 1975, Sobhraj killed an American tourist, Teresa Knowlton, in his Delhi flat and had a sidekick dump her body. A Turkish competitor in the drug trade, Vitali Hakim, was beaten, his neck snapped, his corpse doused with gasoline and set afire. In Bangkok, Charles strangled Hakim's French contact, one Stephanie Parry. A month later, still in Bangkok, he strangled Dutch tourists Cornelia Hemker and Henricus Bitanja on December 16, burning their bodies as a hedge against arrest. Shortly before Christmas, Canadian Laurent Carriere and American Connie Bronzick were found dead in Katmandu, their bodies burned. Sobhraj—traveling as Henricus Bitanja, with his victim's passport—had booked a room at the same hotel, but he slipped out of Nepal after preliminary questioning.

The killer continued his aimless trek across Asia, murdering Israeli Allen Jacobs for his passport at Varanasi, in northern India. A few days later, on January 9, 1976, Sobhraj and two accomplices drugged a trio of Frenchmen at Goa, dumping their bodies at roadside, but all three victims managed to survive. In Hong Kong, Allen Gore was also lucky; he lost $8,000 but kept his life, despite a jolt of Sobhraj's chemical cocktail. Arrested with false passports in Bangkok, Charles was allowed to walk after doling out bribes all around. In Penang, he was arrested for trying to cash stolen traveler's checks, but he managed to talk his way out of jail.

Back in Bombay, Sobhraj slipped a fatal mickey to French tourist Jean-Luc Solomon, moving on from there to more ambitious projects. Shooting for the moon, he drugged an entire class of 60 French engineering students, but miscalculation of the dose sent 20 to a local hospital, and this time police were waiting. Arrested on July 5, 1976, Sobhraj was linked with at least ten homicides spanning the past three years.

Convicted of "culpable homicide" in the Solomon case, Sobhraj was sentenced to seven years at hard labor, with two more years tacked on for drugging the French students. In 1982, he was sentenced to life imprisonment for the murder of Allen Jacobs, but appeals are continuing. Thailand and Nepal have announced their intention to file murder charges if Sobhraj should manage to win his release.

"Son of Sam, The"

New Yorkers are accustomed to reports of violent death in every form, from the mundane to the bizarre. They take it all in stride, accepting civic carnage as a price for living in the largest, richest city in America. But residents were unprepared for the commencement of an all-out reign of terror in July 1976. For thirteen months, New York would be a city under siege, its female citizens afraid to venture out by night while an apparent homicidal maniac was waiting, seeking prey.

The terror came with darkness, on July 29, 1976. Two young women, Donna Lauria and Jody Valenti, had parked their car on Buhre Avenue, remaining in the vehicle and passing time in conversation. If they saw the solitary male pedestrian at all, he didn't register. In any case, they never saw the pistol that he raised to pump five shots directly through the windshield. Donna Lauria was killed immediately; her companion got off "easy," with a bullet in the thigh.

The shooting was a tragic incident, but in itself was not unusual for New York City. There was scattered sympathy, but no alarm among the residents of New York's urban combat zone . . . until the next attack.

On October 23, Carl Denaro and Rosemary Keenan parked outside a bar in Flushing, Queens. Again, the gunman went unnoticed as he crouched to fire a single bullet through the car's rear window. Wounded, Carl Denaro would survive. A .44-caliber bullet was found on the floor of the car, and detectives would match it with slugs from the Lauria murder.

Just over one month later, on November 26, Donna DeMasi and Joanne Lomino were sitting together on the stoop of a house in the Floral Park section of Queens. A man approached them from the sidewalk, asking for directions, but before he could complete the question he had drawn a pistol, blasting at the startled women. Both were wounded, Donna paralyzed forever with a bullet in her spine.

Again the slugs were readily identified, and now detectives knew they had a random killer on their hands. The gunman seemed to favor girls with long, dark hair, and there was speculation that the shooting of Denaro in October may have been "an accident." The young man's hair was dark and shoulder-length; a gunman closing on him from behind might have mistaken Carl Denaro for a woman in the darkness.

Christmas season passed without another shooting, but the gunman had not given up his hunt. On January 30, 1977, John Diel and Christine Freund were parked and necking in the Ridgewood section of New York, when bullets hammered out their windshield. Freund was killed on impact, while her date was physically unscathed.

March 8th. Virginia Voskerichian, an Armenian exchange student, was walking toward her home in Forest Hills when a man approached and shot her in the face, killing her instantly. Detectives noted that she had been slain within 300 yards of the January murder scene.

On April 17, Alexander Esau and his date, Valentina Suriani, were parked in the Bronx, a few blocks from the site of the Lauria-Valenti shooting. Caught up in each other, they may not have seen the gunman coming; certainly they never heard the fusillade of shots that killed them both immediately, fired from pointblank range.

Detectives found a crudely-printed letter in the middle of the street, near Esau's car. Addressed to the captain in charge of New York's hottest manhunt, the note contained a chilling message.

> I am deeply hurt by your calling me a weman-hater *(sic)*. I am not. But I am a monster. I am the Son of Sam . . . I love to hunt. Prowling the streets looking for fair game—tasty meat. The weman *(sic)* of Queens are the prettyest *(sic)* of all . . .

The note describing "Sam" as a drunken brute who beat the members of his family and sent his son out hunting "tasty meat," compelling him to kill. There would be other letters from the gunman, some addressed to newsman Jimmy Breslin, hinting at more crimes to come and fueling the hysteria that had already gripped New York. The writer was apparently irrational, but no less dangerous for that, and homicide investigators had no clue to his identity.

On June 26, Salvatore Lupo and girlfriend Judy Placido were parked in Bayside, Queens, when four shots pierced the windshield of their car. Both were wounded; both survived.

On July 31, Robert Violante and Stacy Moskowitz went parking near the Brooklyn shore. The killer found them there and squeezed off four shots at their huddled silhouettes, striking both young people in the head. Stacy Moskowitz died instantly; her date survived, but damage from his wounds left Robert Violante blind for life.

It was the last attack, but homicide detectives didn't know that, yet. A woman walking near the final murder scene recalled two traffic officers writing a ticket for a car

parked close beside a hydrant; moments later, she had
seen a man approach the car, climb in, and pull away with
squealing tires. A check of parking ticket records traced
an old Ford Galaxy belonging to one David Berkowitz, of
Pine Street, Yonkers. Staking out the address, officers discovered that the car was parked outside; a semi-automatic
rifle lay in plain view on the seat, together with a note that
had been written in the "Son of Sam's" distinctive, awk-
ward style. When Berkowitz emerged from his apartment,
he was instantly arrested and confessed his role in New
York's reign of terror.

The story told by Berkowitz seemed tailor-made for an
insanity defense in court. The "Sam" referred to in his
letters was a neighbor, one Sam Carr, whose Labrador
retriever was allegedly possessed by ancient demons,
beaming out commands for Berkowitz to kill and kill
again. On one occasion, he had tried to kill the dog, but
it was useless; demons spoiled his aim, and when the dog
recovered from its wounds, the nightly torment had redoubled its intensity. A number of psychiatrists describe
the suspect as a paranoid schizophrenic, suffering from
delusions and therefore incompetent to stand trial. The
lone exception was Dr. David Abrahamson, who found
that Berkowitz was sane and capable of understanding that
his actions had been criminal. The court agreed with
Abrahamson and ordered Berkowitz to trial. The gunman
filed a plea of guilty at his court appearance and was sentenced to 365 years in prison.

Ironically, Berkowitz seemed grateful to Dr. Abrahamson for his sanity ruling, and later agreed to a series of
interviews that Abrahamson has published in a book, *Confessions of Son of Sam*. The interviews revealed that Berkowitz had tried to kill two women during 1975, attacking
them with knives, but he turned squeamish when they
screamed and tried to fight him off. ("I didn't want to hurt
them," he explained, confused. "I only wanted to kill
them.") A virgin at the time of his arrest, Berkowitz was
prone to fabricate elaborate lies about his bedroom prow-
ess, all the while intent upon revenge against the women
who habitually rejected him. When not engaged in stalking female victims, Berkowitz reportedly was an accom-

plished arsonist; a secret journal lists the details of 300 fires for which he was allegedly responsible around New York. In his conclusion, Dr. Abrahamson describes his subject as a homicidal exhibitionist with fantasies of "dying for a cause."

There is another side to David Berkowitz, however, and it surfaced shortly after his arrest, with allegations of his membership in a Satanic cult. In letters mailed from prison, Berkowitz described participation in a New York cult affiliated with the lethal "Four Pi Movement," based in California. He revealed persuasive inside knowledge of a California homicide, unsolved since 1974, and wrote that "There are other Sons out there—God help the world."

According to the story told by Berkowitz in prison, two of neighbor Sam Carr's sons were also members of the killer cult that specialized in skinning dogs alive and gunning victims down on darkened streets. One suspect, John Wheat Carr, was said to be the same "John Wheaties" mentioned in a letter penned by Berkowitz, containing other clues that point to cult involvement in the random murders. Carr had been in Houston, Texas, on June 12, 1976—the day Berkowitz purchased his .44 revolver there—and six months after Berkowitz was captured, Carr "committed suicide" in Minot, North Dakota, under circumstances that police now view as willful murder.

Another Carr—John's brother Michael—died in New York City on October 4, 1979, after crashing his car into a streetlamp at 75 miles per hour. An autopsy found Carr to be heavily intoxicated, in spite of his well-known religious aversion to alcohol. Following his death, the "Sam" case was officially reopened, with investigations continuing to this day.

Newsman Maury Terry, after six years on the case, believes there were at least five different gunners in the "Sam" attacks, including Berkowitz, John Carr, and several suspects—one a woman—who have yet to be indicted. Terry also notes that six of seven shootings fell in close proximity to recognized Satanic holidays, the March 8 Voskerichian attack emerging as a sole exception to the "pattern." In the journalist's opinion, Berkowitz was chosen as a scapegoat by the other members of his cult, who then set out to "decorate" his flat with weird graffiti, whipping up a bogus "arson ledger"—which includes peculiar out-of-order entries—to support a plea of innocent by reason of insanity.

On July 10, 1979, David Berkowitz was assaulted by persons unknown in the segregation block at Attica prison, his throat slashed from behind in a near-fatal attack that left him with 56 stitches. Less talkative since his brush with death, he remains in prison, and the case remains technically "open," awaiting development of new evidence that may bring other suspects to trial. (See also: Baker, Stanley; "Four Pi Movement;" Kogut, John; Manson, Charles)

Soto, Erno

Officially unsolved, the case of New York City's "Charlie Chopoff" murders occupied police for more than two years, from March 1972 through May 1974. The files are officially open today, despite the arrest of a promising suspect and his eventual commitment to a mental institution for the criminally insane. While he remains incarcerated and incompetent for trial, the crimes may not be cleared, but lead investigators on the case are quick to note that "Charlie's" random depredations ended when their man was taken off the street.

Erno Soto's marriage seemed to be the root of all his problems. Separated from his wife for several years, he made a stab at reconciliation, but was startled to discover she had conceived a black child in his absence. (Soto and his wife were Puerto Ricans.) He pretended not to care, but as the boy's eighth birthday rolled around, Soto's behavior grew increasingly erratic, resulting in his commitment to Manhattan State Hospital in 1969 and 1970. He would return for further treatment at sporadic intervals thereafter, but the evidence suggests that Soto found his primary relief by stalking small, dark boys on New York's streets.

The first to die was Douglas Owens, black and eight

years old, found murdered two blocks from his Harlem flat on March 9, 1972. Discarded on a rooftop, Owens had been stabbed 38 times in the neck, chest, and back, his penis slashed but still appended to his body by a bloody flap of skin. An anonymous phone tip, received by police on March 23, fingered Soto as a suspect in the case, but it was not pursued.

Another black boy, ten years old, was attacked on the city's Upper West Side, on April 20. Stabbed in the neck and back, he was also sexually mutilated, his penis severed and carried away by the man who left him for dead. The boy survived his injuries and offered homicide detectives a description of the suspect, but the trauma he had suffered limited his value as a witness.

On October 23, another black boy—nine-year-old Wendell Hubbard, was killed in East Harlem, six blocks from the site of the Owens murder. Hubbard was stabbed 17 times in the neck, chest, and abdomen, his penis removed by the killer and carried away from the scene. Five months later, on March 7, nine-year-old Luis Ortiz, a dark-skinned Puerto Rican, vanished on an errand to the corner store. His body—stabbed 38 times in the neck, chest, and back, penis severed and missing—was found in the basement of an apartment house along his route of travel.

The death of Steven Cropper, on August 17, 1973, appeared to break the killer's pattern. Cropper fit the victim profile perfectly—a black boy, eight years old—and while he had been murdered on a rooftop, he had not been stabbed. Instead, the fatal wounds were razor slashes, and his genitals were still intact. Police initially suspected that a second killer was responsible, but they eventually decided it was too coincidental for a pair of slashers to be simultaneously stalking young black boys.

On May 25, 1974, Soto was arrested after bungling the abduction of a nine-year-old Puerto Rican boy, surrounded by neighbors and held for police after the child escaped his clutches. In custody, he confessed to the Cropper slaying, but "Charlie Chopoff's" sole surviving victim refused to pick Soto out of a lineup, saying only that the suspect's appearance was "similar." Officials at Manhattan State Hospital initially provided an alibi, stating that

Soto was confined on the date of Cropper's slaying, but they later admitted he sometimes slipped away from the facility, unnoticed. Found to be insane, the suspect was returned to the hospital under closer guard, the "unsolved" murders terminating after he was locked away.

Speck, Richard Franklin

Born at Kirkwood, Illinois, on December 6, 1941, Speck was six years old when his family moved to Dallas, Texas. Over the next two decades, he would chalk up 37 arrests in Dallas, specializing in public drunkenness, disorderly conduct, and burglary. At age 20, working part-time as a garbage man, he married 15-year-old Shirley Malone and fathered a child. In 1965, he was charged with assaulting a Dallas woman, holding a knife to her throat in a parking garage before neighbors arrived to chase him off. Sentenced to 490 days in jail, he was released early and handed over to state authorities as a parole violator.

Separated from his wife in March 1966, Speck followed the remnants of his family back to Monmouth, Illinois. A drug-dependent alcoholic, Speck was bitter toward his wife, expressing a desire to kill her, but he never found the time. Obsessed with sex, he divided his time between sleazy bars and sporadic work on ore barges plying the Great Lakes. Speck was ultimately prosecuted—and is known today—for the final spasm of violence that claimed eight lives in a single massacre, but evidence suggests that there were actually a dozen victims, murdered in a three-month period of 1966.

The first to die was Mary Pierce, a barmaid and divorcee who rejected Speck's advances. First reported missing on the night of April 10, she was discovered three days later, nude and strangled, in a shed behind the tavern where she worked. On April 18, a 65-year-old woman was robbed and raped by a man matching Speck's description, but the ore boats had carried him away before detectives sought to question him.

Hospitalized for an emergency appendectomy in May, Speck signed on with another barge on June 27, 1966.

Dismissed from his job on July 2, at Indiana Harbor, Speck was in the neighborhood when three girls vanished at nearby Dunes Park, the same day. Police found their clothes in the car they had driven, assuming all three had stripped down to their swimsuits, but no trace of their bodies was ever discovered.

Speck surfaced in Chicago in July 10, dropping by the National Maritime Union hiring hall to seek passage on a vessel bound for New Orleans. Three nights later, a half-block from the union hall, he knocked on the door of Jeffrey Manor, a two-story townhouse occupied by student nurses from nearby South Chicago Community Hospital. High on drugs and reeking of alcohol, he brandished a pistol and knife when 23-year-old Corazon Amurao opened the door. "I'm not going to hurt you," Speck said. "I'm only going to tie you up. I need your money to go to New Orleans."

Moving through the house, he roused five other student nurses from their beds, herding all six into one room, where they were bound and lined up on the floor. Three more came home from dates over the course of an hour, leaving Speck with nine helpless captives on his hands. The possibilities aroused him, and he made his mind up to eliminate them all.

Speck untied 20-year-old Pamela Wilkening first, leading her into another room where she was stabbed in the chest, then strangled with a strip of sheet. He went back next for 20-year-old Mary Jordan and 21-year-old Suzanne Farris, guiding both women into a different bedroom. There, he stabbed Jordan three times—in the heart, neck, and eye—before turning on Farris, stabbing her 18 times and strangling her lifeless body, shredding her underclothes without taking time for rape.

Nina Schmale, age 24, was next, ordered into another room where Speck told her to lie on the bed, afterward slashing her throat and strangling her to death. While he was thus engaged, the other student nurses wriggled under beds to hide themselves, but Speck would find them all . . . except for Corazon Amurao, huddled in a darkened corner, dumb-struck in her terror.

Valentina Pasion, 23, and Nerlita Gargullo, 22, were

the next to die. Directed to an empty bedroom, Pasion was killed with one deep stab to the throat. Gargullo absorbed four wounds before she toppled across Pasion's body, Speck scrambling after her to finish the job by manual strangulation.

Pausing to wash the blood off his hands, Speck returned for Patricia Matusek and carried her, still bound, into the bathroom. Placing her on the floor, he kicked her savagely in the stomach before squatting astride her body and strangling her to death, leaving her where she lay.

Losing count of his victims, Speck spent the next twenty minutes raping Gloria Davy, once pausing to ask, "Would you mind putting your legs around my back?" When he was finished, Speck led the naked woman downstairs and assaulted her a second time, using some unknown object to mutilate her anus before he strangled her to death and left her lying on a couch.

When Speck was gone, Corazon Amurao made her way to the balcony and called down for help. The killer's use of square knots suggested a seaman to police, and Amurao recalled Speck's remark about New Orleans, together with a tattoo—"Born to Raise Hell"—on his left forearm. Hospitalized on July 17, after a bungled suicide attempt, Speck was recognized from the tattoo and police were summoned to make the arrest. Convicted of multiple murder in April 1967, Speck was sentenced to death a month later, his sentence overturned when the U.S. Supreme Court ruled capital punishment unconstitutional. In the wake of that decision, Speck was resentenced to consecutive life terms totaling more than 400 years.

Spisak, Frank G., Jr.

At 32, Frank Spisak was a walking exercise in contradictions. Neighbors on the near East Side of Cleveland knew him as "Frankie Ann Spisak," a frizzy-haired transvestite who looked forward to the prospect of a sex-change operation, but he had another side, as well. When not in drag, Frank Spisak worshipped Adolf Hitler, ultimately casting off his gowns and makeup in a bid to emulate his idol, growing a toothbrush mustache and slicking his hair down in classic Hitlerian style.

In February 1982, Spisak launched a series of "search-and-destroy missions" designed to "clean up" the city. Selecting his targets at random, Spisak invaded the campus of Cleveland State University, shooting a black minister, Rev. Horace Rickerson, to death in a men's room. Four months later, he wounded another black, 55-year-old John Hardaway, rebounding in August with a full-scale rampage. Before the month was over, Spisak killed 50-year-old Timothy Sheehan, assistant superintendent of buildings and grounds at CSU, and 17-year-old Brian Warford, gunned down at a bus stop near campus. A third attack failed, with Spisak narrowly missing CSU employee Coletta Dartt. Both Sheehan and Dartt were Caucasians, but Spisak had suspected the building superintendent of being a Jew.

Arrested in September 1982, after firing a gun from his apartment window, Spisak was released on bail before an anonymous caller advised police to reexamine his .22-caliber weapon. Test bullets matched slugs retrieved from the Warford murder, and Spisak later confessed to the other homicides, gloating that "my aim was pretty good."

Pleading insanity at his trial, in August 1983, Spisak declared that his one-man war had been launched under orders from God, his "immediate superior." Jews were to blame for his earlier transvestite episodes, having "seized control of his mind" when Frank wasn't looking. How, a defense lawyer asked, was his brain working now? "Never better," the gunman replied.

With the results of psychiatric tests in hand, Judge James Sweeney ordered jurors to disregard Spisak's insanity plea for lack of evidence. Convicted after five hours of deliberation, he was sentenced to death on August 10, 1983. Defiant in the face of judgment, Frank addressed the court. "Even though this court may pronounce me guilty a thousand times," he declared, "the higher court of our great Aryan warrior god pronounces me innocent. Heil Hitler!"

Staniak, Lucian

As a young man in Warsaw, Staniak lost his parents and sister in a tragic automobile accident. The driver responsible—a young Polish Air Force captain's wife—was cleared of criminal responsibility, but Staniak remained obsessed with "justice" in the case, and over time he hatched a scheme to punish young, blond women everywhere in Poland. He launched his campaign in 1964, with a letter to the Polish state newspaper. Writing in red ink, with a peculiar style that earned him the nickname of the "Red Spider," Staniak warned: "There is no happiness without tears, no life without death. Beware! I am going to make you cry."

Employed as a translator for the official state publishing house, Staniak traveled widely in his profession, chalking up an estimated 20 female victims in the next two years. The first, a 17-year-old student, was raped and mutilated at Olsztyn, on the anniversary of Polish liberation from the Nazi occupation. The next day, one of Staniak's trademark letters declared, "I picked a juicy flower in Olsztyn and I shall do it again somewhere else, for there is no holiday without a funeral."

His next holiday victim was a blond 16-year-old, who marched at the head of a student's parade on the day she died. An anonymous letter directed police to the body—ravaged, with a spike run through the genitals—in a factory basement not far from her home.

On All Saints Day, Staniak murdered a blond hotel receptionist, mutilating her body with a screwdriver. Next day, he wrote the press that "Only tears of sorrow can wash out the stain of shame; only pangs of suffering can blot out the fires of lust." On May Day 1966, he raped and disemboweled a 17-year-old, dumping her body in a tool shed behind her home, the victim's entrails pooled around her thighs. Police were looking into fourteen other cases when the killer left another victim raped and mutilated on a train, that Christmas Eve. His letter to the press was simple and direct: "I have done it again."

An artist of sorts, Staniak was finally traced by police in 1967, after he slaughtered a fellow member of the Art

Lovers Club. Police became suspicious when they viewed his paintings—mainly crimson, daubed on with a knife and focusing on scenes of mutilation—and they found that Staniak's itinerary for the past two years precisely coincided with the string of unsolved crimes. Arrested on the way home from his final murder, executed in a peevish bid for more publicity, Staniak readily confessed to 20 murders and was sent to an asylum, in Katowice, for life.

Stano, Gerald Eugene

A native of Daytona Beach, Florida, born in 1951 and adopted as an infant, Stano suffered persistent learning and "adjustment" problems in his early school years, complicated by a lack of coordination that resulted in frequent falls. After several years in a Virginia military academy, he graduated from high school in Daytona beach and went to work in his adoptive father's filling station, also working as a cook and waiter on the side. He met a lot of women, but they universally rejected him, increasing Stano's deep resentment toward a world of "bitches." Sometimes they laughed at Stano, but he also recalled that some "pulled my hair" or "threw beer bottles at me." Years later, after killing 41, he would confide to homicide detectives that "I hate a bitchy chick."

According to his own confession, Stano claimed his first two victims in New Jersey, during 1969. He drifted into Pennsylvania in the early 1970s and murdered half a dozen women there before returning to his native Florida, launching a one-man crime wave that would claim another 33 lives between 1973 and 1980. Devoted to the hunt, Stano preyed chiefly on prostitutes and hitchhikers, though one of his victims would be a high school cheerleader. They ranged in age from 13 to the mid-thirties, dispatched by means of gunshots, knives, and strangulation. None were raped, and state psychiatrists suggest that Stano drew his basic satisfaction from the simple act of murder. As one homicide detective summed the killer up, "He thinks about three things: stereo systems, cars, and killing women."

In April 1980, Stano was arrested after an intended victim managed to escape his clutches in Daytona Beach. In custody, he launched a marathon confession, directing officers to the buried remains of 24 identifiable victims and two skeletal "Jane Does," all in Florida. By December 1983, Stano had provided details of 41 murders, drawing eight life terms in Florida. His ninth conviction—for the murder of 17-year-old Cathy Scharf at Port Orange—earned him a death sentence, and he came within hours of the chair before an indefinite stay was granted on July 2, 1986. At this writing, Stano is still on death row, awaiting execution, and authorities believe that they have finally heard the last of his confessions.

Starkweather, Charles and Fugate, Caril Ann

Born to poverty in Lincoln, Nebraska, during 1940, Charles Starkweather was the runt of the litter, myopic and bowlegged, standing five foot two at age 17. Taunted by classmates in school, he lapsed into "black moods" as a child, developing "a hate as hard as iron" against his fellow man. Dropping out of high school to work as a garbageman, he displayed peculiar, anti-social behavior in public, sometimes shouting curses from his garbage truck, at total strangers. The sole exception to his misanthropic attitude was the affection Charlie felt for 14-year-old Caril Ann Fugate, but even that was tarnished by his rage. Caril's family disapproved of the relationship, justifiably unnerved by Starkweather's moods and his habit of carrying a favorite rifle wherever he went.

On December 1, 1957, Starkweather held up a gas station in Lincoln, abducting the attendant, 21-year-old Robert Colvert, and driving him into the countryside, where he was killed by a close-range shotgun blast. No one suspected Charlie of the crime, and his primal satisfaction in the act of murder was amplified by feelings of power when he escaped detection.

Seven weeks later, on January 21, 1958, Starkweather

was visiting Caril Ann's home when he got into a violent argument with her mother, Velda Bartlett. As Charlie recalled the incident, "They said they were tired of me hanging around," and blows were exchanged, Starkweather falling back on his favorite equalizer, blasting Bartlett and her husband where they stood. With Caril looking on, Charles grabbed her sister, two-year-old Betty Bartlett, and choked the girl to death by ramming his gun barrel down her throat. Caril then retired to watch TV, while Charles concealed the bodies and prepared some sandwiches. A sign was posted on the door—"Stay a Way. Every Body is Sick With the Flu"—and the teenaged lovers spent six days in Caril's home, rebuffing relatives and police officers before they finally left, and the crime was discovered.

On January 28, Starkweather's car bogged down on the property of a local farmer, 70-year-old August Meyer. The result was "a helluva argument," climaxed with Charles shooting Meyer and his dog "in self-defense." Leaving their car in the mud, Starkweather and Fugate walked to the highway and stuck out their thumbs, securing a lift from high school sweethearts Robert Jensen, 17, and Carol King, 16. At gunpoint, Charlie made them drive to an abandoned school and ordered them into the cellar, where Jensen was shot six times in the head. King was also shot to death, her genitals slashed with a knife, but Charlie blamed Caril for the crime, citing "jealousy" as the motive.

Escaping in Jensen's car, Starkweather considered surrender, but Caril allegedly talked him out of it. Returning to Lincoln on January 30, they invaded the home of businessman C. Lauer Ward, binding his wife Clara and a maid, 51-year-old Lillian Fencl, before stabbing both women to death in a bedroom. Charles next went after the family dog, breaking its neck before he settled down to wait for Ward's return from work. Blasting the businessman dead on the threshold, Starkweather fled in his limousine, Caril riding shotgun, intent on escaping to Washington state.

On February 1, they stopped at Douglas, Wyoming, after slipping through a dragnet that included 200 members of the Nebraska National Guard. Seeking a new car, they found shoe salesman Merle Collison asleep in his vehicle, and Starkweather pumped nine bullets into the helpless victim. Stuck behind the steering wheel, Collison's body was giving Charlie fits when another motorist stopped to offer help and Starkweather got the drop on him. They were grappling over Charlie's gun when a deputy sheriff arrived, and Caril Ann jumped into the squad car, pointing at Charles as she cried, "He killed a man!"

Outnumbered, Starkweather fled in the Ward limousine, topping speeds of 120 mph as his pursuers radioed ahead for a road block. Concentrated gunfire drove him off the road at last, and Charles surrendered after he was cut by flying glass. In custody, he made a full confession to his crimes, sharing responsibility with Fugate in what some of her friends described as a spiteful last fling. Sentenced to death, Starkweather was electrocuted at the Nebraska state prison on June 24, 1959. Caril Ann drew a term of life imprisonment for her role in the murder spree, winning parole in June 1976.

Sutcliffe, Peter William

A "harlot killer" who proved rather indiscriminate in choosing victims was Great Britain's Yorkshire Ripper, Peter Sutcliffe. While residing in apparent harmony with his beloved wife—herself a schizophrenic who spent time in institutions—Sutcliffe waged a five-year war against the female population of England's northern counties. With his ball peen hammer, chisel, and assorted other implements of slaughter, Yorkshire's ripper claimed a minimum of thirteen victims killed and seven wounded. In addition to the documented body-count, he is believed by some to be responsible for other unsolved murders on the European continent.

The roots of Sutcliffe's homicidal rage are difficult to trace. His family appears to have been torn by dark suspicions, on his father's part, of infidelity by Peter's mother, and the boy's opinion of all women may have suffered in an atmosphere of brooding doubt. As a young man, he found employment with a local mortuary, and was prone to "borrow" jewelry from the corpses; in his comments, easily dismissed as "jokes" by his co-workers at the time, there is a hint of budding necrophilia, more disturbing then the strain of larceny. A favorite outing for the would-be ripper was a local wax museum, where he lingered by the hour over torsos that depicted the results of gross venereal disease. Before his marriage, Sutcliffe frequently expressed his fears of having caught "a dose" from contact with the prostitutes of Leeds and Birmingham.

Sutcliffe's first attacks on women, in July and August 1975, were unsuccessful in that both his victims managed to survive the crushing blows of hammers to their skulls, the slashes he inflicted on their torsos after they were down. October was a better month for Peter; on the 29th he slaughtered prostitute Wilma McCann, in Leeds, and thus officially began the Ripper's reign of terror.

There seemed to be no schedule for the crimes. On January 20, 1976, housewife/hooker Emily Jackson was bludgeoned in Leeds, her prostrate body bearing fifty stab wounds. Sutcliffe did not strike again for thirteen months, attacking Irene Richardson, another prostitute, again in Leeds. He moved to Bradford for the April butchery of Tina Atkinson, another prostitute, found murdered in her own apartment, mutilated after death.

On June 16, the Ripper struck again, but his selection of a victim made the slaying different, more appalling to the populace at large. At sixteen years of age, Jane Mac-Donald was an "innocent," the perfect girl next door, cut down while strolling to a relative's, almost within sight of home. Her murder put the Ripper on a different plane, immediately serving notice that no girl or woman in the northern counties was considered safe.

Maureen Long was assaulted on the streets of Bradford, in July, but she survived the blows that Sutcliffe rained upon her skull. In October, he crossed the Pennines to murder Jean Jordan in Manchester, crushing her skull with eleven hammer strokes, stabbing her twenty-four times after death. When she had not been found within a week, he would return to move the body and slash it further, making its location more apparent to police.

In January 1978, Sutcliffe killed a prostitute named Helen Rytka in the town of Huddersfield. In April 1979, another "innocent," nineteen-year-old Josephine Whittaker, was butchered in Halifax. A civil servant, Marguerite Walls, was murdered at Pudsey in August, and twelve days later Sutcliffe slaughtered co-ed Barbara Leach, in Bradford.

In the middle of their manhunt, homicide investigators were bedeviled by a mocking tape and several letters from "the Ripper." Later, with their man in custody, they learned that all were hoaxes, perpetrated by another twisted mind that found vicarious release in toying with detectives. Countless hours were wasted by police and independent searchers, looking for a man whose penmanship and accent bore no smallest similarity to Sutcliffe's own. The charlatan responsible—suspected in two unrelated homicides—remains at large today.

The Ripper had two more near-misses in October and November, wounding victims in the towns of Leeds and Huddersfield, respectively. Both would survive their wounds, and Sutcliffe took a year's vacation prior to killing co-ed Jacqueline Hill, at Leeds, in November 1980. The latest victim's mutilations were familiar to police, but Sutcliffe also stabbed her in the eye, unsettled by the corpse's "reproachful stare."

On January 2, 1981, police arrested Sutcliffe, with a prostitute, in one of several areas that had been subject to surveillance through the manhunt. Even so, they almost let him slip the net by stepping out of sight behind some shrubbery to urinate, there dropping the incriminating weapons that he carried underneath his jacket. At the station, Sutcliffe finally broke down, confessing everything. Detectives noted that their suspect seemed relieved to have it all behind him. So he seemed, as well, to spectators in court when he received a term of life imprisonment for thirteen homicides and various assaults. (Author David Yallop, in *Deliver Us from Evil*, links the Ripper with four additional murders and seven non-fatal assaults, including crimes in France and Sweden.) From Sutcliffe's truck, detectives had retrieved a written statement that appeared to summarize the Ripper's twisted view of life:

In this truck is a man whose latent genius, if unleashed, would rock the nation, whose dynamic energy would overpower those around him. Better let him sleep?

"3X Murders, The"

Before the 1970s and Son of Sam, the residents of Queens, in New York City, were familiar with another phantom gunman, stalking human targets in their midst. Like "Sam," he kept up running correspondence with the press, explaining his attacks in terms that only he could fully comprehend. Unlike his imitator, the original Queens killer managed to escape detection, and his case remains unsolved today.

On June 11, 1930, grocer Joe Mozynski parked with 19-year-old Catherine May along an isolated lover's lane in College Point, a neighborhood of Queens. They wanted privacy, and they were startled by a stranger who approached the car, produced a gun, and shot the grocer dead without a word of warning. Catherine May was ordered from the car and raped by the assailant; afterward, he searched her purse and burned some letters she was carrying. That done, he walked her to the nearest trolley stop and put her on a homebound car, first handing her a note that had been printed with a rubber stamp, in crimson ink. It read:

Joseph Mozynski
3X3-X-097

Suspicious homicide detectives were still holding May as a material witness when the killer's first letter reached a local newspaper, on June 13. Despite its brevity, it seemed to make no sense at all.

Kindly print this letter in your paper for Mozynski's friends: "CC-NY ADCM-Y16a-DQR-PA . . . 241 PM6 Queens." By doing this you may save their lives. We do not want any more shooting unless we have to.

A second letter arrived on June 14, branding Mozynski "a dirty rat," declaring that the killer accosted his victim "to get certain documents but unfortunately they were not in his possession at that time." Providing a concise description of the murder gun and ammunition, for purposes of verification, the letter closed with a warning that "14 more of Mozynski's friends will join him" if the crucial documents were not delivered.

On June 16, Noel Sowley and Elizabeth Ring were parked near Creedmore, Queens, when a gunman approached their car, demanding Sowley's driver's license. Turning toward the outer darkness, he appeared to flash a coded signal with his flashlight, finally turning back to Sowley. "You're the one we want, all right," he said, "You're going to get what Joe got."

With that, the gunman executed Sowley, rifling his pockets before he turned on the woman. Avoiding rape with the display of a religious medal, Elizabeth Ring was left with a note similar to the one Catherine May had received on June 11.

Next morning, the killer mailed a new letter, with two spent cartridges enclosed. The note described "V-5 Sowley" as "one more of Mozynski's friends," adding that "thirteen more men and one woman will go if they do not make peace with us and stop bleeding us to death."

A massive search of New York City failed to turn a suspect, even with descriptions from the two eyewitnesses. On June 21, the killer surfaced in Philadelphia, mailing threats to Joe Mozynski's brother in an effort to secure "those papers." While the manhunt shifted into Pennsylvania, New York police received another long and rambling letter from the gunman. Describing himself as an agent of an anticommunist group, "the Red Diamond of Russia," the killer proclaimed: "The last document, N.J. 4-3-44 returned to us the 19 at 9 p.m. My mission is ended. There is no further cause for worry."

True to his word, the "3X" killer disappeared without another note or crime to mark his passing. Six years later, during June of 1936, a suspect in New Jersey signed confessions to the murders, but his story was discredited by homicide detectives and he was dispatched to an asylum.

Memories of phantom gunmen were revived by the October 1937 "Lipstick Murders," so-called after high school sweethearts Lewis Weiss and Frances Hajek were shot in their car, circles drawn on the forehead of each victim with Hajek's lipstick, but that case, too, remained unsolved.

The "3X" legend grew with time and distance, swiftly losing contact with reality. As World War II approached, the homicides were blamed by pamphleteers on Axis spies. A generation later, writing of the case in *Open Files,* author Jay Robert Nash described "3X" as "A maniac bomber [who] plagued New York City in the early 1930s by planting various homemade bombs throughout Manhattan, particularly at the sites of major landmarks." In retrospect, there is no need to make the phantom more or less than what he was. The truth is grim enough.

Tingler, Richard Lee, Jr.

Born out of wedlock in December 1940, Richard Tingler was raised by a mother who beat him regularly, interspersing punishment with frequent reminders that her son was "born in sin." Enlisting in the air force to escape from home, Tingler experienced his first run-in with police in June 1959, while stationed in Alaska. Going AWOL with a friend, he was arrested on a charge of burglary in Anchorage, and wound up pleading guilty to four break-ins. Transferred several times during his two-year federal sentence, Tingler was released from Chilicothe, Ohio, in February 1961. Six months later, with the same air force crony, he was busted in Portsmouth, Ohio, on thirteen counts of breaking and entering. Packed off to state prison for a term of one to fifteen years, Tingler was paroled in August 1964. More burglaries sent him back to prison, as a parole violator, but he was finally released in February 1968.

On September 16, early-morning joggers found four bodies laid out side-by-side in Cleveland's Rockefeller Park. The victims, slain by multiple gunshots from two different weapons, included tavern proprietor Joseph Zoldman, two of his part-time bartenders, and a young female prostitute. Authorities surmised that the four had been taken hostage in a tavern robbery, conveyed to the park at gunpoint, and murdered there to eliminate troublesome witnesses.

A month later, on October 20, a lone gunman entered a dairy bar in Columbus, Ohio, near closing time. Scooping $562 out of the register, he ordered manager Phyllis Crowe and two teenage employees—Susan Pack and Jimmy Stevens—into the back room. Binding their hands, the bandit was about to leave when he paused in the doorway, his face contorted by sudden rage, and snarled, "What the hell, I ain't got nothing to lose. I'm gonna kill you all."

Ripping the door of a safe from its mountings, the stranger advanced on Pack and Stevens, pounding their skulls in a frenzy. Turning on Phyllis Crowe, he twisted a coathanger around her neck, choking her into unconsciousness and leaving her for dead. When she woke and struggled free a half-hour later, Crowe found that both her employees had also been shot in the back of their heads. Ballistics tests matched the bullets to one of the guns used in Cleveland on October 20, and Mrs. Crow identified a mug shot of Richard Tingler as her assailant.

Indicted on six counts of murder, Tingler was added to the FBI's "Ten Most Wanted" list on November 8, 1968. By that time, using the name of "Don Williams," he had secured employment on a farm owned by Alvin Hoffman, near Dill City, Oklahoma. Hoffman thought it strange that his employee packed a pistol everywhere he went, but "Williams" was a decent worker, and a love of firearms does not make a man stand out in Oklahoma.

On March 30, 1969, Tingler's photograph was broadcast following an episode of "The FBI" television series. Viewing the program, "Don Williams" realized his time was running short. He became increasingly nervous on the job, and one morning he failed to report for work.

On April 27, 49-year-old Brooks Hutchenson checked into a motel at Gilman, Illinois, accompanied by a new acquaintance, "D.L. Williams." Next morning, the maid found Hutchenson dead in his room, shot four times at close range, with his cash and late-model Ford LTD missing.

On April 29, "Don Williams" returned to the Hoffman farm, driving Hutchenson's car. He left again the next morning, but returned—minus the car—on May 2. By this time, his erratic behavior was drawing attention from neighbors, and Tingler's time was running out.

By mid-May, the Washita County sheriff's office was receiving complaints about "Williams" and his indiscriminate gunfire. A neighbor's dog had been killed without provocation, and the farm hand was fond of shooting glass insulators on high-tension poles lining the highway. Deputies investigating the complaints were warned by locals that the gunman bore a strong resemblance to a wanted fugitive.

On May 19, a team of federal agents joined sheriff's deputies on a second visit to the farm. They found Tingler working in a field, relieved him of an automatic pistol, and took him into custody without resistance. Tried on six counts of murder in Ohio, the fugitive was convicted and sentenced to die.

Tinning, Marybeth

For a devoted mother, Marybeth Tinning seemed to have no luck at all in raising children. In the thirteen years from 1972 to 1985, she lost nine infants in Schenectady, New York, and police would later charge that eight of those were slain deliberately, for motives no one has been able to articulate.

The first to go was daughter Jennifer, a mere eight days old when she died on January 3, 1972. An autopsy listed the cause of death as acute meningitis, and since the baby never left St. Clare's Hospital after her birth, authorities consider her death the only case above suspicion. We may never know what psychic shock waves were triggered in Marybeth Tinning's mind by the death of her new-born daughter, but more of her children soon joined the casualty list.

Less than three weeks later, on January 20, two-year-old Joseph Tinning, Jr., was pronounced dead on arrival at Ellis Hospital, in Schenectady. Doctors blamed his death on a viral infection and "seizure disorder," but no autopsy was performed to verify those findings. Four-year-old Barbara Tinning died six weeks later, on March 20, and autopsy surgeons, lacking an obvious cause of death, attributed her passing to "cardiac arrest." Barbara's death was the first reported to police, but officers closed their file on the case after a brief consultation with hospital physicians.

And the deaths continued. When two-week-old Timothy died at Ellis hospital, doctors were once more unable to determine a cause, tossing his case into the grab-bag of Sudden Infant Death Syndrome (SIDS). On September 2, 1975, Nathan Tinning died at the age of five months, an autopsy blaming his case on "pulmonary edema." SIDS was the culprit again on February 2, 1979, when Mary Tinning died six months short of her third birthday, while no cause was ever determined in the death of three-month-old Jonathan, on March 24, 1980. Three-year-old Michael Tinning was still in the process of being adopted when he was rushed into St. Clare's Hospital on August 2, 1981. Physicians could not save his life, and while they viewed his passing with a "high level of suspicion," the cause of death was still listed as bronchial pneumonia.

The real questions began on December 20, 1985, when three-month-old Tami Lynne Tinning was found unconscious in bed, blood staining her pillow. Rushed to St. Clare's Hospital, she was beyond help, and while doctors ascribed her death to SIDS, they also telephoned the state police. An investigation led to Marybeth Tinning's arrest on February 4, 1986, after she confessed to pressing a pillow over Tami Lynne's face when the child "fussed and cried." In custody, she also confessed to murdering Timothy and Nathan, but staunchly denied harming any of the others. "I smothered them with a pillow," she told detectives, "because I'm not a good mother."

On July 17, 1987, Tinning was convicted of second-degree murder in Tami Lynne's death, jurors acquitting her of "deliberately" killing the child, blaming her for a lesser degree of homicide through her "depraved indifference to human life." With trials pending in two other confessed slayings, husband Joseph Tinning seemed bewildered by the whole affair. In newspaper interviews, he admitted occasional suspicion of his wife, but had managed to push it aside. "You have to trust your wife," he said. "She has her things to do, and as long as she gets them done, you don't ask questions."

"Toledo Slugger, The"

A classic bogeyman, the "Slugger" terrorized Toledo's population during 1925 and '26, assaulting women, beating some of them to death and leaving others gravely wounded in the wake of his attacks. Before the madness ran its course, the faceless suspect also stood accused of lighting fires and planting bombs in a bizarre and motiveless campaign of terror aimed at random targets.

The war of nerves began in 1925, when several lumber yards were torched within a period of hours. Guards were posted, and the unknown arsonist—or someone else—then started bombing homes and tenements. The FBI was called in when explosives wrecked the mailbox of a Catholic priest, and suddenly the bombings ended, as mysteriously as they had begun.

The madman was not finished with his game, however. As contemporary newsmen put their case, "the alleged fiend then turned to attacks upon women," killing three or four and wounding at least five others in a series of brutal rapes, invariably ending with the victim clubbed insensate. Rewards totaling $12,000 were raised for the maniac's capture, with no takers, when suddenly the violence ceased.

It started up afresh in late October 1926, wih two more slayings added to the Slugger's tally in a single day. The first victim was schoolteacher Lily Croy, age 26, bludgeoned and raped within sight of her classroom in the early morning hours of October 26. The second victim, 47-year-old Mary Allen, was discovered in her home that afternoon. Police initially ascribed her death to gunshot wounds, but later changed their story to report that Croy and Allen had been murdered with the same blunt instrument, the evidence recalling other Slugger homicides.

Around Toledo, lapsed rewards were dusted off and boosted by another rash of contributions, while police swept up a crop of local "odd-balls," finding several who had slipped away from mental institutions. Another rash of arson fires erupted on November 23, inflicting $200,000 damage at a single lumber yard, sweeping on from there to damage an ice company ($10,000), two other businesses, the city street department's stable, an apartment building, and a railroad freight car.

Officers got nowhere in their search for the Toledo Slugger, but again, as during 1925, the crime spree ended of its own accord. Was one demented individual to blame for all the rapes and beatings, fires and bombings? Did police create a monster in their bid to "clear the books" on unsolved local crimes? Whatever else he may have been, the Slugger stands reliably accused of half a dozen homicides, together with an equal number of assaults in which his victims lived to tell the tale. He remains unidentified at this writing, another of the ones who got away.

Toole, Ottis Elwood

A native of Jacksonville, Florida, Toole was born on March 5, 1947. His alcoholic father soon took off for parts unknown, leaving Toole in the care of a Bible-quoting mother who had hoped for a daughter and dressed him accordingly, complete with skirts and frilly undergarments. Toole's confusion was exacerbated by his grandmother, an alleged Satanist, who branded Ottis as "the devil's child." Toole ran away from home repeatedly, but always drifted back again. He suffered from seizures, and derived satisfaction from torching vacant houses in his Jacksonville neighborhood. Questioned about his choice of targets, years later, Toole replied, "I just hated to see them standing there."

By his own admission, Toole committed his first murder at age 14. The victim, a traveling salesman, picked him up outside town and drove him into the woods for sex.

Afterward, Toole "got nervous" and ran the man down with his own car.

Classified as retarded, with an IQ of 75, Toole dropped out of school in the eighth grade. His first arrest, for loitering, was logged in August 1964, and others followed, building up a rap sheet filled with counts of petty theft and lewd behavior. He married briefly, but his bride departed after three days time, repulsed by Toole's overt homosexuality.

By 1974, Toole was drifting, touring the western states in an old pickup truck. Acquaintances thought nothing of it, at the time, but later evidence suggests he may have claimed at least four victims in a six-month period. Police suspect him in the death of 24-year-old Patricia Webb, shot in Lincoln, Nebraska, on April 18. Ten weeks later, on July 1, 24-year-old Shelley Robertson disappeared from Golden, Colorado, her nude body recovered from Berthoud Pass, near Vail, on August 21. Ted Bundy is frequently blamed for Robertson's death, but the last innocent person to see her alive—a policeman—watched as she accepted a ride from "a wild-haired man driving an old pickup truck." (In those days, dapper Ted Bundy habitually drove a Volkswagen "bug.")

On September 19, 1974, a lone gunman invaded a massage parlor in Colorado Springs. Employee Yon Lee was stabbed, her throat slashed, before the attacker moved on to rape, shoot, and stab co-worker Sun Ok Cousin. Both women were set on fire, but Lee survived to describe her assailant as clean-shaven, 6 foot 2 and 195 pounds, driving a white pickup truck. Police, for reasons yet unclear, arrested—and ultimately convicted—Park Estep, a mustachioed soldier who stood 5 foot 10, tipped the scales at a mere 150 pounds, and owned a red pickup. Meanwhile, on October 10, 31-year-old Ellen Holman was abducted from Pueblo, Colorado, shot three times in the head, and dumped near the Oklahoma border. Homicide investigators now believe Toole pulled the trigger in that crime.

Two years later, Toole met killer Henry Lucas at a Jacksonville soup kitchen, taking him home for a night of drinking, conversation, and sex. The men had much in common, sharing memories of murder, looking forward to a time when they might hunt together. By 1983, according to police, they would traverse the continent together several times, annihilating random victims at a dizzy pace.

On January 14, 1977, Toole startled relatives by marrying a woman 24 years his senior. The relationship was curious from day one, and Novella Toole soon found herself sharing Ottis with Henry Lucas and other strangers. "A few nights after we were married," she said, "he told me he would get nervous a lot, especially when he couldn't get a man. He'd get angry, he said, and then he couldn't get excited with a woman." They were separated by 1978, Lucas and Toole moving in with Toole's mother, sharing quarters with sister Drusilla Powell and her children, Frank and Frieda.

The homicidal soul-mates found work with a Jacksonville roofing company, Southeast Color Coat, but office manager Eileen Knight recalls that they disappeared frequently, sometimes for weeks at a stretch. "Ottis would come and go," she told Jacksonville newsmen. "We'd hire him whenever he came back, because he was a good worker." Another part-time employer, Betty Goodyear, said of Lucas and Toole, "They went out of town, always disappearing. All (Toole) cared about was that old car. I think they were using it for robbing people, because they always seemed to have a lot of money." Along the way, Toole allegedly introduced Lucas to a Satanic cult, the "Hand of Death," that kidnapped children, practiced human sacrifice, and cranked out snuff films on a secret ranch in Mexico.

Toole's mother died in May 1981, following surgery, and the loss hit him hard. Ottis haunted the cemetery, sometimes at night, stretching out on the ground by her grave and feeling the earth move beneath him. A short time later, his sister Drusilla died of a drug overdose—considered a probable suicide—and her children were packed off to juvenile homes. Alone for once, with Lucas serving time for auto theft in Maryland, Toole brooded, drinking heavily and popping pills. (It was around this time—on July 27—that six-year-old Adam Walsh disappeared from a Hollywood, Florida, shopping mall, his severed head recovered from a Vero Beach canal, on August 10.)

Lucas returned in October, discharged from a Maryland jail, and together the men contrived Frieda Powell's escape from a Polk County juvenile home. By January 1982, authorities were looking for the girl in Jacksonville, and she fled westward with Lucas. They were gone two days before Toole learned of their departure, and he lapsed into "a world of his own," pacing the floor and muttering over Henry's "betrayal." He wandered to forget and killed along the way, reportedly claiming nine victims in six states between January 1982 and February 1983.

On May 23 and 31, 1983, two houses were burned in Toole's Jacksonville neighborhood. Teenage accomplices fingered Toole on June 6, and he freely confessed to setting an estimated 40 fires over the past two decades. Convicted of second-degree arson in August 5, 1983, he drew a term of 20 years in prison.

By that time, Lucas was singing in Texas, and Toole backed his partner up with more confessions. Toole's statements "cleared" 25 murders in eleven states, and he admitted participating with Lucas in another 108 homicides. A practicing cannibal, Toole also dropped hints about his interest in Satanism, but stopped short of naming alleged fellow cult members.

On October 21, Toole confessed to the murder of Adam Walsh, startling Assistant Police Chief Leroy Hessler with details that were "grisly beyond belief." As Hessler told the media, "there are certain details only he could know. He did it. I've got details that no one else would know. He's got me convinced." In spite of that endorsement, officers reversed their stance a few weeks later, issuing statements that Toole was "no longer a suspect" in the crime.

Another troubling case harked back to 1974, and the carnage in Colorado Springs. Toole confessed to the massage parlor attack in September 1984, again providing details of the crime, but embarrassed prosecutors swiftly mounted their counter-attack. After hours of hostile grilling, Toole threw in the towel. "Okay," he told authorities. "If you say I didn't kill her, maybe I didn't."

At this writing, Toole stands convicted of three murders, facing two death sentences in Florida, with a life term in West Virginia for helping Lucas murder a police officer in August 1976. Ironically, Toole's name is seldom mentioned in the controversy over Lucas's confessions and his later change of heart, in April 1985. No effort has been made to challenge Toole's involvement in a score of homicides from coast to coast, and it is just as well, considering his dialogue with Lucas, taped by Texas Rangers in November 1983.

TOOLE: Remember one time I said I wanted me some ribs? Did that make me a cannibal?

LUCAS: You wasn't a cannibal. It's the force of the devil, something forced on us that we can't change. There's no reason denying what we become. We know what we are.

TOOLE: Remember how I liked to pour some of the blood out of them?

LUCAS: Ottis, you and I have become something people look on as an animal. There's no way of changing what we done, but we can stop it and not allow other people to become what we have. And the only way to do that is by honesty.

Toppan, Jane

Born Nora Kelly, in Boston, during 1854, Toppan lost her mother in infancy. Her father, a tailor, soon went insane, and was confined to an asylum after he was found in his shop, trying to stitch his own eyelids together. His four daughters lived briefly with their paternal grandmother, before they were relegated to a local orphanage. Abner Toppan and his wife, from Lowell, Massachusetts, legally adopted Nora during 1859, changing her first name to Jane. The girl excelled in school and seemed completely normal prior to being jilted by her fiancee, years later. After that, she twice attempted suicide and suffered through a period of odd behavior that included efforts to predict the future through analysis of dreams. (A sister, Ellen, joined their father in the lunatic asylum after suffering a mental breakdown in her twenties.)

Briefly stabilizing during 1880, Jane signed on as a student nurse at a hospital in Cambridge, Massachusetts. Once again, she excelled in her class work, but supervisors and colleagues were disturbed by her obsession with autopsies. Dismissed after two patients died mysteriously in her care, she left the hospital without her certificate, forging the paperwork necessary to find work as a private nurse. Over the next two decades, she was hired by dozens of New England families, caring for the ill and elderly in several states, but few of Toppan's patients managed to survive her "special" treatment.

On July 4, 1901, an old friend, Mattie Davis, died under Jane's care at Cambridge, and Toppan accompanied the body home to Cataumet, Massachusetts, for burial. Retained as the family nurse by patriarch Alden Davis, Jane finished off his married daughter, Annie Gordon, on July 29. The old man's death, a few days later, was blamed on "a stroke," and his surviving daughter, Mary Gibbs, was pronounced dead on August 19. Mary's husband demanded an autopsy, and lethal doses of morphine were found in the three latest victims, but Jane was not finished, yet. Before her arrest in Amherst, New Hampshire, on October 29, she fed a lethal "tonic" to her foster sister, Edna Bannister, and she was working on another patient when police cut short her medical career.

In custody, Toppan confessed to 31 murders, naming her victims, but students believe her final tally falls somewhere between 70 and 100 victims. No accurate list of her hospital victims was ever compiled, and various New England families avoided the scandal by refusing official requests for exhumations and autopsies. At trial, Jane's lawyer grudgingly conceded eleven murders, staking his hopes on a plea of insanity. Toppan cinched the case with her own testimony, telling the court, "That is my ambition, to have killed more people—more helpless people—than any man or woman who has ever lived."

Declared insane, Toppan was confined for life to the

state asylum at Taunton, Massachusetts, where she died in August 1938, at age 84. She was remembered by her keepers as "a quiet old lady," but older attendants remembered her smile as she beckoned them into her room. "Get some morphine, dearie," she would say, "and we'll go out in the ward. You and I will have a lot of fun seeing them die."

"Vampire" Murders—Colombia

Between October 1963 and February 1964, at least ten boys between the ages of ten and eighteen were found dead in the city of Cali, Colombia, their bodies discarded on vacant lots around town. Medical examiners blamed the deaths on deliberate extraction of blood, and police declared that they were searching for a black-market "blood ring," members of which were believed to be slaughtering children and selling their blood for $25 a quart.

Commercial vampires had been suspect in the slayings since December 1963, when 12-year-old twins mysteriously vanished, then turned up four days later in weakened condition. The boys told police they had been kidnapped, taken to a house where other boys were being held, and given shots to make them sleep. From that point, speculation took control, with officers assuming blood had been extracted and, presumably, put up for sale.

In truth, the city's modern hospital attracted sufferers from all around Colombia, creating a brisk market in blood required for surgery, transfusions, and the like. Despite top-level prices and police suspicions, though, the Cali "vampire" slayings have remained unsolved, without a shred of solid evidence to build a case in court.

Warner, Karl F.

On August 3, 1969, schoolmates Deborah Furlong, 14, and Kathy Snoozy, 15, rode their bikes to a wooded knoll overlooking their homes in the rugged Alameda Valley section of South San Jose, California. They brought a picnic lunch and meant to spend a quiet afternoon alone, unconscious of the fact that they had trespassed on a killer's private hunting ground.

When neither girl came home for supper, Debby Furlong's father started scouring the woods. He found a crowd of gawkers and police around the mutilated bodies of his daughter and her friend, laid out within a grove of trees from which their homes were visible. The medical examiner stopped counting at 300 stab wounds, all above the waist; in statements to the press, he would declare that "The Nazi sex mutilations during World War II were nothing compared to what was done to these young girls."

Infuriated parents launched patrols in San Jose, without result, while homicide investigators searched for clues. One theory linked the murders with an offshoot of the Manson "family"; another speculated on connections with the "Zodiac," an unidentified serial slayer whose latest mocking letter, on November 8, claimed seven victims rather than the five accounted for by solid evidence. It all came down to nothing in the end; the killer would remain at large for nearly two more years, before a new attack produced the necessary leads.

On April 11, 1971, 18-year-old Kathy Bilek chose the San Jose murder site as a prime spot for birdwatching. The killer found her there, using his favorite knife to stab her seventeen times in the back, thirty-two times in the chest and stomach, carefully avoiding contact with her breasts. Discovered early next morning, Bilek's wounds connected her murder with the previous killings, and police redoubled their efforts.

Two weeks later, armed with fresh descriptions of a suspicious man seen prowling the area, detectives focused their attention on Karl Warner, a former classmate of victims Furlong and Snoozy at Oak Grove High School. Warner lived with his parents, three blocks from the homes of the earliest victims, and he was also suspected in the stabbing of a woman who survived her wounds.

Police secured a warrant and surprised their suspect in the midst of preparation for a college physics test. Their search turned up the murder knife, and Warner pled guilty on all counts in September 1971, receiving a sentence of life imprisonment. A background check eliminated him as a potential "Zodiac," since he had moved to California from Marlborough, Massachusetts, in early 1969, two and a half years after the first Zodiac murder.

Watson, James B.

A classic American "bluebeard," Watson led a life of subterfuge and mystery, with question marks beginning at his birth. Christened Charles Gillam, he was born at Paris, Arkansas, sometime in 1870, his father absent at the time of the event. As a child, he was told of his father's death, discovering the truth—that he had been deserted—at the age of nine. When his mother remarried, she added further confusion to the situation by calling her son "Joseph Olden," after his new stepfather. Man and boy clashed immediately, with cruel punishment prompting "Joseph" to run away from home around age 12.

By all accounts James Watson was a marrying machine, although the number of his brides—and victims—still remains uncertain. Carl Sifakis, in *The Encyclopedia of American Crime,* credits Watson with 40-odd marriages and "at least 25" murders, but Watson's own confession was somewhat more modest, listing 19 wives and seven murder victims. Of course, his memory left much to be desired—the names of two wives had completely slipped his mind, though he recalled their anniversaries—and victims listed in his final affidavit only span the last two years of his career in lethal matrimony. There may well be others, murdered and forgotten during 12 years on the road, but we cannot retrieve their names at this remove.

"Olden" was working on his second marriage by the time he settled in St. Louis, entering the advertising business, but his creative bookkeeping led to criminal indictment around 1912, and he fled into Canada, adopting the Watson alias that would see him through the rest of his life. On June 12, 1913, he married Katherine Kruse in British Columbia, later deserting her without benefit of a divorce. At that, she was one of the lucky ones. As Watson summarized their relationship in his later confession: "No violence attempted on her—had impulse but was able to resist."

He resisted, also, with a certain Mrs. Watts, married at Winnipeg in early 1918. In March of that year, he married Marie Austin in Calgary, Alberta, afterward moving to the United States. Perhaps the first to die, Marie was bludgeoned with a rock, her body weighted down and dumped in a lake near Coeur D'Alene, Idaho. Later in 1918, Watson married a Seattle widow, whose name he could not recall. They honeymooned at Spokane, and Watson cut the relationship short by pushing her over a waterfall. "There was no controversy," he wrote later, "just an impulse."

Drifting around Tacoma in early 1919, Watson married Maude Goldsmith in January and Beatrice Andrewartha a month later. Beatrice survived until spring, when they paid a visit to Lake Washington, near Seattle, and Watson felt "something come over me," compelling him to drown her on the spot.

Watson picked up two more brides, in Vancouver and Sacramento, before marrying Elizabeth Prior on March 25, 1919, at Coeur D'Alene, Idaho. They were touring near Olympia, Washington, when they began to quarrel and Watson "accidentally" knocked her unconscious, seizing the opportunity to finish her off with a hammer.

Three wives later, in June 1919, Watson married Bertha Goodrich at North Yakima, Washington. They were honeymooning near Seattle when Watson bludgeoned her "on impulse," dumping her weighted body into a convenient lake. In July, he was boating with new bride Alice Ludvigson, near Port Townsend, Washington, when she "accidentally" fell out of the boat and was drowned in the St. Joe River. At least two more survivors followed Watson to the altar before he married Nina Delaney at El Centro, California, in December 1919. A month later, her nude body was found outside of town, strangled, her skull crushed, breasts and genitals slashed with a knife.

Jealousy, rather than homicide, proved to be Watson's undoing. In the spring of 1920, wife nineteen suspected him of infidelity and hired a private investigator to check out his background. The detective found a suitcase filled with wedding rings and marriage licenses, deciding he was "dealing with no ordinary criminal." Arrested on suspicion of bigamy in April, Watson was still in custody when an unidentified woman's body was unearthed near Plum Station, Washington. Afraid it might be one of his— ironically, it wasn't—Watson struck a bargain with the prosecutor and issued a detailed confession on May 7, accepting a life sentence three days later. Confined at San Quentin, he died in prison on October 15, 1939.

Watts, Coral Eugene

Born at Fort Hood, Texas, during 1953, Watts grew up on the move, attending public schools in Texas, West Virginia, and Michigan before finishing high school—after a fashion—in Inkster, a Detroit suburb. Despite a tested IQ of 75, he was admitted to Western Michigan University, at Kalamazoo, and was enrolled there when he started acting out his violent fantasies against women in October 1974.

His first two victims managed to survive when Watts came knocking on the doors of their apartments, starting on October 25. Watts choked them both unconscious, leaving them for dead with no attempt at rape or robbery, but he was disappointed when the press reported both of them were still alive. He found knives more efficient, claiming his first fatality on October 30, when 19-year-old co-ed Gloria Steele was stabbed 33 times and discarded near campus.

Identified as a suspect in the non-fatal assaults, Watts had himself committed to a state hospital on the advice of his attorney, refusing to answer any questions in the Steele murder case. Fourteen months after the fact, he struck a bargain with Kalamazoo prosecutors, pleading guilty to one assault in return for dismissal of another similar charge, accepting a one-year sentence in the county jail. Upon release, he moved to Ann Arbor, marrying long enough to father a child, but his deep-seated hatred of women made the relationship impossible, and he was divorced in May 1980.

Meanwhile, Watts was hunting. When his marriage started showing signs of strain, he spent some time with relatives in the Detroit suburb of Grosse Pointe Farms, jogging by night to keep himself in shape. On October 31, 1979, he invaded the home of 35-year-old Jeanne Clyne, slashing her to death—again without attempting rape or robbery—before he fled. Eyewitnesses described a black man jogging near the scene, but homicide detectives had no way of linking their case with a five-year-old series of crimes against women in Kalamazoo.

Back in Ann Arbor, Watts entered criminal history as the ''Sunday Morning Slasher,'' claiming at least three victims in motiveless, random attacks committed between 3 and 5 a.m. on peaceful sabbath mornings. In April 1980, 18-year-old Shirley Small was hacked to death in her own apartment, followed by 20-year-old Glenda Richmond in July and 29-year-old Rebecca Huff in September. Canadian authorities believe Watts may have crossed the border into Windsor that October, assaulting 20-year-old Sandra Dalpe outside her apartment, leaving her near death with multiple wounds to the face and throat.

By that time, Watts had fallen under scrutiny from local homicide investigators. A task force was organized in July 1980, to probe the Sunday slashings, and Watts was placed under sporadic surveillance, a November court order permitting officers to plant a homing device in his car. Despite pursuit by squad cars and a helicopter, though, Watts managed to commit at least one murder while police were on his trail. Fired from his job as a diesel mechanic in March 1981, he moved south to Houston, leaving the murder investigation at loose ends. Michigan authorities alerted their Texas counterparts, but Watts was accustomed to living under surveillance. He found a new mechanics job and started visiting a local church, sometimes living with relatives, other times out of his car.

And the murders continued.

On March 27, 1981, Edith Ledet, a 34-year-old medical student, was stabbed to death while jogging in Houston. Six months later, on September 12, 25-year-old Elizabeth

Montgomery was attacked while walking her dog at midnight, staggering into her nearby apartment before she collapsed. Two hours later, 21-year-old Susan Wolfe was knifed to death outside her apartment, nearby, presumed to be a victim of the same assailant.

The new year brought no respite from horrors in Houston. In January, 27-year-old Phyllis Tamm was found on the campus of Rice University, hanged with an article of her own clothing, and another Rice student, 25-year-old Margaret Fossi, was killed that same month, found in the trunk of her car, her larynx crushed by a powerful blow that produced death by asphyxiation. On February 7, Elena Semander, a 20-year-old co-ed, was found strangled and partially nude in a trash bin, not far from a tavern where she had spent the evening.

In March 1982, Emily LaQua was reported missing from Brookshire, Texas, 40 miles north of Houston, but authorities drew no immediate connection with the spate of unsolved murders. On March 31, 20-year-old Mary Castillo was found, strangled and semi-nude, in a Houston ditch. Three nights later, 19-year-old Christine McDonald vanished while hitchhiking home from a booze party on the Rice campus. Suzanne Searles, 25, joined the missing list on April 5, her shoes and broken spectacles recovered from her car, in the parking lot of her apartment complex. Carrie Mae Jefferson, age 32, vanished after working the night shift on April 15, and 26-year-old Yolanda Degracia was killed the following night, stabbed six times in her home. High school student Sheri Strait disappeared with her mother's car on May 1, the car—and her body—recovered together on May 4. Two weeks later, Gloria Cavallis, a 32-year-old exotic dancer, was found dead in a trash dumpster, her body wrapped in cast-off curtains.

On the morning of May 23, 1982—a Sunday—Watts was caught while fleeing from the Houston apartment where he had assaulted tenants Lori Lister and Melinda Aguilar. Lister was half-drowned in the bathtub, while Aguilar escaped by throwing herself from the balcony, calling for help. Held in lieu of $50,000 bond, Watts was charged with two counts of attempted murder, plus aggravated assault and burglary. (On the morning of Watts's arrest, an

other victim, 20-year-old Michelle Maday, was found strangled to death in the bathtub of her Houston apartment.)

Psychiatrists declared Watts sane, but noted his pathological hatred of women, whom he regarded as evil incarnate.
The feelings dated back to childhood, when a favorite uncle had allegedly been killed by female relatives. Diagnosed as a paranoid schizophrenic, Watts was said to view
the world around him ''as pure fantasies which revolve to
a large extent around the struggle against the 'evil' he sees
everywhere.''

On August 9, 1982, with jury selection under way for
his trial, Watts struck a controversial bargain with the
prosecutor's office. In return for his guilty plea on burglary
charges and acceptance of a 60-year sentence—the equiv-
alent of life imprisonment in Texas—Watts would clear the
books on several unsolved Houston murders while escaping trial for homicide.

With the deal complete, and Watts compelled to serve
a minimum of 20 years before consideration for parole,
the defendant confessed to ten Houston murders, including
the cases of victims Wolfe, Jefferson, Montgomery, Fossi,
Semander, Searles, Degracia, Tamm, Ledet and Maday.
He also threw in some surprises, including the non-fatal
slashing of a Galveston 19-year-old, attacked on January 30,
1982, and the ''accidental'' death of 22-year-old Linda
Tilley, found floating in an Austin, Texas, swimming pool
on September 5, 1981. Other nonfatal assaults were also
cleared in Austin, Galveston, and Seabrook, Texas.

Watts led authorities to the remains of victims Searles
and Jefferson in Houston, directing other searchers to the
body of Emily LaQua, near Brookshire, and he was still
talking when Michigan weighed in with charges in the
murder of Jeanne Clyne. Swapping testimony for immu-
nity, Watts ran his score up to thirteen confessed murders
with the Clyne case, but detectives suggest that his actual
body-count includes a minimum of 22 victims. On September 3, 1982, Watts received his 60-year sentence, the
judge declaring, ''I hope they put you so deep in the penitentiary that they'll have to pipe sunlight to you.''

Webb, Dennis

A racist drifter with his roots in northeast Texas, Webb would travel widely in the service of the outlaw motorcycle gangs to whom he owed his first allegiance. Jailed for a hometown burglary at age 20, in 1972, he reportedly killed his first victim a year later. The victim was gay, selected at random because, as Webb explained, "I don't like homosexuals."

There would be other murders in the years to come. According to his subsequent confessions, Webb agreed to kill a man as part of his initiation to a biker gang, later serving the group as a hired gun, executing at least one murder-for-hire. A black victim was shot down because of his race, and Webb confessed to killing "one or two" others when they interrupted his looting of their homes. Convicted of robbery and aggravated kidnapping in Utah, during 1981, he struck a plea bargain with prosecutors, serving five and a half years before his parole in December 1986.

Webb lasted two months on the street before killing again. On February 5, 1987, he invaded the home of John and Lori Rainwater, in Atascadero, California. Lori was just home from the hospital, with her five-day-old son, but Webb was deaf to her pleas for mercy as he bound both adults with surgical tape, raping man and woman alike before he shot them to death execution-style. (The newborn infant and his 18-month-old sister were unaccountably spared.)

Tried for his latest rampage in June 1988, Webb was convicted on two counts of first-degree murder, with one count each of burglary and robbery thrown in for good measure. During the penalty phase of his trial, on July 15, the defendant removed his shirt in court, displaying the various gang tattoos that denoted his murders, begging the jury to recommend death. Facing the panel impassively, he said, "I have no feelings, ladies and gentlemen. My heart is a block of ice." Taking Webb at his word, jurors deliberated for ninety minutes before granting his wish.

Weber, Jeanne

Born during 1875, at a small fishing village in northern France, Weber left home for Paris at age 14, working various menial jobs until her marriage in 1893. Her husband was a drunkard, and by 1905, with two of their three children lately deceased, Jeanne was also drinking heavily, residing in a seedy Paris tenement with her spouse and a seven-year-old son.

On March 2, 1905, Weber was babysitting for her sister-in-law, when one of the woman's two daughters— 18-month-old Georgette—suddenly "fell ill" and died. Strange bruises on her neck were ignored by the examining physician, and Jeanne was welcomed back to babysit on March 11. Two-year-old Suzanne did not survive the visit, but a doctor blamed the second death on unexplained "convulsions."

Weber was babysitting for her brother, on March 25, when his daughter, seven-year-old Germaine, suffered a sudden attack of "choking," complete with red marks on her throat. The child survived that episode, but she was less fortunate the following day, when Aunt Jeanne returned. Diptheria was blamed for her death—and for that of Weber's son, Marcel, just four days later. Once again, the tell-tale marks of strangulation were ignored.

On April 5, 1905, Weber invited two of her sisters-in-law to dinner, remaining home with 10-year-old nephew Maurice while the other women went out shopping. They returned prematurely, to find Maurice gasping on the bed, his throat mottled with bruises, Jeanne standing over him with a crazed expression on her face. Charges were filed, and Weber's trial opened on January 29, 1906, with the prosecution alleging eight murders, including all three of Weber's own children and two others—Lucie Aleandre and Marcel Poyatos—who had died while in her care. It was alleged that Weber killed her son in March to throw suspicion off, but jurors were reluctant to believe the worst about a grieving mother, and Weber was acquitted on February 6.

Fourteen months later, on April 7, 1907, a physician from the town of Villedieu was summoned to the home of a peasant named Bavouzet. He was greeted at the door by a babysitter, "Madame Moulinet," who led him to the cot where nine-year-old Auguste Bavouzet lay dead, his throat badly bruised. The cause of death was listed as "convulsions," but the doctor changed his tune on May 4, when "Madame Moulinet" was identified as Jeanne Weber. Held over for trial, Weber was released in December, after a second autopsy blamed the boy's death on "typhoid."

Weber quickly dropped from sight, surfacing next as an orderly at a children's hospital in Faucombault, moving on from there to the Children's Home in Orgeville, run by friends who sought to "make up for the wrongs that justice has inflicted upon an innocent woman." Working as "Marie Lemoine," Weber had been on the job for less than a week when she was caught strangling a child in the home. Embarrassed by their own naivete, the owners quietly dismissed her and the incident was covered up.

Back in Paris, Weber was arrested for vagrancy and briefly confined to the asylum at Nantere, but doctors there pronounced her sane and set her free. She drifted into prostitution, picking up a common-law husband along the way, and on May 8, 1908, the couple settled at an inn in Commercy. A short time later, Jeanne was found strangling the innkeeper's son, 10-year-old Marcel Poirot, with a bloody handkerchief. The father had to punch her three times in the face, with all his might, before she would release the lifeless body.

Held for trial on murder charges, Weber was declared insane on October 25, 1908, packed off to the asylum at Mareville. Credited with at least ten murders, she survived two years in captivity before manually strangling herself in 1910.

Weeks, Robert

An Alabama native, born in 1929, Weeks graduated from Mississippi Southern College in 1952, after working his way through school as a mortician and parachute stuntman. Two years later, he married his first wife, Patricia, in Minneapolis, moving to Las Vegas in 1955. Weeks prospered there, opening the city's first limousine service in 1960, but his pathological jealousy made Patricia a virtual prisoner at home, where she was frequently beaten, denied permission to even go grocery shopping alone. On one occasion, in a jealous rage, Weeks beat her elderly piano teacher. In 1968, Weeks finally agreed to a divorce, Patricia taking the family home and Cadillac in settlement, but she vanished that April, her car found abandoned at a local shopping center. Questioned by his daughters, Weeks informed them that their mother had abandoned them.

Weeks sold his limo service in 1971 and married Waunice Hinkle, in Las Vegas, the following year. They were divorced in 1974, but Waunice survived the break-up, probably because of Weeks's new infatuation with 41 year-old Cynthia Jabour. They dated for the next six years, while Weeks maintained his life-style through the sale of phony stock—almost a million dollars worth—in sundry "paper" corporations. By the fall of 1980, Cynthia was anxious to be rid of Weeks, and she agreed to meet him for a final dinner date, October 5, to break the news that they were finished. Her car was found next day, in a casino parking lot, but nothing more was seen of Cynthia Jabour. Interrogated by police, Weeks proved evasive, first agreeing to a polygraph exam, then fleeing the United States and surfacing in Chili.

Weeks returned in 1981, by way of Houston, with a Libyan passport in the name of "Robert Smith." He set up shop in San Diego, launching a construction business, and in 1983 he met Carol Riley on a trip to Colorado, persuading the 43-year-old divorcee to join him in Southern California. Disillusioned with "Smith" over time, Riley was contemplating a break-up when she vanished on April 5, 1986, after a dinner date with Weeks. Her car was found abandoned in a hotel parking lot.

Weeks moved to Tucson, as "Charles Stolzenberg," but he had already attracted national attention. Profiled on an episode of "Unsolved Mysteries," aired by NBC television, Weeks was fingered by neighbors in Tucson and arrested on May 26, 1987. Charged with embezzlement in Arizona, he was held in lieu of $3 million bond.

In April 1988, Weeks was convicted of murdering Patricia Weeks and Cynthia Jabour, in Las Vegas. Jurors fixed his punishment as life imprisonment without parole.

Weidenbroeker, Helmut

A German chemist, born in 1964, Weidenbroeker lived in Broichweiden, while serving his apprenticeship in nearby Aachen. As a student, he had dressed up in his sister's clothes before assaulting elderly women and stealing their purses. Arrested, he confessed but gave no motive for his crimes, earning a sentence of two years in prison. The verdict was under appeal—and Helmut was still on the street—when a two-year series of sex-murders began terrorizing the vicinity.

On May 4, 1982, 19-year-old Marta Habermann, disappeared from a bus stop in Aachen, her body discovered at another stop along the line. Found nude, she had been raped and sexually abused with a beer bottle, then stabbed 17 times in the chest and abdomen.

Eleven months later, on April 19, 1983, 16-year-old Karen Fink disappeared on her way home from school, in Wuerselen. It took a week for searchers to retrieve her body from a nearby pond, where she was dumped after being raped and beaten, strangled, stabbed nine times, her vagina torn by penetration of a foreign object.

On August 30, 1983, 18-year-old Doris Schroeder stepped off a bus in the village of Breinig and promptly vanished. Her body—raped, stabbed 19 times, and violated with a foreign object—was recovered from a manmade lake near the Belgian border. The official cause of death was drowning, indicating that she was alive when thrown into the water.

Elke Braun, age 17, was next, abducted from the town of Rott—two miles from Breinig—on June 3, 1984. Beaten, raped and stabbed, sexually abused with a foreign object, she was still alive when her attacker threw her off a 40-foot cliff, but she was killed by the fall to a stone quarry below.

On March 6, 1986, 18-year-old Beate Goertz disappeared after leaving her bus in Broichweiden. Fished out of the Rur River, near Deuren, on March 18, she had been raped and stabbed, her skull fractured by stomping, before she was drowned. Bus passengers recalled that Helmut Weidenbroeker had disembarked at the same stop on March 6, and he was pulled in for questioning, swiftly confessing to Goertz's murder. Sentenced to life imprisonment on April 10, 1987, the defendant was charged in only one case, but authorities were satisfied of his guilt in all five, noting that the serial slayings ended abruptly with his arrest.

Wilder, Christopher Bernard

Born March 13, 1945, Christopher Wilder was the product of an international marriage, between an American naval officer and his Australian wife. A sickly child from the beginning, Wilder was given last rites as an infant. Two years later, he nearly drowned in a swimming pool; at age three, he suffered convulsions while riding with his parents in the family car, and had to be resuscitated.

By his teens, the boy had problems of a different sort. At seventeen, in Sydney, Wilder and a group of friends were charged with gang-raping a girl on the beach. He pled guilty to carnal knowledge and received one year's probation, with a provision for mandatory counseling. The program included group therapy and electroshock treatments, but it seemed to have little effect.

Wilder married at age twenty-three, but the union lasted only a few days. His bride complained of sexual abuse, and finally left him after finding panties (not her own) and photographs of naked women in a briefcase Wilder carried in his car. In November 1969, he used nude photographs to extort sex from an Australian student nurse; she complained to the police, but charges were ultimately dropped when she refused to testify in court.

Australia was growing too hot for Wilder, so he moved to the United States. Settling in southern Florida, he prospered in the fields of construction and electrical contracting, earning (or borrowing) enough money to finance fast cars and a luxurious bachelor pad, complete with hot tub and a private photo studio. The good life visibly agreed with Wilder, but it did not fill his other hidden needs.

In March 1971, at Pompano Beach, Wilder was picked up on a charge of soliciting women to pose for nude photos; he entered a plea of guilty to disturbing the peace and escaped with a small fine. Six years later, in October 1977, he coerced a female high school student into oral sex, threatening to beat her if she refused, and he was jailed a second time. Wilder admitted the crime to his therapist, but confidential interviews are inadmissible in court, and he was later acquitted. On June 21, 1980, he lured a teen-aged girl into his car with promises of a modeling job, then drove her to a rural area where she was raped. A guilty plea to charges of attempted sexual battery earned him five years probation, with further therapy ordered by the court. Following his last arrest in Florida, the self-made man complained of suffering from blackouts.

Visiting his parents in Australia, Wilder was accused of kidnapping two 15-year-old girls from a beach in New South Wales on December 28, 1982, forcing them to pose for pornographic snapshots. Traced through the license number of his rented car, Wilder was arrested on December 29, charged with kidnaping and indecent assault. His family posted $350,000 bail, and Wilder was permitted to return to the United States, his trial scheduled for May 7, 1983. Legal delays postponed the case, but Wilder was scheduled to appear in court for a hearing on April 3, 1984.

He never made it.

On February 6, Rosario Gonzalez, 20, disappeared from her job at the Miami Grand Prix. Chris Wilder was driving as a contestant that day, and witnesses recall her leaving with a man who fit Wilder's description. Her body has never been found.

On March 4, 23-year-old Elizabeth Kenyon vanished after work from the school where she taught in Coral Gables. She was seen that afternoon, with Wilder, at a local gas station, and his name was found in her address book. Kenyon's parents remembered her speaking of Wilder as ''a real gentleman,'' unlike the various photographers who asked if she would model in the nude. As in the February case, no trace of Kenyon has been found.

Wilder celebrated his thirty-ninth birthday on March 13, treating himself to the peculiar gift of a 1973 Chrysler. Three days later, the *Miami Herald* reported that a Boynton Beach race driver was wanted for questioning in the disappearance of two local women. Wilder was not named in the story, but he got the point. Missing his scheduled therapy on March 17, he met with his business partner the following night, "I am not going to jail," he vowed, tearfully. "I'm not going to do it." Packing his car, Wilder dropped off his dogs at a kennel and drove out of town, headed north.

Indian Harbour lies two hours north of Boynton Beach. On March 19, Terry Ferguson, 21, disappeared from a local shopping mall where witnesses remembered seeing Wilder. Her body was recovered four days later, from a Polk County canal.

On March 20, Wilder abducted a university co-ed from a shopping mall in Tallahassee, driving her across the state line to Bainbridge, Georgia. There, in a cheap motel, she was raped repeatedly and tortured with electric shocks, her eyelids smeared with super glue. Wilder fled after his captive managed to lock herself in the bathroom, screaming and pounding on the walls to draw attention from the other guests.

The killer touched down next in Beaumont Texas. Terry Walden, 24, informed her husband on March 21 that a bearded man had approached her between classes at the local university, soliciting her for a modeling job. She thanked him and declined the offer, but the conversation struck a chord of memory when Terry disappeared March 23. Her body, torn by multiple stab wounds, was recovered from a canal three days later.

On March 25, 21-year-old Suzanne Logan disappeared from a shopping mall in Oklahoma City. Her body was found the next day, floating in Milford Reservoir, near Manhattan, Kansas. Raped and stabbed, the victim had apparently been tortured prior to death.

Sheryl Bonaventura was the next to die, abducted from a shopping mall in Grand Junction, Colorado, on March 29

Another shopper placed Wilder in the mall, soliciting women for modeling jobs, and he was seen with Sheryl at a nearby restaurant that afternoon. She joined the missing list as Wilder worked his way across the country, killing when he paused to rest.

On April 1, 17-year-old Michelle Korfman vanished from a fashion show at the Meadows Mall, in Las Vegas, Nevada. Snapshots taken at the time show Wilder smiling from the sidelines, watching as the teenage girls parade before him in their miniskirts.

At last, it was enough. Linked with three murders, one kidnapping, and four disappearances, Wilder was described by FBI spokesmen as "a significant danger." His name was added to the Bureau's "Ten Most Wanted" list on April 3, 1984.

The following day, he abducted 16-year-old Tina Marie Risico in Torrance, California, raping her that night and through successive evenings as they stayed in various motels, working their way eastward. Subjected to threats and abuse, living continually in the shadow of death, Risico agreed to help Wilder find other victims as he continued his long flight to nowhere.

On April 10, Dawnette Wilt was lured away from a shopping mall in Merrillville, Indiana, raped and tortured through the course of that day and the next. Wilder tried to murder her on April 12, stabbing Dawnette and leaving her for dead outside Rochester, New York, but she managed to survive and staggered to the nearest highway, where a passing motorist discovered her and drove her to a hospital.

Wilder's final victim was Beth Dodge, abducted near Victor, New York, on April 12 and shot to death in a nearby gravel pit. Following the murder, Wilder drove his teenage captive to Boston's Logan Airport, purchasing a one-way ticket to Los Angeles and seeing her off at the gate.

Wilder's sudden attack of compassion remains unexplained, but he wasted no time in searching out another victim. On April 13, he brandished his gun at a woman near Beverly, Massachusetts, but she fled on foot, unharmed. Continuing his aimless hunt, the killer stopped for gas that afternoon in Colebrook, New Hampshire, un-aware that he had reached the end of his run.

Passing by the service station, state troopers Wayne Fortier and Leo Jellison recognized Wilder's car from FBI descriptions. Approaching the vehicle, they called out to Wilder and saw him break for the car, diving inside as he went for his pistol. Jellison leaped on the fugitive's back, struggling for the .357 magnum, and two shots rang out. The first passed through Wilder and pierced Jellison's chest, lodging in his liver; the second snuffed out Wilder's life, resulting in what a coroner termed "cardiac obliteration."

Wilder's violent death, ironically, did not resolve the tangled case. Sheryl Bonaventura's body was recovered in Utah, on May 3, the victim of a point-blank gunshot wound. Michelle Korfman was found in the Angeles National Forest on May 11, but another month would pass before she was identified, her family's fears confirmed. No trace has yet been found of Wilder's early victims in Miami and environs.

With his death, Chris Wilder was inevitably linked with other unsolved crimes. A pair of girls, aged ten and twelve, identified his mug shot as the likeness of a man who snatched them from a park in Boynton Beach, in June of 1983, and forced them to fellate him in the nearby woods. His name was likewise linked with other deaths and disappearances across two decades, in Australia and America.

In 1965, Marianne Schmidt and Christine Sharrock accompanied a young man matching Wilder's description into the beachfront dunes near Sydney; strangled, raped and stabbed, their bodies were discovered in a shallow grave, but no one has been charged to date. In 1981, teen-agers Mary Hare and Mary Optiz were abducted from a mall in Lee County, Florida; Hare was later found, stabbed to death, while Optiz remains among the missing. During 1982, the skeletal remains of unidentified women were unearthed on two separate occasions near property owned by Wilder, in Loxahatchee; one victim had been dead for several years, the other for a period of months.

And the list goes on. Tammi Leppert, teenaged model,

kidnapped from her job at a convenience store on Merritt Island, July 6, 1983. Melody Gay, 19, abducted on the graveyard shift of an all-night store in Collier County, Florida, on March 7, 1984, her body pulled from a rural canal three days later. Colleen Osborne, 15, missing from the bedroom of her home in Daytona Beach, March 15, 1984. Chris Wilder was seen in Daytona that day, propositioning "models."

There was a final, ghoulish twist to Wilder's story. Following an autopsy on April 13, 1984, Dr. Robert Christie, the New Hampshire pathologist in charge of Wilder's case, received a phone call from a man claiming to represent Harvard University. Wilder's brain was wanted for study, the caller explained, in order to determine whether defect or disease had sparked his killing spree. Dr. Christie agreed to deliver the brain on receipt of a written request from Harvard. Two weeks later he was still waiting, and spokesmen for the university's medical school denied making any such request.

Williams, Henry Robert

Sentenced to life imprisonment on his second conviction for rape and murder, Canadian Henry Williams opted for voluntary castration as a form of alternative treatment proposed for his evident mental disorders. Married and the father of two, Williams was advised by his trial judge that Canadian courts lacked the power to mandate emasculation, but he signed the medical release forms willingly, drawing praise from the judge for "insight and courage."

Williams's latest trial concerned the rape and murder of Constance Dickey, a 19-year-old college student, in September 1972. He had been previously convicted and sentenced to life for the sex slaying of Neda Novak, age 16, in October 1973, along with the attempted murder of Julia Gosport, a teenaged visitor from England, in August 1974. All three crimes were committed in Mississauga, Ontario, and Williams confessed that he had raped two other young women in the area, sparing their lives on a whim.

At his last trial, physicians testified that 900 Canadian castrations, carried out over a thirty-year period, had successfully reduced abnormal sex drives in ninety percent of all subject cases. The court offered Williams an option based on reports of inmate attitudes toward rapists and serial slayers of women. In prison, the judge decided, "he runs the real risk of being injured or killed."

Williamson, Stella

No one in the small town of Gallitzin, Pennsylvania, gave much thought to Stella Williamson in life. Unmarried and reclusive, seldom speaking even to her closest neighbors, it was clear that Stella loved her privacy. She made a regular appearance in her local church, but the parishoners knew nothing of her past and little of her present life, beyond the obvious. In 1975, one of Stella's legs was amputated, and she never quite recovered. She was seventy-six at the time of her death, in August 1980, and while the event seemed predictable, its aftermath would spark an uproar in Gallitzin.

Following the funeral, one of Stella's few acquaintances discovered a sealed envelope, marked for opening after her death. The letter within, written in 1960, directed police to the attic of Williamson's house, where an ancient trunk was opened to reveal the withered remains of five human infants. The tiny corpses were wrapped in newspapers from Johnstown, Pittsburgh, and New York City, with dates spanning the decade from 1923 to 1933. John Barron, coroner for Cambria County, reported that four of the infants were newborns, while one was older, perhaps by as much as eight months.

All things considered, there was little that authorities could do about the startling case. It was presumed that Williamson, a lifelong spinster by her own account, had born the children out of wedlock through the years, disposing of them as they came, and that she somehow felt compelled to save the pitiful remains. Details of the case reportedly were offered in her parting message to authorities, but none have been revealed. As Coroner Barron explained to the press, "Everybody involved is deceased. But we have to make sure the obvious is the truth. We have to make sure it's not a coverup."

Wise, Martha Hasel

Born in 1885, by age 40 Martha Wise was an impoverished widow, living alone on a farm near Medina, Ohio. She fell in love with Walter Johns, a man much younger than herself, but members of her family were blunt in their denunciation of the May-October romance, heaping ridicule on Martha for her "cradle-robbing." Furious at her mother's nagging, Martha poisoned the old lady on New Year's Day 1925, waiting a month before she silenced her uncle and aunt, Fred and Lily Geinke, with a double dose of arsenic. Her efforts to annihilate the Geinke family in a single stroke were futile, other members of the clan recovering from grievous illness after several days and taking their suspicions to the local prosecutor.

Under questioning, Martha confessed the three murders, but said, "It was the devil who told me to do it. He came to me while I was in the kitchen baking bread. He came to me while I was working in the fields. He followed me everywhere." She also cleared the books on other felonies, with her confessing to a string of burglaries and arson incidents. "I like fires," she explained. "They were red and bright, and I loved to see the flames shooting up into the sky."

At Martha's trial, sensational reports described her as the "Borgia of America." She pled insanity, and Walter Johns helped out with testimony that Martha had "barked like a dog" during sex, but jurors found her sane and guilty of first-degree murder. Sentenced to life imprisonment, she subsequently died in jail.

Woodfield, Randall Brent

Born at Salem, Oregon, in December 1950, Randy Woodfield was the classic, all-American boy next door.

He made good grades, and high school coaches recognized his natural athletic talents, making him the star of Newport's football team. When Woodfield started to expose himself in public, everybody laughed it off at first, and members of the coaching staff suppressed his first arrest to keep him eligible for the squad. In August 1970, attending college in Ontario, Oregon, he was picked up again, this time for vandalizing an ex-girlfriend's apartment. Two years later, in Vancouver, Washington, he logged his first adult arrest on charges of indecent exposure, receiving a suspended sentence. A similar arrest, in Portland, earned him more suspended time in June of 1973.

Woodfield got a break that year, when he was drafted by the Green Bay Packers, but he could not shake his problems with a trip across the country. In 1974, after a dozen "flashing" incidents called unwelcome attention to Randy, the Packers gave up and sent him home. The local boy-made-good was coming home in failure, a disgrace.

In early 1975, several Portland women were accosted by a knife-wielding man, forced to perform oral sex before they were robbed of their handbags. Policewomen were staked out as decoys, and Woodfield was arrested on March 3, after stealing marked money from one of the officers. In April, he pled guilty to reduced charges of second-degree robbery, receiving a sentence of ten years in prison. Four years later, in July 1979, Woodfield was freed on parole.

On October 9, 1980, a former classmate of Randy's, Cherie Ayers, was raped and murdered in Portland, bludgeoned about the head and stabbed repeatedly in the neck. Woodfield was routinely questioned and refused to sit for polygraph examinations. Homicide detectives found his answers generally "evasive and deceptive," but his blood type did not match the semen found inside the victim's body, and he was not charged.

A short month later, still in Portland, Darci Fix and Doug Altic were shot to death, execution-style, in Altic's apartment. A .32-caliber revolver was missing from the scene, and while the female victim had been formerly involved with one of Woodfield's closest friends, police had nothing to suggest that Randy was the killer.

On December 9, 1980, a young bandit wearing a fake beard held up a gas station in Vancouver, Washington. Four nights later, in Eugene, Oregon, the same man raided an ice cream parlor, rebounding on December 14 with the robbery of a drive-in restaurant at Albany. A week later, in Seattle, the gunman added a new twist, trapping a waitress in the restroom of a chicken restaurant and forcing her to masturbate him. Twenty minutes later, smiling through his phony beard, he robbed another ice cream parlor and escaped with cash in hand.

January was another busy month for the gunman police were already calling the "I-5 bandit," after his apparent highway of preference. On the eighth, he raided the same Vancouver gas station a second time, forcing a female attendant to expose her breasts after looting the till. Three days later, he robbed a market in Eugene, surfacing at Sutherlin, Oregon, on January 12, to wound a female grocery clerk with gunfire. He was wearing the fake beard in Corvallis, on January 14, when he invaded a home occupied by two sisters, aged eight and ten; the girls were forced to disrobe before fellating their assailant. In Salem, four days later, the target was an office building, where he killed Shari Hull and wounded Beth Wilmot, after sexually abusing both women. The bandit rounded off his month on January 26 and 29, with robberies in Eugene, Medford, and Grant's Pass (fondling a clerk and female customer in the latter case).

On February 3, 1981, Donna Eckard, 37, and her 14-year-old daughter were found dead in their home at Mountain Gate, California, north of Redding. Together in bed, each had been shot several times in the head, with lab tests revealing the girl had been sodomized. The same day, a female clerk was kidnapped, raped and sodomized after a holdup in Redding. An identical crime was reported from Yreka, on February 4, and the bandit robbed an Ashland motel that same night. Five days later, in Corvallis, he held up a fabric store, molesting the clerk and her customer before departing. February 12 witnessed a triple-header, with robberies in Vancouver, Olympia, and

Bellevue, Washington—the last two stops including three more sexual assaults.

On February 15, Julie Reitz—a former girlfriend of Woodfield's—was shot and killed at her home in Beaverton, Oregon. The investigation had focused on Randy by February 28, and by that time the I-5 gunman had struck three more times, in Eugene on February 18 and 21, with a final sex assault in Corvallis on February 25.

Interrogation of Woodfield on March 3, 1981, led to a search of his apartment two days later. On March 7, he was taken into custody after several victims picked him from a police lineup. By March 16, indictments were rolling in from various jurisdictions in Washington and Oregon, including multiple counts of murder, rape and sodomy, attempted kidnapping, armed robbery, and possession of firearms by an ex-convict.

The courts in Salem got to Woodfield first, on charges of murder, attempted murder, and two counts of sodomy. Convicted of all counts on June 26, 1981, the all-American killer was sentenced to a prison term of life plus 90 years. By December, conviction of sodomy and weapons charges in Benton County, Oregon, had added 35 more years to Randy's time.

As officers began to follow Woodfield's trail along I-5, they stumbled over other victims. Sylvia Durante, 21, had been strangled in Seattle and dumped beside the highway in December 1979. Three months later, 19-year-old Marsha Weatter and 18-year-old Kathy Allen had vanished while thumbing rides along I-5, outside Spokane; their corpses had been found in May, following the eruption of Mt. Saint Helens. At least four women had died around Huntington Beach, California, while Woodfield was sunning himself in the area, all killed in typical style.

Despite his seeming links with 13 homicides (at least) and countless other crimes, the I-5 killer would not go to court on the majority of his offenses. Unable to afford an endless string of trials, the state was satisfied to know that Woodfield would be off the highways for a century or so.

Yukl, Charles William

A child of divorce, Charles Yukl was 31 years old and married, self-employed as a piano teacher in New York City, when he claimed his first victim in 1966. On October 24 of that year, police responded to a homicide report at Yukl's apartment house, where they discovered the body of 25-year-old Suzanne Reynolds. A student of Yukl's, she had been beaten, stripped and stabbed to death before the teacher "found" her in a vacant flat, investigating after he "noticed" the open door on his way upstairs.

Arrested and charged with the murder next morning, Yukl confessed under questioning, before his attorney arrived at the jail. Months of wrangling over constitutional issues led to a plea bargain in February 1968, with reduced charges of manslaughter earning Yukl a sentence of seven to fifteen years in prison. A model prisoner, Yukl was released on parole in June 1973, two years before the expiration of his "guaranteed minimum" sentence. Objections from the state were overruled, with Yukl cited as "a good risk for parole." He waited fourteen months before he killed again.

On August 20, 1974, the nude and strangled body of Karen Schlegel, an aspiring actress, was discovered on the rooftop of an apartment house in Greenwich Village. She had been dead twelve hours when a janitor discovered her remains, but authorities had no difficulty selecting a suspect. Charles Yukl was a tenant of the house where Karen died, and he confessed to luring his victim with an advertisement placed in a theatrical magazine. Upon arrival, Karen Schlegel had been strangled with a necktie, stripped, and carried to the roof where she was found.

Psychiatrists found Yukl competent for trial, and he was formally indicted on September 6. On June 3, 1976, he managed to strike another bargain with the state, accepting a sentence of fifteen years to life in return for his guilty plea. This time, however, there would be no premature parole. On August 22, 1982, the killer hanged himself in prison with a shredded mattress cover, and his death was ruled a suicide.

"Zebra Murders, The"

For a period of 179 days, between October 1973 and April 1974, white residents of San Francisco were terrorized by a series of random, racially-motivated attacks that claimed 15 lives, leaving another eight victims wounded or raped. By January 1974, authorities knew with fair certainty that the killers were members of a Black Muslim splinter group, the "Death Angels," that required the murder of "blue-eyed devils" as a form of initiation. By their very nature—and the form of the police response—the so-called Zebra murders heightened racial tension by the bay and left a legacy of doubt that time has failed to dissipate.

The first known "Zebra" victims were Richard and Quita Hague, abducted by blacks in a van as they walked down the street on October 19, 1973. Richard Hague was hacked about the head and face with a machete, stunned and left for dead, before the "Angels" raped his wife and finished her with the machete, leaving her nearly decapitated. By some miracle, Richard would survive.

Three days later, gunman Jessie Lee Cooks abducted a young white woman, holding her captive for two hours while he raped her repeatedly and forced her to provide oral sex. Arrested on this and other charges prior to the conclusion of the Zebra case, Cooks—a psychopathic ex-convict—would plead guilty to one count of murder in return for dismissal of other counts. By the time the case broke in 1974, he was already serving his sentence.

On October 29, 28-year-old Frances Rose was shot and killed by a black man who tried to invade her moving car on a San Francisco street. A month later, on November 25, 53-year-old Saleem Erakat was tied up and shot, execution-style, in his small grocery store. Paul Dancik died on December 11, shot three times in the chest while walking to a corner phone booth. Two days later, 35-year-old Arthur Agnos was wounded and Marietta Di Girolamo killed in separate, random shooting incidents. The use of a similar—or identical—weapon in each of the crimes suggested one trigger man, or a group of killers sharing lethal hardware.

Things went from bad to worse near Christmas. On December 20, 81-year-old Ilario Bertuccio was killed while walking home from work, and Angela Roselli was wounded three times as she left a Christmas party. Neal Moynihan, 19, and 50-year-old Mildred Hosler died six minutes apart on December 22, cut down in random attacks. On December 23, a gathering of Death Angels tortured and dismembered an unknown transient in their San Francisco loft, dumping his mangled remains on a beach where they were found next morning. (Never identified, he is listed in homicide files as ''John Doe #169'' for 1973.)

The killers celebrated New Years with a free-wheeling rampage on January 28, killing four persons and wounding a fifth in the space of two hours. The dead included 32-year-old Tana Smith, shot down on her way to a fabric store; Vincent Wollin, killed on his sixty-ninth birthday; 54-year-old John Bambic, shot repeatedly at point-blank range; and 45-year-old Jane Holly, fatally wounded by a gunman who approached her on the street. Survivor Roxanne McMillan, age 23, recalled that her assailant smiled and said ''Hi'' before he opened fire.

On April 1, 19-year-old Thomas Rainwater and 21-year-old Linda Story were gunned down while walking to a neighborhood store; Rainwater was killed outright, while Story survived with permanent nerve damage. Two weeks later, on Easter Sunday, Ward Anderson and Terry White were wounded by black gunmen at a San Francisco bus stop. The last victim, Nelson Shields, was shot three times in the back and killed on April 16, 1974.

Police response to the Zebra murders was almost as controversial as the crimes themselves. A policy of stopping blacks at random on the street and frisking them for weapons led to cries of racism and civil rights violations, while producing no viable suspects. The case was broken in late April, when gunman Anthony Cornelius Harris surrendered voluntarily and made a full confession to police. Turning state's evidence, he named eight ''Zebra'' killers aside from himself, and seven of the suspects were picked up in raids on May 1. (Jessie Cooks was already in prison.) Four of the suspects were ultimately freed for lack of solid evidence, and they remain at large today. Indicted for the Zebra crimes were Jessie Cooks, J.C. Simon, Larry Craig Green, and Manuel Leonard Moore. Harris, Moore, and Cooks had met while serving time in San Quentin on various felony charges, and they had joined the Black Muslim movement while still behind bars.

The Zebra trial set a new record for California legal proceedings, lasting from March 3, 1975 to March 9, 1979. Three of the four defense attorneys were provided and paid by the Nation of Islam, in a demonstration of solidarity with the accused murderers. At the end of the marathon proceedings, jurors took barely 18 hours to convict all defendants on all counts, and the four gunmen were sentenced to life imprisonment.

As for the Death Angels, their existence has never been publicly acknowledged by American law enforcement, and the results of confidential investigations into the cult remain classified. According to author Clark Howard, there were 15 "accredited" Death Angels—those who had earned their "wings" by killing a specified number of whites—in California during 1973. None of them were swept up in the Zebra dragnet, which bagged only prospective members, still short of their tally for final qualification. They, and their brethren of the "church," are presumably still at large. Still hunting.

"Zodiac, The"

California's most elusive serial killer claimed his first victim on October 30, 1966, in Riverside. That evening, Cheri Jo Bates, an 18-year-old freshman at Riverside City College, emerged from the campus library to find her car disabled, the distributor coil disconnected. Police theorize that her killer approached with an offer of help, then dragged her behind some nearby shrubbery, where a furious struggle ended with Cheri stabbed in the chest and back, her throat slashed so deeply that she was nearly decapitated.

In November 1966, a letter to the local press declared that Cheri "is not the first and she will not be the last."

Following publication of an article about the case, on April 30, 1967, identical letters were posted to the newspaper, police, and to the victim's father. They read: "Bates had to die. There will be more."

On December 20, 1968, 17-year-old David Faraday was parked with his date, 16-year-old Betty Lou Jensen, on a rural road east of the Vallejo city limits, in northern California. A night-stalking gunman found them there and killed both teenagers, shooting Faraday in the head as he sat behind the wheel of his car. Betty Lou ran thirty feet before she was cut down by a tight group of five shots in the back, fired from a .22-caliber automatic pistol.

July 4, 1969. Michael Mageau, 19, picked up his date, 22-year-old Darlene Ferrin, for a night on the town. At one point, Mageau believed they were being followed, but Darlene seemed to recognize the other motorist, telling Mageau, "Don't worry about it." By midnight, they were parked at Blue Rock Springs Park, when a familiar vehicle pulled alongside and the driver shined a bright light in their eyes, opening fire with a 9mm pistol. Hit four times, Mageau survived; Darlene, with nine wounds, was dead on arrival at a local hospital.

Forty minutes after the shooting, Vallejo police received an anonymous call, directing officers to the murder scene. Before hanging up, the male caller declared, "I also killed those kids last year."

In retrospect, friends and relatives recalled that Darlene Ferrin had been suffering harassment through anonymous phone calls and intimidating visits by a heavyset stranger in the weeks before her death. She called the strange man "Paul," and told one girlfriend that he wished to silence her because she had seen him commit a murder. Police searched for "Paul" in the wake of Darlene's slaying, but he was never located or identified.

On July 31, 1969, the killer mailed letters to three Bay Area newspapers, each containing one third of a cryptic cipher. Ultimately broken by a local high school teacher, the message began: "I like killing people because it is so much fun." The author explained that he was killing in an effort to "collect slaves," who would serve him in the afterlife. Another correspondence, mailed on August 7, introduced the "Zodiac" trade name and provided details of the latest murder, leaving police in no doubt that its author was the killer.

On September 27, 20-year-old Bryan Hartnell and Cecilia Shepherd, 22, were enjoying a picnic at Lake Berryessa, near Vallejo, when they were accosted by a hooded gunman. Covering them with a pistol, the stranger described himself as an escaped convict who needed their car "to go to Mexico." Producing a coil of clothesline, he bound both victims before drawing a long knife, stabbing Hartnell five times in the back. Cecilia Shepherd was stabbed fourteen times, including four in the chest as she twisted away from the plunging blade.

Departing the scene, their assailant paused at Hartnell's car, to scribble on the door with a felt-tipped pen. He wrote:

Vallejo
12-20-68
7-4-69
Sept 27-69-6:30
by knife

A phone call to police reported the crime, but by that time a fisherman had already discovered the victims. Brian Hartnell would survive his wounds, but Cecilia Shepherd was doomed, another victim for the man who called himself the Zodiac.

On October 11, San Francisco cab driver Paul Stine was shot in the head and killed with a 9mm automatic pistol. Witnesses saw the gunman escape on foot, toward the Presidio, and police descended on the neighborhood in force. At one point in the search, two patrolmen stopped a heavyset pedestrian and were directed in pursuit of their elusive prey, not realizing that the "tip" had been provided by the man they sought.

In the wake of Stine's murder, the Zodiac launched a new barrage of letters, some containing swatches of the cabbie's bloodstained shirt. Successive messages claimed seven victims, instead of the established five, as the killer threatened to "wipe out a school bus some morning." He also vowed to change his method of "collecting souls"; "They shall look like routine robberies, killings of anger, & a few fake suicides, etc." Five days before Christmas, he wrote to prominent attorney Melvin Belli, pleading for help, with the chilling remark that "I can not remain in control for much longer."

On March 22, 1970, Kathleen Johns was driving with her infant daughter, near Modesto, California, when another motorist pulled her over, flashing his headlights and beeping his horn. The man informed her that a rear tire in her car seemed dangerously loose; he worked on it briefly, with a lug wrench, but when she tried to drive away, the wheel fell off. Her benefactor offered a lift to the nearest garage, then took Kathleen on an aimless drive through the countryside, threatening her life and that of her child before she managed to escape from the car, hiding in a roadside irrigation ditch. Reporting the abduction at a local police station, Johns noticed a wanted poster bearing sketches of the Zodiac, and she identified the man as her attacker.

Nine more letters were received from Zodiac between April 1970 and March 1971, but police were unable to trace further crimes in the series. On January 30, 1974, a San Francisco newspaper received the first authentic Zodiac letter in nearly three years, signing off with the notation: "Me-37; SFPD-0."

One officer who took the estimated body-count seriously was Sheriff Don Striepke, of Sonoma County. In a 1975 report, Striepke referred to a series of 40 unsolved murders in four western states, which seemed to form a giant "Z" when plotted on the map. While tantalizing, Striepke's theory seemed to fall apart with the identification of Theodore Bundy as a prime suspect in several of the homicides.

On April 24, 1978, the Zodiac mailed his twenty-first letter, chilling Bay Area residents with the news that "I am back with you." No traceable crimes were committed, however, and Homicide Inspector Dave Toschi was later removed from the Zodiac detail on suspicion of writing the letter himself. In fact, while Toschi confessed writing several anonymous letters to the press, praising his own performance in the case, expert analysis agree that the April note was, in fact, written by the killer.

Theories abound in the Zodiac case. One was aired by author "George Oakes" (a pseudonym) in the November 1981 issue of *California* magazine, based on a presumption of the killer's obsession with water, clocks, binary mathematics, and the writings of Lewis Carroll. Oakes claims to know the Zodiac's identity and says the killer phoned him several times, at home. He blames the Zodiac for an arson fire that ravaged 25,000 acres near Lake Berryessa in June 1981, but *California* editors confessed that FBI agents "weren't very impressed" with the theory. Spokesmen for the California State Attorney General's office went further, describing the tale as "a lot of bull."

Author Robert Graysmith also claims to know the Zodiac by name, calling his suspect "Robert Hall Starr" in a book published during 1986. A resident of Vallejo, "Starr" is described as a gun buff and suspected child molester, confirmed as a prime suspect by several detectives (and flatly rejected by others). Graysmith credits Zodiac with a total of 49 "possible" victims between October 1966 and May 1981, three of whom survived his attacks. In addition to the six known dead and three confirmed survivors, Graysmith includes fifteen "occult" murders linked to one unidentified slayer in northern California, and fifteen other victims killed in close proximity to a solstice or equinox—nine confirmed by police as the work of a single man. Of 40 "possible" victims, 39 are female, variously shot, stabbed, beaten, strangled, drowned, and poisoned . . . perhaps in compliance with Zodiac's promise to alter his method of "collecting slaves."

Zon, Hans Van

Born in April 1942, at Utrecht, Holland, Hans van Zon was a lethargic child, remembered for his exaggerated courtesy toward adults and his preference for younger playmates. An introverted youth, he was dismissed from several jobs for petty theft and seemed to live increasingly in a fantasy world of his own creation. At age 16, he moved to Amsterdam and bought himself a new, expensive wardrobe, settling down to make his way as a con man and swindler. Van Zon's favorite trick was to pose as a student, bilking sympathetic strangers of cash for a "trip home." Handsome and bisexual, he enjoyed affairs with men and women alike.

Van Zon's first known victim was Elly Hager-Segov, murdered after a date on July 22, 1964. Elly had already taken Hans to bed once that night, and when she rejected his new advances he choked her unconscious, stripped her, and cut her throat with a bread knife.

In 1965, Van Zon reportedly murdered homosexual film director Claude Berkeley, in Amsterdam. (A confession to both crimes was later recanted, with Van Zon asserting that he derived his intimate knowledge of the murders from "psychic visions.") A short time later, he married an Italian chamber maid, living on her wages while he continued his affairs with other women. In 1967, Van Zon's wife told police he was planning to kill her, and he spent a month in jail—for violating his probation on earlier charges—before they were reconciled.

On April 19, 1967, Van Zon murdered his occasional mistress, Coby Van der Voort, first drugging her with a supposed aphrodisiac, then bludgeoning her with a lead pipe, stripping her body, and stabbing her with a bread knife. Unsuccessful in his attempt to rape the corpse, Van Zon still bragged of the crime to an acquaintance, ex-convict Oude Nol, and found himself the target of blackmail. In return for his continued silence, Nol demanded that Van Zon "assist" in the murder and robbery of selected victims.

On May 31, 1967, Van Zon entered the fireworks shop run by 80-year-old Jan Donse, clubbing the man to death with his favorite lead pipe before looting the till and dividing the proceeds with Nol. In August, he killed farmer Reyer de Bruin at Heeswijk crushing his skull with the pipe, then slashing his throat for good measure. The crime spree came to an end soon after, when a widow named Woortmeyer—once romanced by Oude Nol—survived Van

Zon's clubbing and fingered him for police. In custody, Van Zon implicated Nol, and both men were held for trial. On conviction of murder, Van Zon was sentenced to life, while Oude Nol drew a term of seven years in prison.

BIBLIOGRAPHY

Abrahamson, David. *Confessions of Son of Sam.* New York: Columbia University Press, 1985.

Adam, H.L. *Trial of George Chapman.* London: William Hodge, 1930.

Allen, William. *Starkweather: The Story of a Mass Murderer.* Boston: Houghton Mifflin, 1967.

Altman, Jack, and Martin Ziporyn. *Born to Raise Hell: The Untold Story of Richard Speck.* New York: Grove, 1967.

Angelella, Michael. *Trail of Blood: A True Story.* New York: New American Library, 1979.

Bakos, Susan C. *Appointment for Murder.* New York: Putnam, 1988.

Berg, Karl. *The Sadist.* London: Heinemann, 1932.

Brussel, James A. *Casebook of a Crime Psychiatrist.* New York: Bernard Geis, 1968.

Bugliosi, Vincent, and Curt Gentry. *Helter Skelter.* New York: Norton, 1974.

Burn, Gordon. *Somebody's Husband, Somebody's Son.* New York: Viking, 1984.

Cahill, Tim. *Buried Dreams*. New York: Bantam, 1985.

Cheney, Margaret. *The Co-Ed Killer*. New York: Walker, 1976.

Clark, Tim and John Penycate. *Psychopath*. London: Routledge & Kegan Paul, 1976.

Cray, Ed. *Burden of Proof*. New York: Macmillan, 1973.

Cross, Roger. *The Yorkshire Ripper*. London: Granada 1981.

Damio, Ward. *Urge to Kill*. New York: Pinnacle, 1974.

Damore, Leo. *In His Garden: The Anatomy of a Murderer*. New York: Arbor House, 1981.

Dettlinger, Chet, and Jeff Prugh. *The List*. Atlanta: Philmay, 1983.

Eggington, Joyce. *From Cradle to Grave: The Short Lives and Strange Deaths of Marybeth Tinning's Nine Children*. New York: William Morrow, 1989.

Elkind, Peter. *The Death Shift*. New York: Viking, 1989.

Emmons, Nuel, and Charles Manson. *Manson in His Own Words*. New York: Grove, 1986.

Fawkes, Sandy. *Killing Time*. London: Hamlyn, 1978.

Frank, Gerold. *The Boston Strangler*. New York: New American Library, 1967.

Freeman, Lucy. *"Before I Kill More . . ."* New York: Crown, 1955.

Gaddis, Thomas E., and James O. Long. *Killer: A Journal of Murder*. New York: Macmillan, 1970.

Gibney, Bruce. *The Beauty Queen Killer*. New York: Pinnacle, 1984.

Godwin, George. *Peter Kurten: A Study in Sadism*. London: Acorn, 1938.

Godwin, John. *Murder USA*. New York: Ballantine, 1978.

Gollmar, Robert H. *Edward Gein*. New York: Charles Hallberg, 1981.

Graysmith, Robert. *Zodiac*. New York: St. Martin's, 1986.

Grombach, John V. *The Great Liquidator*. New York: Doubleday, 1980.

Gurwell, John K. *Mass Murder in Houston*. Houston: Cordovan Press, 1974.

Heimer, Mel. *The Cannibal: The Case of Albert Fish*. New York: Lyle Stuart, 1971.

Howard, Clark. *Zebra*. New York: Berkley, 1980.

Jones, Ann. *Women Who Kill*. New York: Holt, Rinehart and Winston, 1980.

Jouve, Nicole W. *"The Street Cleaner": The Yorkshire Ripper Case on Trial*. London: Marion Boyers, 1986.

Kennedy, Ludovic. *10 Rillington Place*. London: Gollancz, 1961.

Keyes, Edward. *The Michigan Murders*. New York: Pocket Books, 1976.

Kidder, Tracy. *The Road to Yuba City*. New York: Doubleday, 1974.

Klausner, Lawrence D. *Son of Sam*. New York: McGraw-Hill, 1981.

Kuncl, Tom, and Paul Einstein. *Ladies Who Kill*. New York: Pinnacle, 1985.

Langlois, Janet L. *Belle Gunness: The Lady Bluebeard*. Bloomington, IN: Indiana University Press, 1985.

Larsen, Richard W. *Bundy: The Deliberate Stranger*. Englewood Cliffs, NJ: Prentice-Hall, 1980.

Leith, Rod. *The Prostitute Murders: The People vs Richard Cottingham*. New York: Lyle Stuart, 1983.

Levin, Jack, and James Alan Fox. *Mass Murder: America's Growing Menace*. New York: Plenum, 1985.

Leyton, Elliott. *Compulsive Killers*. New York: New York University Press, 1986.

Linedecker, Clifford. *The Man Who Killed Boys*. New York: St. Martin's, 1980.

Linedecker, Clifford. *Thrill Killers*. New York: Paperjacks, 1987.

Livsey, Clara. *The Manson Women: A "Family" Portrait*. New York: Marek, 1980.

Lucas, Norman. *The Sex Killers*. London: W.H. Allen, 1974.

Lunde, Donald T., and Jefferson Morgan. *The Die Song: A Journey into the Mind of a Mass Murderer*. New York: W.W. Norton, 1980.

Marchbanks, David. *The Moors Murders*. London: Frewin, 1966.

Master, R.E.L., and Eduard Lea. *Perverse Crimes in History*. New York: Julian, 1963.

Masters, Brian. *Killing for Company*. London: Jonathan Cape, 1985.

McConnell, Brian. *Found Naked and Dead*. London: New English Library, 1974.

Meyer, Gerald. *The Memphis Murders*. New York: Seabury, 1974.

Michaud, Stephen, and Hugh Aynesworth. *The Only Living Witness*. New York: Simon and Schuster, 1983.

Moore, Kelly, and Dan Reed. *Deadly Medicine*. New York: St. Martin's, 1988.

Moser, Don, and Jerry Cohen. *The Pied Piper of Tucson*. New York: New American Library, 1967.

Nash, Jay Robert. *Bloodletters and Badmen*. New York: Evans, 1973.

Nash, Jay Robert. *Look for the Woman*. New York: Evans 1981.

Nash, Jay Robert. *Murder, America*. New York: Simon and Schuster, 1980.

Neville, Richard and Julie Clark. *The Life and Crimes of Charles Sobhraj*. London: Jonathan Cape, 1979.
Newton, Michael. *Mass Murder*. New York: Garland, 1988.

Nickel, Steven. *Torso: The Story of Eliot Ness and the Search for a Psychopathic Killer*. Winston-Salem, NC: J.F. Blair, 1989.

Norris, Joel. *Serial Killers: The Growing Menace*. New York: Doubleday, 1988.

O'Brien, Darcy. *Two of a Kind: The Hillside Stranglers*. New York: New American Library, 1985.

Olsen, Jack. *The Man With the Candy: The Story of the Houston Mass Murders*. New York: Simon and Schuster, 1974.

Reinhardt, James M. *The Murderous Trail of Charles Starkweather*. Springfield, IL: C.C. Thomas, 1960.

Reinhardt, James M. *The Psychology of Strange Killers*. Springfield IL: C.C. Thomas, 1962.

Rule, Ann. *The I-5 Killer*. New York: New American Library, 1984.

Rule, Ann. *Lust Killer*. New York: New American Library, 1983.

Rule, Ann. *The Stranger Beside Me*. New York: New American Library, 1980.

Rule, Ann. *The Want-Ad Killer*. New York: New American Library, 1983.

Sanders, Ed. *The Family*. New York: Dutton, 1971.

Schechter, Harold. *Deviant: The Shocking True Story of the Original "Psycho."* New York: Pocket, 1989.

Schreiber, Flora R. *The Shoemaker: The Anatomy of a Psychotic*. New York: Simon & Schuster, 1983.

Schwartz, Ted. *The Hillside Strangler: A Murderer's Mind*. New York: Doubleday, 1981.

Sereny, Gitta. *The Case of Mary Bell*. London: Methuen, 1972.

Sifakis, Carl. *The Encyclopedia of American Crime*. New York: Facts on File, 1982.

Spinks, Sarah. *Cardiac Arrest: A True Account of Stolen Lives*. Toronto: Doubleday, 1985.

Sullivan, Terry and Peter Maiken. *Killer Clown*. New York: Grosset & Dunlap, 1983.

Terry, Maury. *The Ultimate Evil*. New York: Doubleday, 1987.

Thompson, Thomas. *Serpentine*. New York: Dell, 1979.

Tobias, Ronald. *They Shoot to Kill: A Psycho-Survey of Criminal Sniping*. Boulder, CO: Paladin 1981.

Wagner, Margaret S. *The Monster of Dusseldorf*. London: Faber, 1932.

West, Donald. *Sacrifice Unto Me*. New York: Pyramid, 1974.

Wilcox, Robert K. *The Mysterious Deaths at Ann Arbor*. New York: Popular Library, 1977.

Williams, Emlyn. *Beyond Belief*. New York: Random House, 1967.

Wilson, Colin, and Patricia Putnam. *The Encyclopedia of Murder*. New York: Putnam, 1961.

Wilson, Colin, and Donald Seaman. *The Encyclopedia of Modern Murder, 1962—1982*. New York: Putnam, 1983.

Winn, Steven, and David Merrill. *Ted Bundy: The Killer Next Door*. New York: Bantam, 1980.

Yallop, David. *Deliver Us From Evil*. New York: Coward, McCann, 1982.

INDEX